Intentions in the Experience of Meaning

D1558674

What do our assumptions about authorship matter for our experience of meaning? This book examines the debates in the humanities and social sciences over whether authorial intentions can, or should, constrain our interpretation of language and art. Scholars in many disciplines assume that understanding of linguistic and artistic meaning should not be constrained by beliefs about authors and their possible intentions in creating a human artifact. Gibbs argues that people are strongly disposed to infer intentionality when understanding speech, written texts, artworks, and many other human actions. Although ordinary people, and scholars, may infer meanings that diverge from, or extend beyond, what authors intend, our experience of human artifacts as meaningful is fundamentally tied to our assumptions of intentionality. This volume challenges the traditional idea that intentions exist solely in the minds of individuals, and formulates a new conceptual framework for examining if and when intentions influence the interpretation of meaning. *Intentions in the Experience of Meaning* presents a clear and concise overview of state-of-the-art research on the role of intentions in meaningful experience in the fields of psychology, linguistics, philosophy, literature, legal theory, art history, and anthropology.

Raymond W. Gibbs, Jr., is Professor of Psychology at the University of California, Santa Cruz. He is the author of *The Poetics of Mind*.

Intentions in the Experience of Meaning

RAYMOND W. GIBBS, JR.
University of California, Santa Cruz

CAMBRIDGE
UNIVERSITY PRESS

PUBLISHED BY THE PRESS SYNDICATE OF THE UNIVERSITY OF CAMBRIDGE
The Pitt Building, Trumpington Street, Cambridge, United Kingdom

CAMBRIDGE UNIVERSITY PRESS
The Edinburgh Building, Cambridge CB2 2RU, UK   www.cup.cam.ac.uk
40 West 20th Street, New York, NY 10011-4211, USA   www.cup.org
10 Stamford Road, Oakleigh, Melbourne 3166, Australia
Ruiz de Alarcón 13, 28014 Madrid, Spain

First published 1999

Printed in the United States of America

Typeface Palatino VIP 11/13 pt.   *System* LaTeX 2_ε [TB]

A catalog record for this book is available from the British Library.

Library of Congress Cataloging-in-Publication Data
Gibbs, Raymond W.
Intentions in the experience of meaning / Raymond W. Gibbs, Jr.
p.   cm.
Includes bibliographical references.
ISBN 0-521-57245-2 (hardcover). – ISBN 0-521-57630-x (pbk.)
1. Meaning (Psychology)   2. Intentionalism.   I. Title.
BF463.M4G53   1999
121'.68 – dc21   98-50661

ISBN 0 521 57245 2 hardback
ISBN 0 521 57630 x paperback

Contents

v

Contents

Acknowledgments

I thank Larry Barsalou, Art Graesser, Julia Hough, Litze Hu, Nicole Lordi, Greg Murphy, and Rosalyn Tantraphol for their many helpful comments on an earlier draft of this book. It is my particular pleasure to, once again, express my gratitude to Julia Hough and the staff at Cambridge University Press for all their support and guidance during the writing and production of this book. Special thanks to Nicole Lordi for accompanying me to all those libraries, bookstores, museums, and bars where many of the topics presented here first came to mind.

Part I

Introduction

Chapter 1

The Controversy over Intentions

Our intentions to say or perform certain acts appear to have an intimate relationship with how people interpret what we are doing. Suppose I ask a good friend *Have you seen the latest Woody Allen movie?* I may have a whole range of intentions and goals that motivate my asking this particular question. For instance, I may intend to engage my friend in a discussion about the movie, I may want to use this utterance as a way of inviting my friend to see the movie with me, I may want to use this question to accuse my friend of not being up on the contemporary movie scene, and so on. But do any of these various intentions play a role in my friend's interpretation of my question?

My friend might simply interpret the meaning of my question about the latest Woody Allen movie not by assessing anything about my specific communicative intentions. She might, instead, determine what my question means from a linguistic analysis of the words in my utterance in combination with her knowledge of English grammar. Perhaps my friend will use her understanding of the context in which I uttered my question to determine its meaning, again, without trying to read my mind as to the intentions behind my question.

Similar questions may be asked about how readers interpret written texts. Imagine that you pick up your local newspaper one morning and see the following headline on the front page: *Drunk gets nine months in violin case.* How might you decide that a reasonable interpretation of this headline is that some drunk person was sentenced to a prison term of nine months in regard to the possible theft of a violin and *not* that some drunk person was

3

put *inside* a violin case for nine months? Do you understand what is meant by this phrase merely by analyzing the words' meanings in the context of what newspaper headlines often express? Or do you try to infer something about the possible intentions of the headline writer in phrasing the headline in the particular way he or she did?

More dramatically, imagine that you are reading the famous poem by Archibald MacLeish entitled "Ars Poetica" that begins:[1]

> A poem should be palpable and mute
> As a globed fruit,
>
> Dumb
> As old medallions to the thumb,
>
> Silent as the sleeve-worn stone
> Of casement ledges where the moss has grown –
>
> A poem should be wordless
> As the flight of birds.

MacLeish may have written these lines to express many ideas. He may have intended for you to understand his vision of poetry as part of nature, or how poetics conveys meaning by spatial language, or even how poems refer to themselves while presenting descriptions of the external world. Once again, you must ask which, if any, of MacLeish's putative intentions play a role in your interpretation of his poem.

This book explores the role that communicative intentions play in people's experience of meaning. My aim is to demonstrate that many aspects of how we understand spoken language, interpret written texts, and make sense of artworks, is to a significant extent influenced by the search for communicative intentions. We do not necessarily seek to recover the specific intentions of the actual person who produces some discourse or artwork. Yet much of what we do when understanding meaning is guided by the assumption that some individual, whom we may not even know, said or created what he or she did for a particular set of reasons that we are to recognize. I will not argue that intentions completely limit both ordinary and scholarly interpretation, but I shall claim that the recovery of communicative intentions is an essential part of the cognitive processes that operate when we understand human action of any sort.

There has been continuing debate on the place of intentions in theories of linguistic and nonlinguistic interpretation. On an intuitive level, it makes good sense to describe communication in terms of intentions and inferences about a speaker's or author's meaning. We ordinarily attribute intentions to other people and animals in a wide variety of everyday interactions. Although there has been a great deal of effort given to understanding human behavior in terms of different systems of signs, as witnessed by the study of semiotics, human behavior is predominately conceptualized in intentional rather than physical terms.

The idea that communication exploits the human ability to attribute intentions to other people has always had great psychological appeal. This is seen most forcefully in how we understand utterances in conversation. Imagine a situation in which my roommate says to me one morning *The cat is on the mat*. I clearly interpret this utterance based on my assumptions about my roommate's likely intentions in saying what she did; for example, that she wants me to go let the cat outside. In this way, my interpretation of *The cat is on the mat* is closely tied to my recovery of the speaker's communicative intentions.

Speakers' intentions can be misunderstood, particularly in certain types of communicative situations where people are trying to get their own way (e.g., when making requests, excuses, explanations of behavior). For example, one couple recalled a typical argument in which both maintained that they had not gone to a party because the other had not wanted to go.[2] Each partner denied having expressed any disinclination to go. In this case, the mixup was traced to the following reconstructed conversation:

Wife: John's having a party. Wanna go?

Husband: OK.

(Later)

Wife: Are you sure you want to go to the party?

Husband: OK, let's not go. I'm tired anyway.

5

When the couple later discussed the misunderstanding, the wife reported that she had merely been asking what her husband wanted to do without considering her own preference. She claimed that she was about to go to the party for her husband's sake and tried to make sure of his preference by asking him a second time. The wife felt she was being solicitous and considerate. The husband said that by bringing up the question of the party, his wife was letting him know that she wanted to go, so he agreed. But when she brought it up again, he thought that she was letting him know that she had changed her mind and now did not want to go. So he found a reason not to go, to make her feel all right about getting her way. Thus, the husband was also being solicitous and considerate. This example shows how people can misunderstand the communicative intentions of others even when both conversants were being attentive and polite.

Of course, there are moments in everyday conversation when listeners openly resist acknowledging their recognition of speakers' intentions. A nice illustration of this is seen in Ingmar Bergman's film *Scenes from a Marriage*.[3] The couple, Marianne and Johann, have decided to end their marriage and meet in Johann's office to sign the divorce papers. As they talk about their relationship, Marianne says:

> Marianne (gently): I want you to know that I'm nearly always thinking of you and wondering if you're lonely and afraid. Every day, several times a day, I wonder where I went wrong. What I did to cause the breach between us. I know it's a childish way of thinking, but there you are. Sometimes I seem to have got hold of the situation, then it slips through my fingers.

> Johann (sarcastically): Why don't you go to a psychiatrist?

Throughout the film, Marianne and Johann talk of their sadness over the deterioration, and ultimate break-up, of their relationship. They express their thoughts and feelings in different ways, but both Marianne and Johann collude to ignore what the other is attempting to communicate. In the above scene, Marianne tries to talk plainly of her feelings to draw Johann closer to her, yet Johann clearly rebuffs Marianne. This practice of ignoring or deflecting speakers' transparent communicative intentions occurs in many discourse situations. Yet the fact that someone's communicative intentions must be dealt with in some way, even if this means resisting them, reveals the salience of speakers' intentions in our understanding of what is said.

Conversations like the above raise the thorny question, once more, of how best to define what constitutes a speaker's communicative intention. Should we distinguish between what a person communicates quite specifically by virtue of what he or she says from what that person hopes to achieve by virtue of the listener's recognizing the communicative intention? I will suggest that it makes good sense to limit communicative intentions to what speakers say (e.g., Marianne talking of her feelings), and not confuse discussion of these intentions with what speakers (or writers and artists) hope to concretely realize by what is said (e.g., Marianne's hope to draw Johann closer to her as a result of his understanding her communicative intention).

Although intentions seem most transparently at play in face-to-face conversation, they also shape our interpretation of written texts where, in most instances, the writer is not physically present. Our reading of what many texts mean seems inseparable from our awareness of who the author is who penned the work. Reading a letter from one's mother, a best friend, or a lover, creates an experience in which we almost hear the author's voice speaking to us. Even when we don't personally know the author, we struggle to understand a writer's communicative intentions when reading most texts. Consider the following example of a letter to a newspaper advice columnist.[4]

Dear Etiquette Expert:

My girlfriend and I are ready to get married in a few months. She has been hounding me to get an engagement ring. But I don't see why it's so important to buy an expensive ring when it's the love that counts. If two people love each other, why does the man have to prove it by buying her an expensive ring?

This letter illustrates that a writer might have a diversity of communicative goals: for example, to get a problem solved, to draw the reader's attention to an issue, to solicit agreement on an argument, to get into print, and so on. Here the etiquette expert has the task of determining which of these goals are primary in order to supply a useful response to the letter writer. Moreover, there are other agents involved in the interpretation of this letter, such as other potential letter writers, readers of the newspaper, the editors and publishers of the newspaper, and so on. Letters like this one are hardly simple and show how, in some cases anyway, understanding what a writer intends to communicate may involve multiple agents with multiple intentions. At the same time, people's interpretations of what a writer says will also differ depending upon their own attitudes and beliefs about the writer. For instance, some readers might think the writer of the above letter is simply "cheap" and unwilling to express his love for his fiancée in the traditional manner. Other readers might have great sympathy with the writer for wanting to place his love for his fiancée above traditional, material values.

There are other cases where we may not personally know the author, but know of the author and his or her beliefs through previous works. In these instances, we often create in our minds a sense of someone familiar talking to us with specific communicative intentions that we are to recognize and appreciate. Consider this example from a popular movie review column, "Joe Bob Goes to the Drive-In," written by Joe Bob Briggs.[5]

> So this flick starts off with a bimbo getting chained up and killed by a bunch of Meskins dressed up like Roman soldiers in their bathrobes... Sixty-four dead bodies. Bimbos in cages. Bimbos in chains. Arms roll. Thirty-nine breasts. Two beasts (giants lizard, octopus). Leprosy. Kung fu. Bimbo fu. Sword fu. Lizard fu. Knife fu. Seven battles. Three quarts blood. A 39 on the vomit meter... Joe Bob says check it out.

Joe Bob Brigg's movie reviews are not exactly inspired literature, and to some readers are quite offensive. But many readers recognize the satirical intent of the writer, whose real name is John Bloom, a young Dallas newspaper reporter. Bloom's idea for his column was to review "bad" movies, but to do so from the vantage point of a viewer who could discriminate between what was good and what was bad in a "bad" film. As a satirist, Bloom allowed his narrator, Joe Bob Briggs, to talk in his own language in order to target contemporary attitudes about "taste." Bloom even gave Joe Bob his own special identity as a redneck working man who at nineteen has been married three times and literally seen sixty-eight hundred movies, which gives him great authority as a drive-in movie reviewer.

Of course, like all satirists, Bloom takes an enormous risk in writing this column. Problems soon arose after he started publishing it as to whether the column was making fun of Joe Bob or of the people Joe Bob writes about (e.g., *Meskins, Bimbos*, etc). Predictably, some readers view Joe Bob as a Southern cracker being satirized for their amusement, while others, such as the Baptists and some feminists, are offended by Joe Bob's passion for violence and sex. Yet other feminists get angry at the angry feminists for not recognizing that the column was simply poking fun at the kind of people who go to the types of movies reviewed in Joe Bob Briggs's column. All of this goes to show how readers' different views about who an author is, and what that author's motives are in writing as he or she does, has an enormous influence on how people interpret the meaning of texts. Moreover, it is clear that a reader's attitudes toward the author and the topic discussed have a great bearing on the interpretations given to any text.

These observations on speech and written texts point directly to the strong conclusion that recognition of speakers'/writers' intentions play an important part in how we understand language. Over the past twenty-five years, much research in cognitive science – which includes parts of the disciplines of psychology, philosophy, linguistics, computer science, neuroscience, and anthropology – has been devoted to the question of whether intentions have a significant role in the experience of meaning, especially in regard to how people interpret linguistic communication.[6] Although other approaches to linguistic meaning are widely pursued, such as truth-conditional semantics, it is widely assumed that understanding many aspects of linguistic meaning crucially depends on recognizing speakers'/authors' intentions. Cognitive scientists have, for example, learned a great deal

9

about how speakers/authors express their intentions and how listeners/readers figure out exactly what it is that others wish to communicate. A variety of theoretical proposals and empirical findings suggest that a critical part of the unconscious and conscious mental activities involved in speaking and listening, and in writing and reading, center on the expression and recovery of communicative intentions. Part of my goal in this book is to illustrate that determining the role of intentions in the interpretation of meaning depends on the recognition that speakers/listeners, authors/readers, artists/observers are engaging in cognitive, psychological activities that can be empirically studied and understood.

Despite our strong intuitions, and much of the evidence from cognitive science, that understanding what a speaker, author, or artist means depends critically on inferring something about that person's communicative intentions, there have for decades been fierce arguments in scholarly and public circles about the role of intentions in the interpretation of linguistic and nonlinguistic meaning. *Intentionalism*, the idea that speakers' or authors' intentions place constraints on linguistic and artistic interpretation, has been most widely debated in the humanities. One quote from Peter Kivy nicely captures the fever of the debate over intentionalism: "The mere mention of the word word 'intention' in regard to any art-critical or art-theoretical question is liable to elicit, these days, the most violent reaction, as if one had just dropped a snake in a crowded room."[7]

Many literary critics in the early twentieth century argued that an author's intentions place significant constraints on how one should interpret the meaning of any literary work. Thus, readers presumably determine the meaning of the opening lines of MacLeish's poem "Ars Poetica" – *A poem should be palpable and mute /As a globed fruit* – based on the recognition of certain intentions that they believe MacLeish wishes them to recover. Readers, especially literary critics, might, for example, try to interpret MacLeish's poem in light of their knowledge of MacLeish, his various life experiences, his pronounced goals as a poet, and so on.

In the 1940s and 1950s, however, intentionalism suffered its first major blow with the rise of New Criticism and its influential doctrine, called the *intentional fallacy*, which states that interpretation of texts should be freed from historical and biographical influences.[8] Thus, when readers formulate a critical interpretation of MacLeish's "Ars Poetica," they should restrict their analyses to the possible meanings *in the text* and neither speculate about MacLeish's possible reasons for writing the poem in the way he did nor refer to any information about MacLeish in passing critical judgment on his poem. With the rise of New Criticism, a whole generation of scholars felt they needed to tiptoe delicately and apologetically around any suggestion that they were interested in authorial intentions as part of their critical analyses of literary texts. As the poets/critics Ezra Pound and T. S. Eliot had argued earlier, textual meaning should be independent of authorial intentions because the best poetry is objective, autonomous, and impersonal and should continue to express meaning long after it has been disassociated from the person who wrote it.[9]

From the 1960s to the 1990s other philosophers and literary critics declared their own beliefs in the intentional fallacy. Poststructuralists such as Roland Barthes, Jacques Derrida, and Michel Foucault announced the "death of the author" as a precondition for the desired "birth of the reader" in literary criticism.[10] Though authors may think they know what they intend, their thought and language are at the mercy of socioeconomic, psychological, and historical forces that cause them to mean something other than what they frequently intend. This blindness makes what authors intend far less interesting than the operation of these external forces as revealed in their work.[11]

Anti-intentionalist theorists and critics have argued that textual meaning can be determined by conducting close analyses of the "meanings in the text," uncovering the hidden political/historical/cultural forces that shape texts, or even deconstructed by recognizing the infinite number of possible meanings that a text can offer in the "endless web of texts past and present."[12] Once again, what an original author might have intended to communicate in writing has little or no value in determining how a text should be construed. Similar claims have been advanced for how critics should interpret artworks, in that what an artist might have intended to convey should pose no limits on the interpretations observers can give to these artworks.

The rise of anti-intentionalism over the past fifty years has not gone unchallenged. Several prominent literary scholars and philosophers since the 1960s have rebutted the contention that reliance on authorial intentions is the *only* way to objectively adjudicate between competing interpretations of a text.[13] Without some appeal to what authors specifically intend to communicate, literary criticism falls victim to needless relativism where every interpretation of a text is about as good as any other reading. Other scholars have gone so far as to argue that the meanings of texts are identical to authorial intentions and, therefore, that there are no theoretical or practical consequences to intentionalism.[14]

How literary texts should be interpreted is not the only arena in which contests over the importance of authorial intentions are fought. The question of how authorial intentions inform our understanding of language has its greatest social significance, perhaps, in debates on the interpretation of legal texts. Jurists and legal theorists face the issue of whether the United States Constitution or, indeed, any legal document should be interpreted according to the original authors' intentions.[15] This battle was brought to the public's attention most forcefully during the 1985 Senate confirmation hearings on President Reagan's nominee to the Supreme Court, Robert Bork.[16] Advocates of "originalism" like Bork argued that the proper aim of constitutional interpretation is to understand and deploy the intentions of the framers. Under this view, interpretation organizes textuality as the place where an author's intentions are represented in language: originalism posits interpretation as a process of deriving, according to the relevant aesthetic/political/moral values, what that intention is, and hence, what the text "means." The originalists propose the doctrine of "original intent" to promote judicial neutrality and fidelity to the Constitution.[17] For example, many originalists argue that the Supreme Court should not support a woman's right to abortion because it was never the intention of the original framers of the Constitution back in 1789 to permit such activities under the Fourteenth Amendment of the Constitution. How

jurists conceive of the place of authorial intentions in textual interpretation clearly affects the lives of ordinary citizens.

The struggle over intentions in our understanding of human
acts is not limited to the domain of linguistic meanings. We also
ask ourselves whether intentions play any role in our experience
of meaning when viewing artworks or listening to music. When
listening to, for instance, Beethoven's Sixth Symphony, do people
sense that Beethoven specifically desired for them to experience
particular aesthetic responses to different parts of his composition? What role, if any, do the composer's artistic intentions play
in people's understandings of avant-garde performances such as
John Cage's silent composition 4′33″? What meanings, if any, did
artists such as Jackson Pollack and Mark Rothko intend for us
to recognize in viewing their various nonrepresentational paintings? Modern painting and sculpture puts into sharp focus the
battle over "authorial" intentions as ordinary spectators and art
critics strive to make sense of an artist's work. People can't help
but ask what artists like Pollack or Cage might have been attempting to achieve when they created their artworks. In a related way,
it is almost impossible for us to view van Gogh's later paintings
and not think about the sliced-off ear, the suicide, and how the
whirling landscapes might be the result of unconscious impulses
that drove van Gogh to paint as he did. Most generally, who a
speaker, reader, or artist is and what he or she might be trying
to communicate seems inextricably a part of the interpretations
people give to speakers, texts, and artworks.

Do speakers, authors and artists have any natural rights over
the interpretation of their creations? Very few critics or scholars
would argue that what a speaker, author, or artist explicitly intended to communicate fixes, once and for all, what any utterance,
text, or artwork means. People clearly bring their own biases into
interpreting human artifacts. It is no surprise that responses to
any specific utterance, poem, or artwork will vary considerably
across individuals.

Yet discussions about what a speaker, author, or artist means
don't easily settle into the radical subjectivist position where
each person creates his or her own meaning. Listeners, readers, observers, and critics of art most often contend that some

interpretations of a human artifact are more correct, or at least more permissible, than others. Few of us, for example, would agree with Charles Manson's reading of the Beatles song "Helter Skelter" as a plea for a race war in America.[18] Part of the reason we reject Manson's interpretation of "Helter Skelter" rests with our tacit belief that John Lennon didn't entertain any such thoughts in writing this song, nor did he wish for us to assume any such communicative intentions on his part. Artists often debate, refute, or outright reject interpretations of their work. This is precisely what Georgia O'Keefe did during her lifetime when she repeatedly denied critical interpretations of both the erotic content and feminist intent of her paintings.

The scholarly debate over intentionalism touches on many interesting questions and topics that will be addressed in the chapters that follow. Are "meanings" and "intentions" similar, related, or entirely different concepts? Are intentions best understood as private mental events that precede individual actions, or are they better characterized as emergent properties of collaborative interactions among people? What constitutes an "author" (e.g., what do we do with texts written by multiple authors with possibly competing intentions, when we have no idea who wrote a text or when it was composed)? Do authors, or even speakers, have any special authority in interpreting what their own texts possibly mean? What criteria should be applied in specifying a person's communicative intentions? Should critics consult the author, her diary, her psychiatrist or even her astrologer? Can people ever, under any circumstances, really know what an individual's true intentions are in saying or writing or creating what he or she did? How can scholars account for metaphor and irony, cases of language that seem to demand that we recognize that speakers/writers intend something different from what their words conventionally mean? Does it *ever* matter who speaks, writes, or creates something? How are we to interpret literary texts or artworks that are claimed to have been created by someone other than the person(s) who actually produced the artwork? What are judges and lawyers to do when they interpret legal texts and apply these interpretations in making judicial decisions? Do people ground their interpretations of meaning differently across cultures? What does it even mean to say that anyone has *interpreted* someone's utterance, text, or artwork?

Despite the tremendous, continuing debates about intentions in the humanities, there is surprisingly little discussion in the cognitive sciences of the possibility that communicative intentions are ephemeral by-products of linguistic understanding rather than the foundation for utterance interpretation.[19] Until now, cognitive scientists have not seriously responded to the current challenges regarding intentions in communication. My aim in this book is to address the controversy over intentionalism from an interdisciplinary perspective, one that acknowledges the variety of viewpoints on intentions, meanings, and interpretations in both the humanities and cognitive science. Much of the debate over whether communicative intentions constrain the interpretation of meaning rests with scholars' very different accounts of what it means to interpret any utterance, text, or artwork. How ordinary readers, listeners, and expert critics understand and form interpretations of meaning requires cognitive effort that takes place in real time, starting with the first moments when people move their eyes across the page, hear the first few notes of a sonata, or glance at a painting, up to later moments when we consciously, deliberatively reflect upon what has been seen or read. Understanding and interpreting are fundamental processes of the human mind. Yet the surprising fact about debates on intentionalism is that critics often ignore considerations of what is known about how people actually experience meaning, including the possibility that people immediately, and unconsciously, seek out authorial intentions when they read, listen, or observe human artifacts.

This book describes in greater detail the extent to which meaningful experience is, and is not, shaped by people's assumptions about the communicative intentions of others. Understanding how people ordinarily create interpretations of the acts they see or hear requires a detailed examination of human cognitive processes as these operate moment-to-moment in everyday life. Fortunately, extensive work in the cognitive sciences reveals important insights into ordinary, unreflective, as well as reflective, cognitive processes, that tell us a good deal about the possible role of intentions in the experience of meaning. My strategy in exploring intentions in meaningful experience adopts what might be called the *cognitive intentionalist premise*:

People bring their ordinary human dispositions to understand what other people are saying or doing in interpreting nonlinguistic, linguistic, and artistic acts. Our interest in communing with the intentions of others is so deeply a part of how people construct meaningful interpretations of artifacts that we sometimes think that the search for intentions is optional and therefore can be abandoned if desired. Yet an explicit search for the psychological underpinnings of human action will reveal the fundamental importance of communicative intentions in many aspects of meaningful experience.

Adopting the cognitive intentionalist premise constrains me to systematically explore the possibility that our assumptions about people as intentional agents place significant limits on both the creation and interpretation of meaningful experience. My exploration of intentions in meaningful experience is guided by two primary commitments: (a) a commitment to seek general principles governing all aspects of how people experience meaning (the generalization commitment); and (b) a commitment to make my account of meaningful experience consistent with what is known about human cognition (the cognitive commitment). I do not assume that meaningful experience *must* always be directly linked to human intentions. But I don't reject the possibility that intentionalism has little to offer in explaining how people create and understand meaning in everyday life, in different cultural contexts, and in special scholarly, interpretive activities.

Of course, many scholars disagree with my strategy in exploring the consequences of intentionalism. They argue that it is nearly impossible to accurately know the intentions of others. For these scholars, it is far better to focus on the meaning in the work itself, apart from considering anything about the human agents who created the work, or to focus on different idiosyncratic interpretive strategies, than it is to propose accounts of meaningful interpretation based on unreliable readings of other people's minds. These scholars maintain that looking solely at human intentions misses the critical contribution of historical, political, and cultural forces in the creation and experience of meaning. Seeking what is meaningful about human artifacts, and the ways they are meaningful, demands the privileged exploration of these different forces.

Yet my concern with understanding the psychological reality of meaningful experience attempts to situate historical, political, and cultural forces within the context of how people actively seek to make sense of their experiences. Many postmodernists, for example, attempt to render invisible the meaning that arises in interpretive experience. These scholars claim to be justified in doing this because they are revealing hidden social and historical forces outside the awareness of the creators and interpreters of human artifacts. However, postmodern scholars only talk about possible theoretical factors rather than focusing on genuine social and historical processes within which people experience meaning. My aim is to show how intentions can be described not as a mere matter of recovering the disembodied meanings in individual minds, but as dynamic, emergent properties of interactive social/cultural/historical moments within which people create and make sense of different human artifacts.

A significant portion of this book is devoted to exploring not just whether assumptions about intentions constrain meaningful experience, but to explaining how people's assumptions and their coordinated, collaborative interactions with others give rise to meaning, even in cases where there is no face-to-face contact between creator and observer (author and reader). I will strongly reject the idea that our experience of meaning rests primarily with locating the meaning "in" human artifacts. Theorists too often seek to find supposedly fixed "meanings" or "thoughts" or "intentions" underlying human discourse, with the entities being described as rules, conventions, representations, or theories. Yet it is something other than rules, conventions, representations, or theories that make communication possible. As Russian linguistic and literary scholar V. Voloshinov put it, "meaning belongs to a word in its position between speakers (at the moment of its utterance), that is, meaning is realized only in the process of active, responsive understanding."[20] Even when we know nothing about the person(s) responsible for an artifact, we still construct interpretations of artifacts, to a large extent, around the belief that some person created an artifact with a communicative purpose in mind. What any human artifact means is best characterized in terms of what a speaker, author, or artist meant to communicate successfully given the linguistic, cultural, and artistic conventions in place at the time the work was created. This account doesn't deny that people sometimes fail to recognize communicative intentions, or that conventions sometimes clash with what people intend to communicate. Yet in each case of meaningful experience, the recognition of what is intentional about human artifacts places significant constraints on how we make interpretive judgments.

The cognitive intentionalist perspective adopted here will not necessarily resolve all of the debates about the role of communicative intentions in the experience of meaning. We will continue to take the paradoxical stance of wanting to ground meaningful interpretation in the communicative intentions of others while, at the same time, not wanting to be limited by what other people intend by what they say, write, or do. My argument, though, is that understanding something about how the human mind constructs meaningful patterns from what is heard, read, or observed should help mediate some of the disputes about intentionalism in contemporary academia and popular culture.

Part II

Searching for Intentions

Part II presents several chapters illustrating the ubiquity of intentions in people's meaningful experiences of language and artwork. I focus on some complexities associated with defining intentions and intentional actions, and argue that people have a strong, natural disposition to attribute intentionality to human action and language. I suggest that intentions need not be viewed only as private mental acts that precede human action, but can profitably be understood as emergent properties of social interactions and thus are not necessarily located in individual minds. It is also important to distinguish between intentions at different levels of unconscious and conscious experience. I describe contemporary research demonstrating the interrelatedness of intentions and ideas about communication and meaning. Moreover, determining the precise role that intentions have in meaningful experience requires acknowledging the diversity of ways that people understand language and artwork.

Chapter 2

Intentions and Intentional Action

What do people's actions tell us about their intentions? Consider the simple situation of a person standing in front of a door, digging into his pockets, and then fumbling with a set of keys. We can easily assume by his actions that the person is looking for the right key to open the door to the room which he will then enter. Until the person actually finds the key and opens the door, we understand what the person is trying to do, or what his intentions are, as a matter of inference from somewhat uncertain information. After all, people can feasibly perform many actions when they stand in front of a door, fumbling with a set of keys. Yet our vast experience, both personal and vicarious, with standing-in-front-of-door activities provides us with the necessary background knowledge to make a reasonable inference about the person's likely intentions in the door-opening scene, even if this person wasn't necessarily trying to communicate anything by his or her actions.

This simple example demonstrates how our understanding of human behavior depends on our ability to make inferences about people's intentions. All actions can be described in purely physical terms, but we rarely talk of human actions in this way. For example, suppose I see Mary waving her hand. To describe Mary's action in purely physical terms, I might say something like *Mary raised her arm slightly, extended her fingers, and moved her forearm and hand from side to side*, etc. Although this statement might precisely describe Mary's action, it doesn't suggest that her hand waving was intentionally performed for the purpose of having others recognize what Mary is doing and why she is doing it. Most people would probably say that *Mary waved* or *Mary waved at us* to express their belief that Mary intentionally waved for a particular communicative purpose.

Determining whether someone performs an action intentionally, or with the intention to communicate something to other people, requires something more than just observing what people do. Intentionality is a social judgment, not an objective fact about the world.[1] Defining what counts as an intention, as distinct from other mental and physical acts, is quite difficult. As one philosopher wrote: "Just what an intention is, in terms of brain processes or anything else, is exceedingly hard to say."[2]

Understanding what intentions are and what function they play in human life is critical to determining their possible role in people's experience of meaning. My aim in this chapter is to briefly consider some ways of characterizing intentions in human action and thought. Later chapters discuss the relations of intentions to questions of meaning and communication, as well as how people infer intentionality from human action and artifacts. I argue here that there are important differences between *intentions* and *intentional actions*. I suggest that it is important to distinguish between intentions at different levels of conscious and unconscious experience. I will also argue that when accounting for meaningful experience it is important to distinguish between the intentions motivating human action and the effects that people hope to achieve as a result of others inferring intentions. Moreover, intentions are not just private mental acts located solely in the minds of individuals, but in many cases reflect emergent properties of interactions between people.

WHAT ARE INTENTIONS?

Cognitive scientists struggle with the concept of intention, but philosophers outline four ways to talk about intentions.[3]

First, there are *expressions of intention*, as when a speaker says, "I shall (am going to) do A in circumstance C." Examples of people's expressing this intention include the following utterances: *I'm going to go to San Francisco tomorrow* and *I promise to mow your lawn this afternoon.*

Second, there are *ascriptions of intention*, as when a speaker says, "Someone has the intention of doing A in C." Examples of speakers expressing this intention are seen in *Jones will run the race* and *Mary wants to marry Louis.*

Third, there are *descriptions of the intention with which some action is done*, as when a speaker says, "His intention in saying X was to do Y." Examples of speakers expressing this intention are seen in *Smith's intention in saying that was to embarrass Gary* and *Bill's intention in closing the door was to keep the noise out.*

Finally, there are *classifications of actions, as intentional or as done with intention*, as when a speaker says, "Someone did X intentionally." Examples of speakers expressing this view of intentions are *Sally shot Harry intentionally* and *Natalie intentionally skipped her appointment.*

This outline makes it clear that the concept of "intention" (and its allies "intent," "intend," and "intentionally") covers a wide range of physical actions and mental events.[4] Part of the debate over the importance of authorial intentions in the experience of meaning stems from the fact that scholars focus on different aspects of intentions when making arguments for, or against, intentionalism.

Yet most scholars more narrowly believe that intentions are closely related to the idea of subjectivity. Intentions are traditionally conceived of in individual, singular terms.[5] Philosophers, psychologists, and others tend to think of intentions as private mental states that are formulated before the performance of behavioral acts. Intentions are purposeful psychological states where the contents of an intention are assumed to be mentally represented. For example, my observation of a person fumbling with a set of keys by a closed door leads me to assume that the person experienced a private mental state, something like "Find key to open door," which precedes his or her taking the keys out and trying to open the door. In a similar way, we believe that a speaker, writer, or artist must have in mind a representation of some set of assumptions which he or she intends to make manifest or more manifest to an audience.

INTENTIONS AND DESIRES

Intentions differ from desires in specific ways. Desires are psychological states that represent what someone wishes for or wants. Desires represent our feelings about possible goals or objectives and are influenced by factors internal to the individual. Intentions are psychological states that represent what someone actually plans to do. They are based on desires but take into consideration which desires actually can be achieved. As a general rule, desires are transformed into intentions before action is taken. Even in the case of impulsive acts, an intention is formed, however briefly. What makes impulsive actions different is that the desire behind the intention arises suddenly and forcefully, often overshadowing previously established intentions.

A good way to concretely illustrate the difference between desires and intentions is to consider the following. If I want someone to be dead, my desire will be satisfied no matter how he dies. If I intend to kill someone, my intention will not be carried out unless I act on that intention and murder him. Consequently, my intention to kill someone will not be carried out if I accidentally run over him, or if he dies of a heart attack. That is to say, the propositional content of an intention is not *it happens*, nor even *I did it*, but *I do it in order to carry out this intention*. It is this feature of intention that is called *causal self-referentiality*, and it is this that distinguishes intention from desire.[6]

FUNCTIONS OF INTENTIONS

Intentions have specific functional roles in people's lives.[7] The mental state of intending usually requires that we believe the achievement of some act is possible and that we can bring about that act by engaging in certain activities. It makes little sense to say that *I intend to leap over that tall building* if I fully know that there is nothing I could really do to achieve that goal. Intentions typically pose problems for future deliberation. For example, if I intend to visit my parents in Boston, I need to determine which activities best allow me to achieve this goal. If my planning does not result in my visiting my parents in Boston, my intentions have not affected me in the right way. In this way, intentions usually require that we find good solutions for the problems they pose. Moreover, prior intentions constrain possible future intentions. If I am intending to go visit my parents in Boston at a specific time, I certainly cannot be somewhere else on the same date.

Intentions provide a *source of admissibility* for adopting others' intentions. A person's desires can be inconsistent with one another (e.g., strongly desiring to go swimming this afternoon while, at the same time, wishing to work this afternoon on writing this book). Yet people don't ordinarily adopt intentions that they believe will conflict with each other either in the present or in a future-directed way. Thus, I can't intend to go swimming this afternoon if I know the swimming pool is closed.

People ordinarily track the source of their intentions and will typically alter their activities when all their attempts to achieve their intentions fail. For instance, I have particular intentions I wish to communicate and have you understand in writing this book. I will often revise portions of each chapter, as indeed I have done, when I believe that any of my intentions have not been successfully realized in what I have written. This process of altering our initial plans to achieve some intentional goal is a commonplace activity in everyday life.

A nice, although slightly mechanistic, description of the function of intentions in human experience is given by psychologist Jerome Bruner:

> What I take for granted ... is that most of what we speak of in common sense term as human action is steered by intentions of the following kind and in the following way. An intention is present when an individual operates persistently toward achieving an end state, persists in developing means and corrects the development of means to get closer to the end state, and finally ceases the line of activity when specifiable features of the end state are achieved. The elements of the cycle, then, comprise aim, option of means, persistence and correlation, and a terminal stop order.[8]

WHAT COUNTS AS INTENTIONAL ACTION?

How should intentional action be characterized? The philosopher Elizabeth Anscombe provided a valuable characterization of intentional behavior: "An act is intentional if it is being done in relation to some future state of affairs and if what is being done is directed towards bringing about that future state of affairs."[9] Although most of what adults do most of the time is intentional, we can't judge the intentionality of an act simply by knowing what was done. The action needs to meet the two conditions of Anscombe's definition: (a) it is done in relation to some future state of affairs, and (b) it is done in an attempt to bring about that future state. Some human actions such as telephoning, calling, groping, paying, hiring, sending, and marrying are clearly intentional. Other actions may or may not be intentional, such as offending, kicking, dropping, coming to possess, and switching (on or off). Thus, I can offend someone without intending to do so. I cannot unwittingly marry someone.

Since Anscombe's pioneering work, philosophers have continued to argue about the conditions that must hold for any particular act to be judged as intentional. They note various complications arise that make it difficult to say whether some actions were performed intentionally. For instance, when people are asked why they did something, they may reply in such a way as to make the act appear unintentional (e.g., *I didn't know I was doing that*) when, in fact, the actor clearly knew what he or she was doing and intended to act in a particular way. On the other hand, when asked about an unintentional act, a person might quickly invent a reason to make the act appear purposeful. For these reasons, philosophers often argue that there is an important distinction between intending something and doing something intentionally. Thus, we may perform many intentional actions without forming an intention to perform them. As philosopher Donald Davidson noted: "It is a mistake to suppose that if an agent is doing something intentionally, he must know that he is doing it."[10] Consequently, many intentions are not formed, if forming an intention presupposes conscious deliberation.[11]

What do people normally think about intentions and intentional action? Chapter 4 describes some of the psychological research on people's judgments of intentionality. But only one set of empirical studies has systematically examined ordinary people's folk concept of intentionality. Psychologists Bertram Malle and Joshua Knobe specifically investigated what kinds of behavior college students viewed as intentional.[12] They first asked students to rate the intentionality of twenty behaviors and found, not surprisingly, that some statements such as *Anne is sweating* or *Anne was yawning during a lecture* were consistently rated as low in intentionality, while other statements such as *Anne stole a pound of peaches* and *Anne invited Sam to lunch* reflected high degrees of intentionality. People evidently, then, are sensitive to differences in the intentionality of various human actions.

Participants in another study were asked *When you say that somebody performed an action intentionally, what does this mean?* People listed four main ideas: Intentions (i.e., he showed a desire to perform the action), Beliefs (i.e., he thought about the act and its effect), Desires (i.e., he did it in hopes of getting some result), and Awareness (i.e., he knew what he was doing). The awareness concept is critical for identifying actions that conform to intentions but were not performed intentionally. Suppose, for example, that Ben forms an intention to call his mother. He also remembers that he is supposed to call his sister. He picks up the phone to call his sister but dials the wrong number and ends up reaching his mother. In this case, Ben's behavior is consistent with his intention of calling his mother, but he did not call his mother intentionally, because he did not perform the behavior with the awareness of fulfilling his intention.

There are other important factors to consider when evaluating whether someone has done something intentionally. Consider the following situation.[13] Imagine that Jerry is a novice at playing darts. He has never played darts before and is not talented at playing games like this. Surprisingly, Jerry hits triple 20 (a very difficult throw) on his first try. A friend dismisses the throw as a fluke, so Jerry tries again, this time missing badly. We can be confident that Jerry wanted to hit the triple 20, but would we say that he hit it intentionally on his first throw? Most people would not. Participants in one of Malle and Knobe's studies clearly distinguished between whether an actor tried to perform a particular action (judgment of intention) and whether he performed it intentionally (judgment of intentionality).

Overall, Malle and Knobe's results revealed five main factors in people's folk concept of intentionality (desire, belief, intention, skill, and awareness). To put these factors all together, imagine that I painted a picture of a cat. I want to paint a picture (desire), I thought that painting a picture of a cat might be a good way of realizing this desire (belief), I therefore decided to paint the picture (intention), I possessed the skill to do so (skill), and I was aware of fulfilling my intention (awareness) while painting the picture.[14]

This five-factor model is especially useful because it clarifies the distinction between *intentions* and *intentional action*. People differentiate attributions of *intention* (based on belief and desire information) from attributions of doing something intentionally (based on intention, skill, and awareness information). People apply the term *intention* to persons (who intend to do something) and the term *intentional* to actions (which are performed intentionally). When speaking of intentionality, people speak of actions that were performed intentionally. By contrast, when speaking of an action that was intentional (i.e., preceded by an intention), people do not automatically infer that such an action was performed intentionally. Thus, if a person lacked skill, or was unaware of his or her skills, this action would be intended but not performed intentionally.

INTENTIONS AND THE UNCONSCIOUS MIND

In everyday life, we are not always consciously aware of what we are doing. Sigmund Freud, in many respects, laid the foundation for a psychology of intention. Freud argued that intentions serve as unconscious links to what appear to be gaps in our conscious experience.[15] Psychologist Keith Oatley described Freud's ideas about intention and psychoanalysis in the following way:

Memory does indeed have a central place in psychoanalysis, but the key to Freud's theorizing about it is his treatment of it as related to human goals, wishes as he called them; how we sometimes act as if we had an intention but deny it. Freud's methods were methods for investigating goals and plans, by listening to patients' stories. A story makes sense only when the goals and plans of the actors are understood. Yes, Freud was interested in restoring memories, but the interpretations that psychoanalysts offer to fill gaps in a story do not fill any old gaps. They fill specifically those gaps left by missing intentions. They suggest goals that might have been forgotten or denied, but which might make sense of otherwise incomprehensible sequences of action.[16]

Freud was interested in many manifestations of unconscious intentions. He described in *The Psychopathology of Everyday Life* how common faulty actions, such as slips of the tongue, the forgetting of familiar names, and mistakes in reading and writing, are not accidents but meaningful events indicative of unconscious psychological conflicts. For example, slips of the tongue express "something one did not wish to say; it becomes a mode of self-betrayal."[17] Freud said that "the suppression of the speaker's intention to say something is the indispensible condition for the occurence of a slip of the tongue."[18] Although the suppression of an intention could be deliberate, as when someone is lying, Freud was most concerned with cases where speakers were unaware of the suppression because of what these verbal accidents revealed about unconscious forces and motivations. Consider the following example from Freud:

> A recently married man, whose wife was concerned about preserving her girlish appearance and only with reluctance allowed him to have frequent sexual intercourse, told me the following story which in retrospect both he and his wife found extremely funny. After a night in which he had once again disobeyed his wife's rule of abstinence, he was shaving in the morning in his bedroom which they shared, while his wife was still in bed; and as he had often done to save trouble, he made use of his wife's powder-puff which was lying on the bedside table. His wife, who was extremely concerned about her complexion, had several times told him not to, and therefore called out angrily: "There you go again, powdering

me (*mich*) with *your* (*deiner*) puff!" He husband's laughter drew her attention to her slip (she had meant to say "you are powdering *yourself* (*dich*) again with *my* (*meiner*) puff") and she herself ended by joining in the laughter. "To powder" ("*pudern*") is an expression familiar to every Viennese for "to copulate"; and a powder-puff is an obvious phallic symbol.[19]

This example illustrates how slips of the tongue are related to jokes and puns, all of which can reveal certain aspects of unconscious intentions/thoughts.

Although consciousness is typically viewed as one side of the conscious/unconscious dichotomy, most psychologists now contend that there are varying degrees of awareness, ranging from minimal states that are "the common sense of being" up to higher levels of consciousness where we can verbally express our motives, plans, and activities. We can consider behavior along a continuum extending from no intent through unconscious to conscious intent. On one extreme of the continuum will be (1) pure accidents, followed by (2) reflex actions, (3) actions motivated by unconscious forces, such as neuroses, (4) behavior under stress, such as panic and hysteria, (5) actions performed under hypnosis and other forms of suggestion, (6) behavior as adaptation to group and cultural norms or resulting from interpersonal transactions, (7) acts with foreseeable consequences but without specific intent, and finally (8) premeditated acts that are carefully planned and executed.[20]

Cognitive scientists have recently argued that consciousness is neither unitary nor continuous.[21] For instance, philosopher Dan Dennett claims that "there is no single, definite 'stream of consciousness' because there is no central Headquarters, no Cartesian theater where 'it all comes together' for the person or a Central Meaner."[22] Our phenomenal sense of a single "stream of consciousness" is "only rather like a narrative because of its multiplicity; at any point in time there are multiple 'drafts' of narrative fragments at various stages of editing in various places of the brain."[23] Cognitive scientist Marvin Minsky argues that the "same person can entertain different beliefs, plans, and dispositions at the same time."[24] It is not simply a matter of different systems of the brain working together to construct a singular view of the world, but of different systems that may be constructing different views at the same time, and different images of the self who is looking out at it.

This contemporary view of consciousness nicely explains why people may be aware of a general goal, yet unaware of the specific intentions for reaching that goal. For instance, you may have a goal of helping someone with some task. As part of this, you may have an intention, usually unconscious, to encode some message in language; an intention, sometimes unconscious, to be seen as nice, smart, or helpful; and an intention based on social norms and obligations to assist other people. Each of these intentions may have been conscious at one time, but they may not necessarily remain at a conscious level because many intentional states become overlearned.

A good example of overlearned intentionality is seen in dance performance. Dancing appears to require that a person have supreme control over his or her body. Yet dancers report that their movements are not guided by mindful intentions. When a dancer's intent is fulfilled, the dancer is his or her own body. Expert dancers report no duality of the conscious mind controlling the body. Even if dancing is movement with aesthetic intent, an experienced dancer need not think about how to move, or about what he or she is doing, for the dancer owns the movement and moves through space with no other purpose than realizing the aesthetic power of the movement.[25]

The multiplicity of conscious states and of intentions makes it reasonable to suppose that a person's conscious awareness may vary along different levels of intention during human action. Some philosophers have suggested that, at the very least, it is crucial to distinguish between "fully intentional" and "half-intentional" actions.[26] Fully intentional actions are deliberate and decided upon under full awareness of the actor. An example of a fully intentional action might be my writing an essay in which many statements arise quite automatically during the "flow" of my making a particular argument. Even though I may not consciously think about each statement written, I am still ultimately responsible for the contents of the final essay. Half-intentional actions typically are not consciously deliberated and thus are not the immediate cause of an actor's behavior, but they are actions for which a person may nevertheless be responsible. Many of my word choices in writing this sentence are half-intentional actions in that the words mostly pop into mind automatically without any conscious deliberation. In general, most of our activities are half-intended.

Many writers and artists have explored how different levels of conscious and unconscious experience influence the production of artworks. For example, several surrealist painters and poets from 1915 to 1930 conducted experiments involving different forms of "automatic painting" and "automatic writing" to see how the unintentional, unconscious mind gives rise to the creation of art. Automatism was seen as a means to liberate the creative spirit from the confines of conventional consciousness. Painters and poets tried to "let the pen or brush wander" or "let words speak for themselves," as if the artist or writer were magically taking dictation from the unconscious mind. For instance, in 1915 André Breton and Philippe Soupault created in collaboration the first automatic novel, *Les Champs magnetiques*. Some of the more beautiful, lyrical sentences from the opening pages of this book include:

> Tonight there are two of us by the river that overflows with our despair ... We think of the glimmering lights of bars, of the grotesque balls in those shattered houses where we left the day. But nothing is more desolate than this light flowing gently over the roofs at five in the morning. The streets diverge silently and the boulevards come to life: a belated walker smiles not far from us. He has not seen our eyes and he passes softly. It is the sound of the milk wagons that dispel our torpor, and the birds soar heavenward in search of divine nourishment.[27]

Not all of the prose and poetry that emerged from the surrealists' "automatic writing" experiments produced such vivid, coherent imagery. And it is unclear to what extent any of the writers or painters who engaged in automatism actually created their works unintentionally and unconsciously. But some of the products of "automatic writing" certainly suggest how different aspects of the cognitive unconscious might find their expression in creative artworks.[28] At the very least, we need to recognize that human intentions are multifaceted and exist along different levels of conscious and unconscious experience.

Any individual speech or artistic event actually reflects a hierarchy of intentions, with each level having a different relationship to consciousness.[29] *High-level intentions* refer to the beliefs, emotions, or behavior that a person wishes to cause in someone else. For example, I utter the expression *Winter is the best season to go surfing in Santa Cruz* with the high-level intention of getting someone to adopt my belief about the best season to surf in Santa Cruz. *Middle-level intentions* are directed toward goals that are the planned means to achieve high-level intentions. In the case of my statement about surfing in Santa Cruz, my middle-level intention is for someone to have a certain perceptual experience in which he or she recognizes my statement as spoken in the English language. Middle-level intentions, therefore, are directed toward chosen sense-experienceable features of the physical object of phenomena. Finally, a person must make decisions about how to produce certain sense experiences for others. These *low-level intentions* are directed toward the means of bringing about the middle-level intentions and in turn the high-level intentions. Thus, I must make certain audible sounds that are recognized as English to get another to adopt my beliefs about the best season to surf in Santa Cruz. Of course, I may accomplish my high-level intention via other middle- and low-level intentions. For example, I might have chosen to get someone to have a certain belief about surfing in Santa Cruz (a high-level intention) by choosing a means, such as expressing a certain pattern of light and dark on a page that is called writing (a middle-level intention), and then choosing a typewriter to produce an instance of this pattern (a low-level intention). These three types of intentions together reflect a hierarchy of different relations between means and ends. Understanding what a speaker, writer, or artist has intended to communicate depends on the ability to infer high-level intentions from low- and middle-level intentions.

OVERT AND COVERT INTENTIONS

People often have several intentions motivating their actions. In some instances, people wish to conceal their true intentions from others. For example, imagine that John and Mary are arguing on the edge of a cliff when John suddenly jumps off as if committing suicide.[30] When the frightened Mary leans over the edge and sees John standing on a small rock a few feet below, she realizes that John has deceived her. The intention that John ostensively displays with a deceitful purpose (i.e., the suicide) is called an *overt intention*, while the actual intention motivating his deceitful act (i.e., to momentarily deceive Mary) is called the *covert intention*. Of course, in the present example, John realizes that Mary will soon come to grasp both his overt and covert intentions.

There are many cases in literature where readers assume that an author has a particular overt intention only to discover that the author also had a covert intention motivating what is written. Consider the following story.[31]

> A pair of suburban couples who had known each other for quite some time talked it over and decided to do a little conjugal swapping. The trade was made the following evening, and the newly arranged couples retired to their respective houses. After about an hour of bedroom bliss, one of the wives propped herself up, looked at her new partner and said *Well, I wonder how the boys are getting along*.

The author has the overt intention here of having readers interpret the story as being about heterosexual relationships, but eventually we discover that the author's covert intention was to convey the opposite interpretation. Readers are momentarily deceived because the story leads us at first to infer certain contextual effects that demand very little processing effort (a cognitive phenomenon called "garden-path"). But as readers soon recognize, another interpretation is equally valid. Speakers, writers, and artists often design their creations precisely to achieve garden-path effects for aesthetic purposes. Chapters 3, 4, and 5 provide many additional examples and discusses how people produce human artifacts with multiple overt and covert intentions in mind.

A significant part of the richness in our experience of meaning depends on our ability to infer both overt and covert intentions and, quite importantly at times, to distinguish between these in making sense of human artifacts.

INTENTIONS AND CONSEQUENCES

One of the major problems in debates over intentionalism in interpretation is that scholars often confuse authorial intentions with the putative consequences of realizing someone's intentions. Suppose, for example, that I intend to warn someone of impending danger by saying *Watch out for that bear behind you!* Although my intention is to warn you of the bear behind you, I may also wish by virtue of my utterance to have you take appropriate action, such as running away from the bear. As will be discussed in the next chapter, my intention here is called an *illocutionary speech act*, which I perform with the aim of my utterance having a *perlocutionary effect* (e.g., getting you to run away). Note that the addressee only runs away from the bear if she first recognizes my communicative intention to warn her. There may be instances, of course, where a listener clearly understands my intention to warn her but doesn't take any of the actions I had hoped she would subsequently perform. For example, the listener may not believe that she is really in danger from having a bear behind her.

This simple example illustrates the difference between recognizing someone's intention and realizing the consequences that person hoped would happen as a result of understanding the intention. Recognizing the distinction between intentions and their consequences will be critical later on in understanding the possible role that authorial intentions play in interpretation and criticism. There are many cases of scholars confusing the understanding of authorial intentions with understanding the concrete actions that speakers, authors, and artists hope to realize as a result of people understanding their language or artworks.

Naturally, people do not always intend all the expected side effects or consequences of their intentions. Imagine that Nancy has a toothache and guesses correctly that she will require a root canal operation. In this case, Nancy clearly recognizes the necessity of the root canal operation and specifically intends to go to the dentist with the aim of having the operation performed despite how unpleasant it may be. Nancy's intention is for the dentist to do the operation, she believes in what the dentist is doing and is willing to put up with the personal discomfort of the procedure, but she doesn't consciously intend to be in pain. Side effects of trying to achieve intentions do not generally play the same role in a person's planning as their intentions do. In particular, side effects are not always monitored by people. If Nancy's plan to get her toothache taken care of doesn't result in the side effect of her feeling additional pain because of the miracles of modern dentistry, she will not go back and try again to achieve that side effect.[32] In general, recognizing the distinction between a person's intentions and the possible consequences that result when that individual's intentions are realized is a critical element in our understanding of human action and communicative meaning.

COLLECTIVE INTENTIONS

Even when people act alone, their particular actions take place in social contexts that presuppose collectivity and a high degree of collective intentionality. For example, although mailing a letter is ostensibly a simple individual act, it is nonetheless premised on a host of assumptions about other people, none of whom the writer need ever meet.[33] Suppose that I deposit into my corner mailbox a letter, along with a check written to purchase a book. In doing so I assume that some uniformed stranger will pick up the mail and do whatever such uniformed strangers typically do to forward it to my addressee, most likely another stranger. I furthermore assume that this addressee will read my letter as a particular sort of letter – that is, as a mail order, and not some peculiar act of trivial philanthropy – and will respond in a particular way – that is, will not rob me blind, but will indeed send me the book I have ordered. Clearly mailing a letter is not a simple individual act. It is a highly contextualized act requiring, indeed assuming, considerable social knowledge on the part of the letter writer. By dropping my letter irretrievably into these public boxes, even into one I've never seen before, I take for granted a complicated set of actions by other people.

This simple example illustrates how an intention to perform certain actions relies on many assumptions about other people's intentions and actions. Although we sometimes talk of ourselves as the authors of our actions, we hardly ever act independently of each other. When a second living person responds to the act of a first, and thus acts in a way that depends on his acts, then the activities of the second person cannot be accounted as wholly his own. Important in all this is the idea that many individual actions are best characterized in collective, rather than purely individual, terms. When two people use language, it is (in its simplest forms) like shaking hands, playing a piano duet, or paddling a two-person canoe. Collective behavior is not just helpful behavior. Engaging in a prizefight is an example of collective behavior in which the pugilists have agreed to cooperate, even if the two contestants are competing. Collective behavior is also not the same as a summation of individual actions, and the difference between them resides in the intentions of the actors. When engaged in collective activity, individuals are guided by collective intentions, called "we-intentions."[34]

John Searle has argued that individual intentionality is not by itself sufficient to account for collective action, including conversation. But how do collective intentions relate to the individual intentions that cause the individual actions constitutive of the collective behavior? Searle argued that collective actions are primitive and cannot be reduced to individual intentions supplemented by mutual beliefs. Instead, each agent *we-intends* to achieve the collective goal by means of having an individual intention to do his or her part. Collective intentionality presupposes that each person assumes the existence of other agents as candidates for collaboration.

The philosopher J. David Velman gives a good example of how individual and collective intentions differ.[35] Imagine that a dean at a university asks the Philosophy department how it intends to fill a faculty position. When the dean does this, she seems only to be asking the seventeen members of the department to form a single intention. She is certainly not envisioning that the different members of the department will arrive at seventeen individual intentions that somehow converge. What rules out this possibility is not that convergence among the particular people is impossible, it's that none of them is in a position to have an individual intention about what the department should do. Each faculty member may have his or her own belief or desire as to what the department should do in filling the vacancy. Yet no individual can form an intention that speaks for the department as to what the department plan should be. Filling the vacancy is up to the department, and so any intention on the subject must be formed and held by the group as a whole.[36]

This example shows how intentions can clearly be viewed as social products created through the interaction of mutual beliefs between relational participants. The ongoing context of interaction is not reducible to either the intentions or actions of individuals. When issues of intent arise, participants negotiate and construct a mutually shared social reality with individual and relational implications. Whether intentions exist as "private mental acts" is beside the point; what is important is that intentions become meaningful only as a basis for cultural exchange between people. Rather than viewing intentions as solely subjective entities, we might better see them as part of the intersubjective quality of human experience as people come to a meeting of minds in everyday life. This point will turn out to be critical in understanding the role of authorial intentions in communication and criticism.

CONCLUSION

This chapter has offered some introductory remarks on the nature of intention and intentional action. Intentions are mostly viewed as purposeful mental states representing what a person plans to do. Yet intentions are not only subjective mental acts located in the minds of individuals, but also reflect the products of people's interactions in different social situations. Later chapters explore in greater detail how communicative meanings arise from people's coordinated, cooperative interaction in speech, written language, and artworks. A second point of interest is that intentions differ from intentional action. People attribute intentions to other persons and attribute intentionality to actions that are performed intentionally. When speaking of an action that was intentional, people do not immediately assume that the action was performed intentionally, especially in cases when the actor lacked skill or awareness of what he or she was doing. Third, people's intentions are realized along different levels of conscious and unconscious experience. Appreciating the diversity of unconscious and conscious experiences shapes our understanding of others' behavior and communicative meanings. Fourth, people recognize a distinction between understanding someone's intention and realizing the consequences that person desired as a result of others understanding the intention. Finally, people also distinguish between overt (i.e., ostensibly displayed) and covert (i.e., what really motivates) intentions. Each of these distinctions will turn out to be very important in determining the possible roles of authorial intentions in the interpretation of meaning.

Chapter 3

Meaning and Communication

Does understanding someone's intentions imply that one has understood that person's meaning? Consider the following brief exchange:

Jean: Can you tell me the time?

Dale: It's half past three.

The goal of Jean's question seems transparent, and Dale responds appropriately by providing Jean with the desired information. Although Jean and Dale must assume a good deal about each other in saying what they do (e.g., Jean must have some idea that Dale is able to provide the information, and Dale must assume that Jean needs only the approximate time), the ability to recognize the intentions in what the other says appears to be a fundamental part of understanding his or her meaning.

But consider now the following segments of dialogue between a woman patient (P) and her surgeon (S) soon after the woman has undergone a mastectomy. The conversation focuses on P's concern that her own illness might be treated as her late sister's cancer was several years earlier.[1]

(P): Well, it's just that I watched this with my sister, and I hate the idea of chasing it all over my body because she ended up dying anyway.

(S): Well, June, I don't know whether you're going to end up dying of this "anyway" anyway.

(P): Yeah.

40

(S): But I do know one thing. Between now and your death, whether it's from cancer or whether it's from an automobile accident, a lot of time's gonna pass. You are not faced with widespread cancer. I'm not in the business here of teaching you how to die. That's not the business I'm about now. I'm in the business of trying to make you a lot more alive. And, we're not in the business of chasing something. You know, taking pieces off you while we're chasing – no, that's not our business. Whatever it was with your sister, we're not your sister.

(P): No, but – when you've watched it happen once – You know, there are many times when the reason she didn't kill herself was because she was so close to my folks. But I thought, "How cruel for her." It would have been so much easier to do it in one lump. I know as a doctor you can't do that.

(S): Well –

(P): But I can.

(Later)

(P): That was another thing that was so sad to me when my sister died. My father kept saying "What did I do to deserve this? Haven't I been a good Jew?" And I said to him, "What has it got to do with anything, nobody's doing anything to you. You're not being punished." But it was his baby.

(S): You remember that too, though..

(P): What?

(S): Nobody's doing anything to you.

(P): No, nobody's doing anything to me ... But I shouldn't be forced to stick around and just ... just be kept, put together with spit for the rest of my life.

(S): Please! Please! I'm looking at you right now, you don't look like you're put together with spit. Now ...

This doctor-patient conversation suggests many levels of complex intentions that each speaker tries to communicate. For instance, the patient expresses concerns about her illness in comparison with that of her sister, feelings of jealousy and envy in the face of her sister's achievements, and her desire to uphold the family's honor in the face of her illness. The surgeon faces the challenge of recognizing this complex set of the patient's communicative intentions. Failure to understand what the patient intends to communicate could negatively impact her recovery. Because she believes that her sister died of the same disease and desperately wishes to avoid the course of her sister's horrible illness, the patient might go to extremes to avoid chemotherapy, radiation, and other types of therapy. Clearly, the surgeon's understanding and appropriate response to the patient's intended meanings is critical to her well-being.

The purpose of this chapter is to discuss the relation between intention, meaning, and communication. I describe a way of thinking about linguistic communication that captures some of the complexities evident in ordinary conversations.[2] My argument is that understanding the meaning of what another person says (or writes or creates) demands some recognition of that person's communicative intentions, even if we sometimes infer meanings different from that person's intended messages. Making sense of what someone else has said cannot be reduced to, or grounded in, considerations of what the artifact naturally, or conventionally, means apart from human intentionality. People use words to convey to each other first and foremost their communicative intentions, not the semantic meanings of the words or the unconscious causes that might underlie such intentions. Nevertheless, in many communicative situations, people will infer meanings as intentional that were only made manifest by speakers in order to enrich the specific mutual cognitive environment (and that were not in the speaker's mind before making his or her utterance).

WHAT IS MEANING?

When someone says "Jean's utterance '*Can you tell me the time?*' means X," what does he mean? Not surprisingly, the term *meaning* is complex and ambiguous. Consider several definitions of *meaning*.[3]

(1) When one thing like a symptom or clue can help to discover or discern another, we sometimes say the first *means* the second.

Clouds in the south mean a storm is coming.
These broken branches mean a large animal was here.
I hope this new desk means I'm getting promoted.

(2) Saying what or how much something *means* is a way of indicating its significance, consequences, or importance.

Losing millions means little to him.
A promotion for me means new shoes for the children.

(3) The *meaning* of something can be its point, purpose, or justification.

Mystics ponder the meaning of life.
What is the meaning of this? (asks the art critic)
Their futile counterattack was a meaningless waste.

(4) A person can *mean* to do something, in the sense of intending or being determined to do it.

Mrs. O'Leary's cow didn't mean to burn down Chicago.
I deserve that promotion, and I mean to have it.

(5) What somebody *means* by something is what he or she intends to express, communicate, or say; and in this sense, what the person means is also the *meaning* of the expressive utterance or act.

Plainly, she meant by her grimace that I should shut up.
The meaning of her grimace was, plainly: "Shut up."
"That's smart!" he taunted, meaning the opposite.

(6) Finally, the *meaning* of an expression or symbol can be what it expresses, represents, or conveys in standard usage. This is what dictionaries try to explain, what careful translations try to preserve, and what the present list distinguishes six of.

What a surprise that "meaning" has so many meanings!
The German word "rot" means the same as "red" in English.
Undeciphered, that code looks like meaningless nonsense.
Idiomatically, "kick the bucket" means "bite the dust."

Each use of *mean* differs in subtle but important ways. Although some scholars argue that some abstract conceptual unity underlies these different surface uses of the term *mean*, the variety of definitions for *mean* have not been generally taken into serious discussion in contemporary debates about the relations between intentions and meaning. The failure to adhere to these definitions has led to significant confusion in trying to explicate the notion of the "meaning" within an utterance, text, or artwork.

Jean's utterance takes on different meanings when these various definitions of *meaning* are applied. One might argue that the meaning of *Can you tell me the time?* is best captured by definition 3 (i.e., what is its point, purpose, or justification of Jean's statement), definition 5 (i.e., what Jean intended to communicate by her statement), or even definition 6 (i.e., what do certain elements in Jean's utterance represent or convey). Each of these definitions sheds different light on the meaning of what Jean said. But to what extent does our experience of meaning depend on the assumptions we have about what the utterance, or what Jean, communicates?

WHAT IS COMMUNICATION?

There are four main ways to characterize human communication, each of which places a different emphasis on meaning.[4] These views mostly describe linguistic communication, but as will be noted throughout this book, many forms of communication are nonlinguistic, including the experience of meaning in artworks. The encoding/decoding paradigm describes meaning as an inherent property of messages. The intentionalist paradigm views meaning as tied to the speaker's intentions. The perspective-taking paradigm sees meaning as determined from the addressee's point of view. The dialogic paradigm characterizes meaning as an emergent property of participants' joint activity.

According to the encoding/decoding, intentionalist, and perspective-taking paradigms, communication consists of speakers' and listeners' autonomous acts. For instance, in the encoding/decoding view, speakers transform their internal thoughts into a public code (i.e., a natural language) which they verbally express, and listeners decode the message to reveal its meaning. In the intentionalist perspective, speakers produce utterances that convey particular communicative intentions, and addressees process these utterances in order to recover speakers' intentional meanings. In the perspective-taking perspective, speakers convey intentions, but addressees understand these meanings from their particular points of view, not those of the speaker. All of these paradigms view speakers and listeners acting autonomously as they separately figure out what to say and how to infer what is meant. However, in the dialogic paradigm, communication is a process in which participants collaborate to produce shared meanings. Under this perspective, feedback is not simply a mechanism by which addressees help speakers generate more informative messages, but is an intrinsic part of the process by which the meanings of messages are established. Thus, communication is a joint activity of the kind that characterizes most social interactions.

The intentionalist, perspective-taking, and dialogic views contribute important ideas to describing people's meaningful experience of linguistic communication. These paradigms are not mutually exclusive. For instance, understanding something about a speaker's communicative intentions occurs as a joint activity in which speakers and listeners cooperate and coordinate to reach mutual understandings of each other's, and their joint, intentions. In some situations, speakers and listeners will coordinate in such a way that a new, emergent meaning will arise that wasn't originally in the mind of either participant.

THE PROBLEM OF LITERAL MEANING

A common assumption among scholars and laypersons is that understanding the meanings of utterances and texts is grounded in literal meaning. Most linguistic theories, for instance, presuppose that the literal meanings of words and sentences can be precisely stated and that literal meaning serves as the foundation for interpretation of what speakers and texts really mean. As I argued in *The Poetics of Mind: Figurative Thought, Language, and Understanding*, this faith in literal meaning as the bedrock for all interpretation is clearly misguided.[5]

Who believes that understanding literal meaning is the ultimate aim of interpretation? Actually, many people do. The Rev. Jerry

Falwell, for instance, described the interpretation of Scriptures as grounded in understanding its plain, literal meaning: "The Bible is absolutely infallible, without error in all matters pertaining to faith and practice, as well as in areas such as geography, science, history, etc. The disintegration of our social order can be easily explained. Men and women are disobeying the clear instructions God gave in His Word."[6] Consider the following small portion of text from the Bible: "Wives, submit yourselves unto your own husbands, as unto the Lord. For the husband is the head of the wife, even as Christ is the head of the church...Husbands, love your wives, even as Christ also loved the church, and gave himself for it." (Ephesians 5:22-23, 25). Falwell, and many other Christians, believe that this text must be understood and accepted in plain, literal terms.[7] This statement may seem alien to many Americans, as does Falwell's belief in the literal truthfulness of the Bible. But as recently as 1980, a Gallup poll discovered that 40 percent of the American public claimed to believe that the Bible is the "actual word of God and is to be taken literally, word for word."[8]

Of course, Christians differ in the extent to which they interpret, and obey, the Bible in strict literal terms. Fundamentalists are confident that every word of scripture (as found, for instance, in the King James Version) must be taken at literal face value. Evangelicals, on the other hand, are more comfortable with the ambiguities of translation and interpretation that arise when Scripture is critically analyzed. Fundamentalist readers of Scripture are confident that they can turn to their King James Bibles to find prescriptions for living; evangelicals are not so sure it is that simple. As one fundamentalist Christian said "It's not a fairy tale. It's something that actually happened."[9] An analysis of discourse among members of a fundamentalist church concluded that the parishioners believed that "Biblical stories are about the one true God and are not the product of human imagination. Likewise, because God is the timeless author of every word and story, the Bible need not be interpreted in a historical or literary context. Each word is equally valid, and each sentence is equally timeless and useful."[10] According to members of this church "anyone who contradicts the 'plain words of scripture' is doing the work of Satan, whether they know it or not."[11]

The belief that language has clearly demarked literal meanings is widespread, regardless of one's view of the Bible. But why does the belief in literal meaning have such currency in both folk and scholarly accounts of language and communication? The belief in literal meaning stems from the folk idea that words contain meaning and that by using words or sentences speakers are able to communicate these meanings to other people. This "container view of meaning" underlies both formal and informal theories of linguistic meaning and communication (i.e., the encoding/decoding paradigm) and presuppose that meaning is independent of the uses words are put to by individuals. The linguist Michael Reddy has demonstrated how pervasive this notion is in ordinary language and has identified the underlying metaphor the "conduit metaphor."[12] According to this metaphor, ideas are conduited from one inner mind to another, transported in small compartments by the train of speech. The listener's task is to extract the ideas of meaning from the words, thereby acquiring internal entities (i.e., meanings) that correspond to the internal entities in the speaker. Presented below are several statements that express the conduit metaphor in action:

> *I can't get anything out of this paragraph.*
> *There are few interesting ideas in Steve's essay.*
> *The poem is impenetrable.*
> *I had to struggle to find the meaning in this sentence.*
> *Please pay attention to what's in the words.*
> *Mary has good ideas that get lost in her prose.*

Despite the folk belief in the conduit metaphor, and its container view of meaning, the literal meaning of any word or sentence is almost impossible to determine. People cannot reach stable, unambiguous literal meanings for texts devoid of context and shared knowledge between speakers and listeners, authors and readers.[13] For instance, consider the adjective *muddy*.[14] The dictionary defines it as "covered, full of, or spattered with mud." Yet when I use *muddy* on a particular occasion, I always mean something more specific. If I told you *My shoes are muddy* I wouldn't just mean they are "covered, full of, or spattered with mud." Depending on the situation, I may mean there is mud on

47

my shoes, or on the leather surface. I am unlikely to mean they are "full of mud." There is an entirely different range of salient occasional meanings for *muddy*, as in *muddy water* (e.g., water with mud dissolved in it), *muddy road* (e.g., road with a surface of mud), *muddy windshield* (e.g., a windshield with mud on the outside surface), and *muddy floor* (e.g., floor with mud patches on it). The meaning of *muddy* on each occasion depends on what a speaker and listener, or writer and reader, might mutually expect given the particular context.

Empirical research, in fact, shows that people's intuitions about the meanings of words and sentences varies considerably across contexts. For example, when people were presented with sentences such as *John bends paperclips* and asked afterwards *How many does he bend?* most people responded *Oh, about three or four* even though the utterance itself does not contain this specific information.[15] Why not six or seven, or a dozen, or twenty? It's unlikely that the lexical entry for *to bend* specifies that "if said about paper clips, three or four, if said about iron rods, at most one, if said about pipe cleaners, five to seven" and so on.

Certain words such as *good, love*, or *a few* seem especially fuzzy even though in context the fuzzy area of denotation is often made precise. One study asked people to state how many of the objects in question would actually be meant when *a few* was used in different situations.[16] People on average estimated the following: *a few people standing before a hut* (4.55), *a few people standing before the house* (5.33), *a few people* (5.72), *a few people standing before City Hall* (6.37), *a few people standing before the building* (6.99). The data reveal the difficulty in defining the literal meanings of many words. It makes no sense to specify the meaning of *a few* in the mental lexicon as being "5.72 if said of people, 4.55 if said of people standing before a hut," and so on. Listeners do not simply look up the particular number associated with *a few*, but construct its meaning given some specific situation.

These observations show that meaning cannot be defined in simple literal terms. Meaning is not something that exists as a code to be listed in dictionaries. Dictionaries do not represent facts of a language that are independent of language users. The fact that a meaning is listed in a dictionary is just evidence that lexicographers observed the word being used in a way consistent with speakers' intending that meaning.

Determining the literal meaning of sentences is also impossible. A traditional view asserts that all sentences have literal meanings that are entirely determined by the meanings of their component words (or morphemes) and the syntactical rules according to which these elements are combined. Certain sentences may have more than one literal meaning, such as ambiguous sentences. Moreover, the literal meaning of a sentence may be defective or ill-specified, such as with nonsense sentences. In addition, the literal meaning of a sentence should be sharply distinguished from what a speaker means by use of the sentence, since the speaker's utterance may depart from the literal sentence in a variety of ways, as in metaphor, irony, indirect speech acts, and other figures.[17] Finally, and significantly, the literal meaning of a sentence is its meaning independent of context. Assuming this goal allows scholars to differentiate between *literal* or *sentence* meaning and *contextual, implied,* or *speaker* meaning, where the former represents a semantic interpretation and the latter a pragmatic interpretation.

Scholars often presume that a theory of literal meaning should provide the foundation for theories of language interpretation, in the sense that people should ordinarily analyze sentences according to their literal meanings as a first step toward understanding what speakers/authors intend by their utterances. Yet the meaning of any sentence, literal or otherwise, can only be determined relative to a set of background assumptions.[18] Consider the sentence *The cat is on the mat.* Determining the literal meaning of this sentence requires that many assumptions be made, for example that the cat and mat are not floating freely in outer space, and that gravitational forces exist. It is only through these kinds of background assumptions that the literal meaning of the sentence can even possibly be determined. However, these assumptions are not specifiable as part of the semantic analysis of the sentence, nor are these assumptions fixed in number or content. It appears impossible to know when to stop the process of specifying which assumptions need hold for determining literal meaning. Each assumption tends to imply other assumptions, which themselves must be specified in some way. For these reasons, it is unlikely that the background assumptions needed to specify the literal meanings of even simple sentences, such as *The cat is on the mat*, can be included as part of the semantics of the sentence.[19]

These problems with defining what words and sentences literally mean multiply when we try to specify what texts literally say. Texts are not static containers of meaning, but provide the common ground for writer and reader from which meaning may arise. Reading requires constant reference to prior knowledge from speech-based culture, not just the application of linguistic rules. For example, when reading legal texts (e.g., interpreting the First Amendment of the Constitution, protecting the right to free speech), meaning is constructed through consideration of the culture of law and the interpretation of human intentions which are brought to bear in the oral forum of the courtroom. This mix of cultural knowledge and speech-based understanding clearly contradicts the belief that any sentence has some sort of autonomous meaning in written language (see Chapter 7). Texts provide enduring opportunities for readers to construct meaning within a non-spatial, epistemological context of shared knowledge and conventions. Each reading of a text may lead to a multiplicity, rather than a singularity, of meanings.

As I comment in *The Poetics of Mind*, "Simply put, there exists no comprehensive account of literal meaning. What we think of as literal depends on a variety of factors including culture, individuals, context, and the task. People often fail to acknowledge that certain knowledge and assumptions drive their judgments of literalness for words, sentences, and texts."[20] Problems in defining what any piece of language means apart from human intentionality are precisely why code-based views (i.e., the encoding/decoding paradigm) fail to explain the complexity of linguistic communication. Chapter 6 describes research showing how people need not analyze the putative literal meanings of sentences as part of their inferring what speakers and writers intend to communicate.

Meaning and Communication

The intentionalist paradigm has been widely embraced, and debated, ever since the philosopher Paul Grice introduced his theory of "non-natural meaning" (i.e., meaning-nn).[21] According to Grice, natural meaning is devoid of human intentionality, as in, for example, *Those spots mean measles* or *Smoke means fire*. Strictly speaking, spots and smoke can't intentionally mean anything. Natural signs, like getting spots on one's face when sick with measles, are really symptoms or direct evidence of something (e.g., that somebody has the measles).

On the other hand, non-natural meaning is roughly equivalent to intentional meaning. For example, consider the expression *Those three rings on the bell (of the bus) mean that the bus is full*. A critical feature of meaning-nn is that it is intended to be recognized in a particular way by a recipient.[22] So we might say that the three rings on the bell has meaning-nn, because it is sufficient for the bus riders to recognize that the conductor (or whoever caused the three bells to ring) produced the rings for the expressed purpose of having the riders recognize his intention.[23]

Grice's work on non-natural meaning has led to the important idea that communication consists of a sender intending to cause a receiver to think or do something just by getting the receiver to recognize that the sender is trying to cause that thought or action. Thus, "communication is a complex kind of intention that is achieved or satisfied just by being recognized" (i.e., recognition-implies-fulfillment intentions).[24]

INTENTIONS AND OSTENSIVE-INFERENTIAL COMMUNICATION

In many interpersonal situations, the mere fact that an intention is recognized may lead to its fulfillment. Anthropologist Dan Sperber and linguist Deidre Wilson provided a nice illustration of this with the following example.[25] Imagine that Mary intended to inform Peter of the fact that she has a sore throat. Merely letting him hear her hoarse voice provides salient and conclusive evidence of her sore throat. Mary's intention can be fulfilled whether or not Peter is aware of it. He might realize that she has a sore throat without also realizing that she intends him to realize this fact.

Suppose now that Mary intended to inform Peter on July 1 that she had had a sore throat on the previous Christmas Eve. Now she could not produce direct evidence of her past sore throat, but could give him direct evidence, not of her past sore throat, but of her present intention to inform him of it. How would she do this, and what good would it do? She might utter the expression, *I had a sore throat on Christmas Eve*. Doing so gives Peter indirect but nonetheless strong evidence that she had a sore throat on the previous Christmas Eve. If Peter assumed that Mary was sincere and if he knew that she had a sore throat on the previous Christmas Eve, he could assume that Mary's intent to inform him that she had a sore throat on this date provides conclusive evidence that she spoke the truth. In these ordinary conditions, Mary's intention to inform Peter of her past sore throat would be fulfilled by making Peter recognize her intention. Thus, Mary intended her utterance *I had a sore throat on Christmas Eve* to produce in Peter the belief that she had a sore throat the previous Christmas Eve, she intended Peter to recognize her intention, and she intended his recognition of her intention to function as at least part of his reason for his belief. Successful communication can only take place if the speaker's communicative intentions (e.g., Mary's intention) has become mutually known to both the speaker and her addressee(s). The addressee may not believe what the speaker says, or may not act in a way that was hoped for by the speaker.

Determining speakers' communicative intentions can be tricky in many situations. To start with a simple case, when I put a sign in my yard that says *New Grass*, there is little doubt that I intend others to recognize that this sign is an artifact and not a natural object, and that my purpose is to convince people that there is new grass. But in this case I surely also intend others believe that there is new grass.[26] Getting people to believe that there is new grass may be a means to a future end, such as getting them to not step on it or, still higher in the means-ends hierarchy, allowing the new grass to grow. There are other means to keep people off my grass, many of which do not necessarily involve consideration of another as a cognitive agent who has beliefs (e.g., enclosing the area with a screened roof and walls keeps people, rabbits, and even hail off my grass). So the sign is a communicative artifact, because it is one means among several that usually serve the overall purpose of letting my grass grow, specifically selected to produce a belief in another person.

Deidre Wilson and Dan Sperber present a theory that describes my putting a sign in the yard that says *New Grass* as one example of "ostensive-inferential communication."[27] Under this view, ostensive-inferential communication consists of two intentions: an informative intention and a communicative one. An informative intention is conveyed by saying something, such as my putting up the sign *New Grass*, and this intention is specifically intended to be recognized by others, such as people who might potentially walk on my lawn (the communicative intention).[28]

Consider now a different type of intention.[29] Imagine that I am sitting on a beautifully crafted wooden chair. The craftsperson who created this chair might well have intended me to believe the chair is good, not just an artifact to sit on. This is an *expressive intention*. How does this belief differ from the belief that I want to instill in others with my sign about the grass? The difference is that in the case of the chair, the intended belief is about the chair, the artifact itself. In the case of the sign, the belief is about the grass, or my desire that you not walk on the grass, a different entity altogether. For something to be a communicative artifact, it must have been made with an intent to cause a belief about an entity other than the artifact itself.

Another type of intention that is not strictly communicative includes cases in which an artifact is intended to produce a belief about its creator. For example, a good chair is intended to produce the belief that its maker is a good craftsperson. In this situation, the craftsperson's intended belief is not about the artifact itself, or about the entity to which the artifact refers (as in the case of the grass sign). Instead, the artifact has been created with the intention of producing a belief about its maker. The intention in this case is expressive, not communicative.[30] People can also say things to impress others with their knowledge, sophistication, and so forth, but these are best described as expressive intentions.

Expressive intentions differ from communicative ones because their recognition does not imply their fulfillment. For example, my intention to make someone think of the concept of justice by saying *Consider the concept of justice* is an instance of ostensive-inferential communication in that someone's recognition of my intention to get the person to think of justice logically implies that he or she think of justice and hence my intention is fulfilled by its recognition. On the other hand, my high-level intention to get a person to believe that winter is the best season for surfing in Santa Cruz is not an intention in which recognition-implies-fulfillment: recognition of the intention does not itself bring about another's believing that winter is the best season for surfing in Santa Cruz. A person might understand my utterance *Winter is the best season for surfing in Santa Cruz* to express a particular proposition (itself an instance of ostensive-inferential communication), but recognition of the contents of the proposition does not itself necessarily lead the person to adopt my belief about Santa Cruz. After all, the person may think that summer is the best time to go surfing in Santa Cruz. The difference between communicative and expressive intentions depends on whether the recognition of an intention implies that the intention has been fulfilled.

A TRADITIONAL VIEW
OF COMMUNICATIVE ACTS

There are perhaps an infinite number of very specific intentions (what Grice referred to as "m-intentions") that people might communicate through their speaking, writing, art, and actions.[31] The philosopher J. L. Austin was the first to draw attention to the many functions performed by utterances as part of interpersonal communication.[32] Austin pointed out that many utterances do not communicate information, but are equivalent to actions. When someone says *I apologize for stepping on your toe*, or *I promise to meet you for lunch tomorrow*, or *I name this ship the U.S.S. Yorktown*, each utterance immediately conveys a new psychological or social reality. Thus, an apology takes place when someone apologizes, and not before. A promise obligates the speaker to perform some future action. A ship is named only when the act of naming is complete. In such cases, to say something is to perform a particular social action. Austin called these utterances "performatives," seeing them as very different from statements that convey information ("constatives"), such as *Snow is white*. In particular, performatives are not true or false in the way that a statement like *Snow is white* can be evaluated for its truthfulness. If someone with the appropriate authority says *I name this ship the U.S.S. Yorktown*, someone else cannot then say *That's not true*!

Austin argued that each utterance conveys three different social actions. First, an utterance conveys the bare fact that a communicative act has taken place: the *locutionary act*. Secondly, every time a speaker utters a sentence he or she is attempting to do something specific with the words, such as declaring, promising, apologizing and so forth: the *illocutionary act*. Finally, a speaker's utterance has a particular effect on the listener, who may feel amused, persuaded, warned, etc., as a consequence: the bringing about of such effects is known as a *perlocutionary act*. It is important to appreciate that the illocutionary force of an utterance and its perlocutionary effect may not coincide. If I warn you against a particular course of action, you may or may not heed my warning.

There are thousands of possible illocutionary acts and several attempts have been made to classify them into a smaller number of types. Such classifications are difficult, because verb meanings are often not easy to distinguish, and speakers' intentions are not always clear. But one influential approach sets up five basic types:[33]

Assertives: The speaker is committed, in varying degrees, to the truth of a proposition (e.g., *I affirm, believe, conclude, deny, report*). Assertives predicate that the speaker is thinking of something that he or she intends for the listener to believe.

Directives: The speaker tries to get the hearer to do something (e.g., *I ask, challenge, command, insist, request*). Directives predicate that the speaker intends for listeners to do something.

Commissives: The speaker is committed, in varying degrees, to a certain course of action (e.g., *I guarantee, pledge, promise, swear, vow*). Commissives predicate the speaker's intention to behave in a certain way under circumstances that are specified or presupposed.

Expressives: The speaker expresses an attitude about a state of affairs (e.g., *apologize, deplore, congratulate, thank, welcome*). Expressives predicate the feeling states of the speaker.

Declarations: The speaker alters the external status or condition of an object or situation solely by making the utterance (e.g., *I resign, I baptize, You're fired, War is hereby declared*).[34] Declarations predicate that the speaker intends for a particular ideational world-model or world-construal to be consensual.

PROBLEMS WITH THE TRADITIONAL VIEW

The traditional view of speech acts suggests that each illocutionary act belongs to only one of the above categories. Yet speakers often say things that express more than a single type of speech act. For instance, when a baseball umpire says to a baserunner sliding into second base *You're out!*, he not only changes an institutional state of affairs because by his words alone the runner is ruled to be out, he also directs the runner to leave the field (i.e., a directive). Many ordinary utterances have this quality of expressing a complex configuration of illocutionary acts.

To take another example, consider the following dialogue between a husband and wife:[35]

Wife: Why were you out so late last night?

Husband: I went out bowling with the boys.

Wife: I thought you hated bowling.

Each utterance can be jointly understood by the wife and husband as reflecting a complex set of intentions. The wife's first utterance, for instance, reflects four interacting goals – to seek information about the location of the husband last night, to seek information about the husband's motivation for staying out late, to express anger over the husband's absence, and to regain equilibrium in the relationship once again. Each of these intentions fit together to produce the wife's initial utterance, and the husband's response is, in part, an attempt to respond to some of these intentions. Thus, when the husband responds he satisfies the wife's goal of seeking information about his location last night, but the goal of seeking information about the husband's motivation for going bowling remains active. This in turn results in the wife's second statement. Conversational utterances are often made to satisfy multiple goals, reflecting the complexity of people's intentions in speaking with one another. The traditional view of speech act theory is unable to account for the multiplicity of speaker's intentions.

Speech act theory holds that speakers get addressees to recognize the illocutionary force behind any utterance by selecting the sentence form most appropriate to the particular speech act performed. So, a speaker would choose a declarative form to make an assertion, an interrogative form to ask a question, an imperative form to make a directive, and an exclamatory form to make an exclamation. But this scheme vastly underestimates the diversity of ways that a person might use any sentence modality to express a specific speech act. For instance, speakers can use imperative forms to make commands (e.g., *To the rear, march*), requests (e.g., *Please pass the salt*), promises (e.g., *Wash the car and I'll take you to the ballgame*), offers (e.g., *Have a beer*), advice (e.g., *To be a good parent, you must have patience*), and many more.

Such problems with speech act theory suggest that, despite its attention to the importance of intentions in communication, this framework is inadequate to account for many of the complexities in people's experience of linguistic meaning. The fundamental problem with the speech act view of intentional communication is that it excludes the crucial role of listeners and readers in both the creation and interpretation of meaning.[36] The meaning of any communicative exchange rests not just in the mind of a specific individual (i.e., the speaker), but emerges from a collaborative process of interaction between participants. Some scholars argue that intentional meaning is primarily a matter of people achieving coordinated social action. The next several sections provide examples illustrating the importance of social interaction in the expression and interpretation of intentional meaning.

SPEAKING WITH MULTIPLE INTENTIONS

Many face-to-face situations do not come with prespecified goal packages. Consider a situation where a parent attempts to get her son to do his homework by saying *We're going to Aunt Sarah's for dinner on Sunday. You'll have to plan around that in doing your homework.*[37] Although actually getting the son to do his homework might be seen as the primary goal, there are other goals that could also be central. A parent could be concerned with motivating her son to take responsibility for his behavior. In this case, getting one's son to do his homework would be only part of a broader goal. Thus, if a parent sees the conversation as a compliance-gaining one, that is, one where the parent was trying to impose his or her preferences on the child, a parent might abandon attempts to get the son to do homework. In this case, although the parent might prefer that her son study more, the recognition that the son is a mature decision maker (relational goal), and that she is able to give her child independence (identity goal), might lead a parent to avoid the subject entirely or broach it in an indirect manner as shown above.

Which intentions must we infer to adequately understand the mother's utterance to her son? Relevance theory provides a possible answer to this question. As Dan Sperber and Deidre Wilson argue, a fundamental mistake in the field of pragmatics (i.e., the study of utterance interpretation) is to suppose that pragmatics "should be concerned purely with the recovery of an enumerable set of assumptions, some explicitly expressed, others implicitly conveyed, but all individually intended by the speaker." But "there is a continuum of cases, from implicatures which the hearer was specifically intended to recover to implicatures which were merely intended to make manifest, and to further modification of the mutual cognitive environment of speaker and hearer that the speaker only intended in the sense that she intended her utterance to be relevant, and hence to have rich, and not entirely foreseeable cognitive effects."[38]

Consider again the mother's meaning in saying *We're going to Aunt Sarah's for dinner on Sunday. You'll have to plan around that in doing your homework.* Under the view of relevance theory, the mother may have had one, or more, communicative intentions in mind when saying what she did. She may have made her utterances to specifically make sure that her son's homework was done by the time the family went to Aunt Sarah's for dinner. But she may also have aimed to make manifest in a wide sense other meanings that she didn't explicitly have in mind when speaking to her son (e.g., that her son should take more responsibility in general about doing his schoolwork before he engages in social activities, that her son should be more responsible in general in meeting his various obligations, that her son should take more responsibility for his actions in general).

Thus, the mother might have in mind a "cognitive content" without explicitly having in mind everything that might be entailed by that cognitive content in question. In many instances, a speaker will agree when asked whether some interpretation of his or her utterance was appropriate even if this reading might not have been exactly what he or she had in mind when the utterance was first spoken. Thus, if the son questioned his mother as to her intentions in saying what she did, the mother could elaborate upon her utterance by mentioning several possible meanings that she did not have firmly in mind at the time when she first spoke. The main point here is that there is no reason not to expand the notion of an intended meaning in exactly this way so that speakers would, in fact, frequently accept as correct interpretations of their utterances various implicatures that they did not specifically have in mind when they originally framed the utterances in question.

One of the important arguments in this book is that many aspects of unintentional meaning are grounded in our understanding of people's communicative intentions. Consider the following exchange between two colleagues:[39]

A: Can you meet up on Thursday?

B: That's when I'm away.

What is the best way to characterize A's understanding of B's utterance? Adopting a relevance theory perspective, B implicates that she cannot meet up on Thursday, assuming that A understands the proposition expressed and combines this with salient contextual assumptions such as that "if B is away then B cannot meet with me." Furthermore, B may be reminding/informing A that she will be away on the Thursday in question. A might also combine the expressed proposition with other relevant contextual assumptions and infer, for instance, that B will not be available to discuss the article she is writing, or that B will miss a particular television program airing that day. These latter inferences are *implications* that are worked out solely on the responsibility of the addressee, A. In contrast to the implicature, B has given A no encouragement to derive this conclusion from the context. Thus, the implications are not part of speaker B's communicative intentions. "Implicatures and implications are both worked out by processing the proposition expressed in the context of other assumptions. The difference between them is that implicatures are part of the communicative intentions – the addresser gives the addressee some encouragement to access, construct, or derive them, whereas implications are worked out on the addressee's own initiative."[40] Nonetheless, the implications derived are extensions from the implicatures received. At least some aspects of unintentional meaning are extensions from meanings understood to be intentionally communicated by the speaker.

ALTERING INTENTIONS IN MIDSTREAM

Speakers sometimes change their intentions about the particular meanings they wish addressees to recognize. Speakers often deliberately offer their addressees a choice of construals, so that when addressees make their choice, they help to determine what the speaker is taken to mean.[41] For instance, a speaker may present an utterance with one intention in mind, but when the addressee misconstrues it, the speaker may then change his or her mind and accept the new construal. Here is an example I recently observed in a local bar. The scene begins with my friend John spilling beer on the table:

John: I wonder if there is a towel behind the bar.

Nicole (goes over to the bar and grabs a towel):   Here you go.

John: Oh thanks! I wasn't actually asking you to get a towel for me. I just was thinking aloud about whether there might be a towel that I could get from the bartender. But thanks.

John initially intends his utterance to be taken as meaning one thing, but changes his mind and accept Nicole's misinterpretation of what he said. Speakers often don't correct listeners' misunderstandings because they deem it too trivial, disruptive, or embarrassing to correct, or because what listeners infer somehow works better in the situation (as in John's case). Still, once an interpretation is grounded, it is taken to be what the speaker meant. Listeners recognize that speakers can change their minds and leave part of the construal of utterances to them.

Consider another example of how people modify their communicative intentions during the course of conversation. This excerpt is from a telephone conversation between Gordon and Shawn in which Gordon talks about breaking up with a girlfriend.[42]

Gordon: Oh actually, I'm glad she got the message because we had nothing in common ... and we would like talk on phone and we'd go

Shawn: Heh hh hh eh eh

Gordon: So

Shawn: Ehh hh

Gordon: Ehh hh hh

Shawn: So you gave her to the big punt huh

Gordon: hhh. Thee old one two kick

Shawn: huh huh Drop kick huh huh

Gordon: huh huh hhhh No. I mean she's a nice girl and everything
         but

Here, shared laughter abounds after Gordon enacts his *having nothing in common* story. In the middle of this shared laughter, Shawn offers a characterization of what has just taken place between Gordon and his girlfriend: *So you gave her the big punt, huh.* Gordon upgrades this characterization by calling it *Thee old one two kick.* Again, Shawn laughs and extends the metaphor by saying *Drop kick.* But Gordon now seems to reverse direction. As he laughs at Shawn's overbuilt rendering of *Drop kick*, he adds disagreement-relevant material to it: *No, she's a nice girl.* The point is that Gordon, who introduced the topic of the breakup, and has to this point encouraged play with it, shifts suddenly and resists Shawn's brusque characterization of the dissolution. This instance displays how interpersonal goals, even once they have been accomplished, may continue to change shape as we recount their accomplishment to new recipients, and as these recipients react to the revelations.

Examples like the ones discussed here support philosopher Marcelo Dascal's comment: "Intentional meanings are not fully defined complete entities before they get from the speaker's mind to her mouth. Rather, once they material into utterances they enter a process of negotiation of meaning where the interlocutor's response plays a crucial role."[43]

MULTIPLE AUTHORS IN SPEAKING

Beyond the fact that speakers often have multiple communicative intentions that they wish others to infer, our experience of meaning is enriched by the fact that we sometimes borrow from what other speakers have said before us. In special communicative situations, as with certain speeches or lectures, the person actually speaking is not the true author of what is said. Newscasters on television and radio rarely write the words they speak. Each year the queen of England presents to Parliament the "state of the nation" address, which is actually written by the current prime minister (although the speech is *really* written by the prime minister's assistants and speechwriters).[44]

For the most part, listeners understand the conventions that prompt a speaker to say things that he or she did not author. However, there are cases when these conventions, when publicly flaunted, cause considerable consternation because people like to pretend that what someone says comes straight from their heart, so to speak. Consider the flap that arose when Senator Bob Dole gave his resignation speech from the United States Senate in May 1996. Many political pundits commented that Dole's speech was one of the best of his entire political career. Soon afterwards, it was revealed that the speech was written by novelist Mark Helprin who said about Dole's performance, "I thought he delivered it as very few people could. It was almost as if I hadn't written it."[45] Of course, everyone in Washington knows that politicians employ speechwriters to spin lovely words for them to deliver. But many Republicans were furious at Helprin for talking openly with many members of the press about his role as ghostwriter and taking credit for Dole's words, if not the emotional performance.

Many linguists, anthropologists, and even literary theorists have stressed that "joint production" not only points to the importance of others as coauthors in determining what speakers say, but to the important role that speakers have as colisteners. As M. Bakhtin and Voloshinov argued, no word or utterance can be spoken without echoing how others understand and have used it before. Bakhtin commented:

> The word in language is half someone else's. It becomes 'one's own' only when the speaker populates it with his own intentions, his own accent, when he appropriates the word, adapting it to his own semantic and expressive intention. Prior to this moment of appropriation, the word does not exist in a neutral and impersonal language (it is not, after all, out of a dictionary that the speaker gets his words!), but rather it exists in other people's mouths, in other people's concrete contexts, serving other people's intentions: it is from there that one must take the word, and make it one's own.[46]

For Bakhtin, individual thought and identity are never separate from language. Thought is not something inside speakers' heads that is then transmitted to listeners through language. Instead, thought is best characterized as something that comes into being as the individual enters the external physical world of language, which is already socially imbued with meaning. Bakhtin's ideas suggest that meaning cannot depend on each speaker and listener alone. People may find that they express their personal opinions, experiences, and feelings in their own unique way when speaking. But speakers rarely notice the extent to which their own utterances are routinized, repetitions of what they have previously heard. Speakers echo past utterances quite frequently in ordinary discourse. Consider the following example from a Thanksgiving dinner conversation:[47]

Chad: I go out a lot.

Deborah: I go out and eat.

Peter: You go out? The trouble with ME is if I don't prepare and eat well, I eat a LOT ... Because it's not satisfying. And so I'm just eating like cheese and crackers, I'll just stuff myself on cheese and crackers. But if I fix myself something nice, I don't have to eat much.

Deborah: Oh yeah?

Peter: I've noticed that, yeah.

Deborah: Hmmmm... Well then it works, then it's a good idea.

Peter: It's a good idea in terms of eating, it's not a good idea in terms of time.

The frequent repetition of words and phrases such as *eat, go out, just, myself, cheese and crackers, yeah, a good idea, a lot*, and *myself* illustrate how speakers take other people's words and weave them into the fabric of the conversation.[48]

The conversation presented above shows how there are several problems in constructing the author as a single individual embodying a unified mind and personality.[49] Our tacit understandings of talk include the assumptions that what is being said is the speaker's position, that the speaker is committed to his or her words, and that the speaker believes what is being said, such that evidence to the contrary is expected to be explicitly marked (e.g., by explicitly framing a statement as a joke). Yet what speakers say in some conversations reflects different aspects of their own identities, which suggests a very complex relation between a person's communicative intentions and what he or she says.

The sociologist Erving Goffman drew the important distinction between the animator, the author, and the principal in the production of communication.[50] The animator has responsibility only for the production of the utterance, not for what is said or how it is said. The production of what is said is the responsibility of the author. The one who stands behind or is committed to those words is the principal. In short, the animator produces talk, the author creates talk, the figure is portrayed through talk, and the principal is responsible for talk. Although the positions of animator, author, figure, and principal can be filled by different people, a single individual can alternate among these positions during the course of his or her own talk. For example, when a speaker quotes his or her own prior words, she is at once the animator and the author of that quote, but when a speaker quotes another person's words, she assigns the authorial role to the original source of those words.

The following segment of conversation illustrates how a single individual can embody several roles at once.[51] Ira and Jan are a lower-middle-class, middle-aged Jewish couple explaining their position against intermarriage between Jews and Gentiles. In the following excerpt, they are contrasting their daughter Beth's experience dating a young man of a different religion with their son's experience with dating a Puerto Rican woman. They tell this story to show how Beth's experience is more in line with their own view.

(1) Ira: Now my daughter went out with eh – she went with a couple of Gentile kids, and she said that

(2) Jan: she would go out with them

(3) Ira: she wouldn't go out with them again

(4) Jan: She said they're too different

(5) Ira: She said that uh ... they're just eh-the-

(6) Jan: They're different.

(7) Ira: They're different.

(8) Jan: She says, "It's not what I'm used to

(9) Ira: So em ... she

(10) Jan: One was a ... his father was a friend of my husband's. And when I heard she was goin' out with him, I said "You're going out with a Gentile boy?" She says, "Well Daddy knows his father." I said, "I don't care." So she introduced him, and they went out, and she came home early, and I said, "Well, y'goin' out with him again?" She says, "Nope." I said, "Did he get fresh?" She said, "No!" She says, "But he's different!" She says, "I'm not used t'Gentile boys." That cured her!

(11) Ira: hhhhhhhhhhhhhh

(12) Jan: She'd never go out with one again.

Personal stories like the one Jan tells demonstrate how narrators display both their current competence as storytellers and their prior competence in whatever role and status had been occupied in the prior experience. Individual speakers have the opportunity to present themselves in three capacities. Listeners' interpretations of Jan's utterance in (11) require a highly complex set of reasoning about which of the different figures Jan displays. First is animator – the producer of talk. Second is author – the author can interpret an experience, arrange evaluative devices, and create story events which contextualize a position in order to convey just those sentiments which highlight that version of the experience most in line with the position being argued for. Third is figure – the figure can act in the story world precisely as he or she might have wanted to act had there been the chance to do so. In short, the audience gains an idealized view of the experience (through the author), and an idealized view of the narrator (through the figure). And the narrator's hope is that these idealized views will lead the audience into acceptance of the position being argued for. Understanding the different ways that Jan presents herself is essential to understanding the range of communicative intentions behind Jan's saying what she does.

But the intentions speakers produce do not necessarily reflect the beliefs of a single self, but rather the different roles that individuals embrace in different situations (or "participation frameworks"). The sociologist Erving Goffman referred to this process as speakers "animating" their various roles during talk. For example, consider the following remarks made by a graduate student in a classroom seminar:[52] *If these are two – if these are two activists talking to each other who have a real strong bugaboo about the police, and the police is very foremost in their mind, yes, I think a large riot armed policeman would be more concrete and would come out in front. I mean, having uttered very similar sentences...*

The student here actually embraces two different roles as speaker in this remark. When the student says the *I* in *I think* he is referring to his role as an intellectual figure in the classroom discussion. But when he says *I* in *I mean, having uttered very similar sentences*, he is referring to his personal, nonclassroom figure as a gay activist. Distinguishing between these two participants roles is critical if listeners are to understand the intentions behind what a speaker is saying. As Goffman once said: "The proper study of interaction is not with the individual and his psychology, but rather the syntactical relations among the acts of different persons mutually presented to one another."[53]

CONCLUSION

There are complex links between people's intentions and the meanings they communicate. First, understanding the meaning of someone's message does not end with, or even necessarily begin with, an analysis of the words and sentences and their putative literal meanings. What often appears to be the plain, literal meaning of a message is just a contextually specified meaning that is so widely shared that it appears to be determined apart from any context at all. Understanding the meaning of someone's message requires, at the very least, that listeners recognize something about the speaker's communicative intentions.

In some cases, determining a speaker's communicative intentions will be relatively straightforward and will itself be sufficient for comprehending a speaker's message. In other situations, listeners infer messages that speakers did not specifically intend, but relate to the speaker's utterance in the sense that it enriches their shared cognitive environment. Finally, listeners must also understand how a single individual may manifest different social roles in saying what he or she does, including the possibility that a speaker can echo previously stated material, originally authored by a different person. In all these cases, inferring something about speakers' intentions is a critical part of our meaningful experience of ordinary conversation. Every communicative act rests on the participants' mutual commitment to a "temporary shared social world."[54]

Chapter 4

Inferring Intentionality
in Experience

Put yourself in my shoes for a moment as I recount an experience I had several years ago entering an art exhibition in San Francisco created by Ann Hamilton called *Privation and Excesses*.[1] Several friends and I walked into the door of a warehouse and entered a large room. On the floor lay a huge rectangular pile of pennies (over 700,000), about five inches in height, arranged systematically in overlapping waves of copper. The pennies were laid on a layer of honey that extended several inches beyond the pennies. A woman sat on a simple wooden chair behind the pennies, staring downward, constantly washing her hands in a basin of honey. Behind the woman to one side there was a wooden pen, the floor covered with hay, containing two live sheep (the smell of the sheep distinctly in the air). On the other side of the woman, also behind her, were two small mechanized mortars and pestles, one slowly grinding up pennies, the other grinding up human teeth.

This clearly was an unusual art installation, to say the least.[2] After walking in silence around the exhibit for several minutes, one of my friends, Ken, came up to me and we had the following conversation:[3]

Ken: What does it mean?

Ray: What do you mean what does it mean?

Ken: Well, the artist must have had some idea as to what all this was supposed to represent or mean. What did she want us to think about when seeing all this?

Ken's question nicely captures what many of us struggle with when we encounter various kinds of visual art, music, theater, and literature, as well as some aspects of ordinary speech. My own experience of the *Privation and Excesses* exhibit suggested a variety of different, perhaps contradictory, readings. The event most generally commented on the banality of Americans' fascination with money, and on the plight of the working artist, or each of us, wringing our hands, grinding our teeth, in anxiety as we face the prospect of earning mere pennies, which seem to be literally eaten up. The particular way the pennies were arranged, shimmering, quite near the golden hay of the sheep pen, evoked images of "amber waves of grain," referring to the American dream, or at least, the futility of trying to attain the American dream. The artist herself, as it turned out, was sitting there, anxiously staring, wringing her hands over the work she had created. The exhibit conveyed a general feeling of enormous uncertainty, as we struggle to make sense of the disparate events in our everyday experience.

My friends debated these off-the-cuff interpretations of the exhibit. We also wondered about the possible message on the link between art and performance, especially in light of the artist herself being a part of the exhibit. A central theme of our discussion focused on whether the artist wanted us to draw specific readings from observing her work. Did it matter at all what the artist intended to communicate? Or was each of us free to create his own idiosyncratic readings regardless of who the artist was or what she might have hoped for us to understand about her artwork? One friend argued that the artist might not even know what any of this meant; it could all be an elaborate, bizarre gag. Yet many of us acknowledged that it is hard not to wonder, even if momentarily, about what the artist must have been thinking about, and what she might have intended for us to understand, as she conceived of, and executed, the artwork. Arranging over 700,000 pennies in a layer of honey is, after all, not done for arbitrary reasons (or is it?).

One reviewer of Hamilton's installation later commented in the *San Francisco Chronicle* that "the meaning of Hamilton's work is obscure. She is more concerned with poetic effects than with the possibilities of discursive readings."[4] The artist Ann Hamilton suggested in another published review: "the sheep, the pen, and the mortars create a triangle ... the pennies combine the animal economy and the human economy ... It is very poetic and metaphoric, I can't say that it means one thing."[5]

This discussion of Ann Hamilton's *Privation and Excesses* illustrates some of the questions we ask ourselves as we search for meaningful interpretations of artworks, literature, and even ordinary speech. To what extent do we, or should we, let our interpretations of meaning be constrained by authorial intentions? How can we be influenced in any way by, say, what an artist like Ann Hamilton explicitly means to communicate, when she herself finds it difficult to say what that meaning really is?

The first purpose of this chapter is to argue that people are strongly disposed to attribute intentions or intentionality to human action. Just as my friends and I immediately discussed Ann Hamilton's possible intentions in creating her artwork, consideration of a wide range of human and nonhuman events clearly shows that the reflex to attribute intentions to other people's actions is a fundamental characteristic of our experience of meaning. I describe some of the empirical research that supports the claim that people automatically attribute intentionality to many behaviors and actions.

The second aim of this chapter is to argue that people's dispositions to infer communicative intentions might vary depending on which aspect of understanding is of greatest interest. For example, my immediate understanding of Hamilton's artwork differed from the interpretations I formed after several minutes of viewing. Even now, years later, I still find myself creating new meanings for aspects of the exhibit (and new versions of Hamilton's possible communicative intentions). Scholars differ over which part of understanding is most important to characterize, one reason, in part, why there is disagreement about intentionalism. I will present a preliminary scheme for thinking about the unconscious and conscious mental activities engaged in the experience of meaning. There are significant differences between various mental *processes* of understanding (many of which occur quickly and unconsciously) and various *products* (most of which we are aware of) that arise from our experiences of meaning. Although my adoption of the cognitive intentionalist premise commits me to explaining both the mental processes of understanding and their meaningful products, different theoretical accounts are required to explain the role that intentions may have in different phenomenological experiences of meaning.

THE DISPOSITION TO INFER INTENTIONS

When do people attribute intentions to the actions of others? Several philosophers have argued that in understanding people's actions, we assume that others possess rational minds and abilities. Donald Davidson claimed that people adhere to the *Principle of Charity*, the idea that if we want to make sense of other people's utterances and beliefs, then we had better start out from the premise that more likely than not they have some reasons – some intelligible grounds – for speaking or thinking as they do.[6] Similarly, Daniel Dennett has proposed the *intentional stance* as a principle to capture something about our understanding of the connection between behavior and intention.[7] The intentional stance is the strategy of interpreting the behavior of an entity (person, animal, artifact) by treating it *as if* it were a rational agent whose actions are governed by considering its beliefs and desires. This stance is the attitude or perspective we routinely adopt toward one another, so adopting the intentional stance toward something deliberately anthropomorphizes it. Dennett argued that to determine intentions, we must first treat the object (a person or the product of a person) whose behavior is to be understood as a rational agent. Following this, we figure out what beliefs that agent ought to have, given his or her purposes and plans in the world. We then determine what decisions the agent ought to make given his or her purposes and plans; and, finally, we predict how that rational agent will most likely act to achieve his or her goals by virtue of his or her beliefs.

The general idea behind the intentional stance is that people make reasonable predictions about the emerging behavior of other persons based on a rational assessment of those persons' beliefs, attitudes, and goals. Of course, people do not always behave rationally; but we still seek some assessment of human behavior within a completely rational perspective about what people are doing, and make our assessment of their behavior as the situation demands. The intentional stance adds the critical impact of prediction to our understanding of the relationship between intentions and behavior, because it assumes that people are by definition intentional systems. By adopting the intentional stance, we can predict people's future behaviors just as we would describe what they have already done.[8]

A terrific demonstration of how strongly people embrace the intentional stance is seen in the following dialogue between a patient and her psychotherapist:

Patient: Men are all alike.

Therapist: In what way?

Patient: They're always bugging us about something or other.

Therapist: Can you think of a specific example?

Patient: Well, my boyfriend made me come here.

Therapist: Your boyfriend made you come here.

Patient: He says I'm depressed much of the time.

Therapist: I am sorry to hear that you are depressed.

Patient: It's true. I am unhappy.

Therapist: Do you think coming here will help you not be depressed?

Patient: I need some help, that much seems certain.

Therapist: What would it mean to you if you got some help?

Patient: Perhaps I could learn to get along with my mother.

Therapist: Tell me more about your family.

Patient: My mother takes care of me.

Therapist: Who else in your family takes care of you?

Patient: My father.

Therapist: Your father.

Patient: You are like my father in some ways.

Therapist: What resemblances do you see?

Patient: You are not very aggressive but I think you don't want me to notice that.

Therapist: What makes you think I am not very aggressive?

Patient: You don't argue with me.

Therapist: Why do you think I don't argue with you?

Patient: You are afraid of me.

Therapist: Does it please you to think I am afraid of you?

Patient: My father is afraid of everybody.

Therapist: What else comes to mind when you think of your father?

Patient: Bullies.

Therapist: Does that have anything to do with the fact that your boyfriend made you come here?

The therapist in this conversation employed a nondirective strategy whereby he tried to elicit feelings from the patient, and then reflected them back to the patient for the patient to recognize and acknowledge. In response, the patient dutifully tried to make appropriate comments that reflected her own thoughts and feelings about the topics raised.

What's especially interesting about this conversation is that it is a segment of dialogue between a person and a computer program, called ELIZA, playing the part of the therapist. ELIZA was written by Joseph Weizenbaum in the 1960s on the presupposition that people interacting with the program would play the role of a patient in nondirective, Rogerian psychotherapy.[9] ELIZA, it seems, can chat about anything the patient wishes to mention, be it boyfriends, bullies, or fathers. But the program itself does not really understand what the patient said to the therapist. ELIZA ignores the semantic content of what is said and only responds in a rote manner to certain phrases it encounters. ELIZA's apparent understanding, or rather its concealment of its total lack of understanding, results from comparatively simple "pattern-matching" rules where the program uses a key word from the "patient's" utterance in formulating its own response.

Weizenbaum was astonished at how quickly and how very deeply people conversing with ELIZA became emotionally involved with the computer and how unequivocally they anthropomorphized it.[10] Weizenbaum's secretary, who had watched him work on the program for many months and surely knew ELIZA to be merely a computer program, once asked Weizenbaum to leave the room after she began, in his presence, conversing with ELIZA. Another time, when Weizenbaum wanted to record people's conversations with ELIZA, he was promptly accused of spying on people's most intimate thoughts. Even knowing of the emotional bonds that people form with machines of all types, it is clear that people are strongly disposed to attributing intentions to many aspects of both human and nonhuman behavior.[11]

Several kinds of evidence illustrate the power of the intentional stance in structuring our experience of both linguistic and nonlinguistic events. The next section describes some of this research.

ATTRIBUTIONS OF INTENTIONALITY

INTENTIONALITY IN NONHUMAN EVENTS

Attribution of intentionality influences people's understanding of nonhuman events. Unless told otherwise, people perceive random events as if they were guided by human intentions. For example, in a classic study, people were asked to describe the random movements of dots in film. Forty-nine out of the fifty participants in this study characterized the actions in intentional terms and stated that some dots "chased" others, while other dots "followed" others.[12] A later study showed that giving participants cues such as "jealous husband" led people to exert considerable ingenuity in explaining why the dots moved as they did in the film.[13] People can distinguish between behavior that is produced by a person and some impersonal agent. For example, participants' strategies in an experimental game have been shown to be significantly affected when they are informed that their partner is either a person or "nature."[14]

An interesting idea proposed by psychologist Paul Bloom is that our perception of many man-made objects depends on assumptions about intentionality.[15] For instance, our understanding of an artifact concept like a chair depends on the recognition that the object is an entity that has been successfully created with the intention that it belong to the same kind as current and previous chairs (or, equivalently, with the intention that it be a chair). Bloom formally states this proposal as: "We infer that a novel entity has been successfully created with the intention to be a member of artifact kind X – and thus is a member of artifact kind X – if its appearance and potential use are best explained as resulting from the intention to create a member of artifact kind X."[16] How assumptions about human intentionality figure in people's immediate perception and categorization of objects has yet to be explored. But Bloom's proposal speaks to the tacit disposition to infer intentionality in nonhuman events and objects.

ATTRIBUTIONS OF INTENTIONALITY
IN RESPONDING TO HUMAN BEHAVIOR

Judgments of intentionality play a large role in people's understanding of others' actions. The law has paid particular attention to intent and its attribution. In criminal law, a person usually cannot be charged with criminal responsibility unless, in addition to proof that he or she committed the act, it can also be shown that the person formed an intention to commit the act. In criminal law, the courts "have devised working formulae, if not scientific ones, for the instructions of juries around such terms as "felonious intent," "criminal intent," "malice aforethought," "guilty knowledge," "fraudulent intent," "willfulness," "scienter," to denote guilty knowledge, or "mens rea," to signify an evil purpose or mental culpability. By use or combination of these various tokens, they have sought to protect those who were not blameworthy in mind from conviction of infamous common-law crimes."[17]

Outside the courtroom, research in clinical psychology demonstrates how people with personality disorders often attribute hostile or nonhostile intent to others. Paranoid people characteristically see malevolence all around them. Patients undergoing conversion (hysterical) reactions seem to attribute less hostile intent to people than do other observers of the same event. But even normal individuals respond to others based on their assumptions about the intentionality of others' actions. For instance, people's perceptions of hostile intent play a major role in determining the aggressiveness of response.[18] In one study, experimental participants responded more aggressively to others when they were told that these people intended to do them harm. Other research shows that aggressive boys evidence a "hostile attributional bias" and are more likely than nonaggressive boys to attribute hostile intent to a person.[19]

Other research from social psychology shows that people receive more praise and more blame for actions that are considered intentional rather than unintentional.[20] People's feelings of gratitude toward a benefactor vary strongly and positively with the degree to which experimenters indicated that the benefactor sincerely and solely intended to benefit the recipient.[21] Moreover, intentional acts of helping are more prone to be reciprocated than are unintentional ones, and intentional acts of aggression are responded to more often than unintentional acts.[22] Furthermore, in a situation in which a husband attributes hostile intentions to his wife's actions, there is an increased risk of violence because such interpretations (e.g., "She is trying to hurt me") may increase the likelihood that the husband will choose a violent response to the situation (e.g., "My violence is a justified retaliation").[23]

In real-world settings, studies reveal, for instance, that workers are more likely to file a formal grievance against management when they perceive their supervisors' actions as motivated by dispositional rather than environmental attributions.[24] For example, worker discipline attributed to an enduring personal disposition of the manager (e.g., personal animus toward the worker) is viewed as less justifiable, and is more likely to provoke a worker to file a grievance. Discipline perceived to be due to environmental coercion (e.g., the manager was simply following rules that required punishment for some specific behavior) were less likely to provoke a worker's filing a grievance. More generally, research on retribution demonstrates that recipients of an attack were more likely to retaliate when the attack was attributed to the personal desires/intentions of the attacker than when it was attributed to characteristics of the attacking situation.[25]

Finally, social psychologists confirm that attribution of another person's intentions is necessary for forming an overall impression of that person and for sustaining social interactions.[26] Research shows, for instance, that the higher a person's social status, the more likely other people are to attribute good intentions to that person's actions.[27] Studies also suggests that attribution of dispositional qualities to another person on the basis of behavior may be made spontaneously, without awareness, upon learning that another person has committed a particular behavior.[28]

CHILDREN'S INTENTIONALITY

The ability to impute intentions to other people's actions is not a special ability that develops in late childhood or early adulthood. Developmental psychologists have shown that even young infants possess some ability to "read other minds" to understand what other people are thinking, feeling, and intending.[29] This intersubjectivity first emerges as an infant and mother take pleasure in eye-to-eye contact and, soon afterwards, share joint attention on common objects. Later on, children and their caretakers achieve a "meeting of minds" as they begin to exchange words. Many studies also show that children develop a grasp of another's intentional states, such as other people's beliefs, promises, desires, and intentions (what is called a child's "theory of mind"). Even twelve-month-old babies have a theory of mind sufficient to predict how other people should act based on their previous goal-directed behavior.[30]

Young children's metalinguistic judgments are more influenced by their knowledge of the information the speaker intends to convey than by the literal meaning of the message.[31] For example, first-graders who were more aware of the information a speaker was attempting to convey were significantly more likely to judge the speaker's ambiguous message as informative than were those who heard the utterance without awareness of its likely intended meaning. It is only under especially salient circumstances, such as when the speaker's intent contradicts something, that four- and five-year-old children display a burgeoning grasp of a distinction between what a person literally said and what that person really meant to communicate.

Developmental research also shows that three-year-old children understand something about the distinction between intentional and unintentional action. One study, for instance, in which children performed actions and were sometimes tricked into making mistakes, showed that three-year-olds could distinguish between intentional and unintentional action both for themselves and for another child that they observed.[32] If the goal and the situation in the world match, three-year-olds can judge that an action was performed intentionally or that the outcome will bring pleasure. If there is a mismatch between the goal and the situation, three-year-olds judge that the behavior was unintentional or that the outcome won't bring pleasure.[33]

More recently, one study has shown that three-year-olds are less likely than five-year-olds to see intentions as means to ends, and to focus on the future directedness of intention.[34] Children were shown pairs of pictures, where one picture of the pair showed a child doing something, and the other showed another child who appeared to be getting ready to do the same thing (e.g., there was a picture of a boy sliding down a playground slide and a picture of another boy climbing up the steps of the slide). For each pair of pictures children were asked one question either about the action (e.g., *Which boy's sliding down?*) or about the preparation for the action (e.g., *Which boy's going to slide down?*). The latter question used different terms to express the intention: going to (or gonna), thinks, (s)he will, wants to and would like to.

Children were asked about eight different pairs of pictures. All the children correctly chose pictures of the children who were acting in answer to questions about actions; but three-year-olds also chose those pictures in answer to questions about intentions, whereas five-year-olds usually chose the other pictures. Choosing the picture of the child acting in answer to the intention question is not incorrect, but five-year-olds were more likely to interpret

79

these questions as referring to future, not present, actions. They distinguished between the means and the end, between the intention and the goal. Moreover, it is not that three-year-olds always choose pictures of the action, whatever question they are asked. If three-year-olds are asked *Which boy's not sliding down?* they correctly point to the boy who is climbing up the steps, but if they asked *Which boy's gonna slide down?* they point to the boy who is sliding down.

What the three-year-old lacks is an understanding of the causal nature of intention. An intention is a mental representation caused by a desire for a goal which itself causes action to bring about that goal. It is not clear that three-year-olds, who can distinguish between intentional and unintentional action, have such a sophisticated concept of intention. Only at four or five years of age do children begin to differentiate intention from desire.

Finally, a variety of research shows that parents respond to infants as if their children's actions were intentional (i.e., that the actions could be said to be purposeful or directed toward something such as a person or object).[35] For instance, mothers will comment *I know, you're trying to tell me you're ready to eat* in reply to an infant's hunger cries, or they interpret the infant's smile as a message of greeting. Some researchers suggest that parents project meaning onto infant behavior. Thus, infants do not possess intentional capabilities, and parents mistakenly treat infant actions as if they were intentional. But other scholars contend that infants do have innate, if rudimentary, forms of intentionality.[36]

THE INTENTIONALITY OF RESPONSE CRIES

There are various verbal messages that are not, strictly speaking, linguistic but which still communicate intentional meanings. Consider the case of someone walking alone down a busy sidewalk, then tripping over a small crack in the pavement and uttering *Oops!* What is the purpose of this cry? People utter a wide range of exclamatory interjections that are not full-fledged words, such as *Brr!, Phew!, Ahh!, Whoops!, Eek!, Ouch!, Oopsadaisey!,* in addition to many different grunts, groans, moans, and sighs. The sociologist Erving Goffman refers to these interjections in ordinary conversation as *response cries*.[37] People normally view response cries, like those listed above, as expressions of "natural overflowing, a flooding up of previously contained feeling, a bursting of normal restraints, a case of being caught off-guard."[38] But these ritualized expressions might alternatively be recognized as different intentionally conveyed meanings.

For instance, *Brr!* is employed when a person wishes to convey to others that he or she is cold or has just come out of a cold environment. *Ahh!* and *Phew!* are used when one leaves a hot place for a cooler one, or when speakers wish to convey to others their satisfaction with their present circumstance after being uncomfortable in another one (e.g., when you unbutton your pants after a large meal). *Oops!* and *Whoops!* are "spill cries," noises that we emit when we have momentarily lost control of something, including ourselves. These sounds alert others to our recognition that a mistake has been made, as when I drop eggs on the kitchen floor while making breakfast, warning listeners to take care until the mistake has been rectified. *Oopsadaisey* is used when a caretaker lifts up a child and playfully tosses her into the air. The cry might be intended to let the child know that the momentary loss of control should not be frightening, as the caretaker knows what he or she is doing. *Eek!* and *Yikes!* warn others of some impending danger or comment on some potential threat that has just been avoided. People say *Eeow!* when they come in contact with something contaminated or disgusting (and it can also be used metaphorically, to allow speakers to comment about other people or situations as if they were decaying food). We make grunts when lifting heavy objects to warn others that we are fully occupied and may not be disturbed in any way. We cry *Ouch!* or *Oww!* when we are in pain and want to alert others to our feelings, or to express empathy to others who have told us of their own physical or emotional pain. Sexual moans and groans are emitted to inform our partners of our pleasures. An adolescent girl might cry *Ooo!* when presented with a lovely gift to express her appreciation to others for the present, while an elderly woman playing a slot machine in Las Vegas yells *Whee!* to let her friends know that she has just hit the jackpot.

All of these response cries are uttered for the express purpose of having others recognize our intentional meanings (i.e., meaning-nn). These interjections are not beyond our emotional and physical control, but reflect our purposive displays to others about our particular states of mind. Response cries are not "purely expressive," "primitive," or "unsocialized," but constitute an important part of intentional communication in everyday life.[39]

INTENTIONALITY IN NONVERBAL BEHAVIOR

People often nonverbally communicate various things to others that are specifically designed to be understood by an audience.[40] For example, a man at a crowded lunch counter who looks straight ahead, or the airline passenger who sits with his eyes closed, are both communicating that they do not want to speak to anybody or be spoken to, and their neighbors usually "get the message" and respond appropriately by leaving them alone.[41] As psychologist Bela DePaulo notes, "In social interaction, people more often exert some control over their nonverbal expressive behavior. This attempted control is not always conscious, and it is not always successful, but it is pervasive."[42]

In most cases of face-to-face interaction, both intentional and unintentional meanings are conveyed nonverbally. There are times when we deliberately intend to send a particular message, but the information we give out at the conscious level may be modified or contradicted by nonverbal signals which we are not aware of sending. This extra information, as it were, leaks out. High-speed photography has enabled researchers to observe the minute and very rapid microframed changes in expressions that occur when people are engaged in communication.[43] In various tests, when people are told not to leak out any emotion and are then exposed to films designed to arouse emotional responses, they are surprised at how much they reveal. This research suggests that despite our intentions we will often betray some of our real feelings in our faces and bodies.

People rely on seven basic types of nonverbal signals to infer both intentional and unintentional meaning. These include: (1) *kinesics*: body movements, including gestures, facial expressions, trunk and limb movements, posture, and gaze; (2) *vocalics* or *paralanguage*: vocal cues other than words themselves, including general features such as pitch, loudness, tempo, pause, and inflection; (3) *physical appearance*: manipulable features such as clothing, hairstyle, costumes, and fragrance; (4) *haptics*: use of touch; (5) *proxemics*: use of interpersonal distance and space relationships; (6) *chronemics*: use of time as a message system, including elements such as punctuality, waiting time, lead time, and amount of time spent with someone; and (7) *artifacts*: manipulable objects and environmental features that may convey messages about their designers or users.

These nonverbal cues play an especially important role in the attention, comprehension, and interpretation of interpersonal messages. Some research shows that adults place greater reliance on nonverbal cues when the verbal and nonverbal messages conflict.[44] For example, when a person says she is happy but looks miserable, we tend to infer that her nonverbal messages most accurately represents her true feelings. Verbal cues are needed for factual, abstract, and persuasive communication. Nonverbal cues are important for relational, attributional, affective, and attitudinal messages.[45]

People appear to have two different capacities for displaying information.[46] *Information given* is information intentionally emitted by a person and recognized by another in the manner intended by the actor. On the other hand, *information given-off* is information interpreted for meaning by another person even if it had not been intended to convey that meaning. Thus, when Jack spies on Sally, he can draw various meaningful inferences about what Sally might be doing even though Sally's gestures and actions are only providing information that is given-off, not intentionally given to Jack.

People can become quite adept at manipulating the supposedly unintentional meanings of their own displays or not interpreting the unintended meanings of others' displays.[47] A great example of this is seen in Bob Woodward and Carl Bernstein's Watergate memoir, *All the President's Men*. In this segment, the two *Washington Post* reporters are trying to get a senior Justice Department official to confirm off the record a rumor that President Nixon's chief of staff, H. R. Haldeman, is about to be indicted:

"I'd like to help you, I really would," said the lawyer. "But I just can't say anything."

Bernstein thought for a moment and told the man they understood why he couldn't say anything. So they would do it another way: Bernstein would count to 10. If there was any reason for the reporters to hold back on the story, the lawyer should hang up before 10. If he was on the line after 10, it would mean the story was okay.

"Hang up, right?" the lawyer asked.

That was right, Bernstein instructed, and he started counting. Okay, Bernstein said, and thanked him effusively.

"You've got it straight now?" the lawyer asked.

By failing to say anything, the lawyer confirmed the story, even though, from the lawyer's point of view, he had not actively violated the confidentiality requirements of his position.

Of course, miscommunication between actors and observers can easily occur. Mismatches may be found in the ways different communities infer specific communicative intentions from linguistic and nonlinguistic material. A tragic example of this is found in an analysis of the discourse between Egyptian pilots and Greek traffic controllers during a period of military tension between Egypt and Greece in the 1970s.[48] When Egyptian pilots radioed their intention to land at an air base on Cyprus, the Greek traffic controllers reportedly responded with silence. The Greeks intended their silence to communicate refusal of permission to land, but the Egyptian pilots understood the silence as assent. This misunderstanding led to the the loss of many lives when Greeks fired on the Egyptian planes as they approached the runway.

Studies show that people can differentiate, even without speech, between gestures that are intended to convey meaning and gestures that only seem to emphasize what a speaker is saying.[49] This conclusion may be extended to suggest that most body gestures, facial expressions and so on, are often specifically produced to be understood as part of a person's overall communicative intentions and must be recognized as such for successful interpersonal interactions to occur.[50]

One popular belief is that people's body "language" can communicate different messages than what people say (e.g., my body says *yes*, while my words state *no*).[51] Psychological and anthropological studies have explored aspects of how people communicate what they truly believe or intend by their body postures, facial expressions, gestures, and so on, in contrast to what their words often express. Many scholars presume that nonverbal behaviors are natural (i.e., they are signs) and therefore not specifically performed with the intention to be recognized as conveying communicative meanings.[52]

People appear to recognize, at least tacitly, whether any nonverbal act carries with it the assumption of the "recognition-implies-fulfillment" condition (or meaning-nn). For instance, the two of us may be seated across from one another at a boring lecture. Suppose that at one point I yawn. Now in some circumstances, such as when I catch your eye before yawning, this gesture/facial expression might be intended to communicate to you that I believe the lecture to be boring, whereas in other circumstances you will simply understand my gesture as being a natural act without any specific communicative purpose (even if you understand from this nonverbal behavior that I am tired).

The proposal that nonverbal behavior may be purposefully encoded has been bolstered by researchers studying communicative functions that can be deliberately achieved through nonverbal channels. When participants monitor their own behavior when sending relational messages of involvement or uninvolvement, people report consistently and purposefully manipulating body lean and proxemics/kinesic attentiveness to connote degree of interest.[53] Body movement and eye contact has also been found to intentionally communicate rapport with a partner.[54] Touch has also been highlighted as a cue used intentionally to communicate relational information.[55] All of these studies suggest that nonverbal cues may be encoded with various levels of control and purpose and are best interpreted as falling along a continuum of intent.[56]

A good example of how gestures are specifically designed to be regarded as communicating some particular intention is shown in the following description of a medical consultation.[57] The patient was describing to her doctor the pain she felt in walking up steps. She said *I was coming up the steps like this.* The listener cannot understand the referent of *this* without seeing some gestural demonstration of the action that the speaker performed in walking up the stairs. But when the patient began to show the doctor, he was busy writing a prescription. To make herself noticed, the patient moved to put herself more in line with the doctor's vision. When the doctor glanced up, the patient made eye contact and then enacted the manner in which she was climbing the stairs.

This example illustrates not only how a gesture may be produced as an object of reference for an utterance, but it also shows how speakers may modify the design of their intentional performance so that it is recognized as such by others. Speaker and recipient work together in paying attention to many gestures that must be perceived in the final context of what the speaker is saying to be understood. Many sociolinguistic studies also demonstrate the importance of gestures in how speakers and listeners collaborate in intimate ways in conversation.[58]

One study directly examined people's interpretation of nonverbal behaviors as intentional actions.[59] Participants in this study were asked to go to banks and discuss opening a new account with an employee. They were then asked by a confederate to discuss the nonverbal messages perceived to be sent by the employee. The results showed that 65 percent of nonverbal messages reported were judged to be intentional. Many nonverbal behaviors, such as immediacy changes, gaze, smiling, facial expressions, silence, tone of voice, and mirroring another's behavior were interpreted as intentional. When messages directed toward the participants were perceived as positive, the participants were more likely to assume that the nonverbal behaviors involved in sending the message were intentional because of some quality that the participant possessed (e.g., *She thought I was attractive and communicated this to me* or *He really let me know that he really wanted my account because I appeared to have a lot of money to invest*). Negative behaviors were more likely to be attributed to situational factors rather than the intent of the actor. Furthermore, these attributions of intent seemed designed to protect or encourage a positive self-image.

Another study that casts doubt on the idea that nonverbal behavior is natural and not intentionally communicated observed the facial displays of bowlers.[60] Observers were positioned both behind the waiting pit and in the back of the pin-setting machine at the end of the lane. This allowed observers to chart the bowlers' behavior as they rolled the ball, watched the ball roll, and as they pivoted to face the members of the bowling party. Subjects rarely smiled when facing the pins, but did smile frequently when they pivoted to face their friends in the waiting pit. The outcome of the roll, which one might expect to affect the bowler's emotion, bears little relationship to the production of smiles.[61]

A different study analyzed the facial displays of Olympic gold medal winners during the award ceremonies. The athletes only smiled when interacting with others and rarely did so alone. Even though the athletes were judged by observers to be very happy, the fact that they only smiled when looking at or talking to others suggests the importance of social motives (e.g., the intention to communicate information about oneself to others) in regulating nonverbal behavior.[62]

Results likes these have led some psychologists to argue that emotional displays are not natural expressions of emotions, but of communicative intentions. Nonverbal expressions have co-evolved with people's abilities to recognize the differences among them. Some expressions signal friendliness, others signal the intention to attack, and so forth. None of these expressions can be understood outside the social context of a person's communicative intentions and how others might recognize these intentions. Facial displays, to take one example, facilitate the negotiation of social intentions. If the function of expressions is largely to communicate intentions to others in social encounters, sometimes there will be a direct link between a facial display and a particular emotion, in other cases not. Like any bodily changes, facial expressions are fleeting; people are rarely aware of them. Since their function is primarily social and the recognition of moment-by-moment interactions – a smile of encouragement, a frown of frustration – there is no reason to suppose that facial expressions necessarily correspond precisely to long-lasting emotional states that we are aware of either in ourselves or in other people.

Another empirical demonstration of the intrinsically communicative function of facial display showed that the timing of a wince of empathetic pain depended on the availability of the display to its intended audience. In one study, an experimenter staged an event where he dropped a color TV monitor onto his apparently already injured finger in full view of the experimental participant.[63] When the experimenter directly faced the participant, the participant frequently displayed a sympathetic wince, but when the experimenter turned away right after dropping the TV, any initial wincing by the participant quickly ceased. Again, many aspects of our nonverbal displays are specifically directed to an audience and timed so as to be recognized by the intended recipient. Even simply imagining someone else as an observer of your facial expressions increases the intensity of your facial reactions to events.[64]

Other research showed that observers can easily identify the type of odor (good, bad, or neutral) from the facial expressions of the raters only when the raters knew that they were being observed, not when they thought they were making their ratings alone.[65] Similarly, people emit few spontaneous facial expressions when eating sweet and salty sandwiches by themselves, but emit many facial expressions when eating these sandwiches with other people.[66] These findings contradict the traditional view that faces are by nature readouts of emotions rather than social, communicative displays.[67]

Finally, one behavior that is widely considered a readout of inner state is that of motor mimicry. We cringe when we hear of another's fear, and grit our teeth with their anger. But we now know that motor mimicry is communicative. One study showed that the pattern and timing of wincing at an experimental confederate's pain was strongly dependent upon eye contact with the ostensible sufferer.[68] It appears that a person's overt nonverbal behavior is not a "spillover" from their inner vicarious experiences, but has a distinctly communicative function.[69]

HOW TO INFER INTENTIONALITY

People clearly have strong dispositions to attribute intentionality to other persons' actions. But how do people make judgments of intentionality? Perhaps the way of determining people's intentions (and to figure out the contents of their minds) is to ask others what they intend to do. As philosopher Elizabeth Anscombe suggested, a simple way for determining whether somebody is doing something intentionally consists merely of asking *Why are you doing X?* or *Why are you X–ing?*[70] If the person is aware that they are doing X, and if they give some plausible account that they are doing X in order to bring about Y, then they are acting intentionally. My friend Ken's comment about Ann Hamilton's exhibit (e.g., *What did she want us to think about when seeing all this?*) nicely illustrates a concrete instance of someone putting Anscombe's questions into practice. Most talk about intentions makes it appear as if these mental states are part of our conscious awareness. For example, I fully and consciously intended to sit down and write these words with the explicit aim that readers will understand the ideas I wish for them to understand.

But people's reports about their own mental states can be wrong. I might swear to have the intention to exercise more than I do, or cut down on my intake of alcohol, but not take any actions to fulfill these stated intentions. Psychologists Richard Nisbett and Timothy Wilson have convincingly shown through experimental research that people are often not aware of the causes of their behavior.[71] People may not be the best judges of what is important about their own acts. I may intend to do something by performing some action, yet my action may have other unintended consequences noticeable only to those who observe what I do or who are affected by my behavior.[72]

Several general conditions facilitate the attribution of intent to the actions of others in everyday life. In the social world, unlike the physical world, a large number of complex variables are grasped easily and immediately, largely because people are perceived as the originators of their behavior in the sense that there is some intention motivating their actions. The attribution of intent to others is an important source for making the world seem relatively stable and predictable.[73] Psychologists have suggested that people attribute intentions to others because they are aware of them in themselves. People make inferences about the intentions behind other people's behavior partly through empathic identification (i.e., the ability to wear someone else's skin, walk in someone else's shoes, or see through someone else's eyes), or through vicarious introspection (i.e., the ability to imagine how someone else actually thinks or feels). Attributions of intent are the essential link between the observed effects of an act and the inferred underlying disposition. People infer from the effects of acts to intentions and from intentions to dispositions, assuming that the other person is not acting indiscriminately or under coercion and has some choice of behavior alternatives.

The psychologist Ellen Langer lists several factors that shape people's attributions of conscious intentionality to other people's behavior:[74] (1) We attribute more consciousness of intent to meanings produced in situations which for both participants are normal; (2) We attribute more conscious intent to people when we observe what we think should be fairly routine behavior being performed with great effort; (3) We attribute more conscious intent to a person when we, as external agent, try to interfere with the completion of an action only to find that the other person seeks to complete it; (4) We attribute more conscious intent to another when our goals or plans or intentions are clearly in conflict with another person's; (5) We attribute more conscious intent in situations when the consequences of the interaction are highly discrepant from similar interactions with the same person; and (6) We attribute more conscious intent to people if they deviate from a social convention they should know.

Most generally, the intent of any specific action or utterance is only understandable within the context of the relationship between the actor and observer given the particular action taking place. Attributing intention to others depends on knowing whether or not the person committing the behavior (the actor) knows the effects that the behavior would produce and has the ability to produce it. Thus, an attribution of intent requires the normal assumption of knowledge, ability, and awareness on the part of the actor.[75]

One difficulty in assigning intentionality to some behavior arises when someone's individual act produces a string of consequences. Should all of the consequences be understood as products of an actor's intention? A classic example of this situation is provided by the case of the assassination of the Archduke Ferdinand of Austria by Gavrilo Princip.[76] This event was widely considered to have triggered the First World War. Princip enacted a plan to shoot and kill the archduke, the presumptive heir to the Austrian empire, in order to hurt Austria and thus avenge his own country, Serbia, for Austrian oppression and interference. In cases such as this, multiple true descriptions can be made concerning the many actions in a complex plan. Like the folds of an accordion, alternative true descriptions of an action can easily be expanded or contracted. Correct answers to the question *What did Princip do*? include *He pulled his finger, He fired a gun, He shot the archduke, He killed the archduke, He hurt Austria, He started World War I*, and so on. Only some of these multiple action descriptions may have been intended. Such cases are considered puzzling, because it is unclear how many actions had actually been performed and how the intentionality of each should be assessed.[77]

MISATTRIBUTIONS OF INTENTIONALITY

There are several ways in which people misattribute intentionality to other persons. First, a person might overestimate other people's ability to infer some aspects of his or her own behavior. In everyday conversation, for instance, speakers do not fully realize the ambiguity of their own utterances. When we produce an ambiguous message, the knowledge of our own intentions makes that statement seem less ambiguous to us than to others. One empirical test of this idea provided people with syntactically ambiguous sentences such as *The man is chasing a woman on a bicycle*.[78] The sentence might mean that the man is chasing a woman and the woman is on the bike, or that the man is using a bike to chase the woman. Speakers were provided with a picture that disambiguated the sentence – for instance, a picture showing a man running after a cycling woman. The speaker spoke the sentence to addressees, trying to convey the meaning expressed in the picture, and then predicted which of the two meanings the addressee would actually understand. The addressees, who did not have the picture, chose the meaning they thought the speaker intended. The majority of the speakers overestimated how often they would be correctly understood by others. Moreover, when speakers' utterances were recorded and later played back to the speakers, they were not always successful in detecting their original intentions.

A nonverbal demonstration of how people sometimes overestimate their communicative powers was seen in a study where people were asked to finger tap a popular song so that an audience would be able to identify it.[79] After tapping out the song, the tappers were asked to estimate how many people in the audience would recognize the song, and this figure was compared to the actual number of people who correctly identified the song. Tappers consistently overestimated their success in conveying the song to the audience. Apparently, having the song in mind when tapping makes the tapping seem much less ambiguous than it really is.

Even when people pay close attention to the intentional nature of any human action, there are circumstances when individuals mistakenly attribute intentionality to an action that was not truly done intentionally. People's inflated belief in the importance of personality traits and dispositions, together with their failure to recognize the importance of situational factors in affecting behavior, has been termed by social psychologists the *fundamental attribution error*.[80] A variety of empirical studies indicate that the fundamental attribution error underlies several aspects of human behavior. For example, one study randomly assigned participants in a "College Bowl" quiz game to the roles of questioner and contestant, with the former told to select difficult questions for the latter.[81] The questioners often took advantage of their role to display their expertise about some topic (e.g., "What is the sweet-smelling liquid that comes from whales and is used as a base for perfume?"). After the game, both the contestants and observers rated the questioners' and contestants' general knowledge. Although the questioners had a clear advantage in being able to display their knowledge through the questions they selected, both the contestants and the observers rated the questioners as far more knowledgeable than the contestants, overlooking the advantages that the questioners had in choosing questions from their own areas of expertise. People appear blind to the importance of a person's social role in making their attribution judgments.

Consider the classic study demonstrating that people fail to be sensitive to situational constraints in attributing intentionality to others.[82] College students read essays presumably written by fellow students. The participants were told that the authors had been assigned to write essays expressing a particular view. For instance, the participants were told that the essay was produced by a political science student assigned to write an essay defending Castro's Cuba or that he or she was required to write an essay attacking the proposition that marijuana be legalized. Despite the fact that participants clearly understood the situational constraints under which the essays were written, their estimates of the authors' true opinions were influenced by the specific view the author had espoused. Thus, participants rated one author as sympathetic to Castro and another writer as opposed to the legalization of marijuana. These findings reveal how people tend to attribute behaviors to dispositional factors (e.g., a person's beliefs and attitudes) while underestimating the power of the situation. Other studies showed that the fundamental attribution error explains the tendency to attribute road accidents to "human factors," instead of to the characteristics of road vehicles or of the roads themselves.[83]

A dramatic, highly publicized case of people misattributing intentionality to others' behavior has emerged over the last decade in the debates over *facilitated communication*.[84] Facilitated communication was developed as a technique to assist individuals with communication problems, especially people with mental retardation and autism. Facilitated communication employs a manual or electronic letter display by which the nonverbal, or expressively limited, person spells out messages. The person known as the facilitator provides hand-over-hand support to the client, ostensibly to facilitate message generation. The support presumably enables the client to execute the movement patterns involved in the selection of specific letters.

Proponents of facilitated communication argue that the "natural language" produced through this technique challenges the common belief that autism is due to intellectual impairment. Indeed, there have been many purported success stories of autistic individuals communicating a wide range of thoughts via facilitated communication, including poetry and deeply emotional, personal stories about childhood sexual abuse. Many scholars, parents, and facilitators have heralded facilitated communication as the savior for autistic individuals, allowing these individuals to express their previously inaccessible thoughts and communicative intentions. Reading transcripts of conversations between clients and facilitators suggests to many the opening up of the clients' intentional minds.

Consider the following letter written by a fifteen-year-old autistic girl, Maggie, to her mother using facilitated communication.[85]

Do you mind if two of my friend at school style my hair next week? Kathleen and Molly will put some interesting things in my hair like a pony tail and curl my bangs up in the air. They are nice friends that have been teaching me how to dance and all about music and their tapes. They tell me about the things they do at home and together. I wish I could tell them about my life. We do some sharing when we play games but its not the same as real friends. It is so hard for me to develop normal friends since I can't laugh and talk about clothes I wear and boys I like or the concerts I've been to. So I wish I was not autistic. I wish I could do all the things that the other kids do. I guess I'm getting closer to normal but I am still so far away. Please keep pushing me forward. I need your support and strength. Getting the most out of life and producing the most good is my goal. I want to be an active member of society and just not get dragged down by my handicap. I love you mom.

This is an impressive letter from a girl diagnosed with autism who cannot speak the words she says here and who had only been using facilitated communication for about one year. Maggie demonstrates the ability to type, via her facilitator, almost perfectly, to talk about everyday concerns, her relationships with friends, her feelings about being autistic, and her hope that her mother would continue to push her forward. The major proponent of facilitated communication in the United States, Douglas Bilken, argues that cases like Maggie's have led him to adopt a "new point of view, seeing communication difficulties in autism as arising from a neuromotor problem rather than a problem of cognition."[86]

Is it reasonable to attribute genuine intentionality to what Maggie has written via facilitated communication? Consider another exchange between one client, a twenty-seven-year-old male with a diagnosis of moderate mental retardation and infantile autism, and his facilitator, a woman who only started working with autistics when she trained to do facilitated communication.[87]

Client: YESMMMMMMMMMMMMMMMMMMMMMM
MMMMMMMMMMMMMMMMMMMMMMMMM
MMMMMMMMM

Facilitator: You seem excited about typing today, so why don't you start?

Client: i am ex citred aboutc typibg ttoday
you look nice
you look bdautiful
i like your dress
you look beautiful

Facilitator: Well, you are full of compliments today. You're looking pretty good yourself. Did you get a haircut?

Client: yes i did
you are having some trouble at home
read to me cplease

Facilitator: We'll read in awhile. What makes you think that i'm having trouble at home?

Client: because you were tlaking to (name of person) about locks doc you need some new locks

Facilitator: Yes i think I do need some more locks to be safe.

Client: safe from who you feel unsafe ffrom
             who

Facilitator: I want them just as a precaution from anyone who
             might try to get into the house.

Client: you need to have (name of person) there with you.

Facilitator: You have a solution to everything. Sounds real nice,
             but not possible right now.
             I'm changing the subject now – what happened with
             (name of person) last Friday?

Client: i broek his glasses

Facilitator: why?

Client: because i wsas upset with him

Facilitator: why?

Client: he took my lunch.

Facilitator: Is this the truth?

Client: no

Facilitator: What is the truth about this?

Client: he bugs me

Facilitator: In what way does he bug you?

Client: he puts his nosde in what im doing

Facilitator: Does breaking his glasses help this?

Client: no

Facilitator: What would be a better way to handle this?

Client: tell him to stop

On the surface, this seems like a reasonable conversation between the client and the facilitator (again noting that the client's
output is facilitated by the facilitator). But this seventeen-year-
old client, who exhibited a history of significant learning and
behavioral problems, initially learned to use the keyboard with
reasonably appropriate spelling and spacing in a mere matter

of days (an accomplishment that would be impressive even in individuals without mental and motor problems). Furthermore, there was a great disparity between the relative cogency of his facilitated messages, his typing skills, and his overt behavior. For instance, this client was able in interviews with a reporter from a national magazine to talk about his life in an institution and the course of his own behavior program. Yet his highly aggressive nonverbal behavior, and his inability to learn other skills, stand in marked contrast to his high level of success in communicating with others through facilitated communication.[88]

Does facilitated communication enable autistic individuals to express their intentions to others? Are facilitators and others correct in attributing sophisticated intentionality to the linguistic output produced in facilitated communication interchanges? Much research has now shown that clients' manual output is due primarily to facilitators' unconscious assistance in spelling out words, sentences, and stories. Thus, the tremendous verbal outpouring from autistics reflects very little about the clients' putative communicative intentions.[89] As one group of researchers concluded, "at present, there is no scientifically controlled studies that unambiguously support benefits in expressive language function for people with mental retardation or autism by taking part in FC."[90] It appears that the strong belief, or hope, that autistic individual can communicate through facilitated communication has led to a widespread misattribution of intentionality to their so-called linguistic output.

EXPERIENCES OF UNDERSTANDING

Recall my visit to Ann Hamilton's exhibit *Privation and Excesses*. My initial experience of trying to understand Hamilton's artwork occurred over the course of about thirty minutes, during which I quickly formed, and often rejected, several hypotheses about what the piece might mean (or whether the exhibit gave rise to any coherent readings at all). When I talked to my friends at the exhibit, and when I wrote these paragraphs about Hamilton's artwork, I focused on those thoughts that were most conscious in my mind. However, my actual experience of this artwork as I observed it was mostly outside of my conscious awareness. I wasn't especially aware of how I initially identified any of the objects, sounds, and persons present, how these different entities made contact with my autobiographical memories and conceptual knowledge, or how I decided what aspects of what I was observing were most relevant to the different hypotheses I formed about the exhibit. All I was consciously aware of was what was foremost in my conscious mind as I walked around looking at the artwork and later debated the merits of the exhibit with my friends.

Most of our understanding of artwork, a writer's text, or a speaker's utterance occurs very quickly, outside of awareness, and outside of our control. Much of our experience of meaning lies in the unconscious mind. The cognitive unconscious is the vast system of concepts and cognitive mechanisms that operate beneath the level of consciousness, structuring both our experience and our mode of conceptualizing the world. The existence of the cognitive unconsciousness means that most of human thought is not accessible by traditional philosophical and literary methods. Empirical methods of uncovering the cognitive unconscious are necessary if scholars are to understand and appreciate human experience. Many aspects of intentional understanding lie within our unconscious minds and are not easily understood by conscious introspection alone. Acknowledging the power and prominence of our unconscious minds will in most cases illustrate the importance of intentional understanding in our ordinary and scholarly experience of meaning.

One way of resolving some of the debates over intentionalism is to better appreciate people's phenomenological experiences during the time when they are making sense of any given utterance, text, or artwork. This appreciation includes, most importantly, the fact that much of what occurs when people experience meaning, or construct meaningful experiences, occurs unconsciously. Consider the diversity of understanding experiences one might have in reading the opening stanza of the poem "The Hollow Men" by T. S. Eliot.[91]

> We are the hollow men
> We are the stuffed men
> Leaning together
> Headpiece filled with straw. Alas!
> Our dried voices, when
> We whisper together
> Are quiet and meaningless
> As wind in dry grass
> Or rats' feet over broken glass
> In our dry cellar.

Eliot likens voices to wind in dry grass and to rats' feet running over broken glass, with both metaphors giving rise to detailed mental images. But what is the best way of talking about our understanding of these metaphors? When I first read these metaphors in Eliot's poem, I was consciously aware of several interpretations that appealed to me, yet upon further readings I discovered new meanings that Eliot might, or might not, have intended readers to understand.

My understanding of Eliot's poem as I first read it, and later thought about it, cannot be described as a single experience of understanding. Instead, there were different understanding experiences, each of which might correspond very roughly to different temporal moments underlying the conscious and unconscious interpretation of the poem. All understanding, be it linguistic or nonlinguistic, takes place in real time ranging from the first milliseconds of processing to long-term reflective analysis. This temporal continuum may roughly be divided into moments corresponding to our comprehension, recognition, interpretation, and appreciation of linguistic utterances or artworks. My basic claim is that the recovery of what an author intends to communicate may play a role in any one of these different temporal moments. Some of these are difficult to evaluate through conscious introspection, one reason why scholars must be careful in arguing against the idea that authorial intentions play no role in the interpretation of language or artwork. Recovery of authorial intentions, at the very least, might be essential in earlier cognitive processes of interpretation, but not later products of understanding.

Consider some key parts of the temporal continuum of understanding. These different parts lie along a continuum of processes and should not be viewed as constituting separable aspects of the understanding process.

Comprehension refers to the immediate moment-by-moment process of creating meanings for utterances. These moment-by-moment processes are mostly unconscious and involve the analysis of different linguistic information (e.g., phonology, lexical access, syntax), which, in combination with context and real-world knowledge, allow listeners/readers to figure out what an utterance means or a speaker/author intends. For example, when reading the metaphors *Our dried voices ... Are quiet and meaningless/As wind in dry grass/Or rats' feet over broken glass*, readers may very quickly, with little conscious reflection, come to understand something about what the writer means by this expression. Such a comprehension process is facilitated by contextual information or, more specifically, the common-ground context that exists between speaker and listener, or author and reader, at any one moment. Contemporary psycholinguistic research suggests that comprehension processes operate within the time span of a few hundred milliseconds up to a few seconds at most.

Recognition refers to the conscious identification of the products of comprehension as types. For example, a reader may judge a particular expression as metaphorical. Even though many literary theorists and philosophers assume that recognition (e.g., that some utterance is metaphorical as opposed to literal) is a requirement for understanding what an utterance or text means, it is by no means clear that recognition is an obligatory stage in people's understanding of what utterances mean or of what speakers/authors intend. Listeners, for instance, probably do not have any awareness or conscious recognition that different utterances in conversation are ironic, idiomatic, hyperbolic, literal, and so on. Nor would they normally recognize each utterance as an exemplar of a particular illocutionary act (e.g., assertive, directive, commissive, verdictive, and so on). For instance, ordinary readers can easily arrive at a figurative meaning for the lines *Our dried voices...* without having to first recognize that these were metaphors in any way. Readers, especially critics, may at a later point recognize the lines from Eliot's poem as metaphorical expressions. But our appreciation of these different metaphorical meanings need not require that we categorize the statements as metaphors.

Interpretation refers to analysis of the early products of comprehension as tokens (i.e., as specific instances of some general type of meaning). One can consciously create an understanding for a particular type of text or utterance as having a particular content or meaning. Thus, hearing the lines *Our dried voices ... are quiet and meaningless / As wind in dry grass / Or rats' feet over broken glass* might at some point in time result in a listener understanding a particular set of entailments about the ways that men's voices can be similar in various ways to the sounds of wind in dry grass or rats' feet moving over broken glass. A rich set of entailments can be drawn from any metaphor. Some of these entailments might be specifically intended by the speaker or author of the metaphor. Others meanings might be unauthorized but still understood as being reasonable. Interpretation refers to the various late products of understanding that may or may not be intended by speakers/authors. The process of arriving at some of these interpretive products may be quite elaborate, requiring lengthy, conscious analysis. For instance, astute readers might differ on the questions of wind in dry grass as opposed to the sounds of rats' feet over broken glass (wind in dry grass makes whooshing sounds while rats' feet over broken glass makes rapid clicking sounds). Interpretation processes like this operate at a later point in time than comprehension processes and usually require conscious reflection about what a text or speaker possibly means.

Finally, *appreciation* refers to some aesthetic judgment given to a product either as type or token. This, too, is not an obligatory part of understanding linguistic meaning because listeners/readers can easily comprehend utterances or texts without automatically making an aesthetic judgment about what has been understood. For instance, a reader might especially appreciate the aptness or aesthetic value of an expression in which men's voices are compared to the sounds of wind in dry grass or to the noise of rats' feet rapidly moving across broken glass. When people appreciate some figurative utterance as having a certain aesthetic value, they are reflecting on some meaning as a product. Psychological evidence shows that comprehension and appreciation refer to distinct types of mental processes.[92]

In general, understanding begins from the first moments with comprehension processes, and proceeds in time to the later moments of recognition, interpretation, and appreciation. Much of what takes place when language is normally understood in everyday speech, and even during the understanding of some literary texts, does not demand cognitive effort beyond comprehension. For instance, readers may rapidly comprehend the meanings of a poem without consciously recognizing that the utterances are metaphorical, ironic, idiomatic, and so on. Readers may also correctly interpret a literary poem without necessarily attaching any particular aesthetic value (or appreciation) to it. Whatever set of mental activities operate during the understanding of literature, as well as of any ordinary utterance or any work of art, it is clear that each part of the temporal continuum of understanding demands a unique theoretical explanation.

Critics and theorists too often make the mistake of assuming that a theory constructed to explain one temporal moment of understanding can be generalized to account for *all* aspects of understanding. The time-course of understanding for language and art requires different kinds of theories at different temporal moments. For instance, a theory of the early *process* of language comprehension does not necessarily lead to a theory of the late *products* of poetic interpretation. The failure to acknowledge the distinction between the processes and products of understanding has important consequences for the debates on intentionalism in understanding language and art.

Determining the role of communicative intentions in interpreting language depends partly on which aspect of the temporal experience of understanding scholars most closely study. Philosophers, linguists, anthropologists, and literary theorists have focused their attention on the later products of conscious interpretation and have not generally concerned themselves with quick, unconscious comprehension processes. Cognitive scientists, especially cognitive psychologists and psycholinguists, have usually focused on the fast "on-line" mental processes that occur during the first several seconds of linguistic processing. The issue here is whether it is appropriate to infer something about early, unconscious mental processes from an analysis of later, reflective products, and vice versa. It may be inappropriate to infer something about the role of speakers' or authors' intentions in early on-line processing from an analysis of whether speakers' or authors' intentions constrain textual meaning.

My claim is that such reasoning is faulty and has led to the opposing conclusions of cognitive scientists and humanities scholars in the controversy over intentions in interpretation. Many theorists have mistakenly assumed that a theory constructed to explain one temporal moment of linguistic understanding can easily be generalized to account for *all* aspects of understanding. It is incorrect to conclude that speakers' or authors' communicative intentions are irrelevant to the early processes of language comprehension simply because people can, at times, consciously interpret an utterance without direct appeal to what they think a speaker really intended. To say that people do not seek communicative intentions because they interpret an utterance in a way that apparently deviates from a speaker's or author's intention makes an unwarranted inference about an early process of understanding from an examination of a later product of understanding. Philosophers and literary critics have simply been wrong to proclaim that the "death of the author" eliminates *any* consideration of how authorial intentions constrain people's reading of texts.

In fact, there is experimental evidence demonstrating that people find it easier to understand written language if it is assumed to have been composed by intentional agents (i.e., people) rather than by computer programs without intentional agency.[93] Participants were presented with various comparison statements and were told that they had been either written by famous twentieth-century poets or randomly constructed by a computer program. The participants' task in one study was to rate the "meaningfulness" of the comparisons; in another study they read and then pushed a button when they had comprehended the statements. Readers found metaphorical expressions, such as *Cigarettes are time bombs*, more meaningful when such statements had supposedly been written by twentieth-century poets, intentional agents, than when these same metaphors were seen as random constructions of a computer program. People also took much less time to comprehend the comparisons when they were told that the statements had been written by poets rather than by the computer program. Moreover, readers took longer to reject as "meaning-less" anomalous utterances supposedly written by poets. Read-ers presumed that poets have specific communicative intentions in designing their utterances, an assumption that does not hold for unintelligent computer programs. Consequently, people spent much more effort trying to understand anomalous phrases, such as *A scalpel is like a horseshoe*, when they had supposedly been written by poets. But people more quickly rejected as "meaning-less" these same anomalous expressions when told they had been written by a computer program, because computers are assumed to lack communicative intentions. These data have shown the powerful role of authorial intentions in people's immediate un-derstanding of written expressions (also see Chapters 7 and 9).[94]

Scholars in the humanities and the cognitive sciences who adopt different positions on intentionalism presuppose a great deal about the cognitive *processes* and *products* in the experience of meaning. For instance, understanding the role of speakers' or au-thors' intentions in determining the meaning of a text assumes that certain mental processes *must* occur for a meaning to be un-derstood in the first place. Similarly, understanding the role of speaker or authorial intentions in the processing of utterances as-sumes something about the end-point of that processing when a listener or reader arrives at some kind of meaning or interpre-tation. The scholarly quest for defining what a text means and for understanding how people process linguistic utterances both involve the study of interpretive activities by either critics or or-dinary listeners or readers. To say that a text has a particular meaning requires that a critic employ various cognitive/linguistic processes to construct that interpretation, in the same way that ordinary listeners or readers use various unconscious and con-scious mental processes to understand linguistic expressions. In this way, both the advocates and critics of the intentional view of communication implicitly assume a good deal about the mental activities involved when people listen to or read language (or interact with artworks).

The scholarly study of these various temporal moments of linguistic understanding will require substantially different methodologies for analyzing what role speakers' intentions play in the understanding of what utterances mean. Philosophers of language, for example, might provide articulate, rational analyses of the immediate, unconscious mental processes used in ordinary language understanding. But traditional philosophical methods of rational argument and analysis are clearly insufficient for tapping into the "on-line" mental computations that occur when people understand language in everyday speech and when they read. More indirect, scientific techniques, such as those employed in experimental psycholinguistics, are necessary to determine the psychological reality of immediate comprehension processes and products. Such methods provide good evidence to suggest that understanding language begins, at the very least, with the attempted recovery of speakers'/authors' communicative intentions. The mistake made by many theorists in both the cognitive sciences and the humanities is that a theory constructed to explain one temporal moment of linguistic understanding can somehow be generalized to account for *all* aspects of understanding. We must recognize the need for different theories to account for different aspects of both the processes and products of linguistic interpretation. In this respect, the plurality of ideas found in the interdisciplinary study of meaning and interpretation do not necessarily compete with each other, but simply reflect different aspects of the psychological activity of language understanding.

Needless to say, this argument about the experience of linguistic meaning also extends to how people create meaning when interacting with artworks. Observing and interacting with artworks, such as my seeing Ann Hamilton's *Privation and Excesses*, takes place over time with different unconscious and conscious mental processes operating throughout this experience (never mind the deliberative thought I have expended on the work since I saw it many years ago). Describing the role of communicative, as well as expressive, intentions in our experience of artworks also demands several different kinds of theoretical explanation depending on which temporal moment of experience we are attempting to describe.

CONCLUSION

People are strongly disposed to attribute intentionality to human, and sometimes to nonhuman, action. This disposition is a fundamental part of the cognitive unconscious and provides one of the important reasons why people experience human actions, and the artifacts that arise from these actions, as meaningful. We do not always successfully communicate our intentions to others, and may misattribute intentionality to behavior that is best explained by nonintentional, situational factors. Yet people's bias toward assuming intentionality strongly outweighs any tendency to view human action in nonintentional terms. Of course, some aspects of meaningful experience are not intentionally tied to understanding the intentions of others. People may infer meanings of utterances, texts, and artworks that deviate from what others intended to communicate, especially at later temporal moments in the experience of understanding. But as I argued in Chapter 3, inferences about unintentional meanings are often grounded in our understanding of intentional communication. For example, making sense of Ann Hamilton's *Privation and Excesses*, certain elements of what I observed focused on Hamilton's possible overt and covert intentions. My meaningful experience viewing this exhibit was also based on my assumptions about Hamilton's beliefs and desires, and her awareness and skills in creating the exhibit. Yet my interpretation of Hamilton's work does not necessarily imply any belief that Hamilton's clearly worked out thoughts were perfectly realized in the work itself. Instead, my experience of *Privation and Excesses* felt more like a conversation between the artist and myself, where intentionality emerged from our interaction via the work, rather than my recovery of specific, articulated, private thoughts in the artist's mind. Parts III and IV consider several implications of this idea.

Part III

Intentions in Discourse

The chapters in Part III examine exactly how intentions play an important role in the mental processes by which people construct meaningful interpretations of spoken and written language. I describe in some detail how speakers and listeners cooperate and coordinate with each other to achieve successful communication. In doing so, I emphasize that interpretation is probabilistic in the extent to which communicative intentions shape the experience of meaning. One of the great obstacles in the debates over intentions in interpretation is that it is assumed that people either always or never infer authorial intentions. Yet authorial intentions may contribute only partial information to people about how to interpret speech and texts. In many cases, people infer unintended meanings of messages that still fit the context, but these meanings, nonetheless, depend on the recognition that speakers have some other meanings they are trying to express. Writing and reading, just like speaking and listening, are best characterized as social transactions which include the specific attempt to achieve successful communication of intentional meanings.

Chapter 5

Spoken Language

Consider the following exchange between two college students:

Joe: Are you going to take the semantics course next semester?

Sue: Didn't you hear that Prof. Allen is teaching it?

How does Joe interpret Sue's response to his question? Although Sue's response is itself a question, it is considered an appropriate answer to Joe's original question. But in different circumstances it would convey different answers. For example, on the assumption that Sue likes Prof. Allen, the implied answer will be yes, whereas on the assumption that she wants to avoid him as an instructor, the implied answer will be no. The fact that the listener (Joe) presumably knows, for example, that Sue doesn't like Prof. Allen (or at least is aware of the belief that Prof. Allen is, say, an unusually difficult instructor), allows Joe to easily deduce that Sue really means that she won't be enrolling in the class.

How should we characterize the process by which people understand utterances? And what role does recognition of a speaker's intentions play in the comprehension process? My general claim is that language understanding is not grounded in understanding the meanings of the words spoken, even in context. Nor do speakers produce utterances and listeners understand them independently of one another. Instead, speakers and listeners cooperate and coordinate with each other to understand their individual and joint intentions in face-to-face interaction. Describing how this is accomplished is the primary goal of this chapter. A variety of empirical evidence shows that recovery of people's communicative intentions plays a major role in how participants successfully cooperate and coordinate during ordinary language use. I will also suggest that inferring *unintended* meanings depends on the recognition that some other meaning was likely intended by a speaker in some context.

TRADITIONAL APPROACHES
TO LANGUAGE UNDERSTANDING

There have been in the cognitive sciences three major theoretical views of language understanding.[1] The *independence view* asserts that the literal or direct meaning of a sentence is arrived at by various computational processes which do not extend to supplying referential and real-world knowledge.[2] This view assumes that there is an autonomous stage of linguistic processing wherein the literal meaning of a sentence is analyzed (e.g., the proper domain for the study of meaning or "semantics") before contextual, real-world information is brought in to determine how the utterance of a sentence is used in some situation (e.g., the proper domain of use or "pragmatics"). The *constructivist view* states that elaborate mental edifices are built up for the situation a sentence describes including contextual and real-world information.[3] This view acknowledges the constraining influence of real-world knowledge in the interpretation of context-sensitive meaning. Finally, the *intentional view*, which lies between the other views, sees comprehension as a process by which people arrive at the interpretation a speaker/author *intended* them to grasp for that utterance in that context.[4] Unlike the independence view, the intentional view requires listeners/readers to draw inferences that go well beyond the literal or direct meaning of a sentence. But unlike the constructivist view, this view limits the inferences to those that listeners/readers judge the speakers/authors intended them to draw based on the common ground – the knowledge, beliefs, and attitudes that are thought to be shared by speakers/authors and listeners/readers – at any one moment in a discourse situation.[5]

These different views of comprehension do not necessarily compete with one another, because each position reflects a concern for a different aspect of meaning. The independence view's primary aim is to characterize sentence meaning, the constructivist view characterizes utterance meaning, while the intentional view describes understanding of speaker meaning. In general, there has been a historical progression in cognitive science from looking at language understanding as primarily a question of how people understand sentences to examining how people determine what speakers/authors mean by their use of utterances in discourse. But as described in earlier chapters, the intentionalist view embraces aspects of the dialogic paradigm where communication is viewed as a joint product of speakers and listeners working in collaboration. My adoption of the cognitive intentionalist premise is consistent with this trend.

UNDERSTANDING WHAT IS INTENDED RATHER THAN WHAT IS SAID

People ordinarily focus on what speakers intend, rather than on what they say. A terrific illustration of this comes from the satirist Erma Bombeck, who once wrote in one of her newspaper columns about her daughter's difficulties finding a suitable roommate.[6] Consider what Bombeck says as she quotes her daughter:

> We thought we were onto a steam iron yesterday, but we were too late. Steam irons never have any trouble finding roommates. She could pick her own pad and not even have to share a bathroom. Stereos are a dime a dozen. Everyone's got their own systems. We've just had a streak of bad luck. First, our Mr. Coffee flunked out of school and went back home. When we replaced her, our electric typewriter got married and split, and we got stuck with a girl who said she was getting a leather coat, but she just said that to get the room.

It seems odd, literally speaking, to talk about steam irons not having trouble finding roommates or electric typewriters getting married. Traditional theories of parsing will fail to handle many of these phrases even though we, for the most part, can easily understand what Bombeck's daughter is saying.[7] Consider the sentence *Steam irons never have any trouble finding roommates*. Most parsers will search their lexicons for the sense of *steam irons* that is intended, namely "a person who owns a steam iron," and will fail to find anything like this meaning. But the fact that we think about and talk about people in terms of *steam irons, stereos, Mr. Coffee*, and so on reflects the common metonymic mapping whereby we use a salient aspect of an object or event to stand for the thing or event as a whole.

English has many *contextual expressions*, constructions that have in principle an infinite number of potential senses.[8] Among some of the notable ones in English are: indirect descriptions (e.g., *Stereos are a dime a dozen* or *Please do a Napoleon for the camera*), compound nouns (e.g., *Sit on the apple-juice chair, I want a finger cup*), denominal nouns (e.g., *She's a waller, He's a cupper*), denominal verbs (e.g., *She Houdini'd her way out of the closet* or *My friend teapotted a policeman*), denominal adjectives (e.g., *He seems very California*), and possessives (e.g., *That's Calvin's side of the room, Let's take my route*). All these expressions undermine the idea that sentence meaning is primary to understanding language. They also highlight the centrality of authorial intentions in how people ordinarily comprehend what others say and write.

Several other examples from real-life discourse clearly illustrate how listeners form their interpretations around what is intended and not simply what is said. Consider the following sentence describing New York Yankee pitcher David Cone's performance in a key game: "Before the game, he had said that he would omit the split-finger, sparing his arm, but he threw an absolute Vermeer to Harold Baines in the fourth, and then struck-out the next man, Robin Ventura, with another beauty."[9]

This sentence has several interesting features. The phrase *omit the split-finger* refers to a specific type of fastball pitch, while the expression *threw an absolute Vermeer* certainly doesn't mean that Cone tossed a seventeenth-century Dutch painting by Johannes Vermeer at the batter. Readers easily recognize that the writer intended to communicate something about the beauty of Cone's pitch to Baines and that he uses Vermeer as a denominal verb to make this point. People don't react to this sentence by saying it is literally nonsensical, because they read it seeking the writer's intended meaning.

Consider now a sign discovered on the wall of a London hospital: *No head injury is too trivial to ignore.*[10] This sentence means "There is no head injury that is so trivial that it cannot be ignored," a reading that clearly makes no sense. The sign should have read *No head injury is too trivial to treat*, but for years people interpreted the original sign as "No head injury is too trivial to treat." To do that, they must have created a plausible speaker meaning without determining the sentence meaning.

Does experimental evidence imply that people ordinarily seek communicative intentions when they understand both oral as well as written language? Consider a phenomenon known as the *Moses illusion.*[11] When people are asked *How many animals of each kind did Moses take on the ark?* most of them answer *two* without noticing that it was Noah, not Moses, who was chosen to captain the ark. Most of us immediately focus on our assumptions about the speaker's intentions in asking the question.

Other psychological experiments examined shifts in memory for what is said as evidence for inferences about communicative intentions made during discourse comprehension. Many studies have shown that people are very likely to remember a pragmatic implication of an utterance rather than the utterance itself or what it directly asserts or logically implies. For instance, people hearing sentences such as *He dropped the delicate glass pitcher* and *The housewife spoke to the manager about the increase in meat prices* often remembered them according to their pragmatic force, as in *He broke the delicate glass pitcher* and *The housewife complained to the manager about the increase in meat prices.*[12] In each of these experiments, listeners encoded inferences that went beyond the explicit information contained in the sentences, but which were in accord with the speakers' probable intentions in making these utterances. The intention behind the speaker's utterance is encoded and represented in memory, not the sentence or utterance meaning.

Pairs of participants were asked to act out several dialogues.[13] After each acted version, the participants either judged whether particular sentences from a comparison dialogue were the same or different from the acted dialogue, or, in another experiment, choose between two intentions suggested for some of the acted sentences. The results showed that participants best recognized the test sentences which conveyed the intentions of utterances previously stated. Other data show that intentions produce a distinct form of memory for both linguistic and nonlinguistic activities.[14]

These data and observations on the primacy of speaker's intentions in memory for discourse do not specifically bear on either the issue of how to define sentence meaning or what constitutes a speaker's intentions in the first place. One could argue that these empirical findings only demonstrate the tendency to draw certain inferences about situations (i.e., that when someone drops a glass it usually breaks), and have little to do with listeners imputing anything about speakers' intentions. But recent psycholinguistic research suggests that people do not automatically draw many kinds of inferences appropriate to situations when reading texts.[15] It appears that listeners' memory for sentences is clearly organized around the intentions they attribute to speakers in saying what they do in discourse.

The context in which people hear utterances surely influences their immediate comprehension of what speakers intend to communicate. Context includes not only the surrounding discourse, but also listeners' knowledge of the physical-social situation and knowledge of the speakers' plans, goals, and likely intentions. However, most psychological theories have assumed a view of context in which similarity between speaker and listener is taken for granted due to their being embedded in the same social-linguistic context. This orientation suggests that understanding discourse involves the listener's finding the right knowledge represented in memory to make sense of linguistic events (e.g., the constructivist view).

But this characterization of context and the resulting picture of language understanding is impoverished. Language understanding requires that listeners must not only utilize a context which includes their own information about what the speaker believes, they must also recognize that *speakers* know that they know this as well. Understanding, and the criteria by which listeners judge that they have understood, is a joint product requiring coordination and cooperation between participants' individual and mutual intentions. The context for understanding verbal discourse lies within the set of mutual beliefs, knowledge, and presuppositions that speakers and listeners share. Many cognitive scientists have advanced this point as part of their support for the intentional view of communication.

GRICE'S VIEW

Recall the conversation between Joe and Sue, described above. Successful interpretation of Sue's response *Didn't you hear that Prof. Allen is teaching it?* demands that the listener make an inference about what the speaker meant. But such recognition of the speaker's intention is of a special kind, what the philosopher H. Paul Grice called an *m-intention*.[16] An m-intention is a speaker's intention to produce an effect in the listener by means of the hearer's recognition of that intention. For instance, Sue intends for Joe to recognize that she isn't going to take the course precisely because Prof. Allen is teaching it in part by means of the listener's recognition of that intention. If the listener successfully recognizes this intention, he or she will have drawn the "authorized" inference.[17] Any other inferences drawn – for example, that Sue is going to enroll in the semantics seminar – is "unauthorized" or not m-intended.

The following examples illustrate the role of mutual beliefs in distinguishing "authorized" from "unauthorized" inferences.[18] The first case seems simple but really involves some complexity. Rick is sitting in the living room reading a book when Sally walks in leaving the door open. Rick says to Sally *It's cold in here.* He means for Sally to understand this as a polite request to close the door, and she understands him to mean just that. Sally has therefore drawn an "authorized" inference, one which she believes Rick meant for her to draw. Sally derives this correct inference because she assumes that both she and Rick know that leaving a door open will cause a draft making the room feel cold. Sally uses this piece of shared knowledge in conjunction with the cooperative principle to infer exactly what m-intention Rick wishes for her to recover.

The second example is even more complex. Helen and Karen were talking on the telephone about their upcoming final examinations. Karen asked Helen *How's the studying going?* and Helen replies *I've been smoking a lot of cigarettes.* Although Helen's answer is not a direct response to the question, she intends Karen to understand it to mean "I'm studying quite hard" because Helen always smokes cigarettes when she studies. Karen knows this, it is information shared between Helen and Karen, and Karen correctly infers that Helen intends her to use this shared knowledge in understanding the response to her original question. The inference that Karen draws then is "authorized." Note that if Karen incorrectly believes that Helen isn't studying very hard because she's spending all her time smoking cigarettes due to anxiety, then she probably will draw the "unauthorized" inference that Helen meant "I'm not studying very hard" by her response.

There is various evidence that listeners are generally quite good at drawing authorized inferences about what speakers intend by their words. To take just one example, when thirty San Francisco merchants were asked over the phone *Do you close before seven?*, only four of them just answered the question. The others provided the information about the actual closing time, which is what they assumed the questioner wanted to know.[19] Listeners correctly recognized the speakers' goals in asking the question and answered accordingly. Any presupposition a listener has about a speaker's plans, goals, and likely intentions will act as part of the context for understanding.

How do listeners draw the correct authorized inference about what a speaker means? To determine what a speaker means, listeners must go beyond their understanding of what a speaker explicitly says. Thus, when Sue and Joe were talking about the semantics course, Sue's response to Joe's question was itself a question (i.e., *Didn't you hear that Prof. Allen is teaching it?*). Yet Sue intended to communicate something more than the fact that she was asking a question; she was also conveying, via her rhetorical question, a specific assertion. Understanding that Sue's comment is meant as a particular answer to Joe's question requires that Joe go through a chain of reasoning regarding Sue's intentions because her answer does not logically follow from his question. Grice called the intended message behind Sue's utterance an *implicature*.[20] He proposed that implicatures are a natural outcome of speakers' and listeners' cooperation in conversation because all speakers adhere to the *cooperative principle*. This states that as a speaker you must "make your conversational contribution such as is required, at the stage at which it occurs, by the accepted purpose or direction of the talk exchange in which you are engaged."[21] Thus, when Sue says what she does, Joe should take Sue's response as being cooperative and therefore as implicating something beyond what the response literally means.

The cooperative principle carries with it four maxims:

Maxim of Quantity: Make your contribution as informative as is required, but not more so, for the current purposes of the exchange.

Maxim of Quality: Do not say anything you believe to be false or for which you lack adequate evidence.

Maxim of Relation: Say only what is relevant for the current purposes of the conversation.

Maxim of Manner: Be brief, but avoid ambiguity and obscurity of expression.

These maxims constitute what it means for a speaker to be cooperative. Part of the context for understanding verbal interaction is the shared assumption that speakers and listeners will each uphold the cooperative principle and its associated maxims. Listeners use the cooperative principle to their advantage in determining what speakers mean because they assume that speakers tailor their remarks to satisfy this principle. As such, the cooperative principle and its maxims constitute a sort of shared reality which constrains the interpretation process and plays a crucial role in what listeners recognize as the "click of comprehension."

Grice notes that speakers do not always uphold these maxims. As long as speakers generally adhere to the overall cooperative principle, they can "flout" any of these maxims to produce certain implicatures. That is, speakers can deliberately violate a maxim and specifically intend for their listeners to recognize the deliberate violation. For example, Sue's response to Joe's question with another question can be seen as a deliberate violation of the convention that questions should be responded to with assertions. In this case Sue is obviously flouting the maxim of manner in order to implicate that she is not going to enroll in the semantics seminar. According to Grice's analysis, Joe would not consider Sue's response to be uncooperative.[22] Instead, Joe would continue to assume that Sue's rhetorical response was cooperative and would seek an interpretation given what he assumes about Sue, and what he believes Sue assumes about him, in order to derive an acceptable and "authorized" interpretation. As Grice argues, the cooperative principle is a device for enabling listeners to draw only inferences "authorized" by the speaker.

Grice's view on utterance interpretation has had enormous influence on cognitive science theories of linguistic understanding. His theory argues that listeners' interpretations of speakers' utterances will be sufficiently constrained by the shared reality provided by the cooperative principle. Note, however, that the cooperative principle itself does not sufficiently limit what meanings listeners recognize. Speakers and listeners must share more specific beliefs if they are to communicate the wide variety of meanings often conveyed in everyday conversation.

RELEVANCE THEORY

Understanding what a speaker intends to communicate requires, among other things, that a listener find a context that provides the best framework for interpreting what the speaker meant.[23] What was the speaker's intended attitude toward what was said or implied? Sometimes, it is clear what the speaker intended to say or imply, but less clear what his attitude is toward what he has said or implied.

Suppose, for example, that Joe and Sue have in their common ground, the idea that Prof. Allen is a notoriously bad instructor. In this situation, then, the most natural interpretation of Sue's utterance is that she intended to supply the assumption that Prof.

Allen is teaching the course and that she will therefore not enroll in the seminar. But while Sue clearly intended to commit herself to the claim that Prof. Allen was going to teach the seminar, it is less clear that she seriously intended to commit herself to the truth of the assumption that Prof. Allen is a poor instructor and the conclusion that she will not be taking his semantics seminar. Perhaps she was merely being playful, encouraging her audience to entertain the stereotype about Prof. Allen without actually endorsing it.

When Joe understands Sue's utterance he must answer these questions: (a) What did Sue intend to say; (b) What did Sue intend to imply; and (c) What was Sue's intended attitude toward the propositions expressed and implied? One theory that provides a framework for answering these questions is Sperber and Wilson's *relevance theory*.[24] The relevance-theoretic account of utterance interpretation proposes that a fundamental assumption about human cognition is that people pay attention to information that seems most relevant to them. Every utterance starts out as a request for someone else's attention, and this creates an expectation of relevance.[25] This expectation of relevance provides the criterion for evaluating possible interpretations of a speaker's utterance. Yet different interpretations of what a speaker says will be relevant in different ways (i.e., some will not be relevant at all, some will be fairly relevant, some will be very relevant). For instance, when Joe interprets Sue's rhetorical question *Didn't you hear that Prof. Allen is teaching the course?* he may consider various meanings that might be more or less relevant to the specific context (e.g., that Prof. Allen is handsome and so Sue will take his course even if he is a lousy teacher, that Prof. Allen is the best teacher and so Sue will certainly take his course, and so on). The specific interpretation Joe will choose is the one that best satisfies his expectation of relevance.

What does it mean to say that an interpretation of a speaker's utterance is optimally relevant? Relevance is defined in terms of *contextual effect* and *processing effort*. Contextual effects are achieved when newly presented information interacts with the context of existing assumptions in one of three ways: by strengthening an existing assumption, by contradicting and eliminating an existing assumption, or by combining with an existing assumption to yield a contextual implication – that is, a logical implication derivable neither from the new information alone, nor from the context alone, but from the new information and the context combined. Newly presented information is relevant when it achieves contextual effects in a specific discourse situation, and the greater the contextual effects, the greater the relevance.

Consider the following exchange:

Peter: Would you like some coffee?

Mary: Coffee would keep me awake.

When Peter interprets Mary's utterance, he would normally be expected to supply the contextual assumption that Mary doesn't want to be kept awake and derive the contextual implication that Mary doesn't want any coffee. Notice that this implicature is not the only possible interpretation of Mary's utterance. If Peter and Mary are just about to attend a boring lecture, for example, the possibility that Mary wants to stay awake and wants some coffee to help her stay awake is a very reasonable interpretation.

But how does a listener, like Peter, know which interpretation the speaker, Mary, intended? The answer again follows from the definition of optimal relevance. If in a given situation, a contextual assumption is highly salient, and leads on to a satisfactory interpretation of an utterance then this is the only interpretation that the speaker is free to intend and the listener to choose. Thus, if the contextual assumption that Mary wants to stay awake is quite salient, and this leads to the the inference that Mary wants some coffee, then that will be mutually understood as the authorized meaning. Most generally, the first interpretation tested and found consistent with the principles of relevance is the only interpretation considered. All other interpretations are, at least momentarily, suppressed.

A second consequence of the definition of relevance is that extra effort needed to process an utterance implies extra contextual effects. Consider, again, a situation in which Mary says *Coffee would keep me awake*, intending Peter to supply the assumption that she does not want to stay awake and derive the conclusion that she does not want any coffee. Would Mary's utterance, on this interpretation, be consistent with the principle of relevance? If this were all she wanted to communicate, the answer would be *No*.[26] After all, Mary could have simply responded *No* to Peter's offer. But Mary must have intended the indirect answer *Coffee would keep me awake* to achieve some additional contextual effects, not achievable by the direct answer *No* alone. By saying that coffee would keep her awake, Mary not only refuses the coffee, but gives an explanation for her refusal.[27]

Relevance theory offers a significant advance over the Gricean view of utterance interpretation, especially to the degree that it seeks to tie together pragmatic language use and cognition. Only a few experimental studies have directly tested the psychological plausibility of relevance theory as an account of human language understanding.[28] But relevance theory holds much promise and should clearly be the focus of additional empirical research. One idea from relevance theory that is especially important is that many aspects of what listeners infer can best be described as weak implicatures. I introduced the idea of weak implicatures in Chapter 3 to suggest how some aspects of what listeners infer may not have been specifically intended by speakers. I'll say more about this idea in this and later chapters.

PRINCIPLES OF SUCCESSFUL
COMMUNICATION

Psychologist Herb Clark and his associates have offered a different set of ideas to explain intentional speaking and understanding. Clark contends that several specific principles guide speakers and listeners as they strive to recover a speaker's communicative intentions.[29] These principles form the basis on which speakers and listeners coordinate and cooperate to understand each other, and their joint communicative intentions.

The first is the *principle of speaker meaning*: Speakers and their addressees take it for granted that the addressees are to recognize what the speaker means by what they say and do. When Moe says to Larry *Shut up!* he means something that he wants Larry to recognize, specifically a demand that he stop talking. Recovery of what a speaker means is primary for communication.

The second is the *principle of utterance design*: Speakers try to design each utterance so that their addressees can figure out what they mean by considering the utterance against their current common ground. Under this principle, common ground divides roughly into cultural common ground and personal common ground. Two people's cultural common ground draws on information that is common to the cultural groups they belong to. Their personal common ground draws on joint personal experiences as viewed against their cultural common ground.

Consider the following example. When Barbara and Greg meet at a party and as they establish the cultural groups they have in common, they can each assume an enormous body of cultural common ground. Once they realize that they are both university graduates, for example, they can assume as common ground all those facts and beliefs they assume university-educated people take for granted. These range from theories of gravity, light, and biological systems to the basic facts of geography, history and social organization. As two speakers of American English, they can assume as common ground the phonology, syntax, and vocabulary of that language. As two baseball fans, they can assume as common ground the names of the major players, their statistics, and such jargon as RBI and ERA. Common cultural communities include language (English, California dialect, Santa Cruz high school argot), education (grade school, high school, university, postgraduate), geography (United States, California, Santa Cruz, Beach Flats), profession (psychology, plumbing, law, sheep ranching), avocation (volleyball, professional football fan, jazz).

Once two people jointly establish their membership in any of these communities, they are licensed to add vast quantities of information to their common ground. Barbara and Greg build up their personal common ground as they talk and experience things together. They add to it when they jointly witness a car hit a tree or hear a soprano sing an aria. They also add to it each time one of them asserts something to the other. Personal common ground is established from joint perceptual and linguistic experiences interpreted against cultural common ground. But exactly how do Barbara and Greg build common ground?

In ordinary conversation, common ground accumulates in a highly systematic way, as expressed in the *principle of accumulation*: in a conversation, the participants add to their common ground each time they contribute to it successfully.[30] When Barbara speaks, Greg interprets her utterance against their initial common ground, and then they both add the content of what she says to that common ground. Then when Greg speaks, Barbara interprets him against their updated common ground and the two of them update their common ground once more. And so it goes. Every successful contribution adds to the common ground of the participants.

A fundamental part of everyday language use is a process called *grounding*.[31] When Barbara and Greg talk to each other they work to formulate utterances that express what they mean, but by the principle of accumulation they must make sure what they say becomes part of their common ground. Barbara and Greg insure that what is said becomes part of their common ground through the *principle of grounding*: for each contribution to discourse the participants try to reach the mutual belief that the addressees have understood what the speaker meant to a criterion sufficient for current purposes. Thus, when Barbara speaks she looks for evidence from Greg that he has understood her. Greg in turn tries to provide that evidence by saying *Ah ha*, nodding his head, or taking the relevant next turn.[32] If he hasn't understood her, he will ask her to repeat, confirm, or paraphrase what she said.[33] What Barbara and Greg accomplish in this process is a shared construal of what Barbara meant.

The importance of inferring mutual belief in discourse necessitates that we think of conversation in terms of a series of *joint acts* rather than as a series of individual utterances. Psychologists and linguists refer to joint acts as *contributions*.[34] A contribution to a conversation consists, most simply, as a joint act where a speaker (the contributor) says something to an addressee who offers some sign that the speaker's intended message has been reasonably understood (e.g., when Barbara says something to Greg and Greg shows in some way that he has understood her intended meaning). Listeners signal their understanding of speaker's communicative intentions through their continued attention, acknowledgments such as saying *uh huh, yeah,* or *right,* facial expressions such as raised eyebrows, completing what a speaker has begun to say, initiating the next relevant contribution, or nonverbally demonstrating that the message has been understood (e.g., when an addressee actually passes the salt to a speaker after hearing *Can you pass the salt?*).[35]

Speakers' and listeners' continual monitoring of their discourse is what makes conversations collaborative joint acts. When making contributions, speakers and listeners will work together to ensure the mutual belief that their partner has understood what the contributor meant, at least to a degree sufficient for their current purposes. The mutual belief that the speaker and listener, at least on some level, understand what is meant forms part of their common ground, along with the specific information, beliefs, or attitudes that the contributor intended his or her utterance to supply.[36]

According to the collaborative view, the meaning of an utterance emerges from the process of interpretation and the meaning of an expression is what the participants (implicitly) agree that it means. Clark and colleagues contend that communicators attempt to formulate utterances that minimize their collaborative effort, underscoring the contrast between the intentionalist approach with its emphasis on individual communicative acts, and the collaborative or intentionalist view as a dialogue approach.

A final example showing the necessity of mutual beliefs in language use comes from a "Seinfeld" television program. In one episode, George is having lunch with his new girlfriend when she says to him: *My ex-boyfriend dropped by last night just as I was getting out of the shower and yadda yadda yadda, I felt very tired this morning.* Poor George quickly infers that his girlfriend had sex with her ex-boyfriend. So what does *yadda yadda yadda* mean? As this "Seinfeld" episode cleverly indicated, it can mean anything speakers intend it to mean given whatever common ground has been established with their addressees. *Yadda yadda yadda* is used whenever speakers are confident that such a mutual belief exists, so that speakers need not spell out all the boring, or unpleasant, details of some event.

COLLABORATION IN CONVERSATION

Empirical research in the cognitive sciences has provided a great deal of evidence to support the claim that speakers and listeners collaborate about what is mutually known or manifest to facilitate understanding of speakers' intentions in conversation.

Some research demonstrates that speakers design their utterances with their addressees' perspectives in mind. One study, for instance, examined the assumptions speakers had about an addressee's community membership.[37] An experimenter stopped randomly selected male pedestrians in downtown Boston and asked for directions to Jordan Marsh, a large department store about six blocks away. To a third of the men, the experimenter asked *Can you tell me how to get to Jordan Marsh?* To another third, the experimenter said *I'm from out of town. Can you tell me how to get to Jordan Marsh?* To the remaining third, the experimenter asked *Can you tell me how to get to Jordan Marsh?*, but did so employing a rural Missouri accent. The men's responses were secretly tape-recorded and analyzed for the total number of words in the respondent's directions and the number of places en route that he referred to. When the experimenter prefaced his question with *I'm from out of town*, the men responded with significantly more words and more place names than when asked this question without the preface. Alerting the addressee to the fact that the speaker doesn't share the same kind of community membership clearly gets respondents to design their directions differently. But respondents also gave longer, more detailed directions when the experimenter asked his question without the *I'm from out of town* preface but spoke with a Missouri accent. Thus, hearing a different accent made respondents place the speaker into a different community-membership category, which also influenced the way they verbally responded to the request for directions.

There is a significant body of research showing that speakers take the addressee's perspective into account when designing their utterances.[38] In fact, studies show that perspective-taking influences speaking at many levels of language use, including phonology, syntax, lexical choice, and semantics.[39] Other studies demonstrate that messages addressed to a particular person communicate less well to other listeners than they do to the addressee.[40] This seems especially true when the speaker and listener are friends and the other listeners are strangers. Friends talk in ways that reflect certain kinds of mutual knowledge, acquaintances talk in ways that reflect their lack of knowledge, and this difference is apparent to almost anyone who listens. To illustrate this point, consider the following two conversations, one between friends and the other between acquaintances.[41] These are conversations between college students who were asked to talk on a topic of their own choosing.

Conversation Segment 1:

> A: My roommate's name is Tad. I always kid him, man. Like it's a big thing on campus ... Well, I'm not in any fraternity or anything, but a lot of my friends are Sigma Chi's, what have you. And, And, like, they all changed their names. For instance, Saul, my roommate, decides to call himself Tad, I'm like....
>
> B: His name is Saul?
>
> A: His name is Saul, but you call him Tad.

Conversation Segment 2:

> C: I've got all the tables and stuff worked out. Brad's stressing on it. He came by about 20 minutes ago. "Are we supposed to make a graph or a table for this one?" I'm like, "I don't know, man." Cause she's in class today, "I want graphs and tables and all these summaries and stuff," and I'm just going, "Oh, man," So....
>
> D: You might be able to rig something up on Kev's computer.

The difference between these conversations in terms of mutual knowledge should be obvious. Person A assumes that Person B does not know things that friends ought to know about one another: that his roommate's name is Tad (changed from Saul) and that he is not in a fraternity. Acquaintances have to explain these things. Person C, on the other hand, assumes that Person D knows who Brad is and Person D assumes that Person C knows who Kev is and that he has a computer. Friends tend to know each other's friends, or at least know about them. These kinds of examples are commonplace in conversation.[42]

One of the largest areas of research on perspective-taking and collaboration in language use looks at how people establish and maintain reference in naturalistic dialogue.[43] In these studies, two people, who could not see each other, conversed about the arrangement of Tangram figures (geometric shapes that are vaguely suggestive of silhouettes of people and other objects). One person (the director) had an ordered array of these and had to explain their arrangement to the other (the matcher) so that the other person could reproduce the arrangement. Each director-matcher pair did this six times.

How do participants manage this task? One possibility is that people should generally not waste their breath because the existence of common ground leaves less to be explicitly stated. As common ground is established between the director and matcher during the conversation about the Tangram figures, it should be easier for them to mutually determine where each figure should go. There was ample confirmation of this idea in the fact that the number of words used per Tangram figure fell from around forty on the first trial to around ten on the last. For instance, a speaker referred to one figure on Trial 1 by saying *All right, the next one looks like a person who's ice skating, except they're sticking two arms out in front*, while on Trial 6 the speaker said *The ice skater*. A similar decline was observed in the number of turns required to complete the arrangement task, showing that the interchange became more economical as common ground was established. These data demonstrated that the assessment of common ground has an integral part in facilitating listeners' recovery of speakers' intentions.

Another version of this card-arranging task examined the role of expertise.[44] In these studies, pairs of people, some being from New York (experts) and some not (novices), attempted to arrange a set of postcards with pictures of different buildings and places in New York City. To the extent that the director and matcher could establish that each was from New York, more proper names (e.g., the Chrysler Building, Rockefeller Center) would be used to describe the postcard scenes. If both conversants were novices (not from New York), far fewer uses of proper names would be expected. If an expert and a novice were paired, then the use of proper names would increase over time (or trials) as the experts taught the novice something about the names for different postcards.

These general predictions were shown to be correct. There was also an increase in the efficiency of the conversation as shown by a decrease in the overall number of words used and the number of turns required to complete the task. Thus, in conversations between experts, proper names were used about eighty percent of the time while proper names were used less than twenty percent of the time in conversations between novices. When an expert was talking to a novice, the number of proper names initially decreased as it became clear to the expert that the novice did not know what some of the names referred to. When novices talked to experts, the number of proper names increased as some of the expertise "rubbed off" and the names of landmarks were learned from the expert partner. Experts and novices seem to have discovered they were talking to other experts or novices by the way the conversation proceeded, because in only six of thirty-two pairs did a participant actually ask or tell the other person whether they were New Yorkers.

Participants in real-life conversation sometimes design their utterances with the intention of excluding some person from understanding their communicative intentions. Listeners who are intentionally involved are called *side participants*, while those who are excluded intentionally or by accident are *overhearers*. Speakers consciously distinguish between participants and overhearers and do so by the information that they take to be mutually known to various hearers.

Consider a situation in which Chris and Nancy had previously agreed that they will leave a party whenever Karen arrives. Chris says to Nancy in front of Krystal *Oh look, Karen is here*. In this case Nancy, but not Krystal, will understand that Chris intends to communicate more than a simple observation about Karen's arrival at the party. When speakers are successful, listeners will not ordinarily be aware that they are overhearers rather than side participants. Thus Krystal should not be aware that Chris's utterance has been designed specifically to exclude her from perhaps its most important implications. To be sure, there are circumstances in which overhearers explicitly know that they have been excluded from understanding a speaker's true intentions. Consider the situation where Chris says to Nancy on a crowded bus, *Do you remember that thing about you know who that we were talking about last week? Well, it happened.* An overhearer of this remark could only have the vaguest understanding of what Chris specifically intended for Nancy to understand. The overhearer will recognize that Chris does not want someone other than Nancy to understand his particular meaning.

One set of experiments explored the situation in which two people are speaking to each other but wish to conceal what they are talking about from a third party (i.e., an overhearer).[45] In this particular case, participants in a card-arranging task had to communicate the ordering of photographs of Stanford University scenes, but unlike the previous experiment about New York, there was a third person in the room, provided with the same set of pictures, and the two conversants had to try to ensure that the third person did not succeed in the task. Thus, the speaker had to ensure that the addressee understood, but had to conceal his or her meaning from the overhearer. All three participants were Stanford University students (i.e., "experts"), but the two conversants were friends while the overhearer was unknown to them.

Because the three participants had the same community membership, which prevented concealment by using communal knowledge, it was expected that conversants would use *private keys* or information that is part of their particular common ground, but which is unknown to the overhearer. Although there were certain instances when a speaker would slip and refer to a photograph by its widely known name, the vast majority of the references contained these private keys. For example, a speaker referred to a fountain as *where someone wanted to put my teddy bear in*. Overall, addressees were twice as successful in correctly arranging the photographs as were the overhearers.[46]

A different type of experimental study examined how readers use community membership to disambiguate utterances.[47] Students from Yale University read stories such as one about a football game between Yale and Brown Universities. The readers had to imagine that after the game either a friend or stranger said to them *That game was a disaster*. When readers were asked about the final utterance, they were more confident in their interpretations of what the speaker meant when that person was a friend than when he or she was a stranger. Additional experiments showed that people took longer to read *The game was a disaster* when this was spoken by a stranger than when stated by a friend. These findings provide additional evidence that common ground (in this case "community membership") constrains both the interpretation of speaker's messages and the speed with which people comprehend those messages.

These observations and empirical data suggest that understanding what a speaker intends to communicate, and the criteria by which listeners judge that they have understood, is a joint product requiring coordination and cooperation between listeners and speakers. This more sophisticated characterization of context assumes that speakers and listeners constantly assess what information is in their "common ground" (i.e., their mutually shared beliefs, knowledge, and attitudes), which influences not only what speakers say, but also how listeners determine what is specifically meant in a discourse situation.[48]

GOING BEYOND INTENTIONAL MEANING

Many matters of communication assume a cooperative listener who is prepared to adopt the speaker's point of view.[49] But the goals of speakers and listeners in cooperative tasks are not always consistent at a given moment in time.[50] For instance, listeners occasionally "overinterpret" what a speaker says. An ironic thrust can be taken as a compliment, a compliment can be taken as an ironic insult, a friendly tease can be taken for a hostile act, and even a mild reproof can be taken as a major insult and offense.

People certainly can draw "unauthorized" inferences about what a speaker intended to communicate. For instance, Pierre is having a romantic dinner one evening with his girlfriend Laura and at one point asks her, *Are you wearing a different perfume tonight?* intending this as a serious question because he thinks the perfume is particularly pleasant. Laura, on the other hand, believes that Pierre is being critical of her perfume and responds by saying *I'm sorry if you don't like it.* This shows that Laura clearly made an "unauthorized" inference about Pierre's question, because Pierre did not intend for Laura to draw a negative impression about his comment. Pierre could have intended his utterance as a negative comment about her perfume and might have done so if he could assume that Laura shared the right belief with him about his preference for various perfumes. But, Pierre's original intention was to compliment Laura's perfume. Pierre incorrectly assumed that Laura shared his own particular beliefs and that she could understand his comment as a positive remark.

A wonderful example of how listeners can create interpretations that vastly overinterpret what speakers intend to communicate is seen in Jerzy Kosinski's novel *Being There*. The protagonist in the novel is a gardener named Chance who has spent his entire life in the employment of a rich man, tending his garden. Chance is unable to read or write and knows what he does only from watching television. After his employer dies, Chance, through a series of accidents, moves in with a rich, influential businessman and his wife, who mistakenly believe Chance to be a successful entrepreneur named Chancey Gardiner. When Chance first meets the old businessman, Mr. Rand, the man asks whether his accident prevents him from attending to his business. Chance responds:[51]

> "As I have already told Mrs. Rand," Chance began slowly, "my house has been closed up, and I do not have any urgent business." He cut and ate his food carefully. "I was just expecting something to happen when I had the accident."

When Chance realizes his response was not satisfactory, he continues:

"It is not easy, sir," he said, "to obtain a suitable place, a garden, in which one can work without interference and grow with the seasons. There can't be too many opportunities left anymore. On TV," he faltered. It dawned on him. "I've never seen a garden. I've seen forests and jungles and sometimes a tree or two. But a garden in which I can work and watch the things I've planted in it grow." He felt sad.

Mr. Rand leaned across the table to him. "Very well put, Mr. Gardiner – I hope you don't mind if I call you Chauncey? A gardener! Isn't that the perfect description of what a real businessman is? A person who makes a flinty soil productive with the labor of his own hands, who waters it with the sweat of his brow, and who creates a place of value for his family and the community. Yes, Chauncey, what an excellent metaphor! A productive businessman is indeed a laborer in his own vineyard!"

Later on Chance gets to meet the president of the United States and in one conversation the following exchange occurs in which the president asks Chance:

"And you, Mr. Gardiner? What do you think about the bad season on the Street?" Chance shrank ... He stared at the carpet. Finally he spoke: "In a garden," he said, "growth has its season. There are spring and summer, but there are also fall and winter. And then spring and summer again. As long as the roots are not severed, all is well and all will be well."... The President seemed quite pleased. "I must admit, Mr. Gardiner," the President said, "that what you've said is one of the most refreshing and optimistic statements I've heard in a very, very long time."... "Many of us forget that nature and society are one! Yes, though we have tried to cut ourselves off from nature, we are still part of it. Like nature, our economic system remains, in the long run, stable, and rational, and that's why we must not fear to be at its mercy."

These passages beautifully demonstrate how listeners can completely misunderstand a speaker's actual intentions. Chance's simple, literal speech is interpreted metaphorically, with listeners attributing far greater sophistication and more complex communicative intentions to Chance than he actually has or desires.[52]

In one sense, examples like this illustrate, again, how people are strongly disposed to attribute intentions to what speakers say. Yet, in a different way, listeners' misunderstandings of intentional meanings may still be contextually appropriate. One can easily find other examples where listeners derive meanings that go beyond what speakers specifically intend to communicate. In these situations, it is not the case that listeners misunderstand what a speaker intends, as in the case of Kosinski's *Being There*. Instead, listeners understand what a speaker intends to communicate, but also infer additional meaning that might even be more appropriate to the context. Consider the following two situations:

John and Bill were taking a statistics class together.
Before the final exam, they decided to cooperate during the test.
So they worked out a system so they could secretly share answers.
After the exam John and Bill were really pleased with themselves.
They thought they were pretty clever for beating the system.
Later that night, a friend happened to ask them if they ever tried to cheat.
John and Bill looked at each other and laughed, then John said,
I would never be involved in any cheating.

John and Bill were taking a statistics class together.
They studied hard together, but John was clearly better prepared than Bill.
During the exam, Bill panicked and started to copy answers from John.
John didn't see Bill do this and so didn't know he was actually helping Bill.
John took the school's honor code very seriously.
Later that night, a friend happened to ask them if they ever tried to cheat.
John and Bill looked at each other, then John said,
I would never be involved in any cheating.

Both of these situations end with the identical statement that in each case is understood as verbal irony. The speaker in the first story specifically intends for his audience to understand what is said as ironic, but the speaker in the second situation does *not* intend for his utterance to be understood ironically. In the second story, only the addressees and overhearers see the irony in what the speaker actually says. It is quite possible for people to understand a speaker's utterance as irony even though the speaker did not intend the utterance to be understood as irony.

Several experimental studies show that people understand utterances in stories like the second one above as having ironic meaning even if the speaker did not intend for the utterance to be understood in this way.[53] In fact, readers rated the final statements in the unintentional stories as being *more* ironic than were the final statements in intentionally ironic stories. Thus, although irony often reflects speakers' communicative goals to identify aspects of ironic situations, speakers may unintentionally create irony by what they say.

These studies on understanding unintentional irony demonstrate an important point about cognitive processes in ordinary language interpretation. People not only can misunderstand a speaker's communicative intentions, they can also consciously recognize, in some cases, that the meaning they have inferred diverges from what speakers intended to convey. The fact that people can both understand what a speaker meant and some *other* unintentional meaning suggests that some aspects of understanding unintended meanings are connected to people's interpretations of what speakers meant to communicate. In the irony studies just described, people may have specifically drawn "unauthorized" inferences by virtue of first recognizing the speaker's communicative meaning in context.

Exploring the link between intentional and unintentional meaning demands a cognitive account that is sensitive to the temporal characteristics of how people create interpretations in the experience of meaning. No studies have yet examined whether people necessarily recover a speaker's communicative intentions before deriving other, unintended but still contextually relevant, meanings. One possibility is that listeners draw intentional meanings quite quickly as part of their ordinary comprehension processes and infer unintentional meanings (or weak implicatures or implications) at later moments of linguistic interpretation. Of course, a great deal of psychological evidence shows that many kinds of meanings may be processed in parallel during ordinary linguistic understanding (see Chapter 6). There is obviously much work still to be done.

Is the expression and recovery of speakers' communicative intentions fundamental to how people use language in all cultures? The relationship between people, their thoughts, and their actions is the major topic of cultural anthropology. Most theories within the Western intellectual tradition view the interpretation of meaning as a process that focuses on an individual's mind and on how a person's acts reflect, or are the consequences of, his or her mental states. For example, speech act theorists posit a kind of private, intentional world as a starting point in their analyses.[54] This line of reasoning leads them to consider issues such as "the true intention expressed by some utterance," where "true intention" presumably enjoys some kind of privileged, a priori status as the private property of an individual.

I have already suggested that this view of intentions inaccurately portrays the collaborative, coordinated nature of spoken and written communication. Intentions are not simply in the sole possession of speakers, but emerge from interactions of speakers and listeners, writers and readers, in particular social and historical settings. Cultural anthropologists have provided a different critique of the traditional view of intentional meaning in conversation. Many of these researchers argue that the primary focus on an individual's communicative intentions reflects a Western, especially white middle-class, bias about the nature of selfhood and meaning. For instance, the anthropologist Elinor Ochs has argued, "The emphasis on personal intentions in Anglo society and scholarship is tied to a cultural ideology in which persons are viewed as individuals, i.e., coherent personalities, who have control over and are responsible for their utterances and actions."[55] A culture's assumptions about how language works are likely to reflect local folk theories of human agency, personhood, and linguistic communication.[56] The belief that a person can know what someone else is thinking, or have access to his or her mental processes, is not shared across cultures. Although many cultures appear to focus on speakers' subjective mental states (i.e., their thoughts, desires, beliefs, and intentions), other cultures focus on the consequences of a person's talk, not on what a speaker intended to communicate.[57]

A number of anthropologists in recent years have claimed that the intentional view of communication vastly overemphasizes the psychological state of the speaker, while giving inadequate attention to the social sphere.[58] I want to consider this claim and respond by noting the importance of the time-course perspective in exploring the role of intentions in meaningful experience (again, in line with the cognitive intentionalist perspective).

Students of Austronesian languages have been especially critical of the influence of personality theories of action on theories of language use. One of the most heavily studied cultures in this regard is that of Samoa. Samoans do not appear to conceive of the person as an integral unit with a single, controlling will, but instead as an arena from which different behaviors, traits, and images manifest themselves. Samoans generally attribute responsibility for people's actions to interpersonal relationships and situations rather than to individual agents. For instance, problem children are seen as not being properly taught by their parents, a youth is viewed as stealing objects because he momentarily forgot about his relationship with his sisters, or a son was possessed by a ghost when he spoke harshly to his father. Individual behaviors are understood in interpersonal terms, not in light of what a person may have intended to do or say.

Linguistic anthropologists have examined how Samoans interpret linguistic meaning in various social contexts. For instance, Alessandro Duranti has looked at how speakers' utterances are interpreted within particular Samoan social events, called *fono*, which are formal meetings to resolve disputes and make laws. A Samoan orator may acquire great prestige and material goods by speaking on behalf of a powerful party at a fono. But there are cases where an orator can be held responsible if he announces something on another person's behalf that doesn't come true. The speaker's own understanding of the event, and his personal motivations and intentions in saying what he did, are deemed irrelevant.

What an utterance means depends on what others take it to mean. Consequently a Samoan speaker will not reclaim the meaning of his words by saying *I didn't mean it*. The audience sometimes is more likely to be asked to say more about what something means than is the original speaker. Samoans ignore the orator's alleged intentions and concentrate on the social consequences of a speaker's words. Listeners do not speculate on what a speaker meant to say (a phrase that cannot be translated into Samoan), but rely on the dynamics between the speaker's words and the surrounding circumstances, which include the audience's responses, to assign interpretations. Samoans practice interpretation as a way of publicly controlling social relationships rather than as a way of figuring out what a given person meant to say.[59]

Duranti presented several excellent examples showing how Samoans are not primarily concerned with the intentions of others in fono. In one meeting, one of the two highest ranking orators, Iuli, proposed to fine the orator Loa for having earlier announced that the newly reelected district M. P. would visit the village and present some goods to the people. But the M. P. did not come, and Iuli argued that Loa should be responsible for the villagers' not receiving the gifts and thus losing face. Presented below is the relevant part of the discourse:[60]

Iuli: This topic is about Loa ... About the day our village got together to wait for the M.P. Things like that are a humiliation for a village.

Loa: Well said!

Iuli: And our village is ridiculed ... Our village was tired of waiting... the M.P. not come. But Loa just sits there (instead of) bringing some food for the village.

Loa: Well said!

Iuli: This is what I believe ... Loa should be fined ... He should have made sure. Because Loa are related. If he said that to

you. Well, one must be very clear about it ... bring something
for the village to eat then (Loa), if the M.P. doesn't come....
This is what Loa did ... Perhaps a cow, from Loa and 100
dollars. Get out of this village.

Loa: Well said.

Iuli suggested that Loa was responsible for the village's loss of
face when the M.P. (Loa's relative) did not show up for the antic-
ipated visit. Although Loa was not responsible for the M.P.'s not
coming, he should have tried to remedy the situation by providing food for the village. Iuli does not consider that it wasn't Loa's
intention to mislead the village, or to have the M.P. not show up,
or for the village to lose face. What matters are the consequences
of people's actions and not what they privately intended to accomplish by their speech or actions.

Differences between how Westerners and Samoans respond
to speakers' communicative intentions are further contrasted in
the character of their caregiver-child interactions.[61] When a young
child has said something unintelligible, American middle class
caregivers guess at what meaning the child *intended*, while Samoan
caregivers rarely do so. The American caregivers' linguistic interactions conform to a cultural theory of communication in which
speakers' personal intentions are critical to the interpretation of
an utterance or action. But this theory is limited to certain cultural
practices and does not accurately reflect the linguistic practices of
many other non-Western societies. Samoans will rarely turn to a
caregiver and ask *What does the child mean?* if there is any ambiguity about what the child said. Samoan caregivers treat infants' acts
and vocalizations as physiological reflexes (e.g., hunger, discomfort, pleasure) and never assign personal intentionality to these
acts. Samoans do not guess at what might be going on in another
person's mind.[62]

There are some occasions when Samoans might attempt to infer the communicative intentions of speakers. In the context of
political meetings of titled persons, high chiefs and high-status
speakers are viewed as individuals with personal intentions.[63]
But most generally, recovery of speakers' intentions is "not the
only route and ... participants seem more eager to act upon

convention, consequences, action, public meanings, rather than upon individual intention."[64] Duranti concluded: "The Samoan ideology and practice of doing things with words cannot be explained on the basis of the notion of intentional meaning."[65]

Various other anthropological research supports Duranti's conclusion. The Ilongots, a group of slash-and-burn horticulturalists of the Philippines, appear less interested in considerations of sincerity, truth, and focus, than they are with social bonds and interactive meanings.[66] As anthropologist Michele Rosaldo has written: "Among the Ilongots, personality descriptions are extremely rare, as are strategic reckonings of motivation. Accounts of why particular persons acted as they did refer almost exclusively to public and political concerns – surprising actions giving rise to the despairing claim that one can never know the hidden reaches of another's heart." Ilongots do not discern intentions, trace responsibility, or reckon blame by asking if offenders "knew" that they wronged others through their actions.

Conversation among the Gusii people of Kenya contains few references to speakers' intentions for their words or actions.[67] The Gusii avoid "psychologizing," preferring to talk about the overt behavior of adults and children. Along the same lines, in traditional Tahitian society, the primary emphasis is given to a person's actions, not to the intentions that underlie those actions or the words the person speaks.[68] However, in the modern, Christianized, urbanized Tahiti, intentions have become primary and a person's actions are not judged for themselves. "The moral emphasis now shifts from acts to intentions, for the consequences of the act cannot be judged solely by the ordinary and traditional concerns of hurt to others, or of respect for traditional goals and limits expressed in law and custom."

Many cultures see little reason for speaking truthfully and objectively about people's intentions and inner mental states. Among the Sherpas of Tibet and Nepal ongoing social harmony is protected by a tacit agreement not to speak too plainly about certain aspects of reality. As long as people act reasonably within the bounds of cultural expectations, "no one gains from insisting on knowing whether anybody really meant what they did or said way down deep in their heart."[69]

Anthropologist Roy Wagner concluded from his study of the Darabi people of highland New Guinea that most social acts are so fraught with uncertainties that normal attributions of intent to others quite rare. For the Darabi, intentions may not necessarily precede social acts, because a person may form, or come to the recognition of, an intention as a result of engaging in a particular act.[70] For instance, people will say things or behave in certain ways, yet only later, if at all, attempt to characterize the possible reasons for their linguistic and social actions. This possibility raises the more general question of whether anyone can ever really know his own intentions until some undertaking has occurred that brings them into the world of action.[71] People may only know their intentions through unreflective actions that cast up some image of what they are doing.[72]

These anthropological studies illustrate the important point that people's experience of meaning is not exclusively, or even primarily, constructed around the communicative intentions of others. People in many cultures experience what speakers say, and the actions they take, as meaningful apart from any conscious search for what someone intends or intended. Some work from the United States has even demonstrated that for the community of black speakers, the pragmatic effect on the listener takes precedence over the speaker's intended meaning.[73] As in many other societies, people often speak ambiguously about what is meant, leaving it to listeners to decide which meaning is most appropriate for the particular social situation. Based on his studies of divination, John DuBois has argued not only that intentionality does not act as the criterion for understanding language, but that in certain types of language use, the point is precisely to produce meaning without intention.[74] In fact, formulating meaning independent of intentions of the person speaking is the primary goal of much ritual speech.

This discussion of the anthropological evidence shows that recovery of a speaker's intentions is not essential to all aspects of language understanding. But it is important to note that the anthropological evidence supporting this conclusion comes only from an analysis of what people say or do in response to what other speakers say (i.e., from looking at the *products* of understanding). These studies have not examined whether recognition of a speaker's intentions plays some constraining role in people's mental *processing* of linguistic meaning (see Chapter 4). Listeners might immediately and unconsciously seek to recover speakers' intentions but then go beyond these intentions when they publicly respond to what has been said. In other words, it is quite possible to derive meanings from utterances that vary from what speakers intend when making these utterances. No one questions this possibility, and the analysis of certain non-Western discourse patterns clearly shows that speakers' unauthorized meanings can be of primary concern. The analysis of what listeners do or say in response to speakers' messages can be informative about conversational practices, including whether or not what speakers intend is of central importance in the conduct of social affairs. Yet it is a serious error to assume from this evidence that recovery of speakers' intentions is not a critical part of what listeners do when they understand discourse. While it is indeed true that a listener's eventual interpretation of a speaker's utterance may have little to do with that person's communicative intentions, this does not mean that listeners disregard communicative intentions at all stages of linguistic processing. Samoan listeners, for instance, probably seek to understand speakers' communicative intentions at some point early in their on-line processing of utterances in conversation *even if* their eventual interpretations of speakers' utterances are not limited by these intentions. Of course, simply asking listeners if they have understood what a speaker intended to communicate is difficult. People are unaware of most of the very rapid, unconscious mental processes that can produce some immediate, if temporary, understanding of intentional meaning.

My conclusion about the role that communicative intentions may play in language processing, and the role that they may not play in language interpretation, is not inconsistent with the studies discussed earlier. Much empirical research demonstrates that intentional meaning often emerges as the product of social interactions between speakers and listeners. People in Western cultures often speak indirectly and ambiguously and rely on listeners to provide their own interpretations of what is said given the social context and their personal goals. But the cross-cultural data puts in sharper contrast how people's experience of meaning is certainly not entirely dictated by what individual speakers intended a priori to communicate.

CONCLUSION

People's meaningful experience of spoken language depends critically on their recovery of the communicative intentions of others, and clearly isn't grounded in the meanings of words or utterances themselves. Speakers and listeners actively collaborate and coordinate their beliefs and knowledge to achieve mutual understandings in different contexts. This collaboration and coordination between speakers and listeners occurs quickly in real time and reflects the operation of very rapid, mostly unconscious comprehension processes. Conversational participants are rarely aware of the cognitive and linguistic processes that underlie their understanding of others' communicative intentions. Only when the attempt to coordinate fails do people seem cognizant of their misunderstandings of what someone has intended to convey by the words he or she says. On certain occasions, listeners will infer meanings that are not specifically intended by speakers. And in some cultural settings, what speakers intend to communicate may not immediately guide how others verbally respond. Yet the process by which people draw inferences about unintended meanings appears to involve, at least in some cases, recovery of what the speaker intended to communicate, particularly as part of their immediate comprehension of utterances. Once again, acknowledging the diversity of people's phenomenal experience in speaking and listening provides for a more complex, yet more realistic, picture of the role that authorial intentions play in the communication of meaning. [75]

Chapter 6

Saying What We Don't Mean

No event captured the attention of the American public in 1995 more than the O. J. Simpson trial. Did O. J. murder his ex-wife Nicole Brown Simpson and her friend Ronald Goldman on the night of June 12, 1994? One of the key prosecution witnesses was Los Angeles police detective Mark Furman, whose testimony that he found the infamous "bloody glove" on the grounds of Simpson's estate was seen as a crucial piece of evidence against Simpson. When Furman first testified in March 1995, defense attorney F. Lee Bailey forcefully questioned him about rumors of past racist statements in the hopes of bolstering the defense's contention of a racially motivated police conspiracy against O. J. Simpson. Furman denied these allegations and specifically responded that he had not used the term *nigger* during the previous ten years.

But in late summer 1995, O. J. Simpson's lawyers discovered that Furman had previously given a series of extensive interviews to a screenwriter in which he talked about his experiences as a Los Angeles policeman and boasted of fabricating evidence, beating suspects, and singling out minorities for mistreatment. The tapes and transcripts of these interviews revealed that Furman had used the term *nigger* as many as 30 times. This "bombshell" revelation was a significant boost to the defense's conspiracy theory. As the legal battle developed over the relevance and admissibility of the "Furman tapes," various members of the prosecution team, along with Furman's own attorneys, argued that Furman's comments did not reflect his own opinions or experiences, but merely his role-playing a "bad-boy" cop to assist the screenwriter.

How do people decide what Furman really intended to mean by his various statements to the screenwriter? Consider a few brief excerpts from these transcripts.[1]

> I used to go to work and practice movements. Niggers. They're easy. I used to practice my kicks.
>
> Go to Wilshire division. Wilshire division is all niggers. All niggers. Niggers training officers, niggers ... with three years on the job.
>
> How do you intellectualize when you punch the hell out of a nigger? He either deserves it or he doesn't.
>
> Leave the old station. Man, it has the smell of niggers that have been beaten and killed in there for years.

What were Furman's intentions in making these remarks? Did his comments reflect his true personal views or was he only pretending to speak seriously? Furman wrote in his book *Murder in Brentwood* how he came to use the "n-word" so frequently in his interviews with screenwriter Laura Hart McKinney:

> We began a series of interviews where I laid out police procedures, stories, characters and situations. These were all on tape. I let my imagination run wild. Throughout the interviews I was creating fictional situations, sometimes loosely based on true incidents. Characters were developed from composition of many people, from police management down to the lowest criminals. Dialogue in the screenplay was a mix of conversations I remembered, and others that were imaginary.
>
> When I was making up dialogue, I spoke in the first person. But these weren't my own words, my own experiences, or my own sentiments. They were the words of fictional characters I had created based on my imagination and experience. I know I had to exaggerate things to make the screenplay dramatic and commercially appealing.[2]

Later on, Furman said, "If I must be judged, I wish it were on the basis of my record as a police officer, and not on my play-acting, intentionally shocking comments to an aspiring screenwriter."[3]

The controversy over Mark Furman's statements illustrates just one of the perplexing problems in understanding the role of intentions in the experience of meaning. People often say things they don't literally mean and wish for others to infer their true communicative intentions. I suspect that most Americans doubt Furman's explanation that his racist comments only reflected his "play-acting" a bad Los Angeles police officer. But how do people know when a speaker is sincere in what he or she says? And how do listeners infer a speaker's intended meaning when his or her words convey a different message?

My aim in this chapter is to consider some of the ways speakers' messages diverge from what they seem literally to say. Extending the conclusion from the previous chapter, I argue that speakers and listeners are quite capable of coordinating their mutual beliefs and knowledge for the purpose of communicating intentional meaning indirectly. People often use figurative language, equivocation, evasive speech, deception, and "off-record" devices, precisely to communicate social and relational meanings. These different indirect forms of language are ubiquitous in everyday communication. Literal speech (however one defines it) is clearly not the norm in ordinary talk. Listeners readily infer what people intend to communicate when they speak indirectly and do not merely focus on the meanings of the words or utterances themselves. More importantly, people even appear to infer what speakers intend to communicate by their indirect messages without necessarily having to analyze what speakers literally say.

STAGED COMMUNICATIVE ACTS

Speakers often say things to others that seem, on one level anyway, not to accurately reflect what they really intend to communicate. Consider the following conversation between two parents (Bill and Pat) and their teenage son (Grant) from the documentary film series *The American Family*. The conversation takes place in the family's backyard beside the swimming pool. Grant already knows that his parents want to talk about his apparent disinterest in summer work. In the preceding scene, Grant has complained to his sister, Delilah, about his parents' request to have this chat, so it is clear that Grant – and his parents to some extent – was not looking forward to this confrontation. The conversation starts with Bill summoning Grant over to where Bill and Pat are sitting by the pool.

(1) Bill: Come over here a little closer ... I think

(2) Grant: Well, I'd rather stay out of this.

(3) Bill: You ... want to stay out of swinging distance.

(4) Grant: Yeah, I don't want to hurt you.

Right away, in the opening moments of the conversation, we see how the participants, via their use of teasing and irony, attempt to express a variety of communicative intentions that differ from what they literally say. When Grant says in (2) that he would rather stay out of the conversation, which is likely a serious comment reflecting his unhappiness about having this chat, his father, Bill, in (3), provides in a nonserious manner a reason why Grant might not wish to come closer to sit down and talk. In making his assertion, Bill is only pretending that he and Grant may get into a physical fight, which Grant would, in this hypothetical scene, wish to avoid. In (4) Grant continues the pretense by saying that he doesn't wish to hurt his father, assuming, of course, that this would happen if a physical fight did break out. Grant's comment in (4) might be intended literally or seriously on one level, but his action here is to join in the pretend by remarking in a jocular manner how he might possibly hurt his father if a fight did occur. All of this teasing and irony fulfills the need for father and son to defuse what must be mutually recognized as a potentially uncomfortable situation – the parents criticizing Grant for his unwillingness to work.

What's remarkable about even this brief bit of conversation is that the participants (and we as audience) don't appear to experience any difficulty interpreting what is meant by any of these nonserious utterances. In no sense were these expressions conscious, calculated risks on the part of the participants; they seemed to fit easily into the natural flow of the conversation. Nonserious language like that seen in this brief exchange between Grant and his father, where speakers say what they don't actually mean, seems especially useful in informing others about one's own attitudes and beliefs in indirect ways. Speakers do not always want to make explicit what they think, and so say things in such a way that listeners must infer their true beliefs.[4] People frequently use deception, tease one another, speak ironically or sarcastically, use understatement, and equivocate in ways that are not meant to be understood literally.

Psychologist Herb Clark dubs nonserious language, such as speaking ironically, deceptively, or evasively, *staged communicative acts*.[5] The key ingredient in these acts is pretense. For example, in Grant and Bill's brief exchange, Bill pretends that a physical fight is likely to break out, and Grant immediately extends the pretense by claiming that he'd hurt his father if such a fight were to occur. This scenario is staged in the sense that the speaker, Bill, creates for his audience, Grant and Pat, a brief improvised scene in which an implied Bill (the actor in the scene who might start the fight) makes an assertion to an implied Grant (the actor in the scene who would be the recipient of implied Bill's punches). When Grant continues the pretense, he assumes the role of coauthor of the hypothetical scenario by making an assertion in which an implied Grant (the recipient of Bill's opening punch in the fight) performs a sincere utterance within the play, as it were, for an implied Bill (the one who would get hurt in the play should Grant fight back). As coauthors of this hypothetical scenario, both Bill and Grant want the other, and perhaps Pat as a side-participant, to imagine the scene and to appreciate their pretense in staging it. Pretense is fundamental to the teasing and jocular irony that Bill and Grant communicate. By engaging in pretense, Bill and Grant enable themselves to conceptualize the upcoming serious conversation in a nonserious manner, which should, even if momentarily, help defuse the potentially emotional confrontation between Grant and his parents.[6]

Mark Furman wanted people to believe that his racist comments to a screenwriter about his experiences as an L.A. police officer were also staged, in the sense that he was only pretending to adopt the beliefs held by the hypothetical character he portrayed. Again, people may not find Furman's interpretation of his own message very convincing. Yet the fact remains that speakers often engage in staged communicative acts in their everyday conversation.

The most typical way for people to express their communicative intentions indirectly is to employ figurative language. Among the common forms of figurative language, often referred to as "tropes" or "figures of speech," are: *metaphor*, where ideas from dissimilar knowledge domains are either explicitly, in the case of *simile* (e.g., *My love is like a red, red rose*), or implicitly compared (e.g., *Our marriage is a roller-coaster ride*); *metonymy*, where a salient part of a single knowledge domain is used to represent or stand for the entire domain (e.g., *The White House issued a statement*); *idioms*, where a speaker's meaning cannot be derived from an analysis of the words' typical meanings (e.g., *John let the cat out of the bag about Mary's divorce*); *proverbs*, where speakers express widely held moral beliefs or social norms (e.g., *The early bird catches the worm*); *irony*, where a speaker's meaning is usually, but not always, the opposite of what is said (e.g., *What lovely weather we're having*, stated in the midst of a rainstorm); *hyperbole*, where a speaker exaggerates the reality of some situation (e.g., *I have ten thousand papers to grade by morning*); *understatement*, where a speaker says less than is actually the case (e.g., *John seems a bit tipsy*, when John is clearly very drunk); *oxymora*, where two contradictory ideas/concepts are fused together (e.g., *Parting is such sweet sorrow*); and *indirect requests*, where speakers make requests of others in indirect ways by asking questions (e.g., *Can you pass the salt?*), or by stating a simple fact (e.g., *It seems cold in here*, meaning "Go close the window").

People speak figuratively to be polite, to be humorous, to avoid responsibility for the import of what is communicated, to express ideas that are difficult to communicate using literal language, and to express thoughts in a compact and vivid manner. Yet speakers employ figurative language assuming that listeners will be capable of inferring what they intend to communicate from what they say. Many philosophers, educators, and scientists have historically been suspicious of figurative language because of the long-standing belief that to think or speak figuratively is to adopt a distorted stance toward the ordinary world. But figurative language is ubiquitous in oral speech, literature, poetry, and even scientific writing.[7]

How do listeners comprehend what people intend to communicate when they speak figuratively? Many of the "off-record" communicative acts, such as irony, sarcasm, teasing, hyperbole, understatement, and indirect speech acts, are traditionally viewed as classic tropes. The most influential ideas about trope understanding come from the philosopher H. Paul Grice's theory of conversational implicature.[8] As described in Chapter 5, Grice notes that much of the information conveyed in conversation is implied rather than asserted. He argues that speakers and listeners expect each other to interpret their utterances as if they were acting in a rational and cooperative manner (the *cooperative principle*). To do this, speakers and listeners operate according to several maxims that include Quantity (make your contribution as informative as needed), Quality (do not say what you believe to be false), Relevance (be relevant), and Manner (avoid ambiguity).

For example, when a speaker says *Criticism is a branding iron*, he or she does not literally mean that criticism is a tool to mark livestock. Rather, the speaker intends this utterance to have some figurative meaning along the lines that criticism can psychologically hurt the person who receives it, often with long-lasting consequences. How do listeners comprehend figurative utterances such as *Criticism is a branding iron*? Listeners presumably determine the conversational inferences (or "implicatures") of nonliteral utterances by first analyzing the literal meaning of the sentence. Second, the listener assesses the appropriateness and/or truthfulness of that literal meaning against the context of the utterance. Third, if the literal meaning is defective or inappropriate for the context, then and *only* then, will listeners derive an alternative nonliteral meaning that makes the utterance consistent with the cooperative principle. Grice assumes, then, that figurative language requires additional cognitive effort to be understood because such utterances violate one of the conversational maxims (usually Quantity and/or Quality).[9] In general, the Gricean view follows the centuries-old belief that literal language is a veridical reflection of thought and the external world while figurative language distorts reality and only serves special rhetorical purposes.[10] More specifically, the Gricean view suggests something about the immediate cognitive processes used in understanding figurative language (i.e., comprehension processes) that lead to the conscious judgment that some utterance has a particular figurative meaning (i.e., recognition and interpretation products).

The standard view that figurative language violates various communicative norms suggests three related claims about how tropes are understood.[11] First, the analysis of a sentence's literal meaning is obligatory, and always derived before other figurative meanings can be determined. However, the results of many psycholinguistic experiments have shown this claim to be false.[12] Listeners/readers can often understand the figurative interpretations of metaphor (e.g., *Billboards are warts on the landscape*), metonymy (e.g., *The ham sandwich left without paying*), sarcasm (e.g., *You are a fine friend*), idioms (e.g., *John popped the question to Mary*), proverbs (e.g., *The early bird catches the worm*), and indirect speech acts (e.g., *Would you mind lending me five dollars?*) without having first to analyze and reject their literal meanings, when these tropes are seen in realistic social contexts.

A second implication of this standard view is that understanding tropes requires that a defective literal meaning be found before searching for a nonliteral meaning. Figurative meaning can be ignored if the literal meaning of an utterance makes sense in context. But people apprehend the nonliteral meaning of simple comparison statements (e.g., *Surgeons are butchers*) even when the literal meanings of these statements fit perfectly with context.[13] Even without a defective literal meaning to trigger a search for an alternative figurative meaning, metaphor (to take one example), can be automatically interpreted.

A final claim of this view is that additional inferential work must be done to derive figurative meanings that are contextually appropriate. However, understanding metaphor, metonymy, irony, and indirect speech acts requires the same kind of contextual information as understanding comparable literal expressions.[14]

These different experimental findings are quite damaging to the claim that people understand tropes in a series of steps, because figurative language always violates conversational maxims. Similar psychological mechanisms appear to drive the understanding of both literal and figurative speech, at least insofar as very *early* cognitive processes are concerned (i.e., comprehension processes). Listeners and readers may at later points reflect on the *products* of trope understanding and make different judgments about the meanings or interpretations of metaphor, metonymic, ironic statements, and so on (i.e., interpretation and appreciation processes). But again, the fact that people may, on occasion, consciously focus on figurative meanings does not imply that such language is "special" or "deviant" in any way. The experimental psycholinguistic evidence indicates that from the earliest moments of processing, figurative language comprehension does not differ in kind from the understanding of literal language. From this vantage point, there is no need to postulate any special cognitive mechanism to explain how people understand metaphor, irony, and so forth. Figurative language can, in many cases, be understood effortlessly without conscious reflection.

Consider, finally, an example of sarcastic language to see how speakers and listeners coordinate their beliefs to infer each other's communicative intentions. In the same *American Family* conversation discussed earlier, the father, Bill, is telling his son, Grant, about his responsibility as a father to teach Grant how life is going to be:

(1) Bill: Well that's my job I think ... if, ah, I don't why nobody else will and that's what I'm here for you ... is to kind of see that you get off to a good start ... lucky you may be with the deal, that's my job is to see that you get to see how life's going to be

(2) Grant: Yeah.

(3) Bill: and, ah, if I don't then nobody else will ... a lot of kids go around don't even have that privilege of having a mean old man

(4) Grant: Yeah, sure is a privilege too.

151

In (4) Grant echos his father's previous statement that *most kids don't have the privilege of having a mean old man* by saying *Yeah, sure is a privilege too* and by doing so constructs a pretend scenario with two layers: layer 1 makes a serious assertion about how Grant believes he should feel about having Bill as his father, while in layer 2 Grant only pretends to feel privileged in having a mean old man as his father. The contrast between these two layers produces the irony and communicates Grant's mockery of his father's beliefs about what kind of father he is to Grant.

Later on in the conversation, the mother, Pat, criticizes Grant for other alleged "crimes" committed during his summer of non-work:

(5) Pat: Okay, I'll tell you what, you are totally revolting around the house, you never do anything you're supposed to do.

(6) Grant: Now let's get into the heavy stuff, Mom, really start going now.

(7) Pat: You are, you don't clean up after yourself.

(8) Grant: That's not true, you know that's not true.... that's not true.

(9) Bill: Well

(10) Pat: Alright, you see it ... let me say this: you see it one way and I see it another ... now if you'll ask Delilah

(11) Grant: And you're older than me and you know more than me so that's, you know you're right so the you see it is right.

In (11) Grant doesn't explicitly echo any of his mother's statements in the present conversation, but is very likely echoing aspects of her earlier stated beliefs about her being older and wiser than Grant. Again, by echoing such beliefs, Grant constructs a pretend situation in which his mother adopts the belief attributed to her, which contrasts directly with the present situation of Grant's arguing for a different view, thus producing an ironic effect.

Both of Grant's sarcastic utterances in (4) and (11) require sophisticated metarepresentational reasoning to understand what the speaker intends to communicate, because the thoughts interpreted are interpretations of some further thought or utterance, attributed to someone other than the speaker (i.e., Pat). Some empirical studies indicate that both children and adults interpret irony/sarcasm by drawing complex metarepresentational inferences.[15] Many ironic remarks merely remind listeners of the attitudes and expectations that they might share with speakers.[16]

The psycholinguistic work on figurative language is extremely important in showing how people's primary concern with understanding the communicative intentions of speakers, or writers, shapes unconscious mental processing. People are driven toward understanding what others intend to communicate and do not necessarily focus on what is literally said. This reflexive attempt to infer what speakers' intend to communicate is part of the reason why listeners can easily comprehend (via early temporal processing) what speakers mean when using indirect and figurative language.

DECEPTION

Typical communicative exchanges rest on the assumption that people are essentially honest and don't try to mislead others by what they say or do. But people rarely are completely honest and often speak indirectly to achieve personal and social goals. Consider the following dialogue between a pediatrician and a child's mother about the arteriovenous malformations (i.e., abnormal blood vessel connections) in her child's brain.[17]

Mother: I've often wondered about how

Physician: mhm

Mother: dangerous they are to her right now.

Physician: Well, um, the only danger would be from bleeding. From them. If there was any rupture or anything like that which can happen, um, that would be danger for that. But they're

Mother: mhm

Physician: mm, not going to be something that will get worse as
time goes on.

Mother: Oh I see.

Physician: But they're just there. Okay?

The physician plays down the severity of the child's ailment to
the mother. Yet contrast the above conversation to the pediatrician's comments about the same case at a meeting of the medical
staff at the hospital.[18]

Physician: ... uh I'm not sure about how much counseling has
been done ... with these parents around ... the issue
of the a-v malformation ... and I think that this is uh uh
an important point. Because I don't know whether the
possibility of sudden death, intracranial hemorrhaging
... if any of this has ever been discussed with these
parents.

Should we criticize the physician for being somewhat deceptive when she talked to the child's mother about the child's condition, given what she tells her colleagues? Honesty might not
always be the best policy. Some physicians deliberately choose
to limit the kinds of information they tell patients so as to reduce emotional trauma, which might inhibit the healing process.
Yet one can't help wonder about the pediatrician's intentions in
talking to the mother in the way she did. The fact that people
are often deceptive provides a challenge to intentionalist theories of meaning. Deceptive speakers clearly do not wish others to
recognize their covert intentions. But it is precisely because listeners strongly focus on a person's overt communicative intentions
that speakers are able to deceive others. Nonetheless, deception
is not a specific kind of communicative act, but rather has many
facets.[19]

There are several reasons why people are not obligated to be
completely honest.[20] People have rights to certain information,
but they aren't entitled to all information. Moreover, not all people
share these rights equally. Truth telling naturally goes along with
most voluntary agreements, but when you involuntarily get into
a situation with another person, you have to choose whether truth

telling is reasonable. People normally try to avoid harming others when possible and to help others when they can. There are also great pressures on all individuals to transmit inaccurate, or less than accurate, information as a means of survival (e.g., citizens in Europe hiding Jews during the Nazi period).

Not all deceptive speech acts are morally wrong or undesirable. There are at least five types of deceptive acts, each of which reflects a different way of saying something that a speaker doesn't fully believe or directly wish to communicate: (1) *lies* represent direct acts of fabrication intending to create a belief in the receiver contrary to the truth or facts; (2) *evasions* are behaviors intended to sidestep or redirect communication away from sensitive topics; (3) *concealments* attempt to hide or mask the speaker's true feelings or emotions; (4) *overstatements* are deceptive acts intended to exaggerate or magnify facts or data; and (5) *collusions* are behaviors in which deceiver and target cooperate, at least initially, in allowing deception to succeed.

These five deceptive acts differ considerably in the extent to which speakers' messages reflect their persuasive goals. Nonetheless, the speaker's communicative goals for each type of act still require that addressees recover something about their communicative intentions. Because a person's communicative intent to mislead is central to deception, it is often difficult to know whether any particular statement is deceptive or not. Consider former President Ronald Reagan's denial of knowledge about the illegal channeling of U.S. funds to the Contras in Nicaragua. Some people believed that Reagan was indeed lying, but others assumed that Reagan was simply misinformed, or didn't quite understand the consequences of his general consent to the National Security Council to divert U.S. funds to the Contras through the illegal sale of arms to Iran.

Most deception scholars argue that conscious, deliberate intent to deceive is the central defining characteristic of deceptive communication.[21] Recall the popularity of Lt. Col. Oliver North during his testimony in 1987 before the U.S. Congress about the Iran-Contra affair. The following exchange occurred between North and George Van Cleve, minority counsel for the Senate committee investigating the affair.[22]

Van Cleve: You've admitted before this committee that you lied to representatives of the Iranians.

North: I lied every time I met the Iranians.

Van Cleve: And you admitted that you lied to General Secord with respect to conversations that you had with the President? Is that correct?

North: In order to encourage him to stay with the project, yes.

Van Cleve: And you admitted that you lied to the Congress. Is that correct?

North: I have.

Van Cleve: And you admitted that you lied in creating false chronologies of these events. Is that true?

North: That is true.

Van Cleve: Can you assure this committee that you are not lying to protect your Commander-in-Chief?

North: I am not lying to protect anybody, counsel. I came here to tell the truth.

Ignoring the irony in North's last statement, his testimony to Congress clearly reveals how deceiving others is essentially an act of persuasion undertaken with deliberate intent. People lie not just for the sake of being deceitful, but to achieve some other goal. Consider several typical deceptive situations where it is possible to distinguish between the person's deceptive aim and his or her persuasive goals.[23]

• A used-car salesman tells a potential buyer that the mileage on a car's speedometer is accurate, when in fact he knows that the mileage has been turned back. The salesman's deceptive aim is to induce the potential buyer to believe that the mileage showing on the speedometer is accurate. But the salesman's persuasive goal is to get the potential buyer to pay "top dollar" for the car, thus ensuring a substantial commission for the salesman.

• A son tells his parent he does not know how a window was broken, when in fact he broke it. The son's deceptive aim is to get his parents to believe that he is innocent of any wrongdoing. But the son's persuasive aim is to avoid sanction or punishment, and to maintain a positive image in his parents' eyes.

• A scientist reports important findings at a conference when, in fact, the data for the research are falsified. The scientist's deceptive aim is to get others to accept the authenticity of the falsified data. But the scientist's persuasive aim is to impress others with his acumen, thereby enhancing his professional career.

• A woman tells her husband she likes a new painting he has purchased, when in fact she finds it aesthetically displeasing. The woman's deceptive aim is to induce her husband to believe that she likes the painting when, in fact, she does not. Yet the woman's persuasive aim is to reinforce positively her husband's perception that their aesthetic tastes coincide, and to maintain the positive tone of their relationship.

Deceit is not the primary objective in any of these situations. Yet each speaker specifically stages a communicative act so that his or her addressee(s) will accept what is said at face value (i.e., the speaker's overt intention), in order to persuade listeners to adopt a particular, mostly false, belief (i.e., the speaker's covert intention). Empirical studies reveal that people give eight primary reasons for deceiving others:[24] (a) deception used to acquire or protect resources, (b) deception used to manipulate interaction with others, (c) deception used for protecting image or avoiding self-disclosure, (d) deception to avoid confrontation, lectures, or questions of fidelity, (e) deception to prevent harm, worry, or discomfort for others, (f) deception used to create guilt or sympathy, or to control another's behavior, (g) deception to extricate oneself when one has failed at doing something, and (h) deception for the purpose of teasing others.[25]

Although most scholars believe that outright deception is socially reprehensible, generally harmful to the receiver, and an undesirable communicative strategy, deception is more prevalent than our cultural morality implies. Many people find the ability to successfully deceive others an indispensable strategy for acquiring goods and services, developing and managing social relationships, and creating desired images. For instance, a nationwide survey of 5,700 people revealed that 97 percent of respondents had lied and nearly one-third of married respondents had cheated on their spouses.[26] In 1981 *Psychology Today* polled its readership (24,000 returned questionnaires) and determined that 88 percent had told white lies and one-third had deceived their best friend about something significant.[27] A study reported in the *New England Journal of Medicine* indicated that a large percentage of sexually active individuals have lied in order to have sex, including deception about sexual history, sexual partners, results of HIV tests, and the existence of current sexual partners.[28] These studies suggest that deception is often used as a communication strategy to ensure personal satisfaction at the expense of the person(s) deceived.

Are all deceptive speech acts performed for selfish reasons? A recent study of college students and ordinary citizens near a college community asked participants to keep a diary in which they recorded their social interactions and the lies they told every day for a week. An analysis of these diaries showed that lying was an everyday event. College students lied in approximately one of every three social interactions, and people from the community lied in one out of every five social situations.[29] Although some of the liars reported concern for the other person, over 80 percent of the lies people reported in this study concerned the feelings, achievements, actions, and possessions of the liars, not the person(s) being deceived.

When the participants were asked about the motives for their lies, over twice as many people reported self-serving lies rather than lies to benefit other people. Most of the self-serving lies did not benefit the liar materially, but were told for psychological reasons (e.g., to try to make the liar appear sensitive or kind, to protect the liar from embarrassment or conflict with others). The substantial number of lies regarded as benefiting others were meant to protect other people from embarrassment, worry, or from having their feelings hurt. Interestingly, when participants were asked to rate the degree to which they were protecting their own feelings by telling lies, they described themselves as being more concerned with the feelings of others (i.e., the people deceived) than with their own feelings.[30] Finally, the vast majority of the lies were rated by the participants as being of little importance or consequence. Serious lies, which involve a significant breech of trust, certainly occur. But these are far less common and are not usually part of the lying that goes on in everyday life.[31]

How do people know if a speaker intends to deceive them? People can't tell simply by thinking about the words spoken (e.g., *What a lovely dress you are wearing*). Conventional wisdom and cultural stereotypes suggest that looking someone straight in the eye will reveal whether that person is speaking the truth. The relevance of nonverbal behavior to deception derives from the assumption that their behavior will leak information that a person is trying to hide. According to psychologist Paul Ekman: "When emotion is aroused certain changes occur in the face, body, and voice which can be considered automatic."[32] These automatic leaks present a problem for deceivers because they must override them to avoid being detected. Some nonverbal cues are more likely to be controlled than others. Words and facial expressions are easier to control than are body movements and tone of voice.[33]

Most of the contemporary research on deception investigates how people make false verbal statements with an intent to deceive. Researchers have been interested in the cues sent by deceivers and the cues used by those deceived to detect deception. The cues consist, for the most part, of nonverbal behavior coded systematically from replays of videotaped simulated performances usually acted by college students. For instance, student nurses in one study were shown slides both of beautiful landscapes and of badly injured burn victims. The nurses were asked to report what they were feeling (e.g., happy, sad, depressed, relaxed) as they saw each slide, but were instructed to tell the truth about their feelings when viewing the pleasant slides and to lie when viewing the unpleasant ones. To motivate the nurses to lie, they were told that this test was similar to what they might have to do with patients in order to deceive them about their condition or treatment. The nurses were also informed that their responses would be judged by others as to the truthfulness of each response. In fact, the nurses complied quite well. They often indicated that they were feeling happy and relaxed when viewing the slides of burned victims, even though most people find the slides very disturbing.

But empirical research paints a mixed picture about the reliability of nonverbal cues in detecting deception.[34] Few visual cues are consistently present when people lie. Certain vocal cues, however, seem to be related to deception. Compared to truthful messages, deceptive statements are often shorter in length, more general, spoken in higher pitch, and contain more speech errors and hesitations. Nonetheless, empirical research shows that people are generally poor lie detectors. Folk wisdom about how deceivers are supposed to act (e.g., less gaze, smile less, postural shifts, longer response times) are not diagnostic of deception. For samples of college students, there is a discernible bias in favor of judging messages as truthful when the frequency of lies and truth is about 50-50.[35] Even individuals specifically trained to detect deception (e.g., customs agents, robbery investigators, judges) experience great difficulty making accurate judgments about whether someone is lying. People who are professional lie detectors evince a "deception bias," that is, they judge most (truthful and deceptive) messages as being deceptive.[36] Overall, though, both samples usually do no better than chance in accurately detecting deception, even though both groups of people indicate high confidence in their judgments.[37]

These data quite generally point out the difficulties people have in detecting intentional deception. Yet deception is not a single kind of social act, but varies along a number of linguistic and interpersonal dimensions. People appear able at times to successfully deceive others by what they say precisely because listeners are driven to recover their overt, and not their covert, communicative intentions.

EQUIVOCATION

A different way of expressing what you mean without literally meaning what you say is to engage in equivocation. Speaking equivocally allows people to be deliberately ambiguous as to their communicative intentions. Whenever a speaker says something deliberately ambiguous, the listener must determine which of two (or more) possible meanings he or she prefers to impute to the speaker. Equivocal messages often contain words or phrases with double meanings. This kind of speech is not deceptive, nor uncooperative, because the addressee's wishes are not subverted. For example, in the movie *Amadeus*, Salieri asks Mozart about his impressions of the Salieri opera that Mozart has just heard, and Mozart replies *I never thought such music was possible*. Salieri does not know whether Mozart has praised or criticized his music, because both interpretations are possible and, perhaps, equally relevant.

People equivocate quite frequently in everyday life. Consider the case of a firefighter who helps a woman retrieve her cat from a tree. Afterwards, the two of them start up a conversation. The woman is attracted to the firefighter but doesn't wish to be too forward in expressing this and doesn't wish to say anything inappropriate, especially while the man is still on duty. So she presents a staged act by saying *I probably shouldn't ask you in for a drink*, and thus pretends at one level that she really shouldn't ask the firefighter in, while communicating at another level that she really would like it if the firefighter accepted her implied invitation. The firefighter can't be shocked or insulted by the woman's statement, because if he refuses a drink he actually agrees with her. On the other hand, the firefighter might comment that it would be fine for the woman to ask him in for a drink. In some cases, a listener will recognize only one of the two (or even more) possible interpretations of what a speaker has said. At other times, a person will clearly see how the speaker intends to communicate both meanings, leaving it up to the listener to decide which meaning should guide the interaction.

Speaking equivocally is an important form of talk when people are caught up in *conversational dilemmas*, such as when people feel that they are bound to lose face no matter what they say.[38] Although conversational dilemmas are not necessarily everyday occurrences, almost everyone has been caught in them. Consider the following example:[39]

Tom: Why are you moping around?

Sally: You told me I was stupid.

Tom: I really didn't mean it. I was angry at the time.

Sally: I know you really do think I am stupid.

Tom: That just isn't true. I was angry.

Sally: You always say that when people are angry they express their true thoughts.

At this point in the conversation, Tom is in a difficult bind. He has limited options for responding to Sally's assertion or accusation. Denying he was angry contradicts what he just said. Suggesting that he was wrong about what he said before contradicts what he has previously argued. Saying that Sally misunderstood what he meant can easily be construed by Sally as an attack. In short, Tom is trapped in a conversational dilemma.

How can people escape from conversational dilemmas, verbally extricate themselves from "double-bind" situations like that Tom finds himself in?[40] Most individuals attempt to be polite and create an appropriate staged act. For example, probably all of us have received a terrible gift from a dear relative we care deeply about. When asked how we liked the gift, we appear to only have two choices: we can be truthful and tell the person that the gift is awful, or we can lie and say that the gift is wonderful. Both of these options have negative consequences. The first option conveys a message that we don't care about the other person's feelings, and the second option (lying) may go against our personal values and runs the risk of detection. A different way of dealing with conversational dilemmas is to speak equivocally by saying something that is deliberately ambiguous. In the case where someone presents us with a gift we don't like, for example, we might equivocate by saying something like *You are so thoughtful*.[41]

Experimental research shows that people are quite capable of equivocating in appropriate ways when the situation demands that they do so. For example, one study asked participants to write a message to a friend who had sent a gift so bizarre that it was not clear whether the gift was serious or meant to be a joke. If a person replies *I got a kick out of your gift. It was what I would have expected from you,* the message is sufficiently vague to cover both possibilities. Equivocal messages sometimes contain contradictions, as shown in both experimental studies and analyses of disqualified messages produced in families of schizophrenics.[42] Consider the following examples: *It was okay, but sometimes I wasn't sure what you were getting at. It's great but a little strange.* In both cases the messages begin with a positive phrase followed by a criticism. Contradictory statements render the speaker's communicative intentions unclear. Contradiction is frequently used as a politeness strategy in conveying complaints or criticism.[43]

Equivocal messages may also be characterized by ambiguity about who is responsible for the ideas being expressed. The Mark Furman tapes are an excellent example in which it is unclear whether Furman's racist and sexist comments reflected his own beliefs, or those of the Los Angeles police force in general. A person can deny responsibility for the ideas being expressed by prefacing the message with *They believe* or *It would appear.* Such prefatory phrases imply that the speaker is not the source of the message, although he or she is clearly saying or quoting the message. This duality makes it unclear whether speakers agree with the idea mentioned or quoted, or are merely expressing what others believe. Politicians often employ this strategy when responding to questions that they don't wish to truthfully answer.

A different source of equivocation centers on ambiguity as to whom a message is intended for. I might say to a group of people *Will someone please close the window?* leaving it up to the group to determine which person actually fulfills the request.[44] People may design their messages so that only individuals who fit certain criteria should respond. Thus, in the following advertisement, there is a suggestion that only certain individuals should consider purchasing the car: *For sale. 1966 Volkswagen. Very cheap. Person who likes working on cars would be wise to buy this car.*[45]

Finally, many communicative acts are performed only for the sake of politeness and are not to be taken seriously. Consider the following situation.[46] Two college friends, Ross and Cathy, made a date to study one night. But before the date, some friends of Ross call to ask him to a basketball game at another university, and Ross accepts the invitation. Ross then telephones Cathy and explains the situation to her. They then have the following exchange:

Ross: You want to come?

Cathy: That's all right. I'll pass.

Ross: Okay.

As they later reported, Ross and Cathy both understood that Ross issued the ostensible invitation to Cathy only to be polite. But this polite act was very much appreciated by Cathy, because it demonstrated that Ross still cared for her.

Psychologist Herb Clark argued that ostensible invitations are communicative acts with two layers. For the above conversation, Ross's utterance communicates in layer 1 that implied Ross is sincerely inviting implied Cathy to go to the basketball game, while in layer 2 Ross and Cathy jointly pretend that the event in layer 1 is taking place.[47] This two-layered act allows Ross to communicate that he doesn't really want her to go to the game, yet avoids having to make this statement openly. By making an ostensible invitation, Ross doesn't deny either that he really wants Cathy to go to the game, or that he doesn't. Yet Ross assumes that Cathy will collude with him by pretending to take the invitation seriously and declining. Many routine exchanges in conversation include ostensible acts where a speaker doesn't explicitly say what he or she really intends to communicate (e.g., greetings, congratulations, apologies).

EVASION

There are many occasions where people wish to avoid responding to the intended meaning of another person's message. In situations like this, speakers attempt to cleverly evade the topic, or evade the direct implication of what someone else has said. Overt evasions are those where the speaker more or less directly suggests that he or she is not going to give a cooperative answer. For instance, a speaker may challenge the listener by condemning the original question. Consider the following exchange:

Congressman Smith: Do you want stiffer sentences for adult crim-
inals?

Congressman Jones: It's not a question of whether they are stiff or
not, it is a question of what the appropriate
sentence is.

Jones openly states that Smith's question is flawed, so he will
not attempt to answer it. Speakers often use evasion like this to
control the flow of the discourse. Consider another example in
the following exchange:[48]

Rick: How old are you?

Joan: Don't worry, they'll let me into the bar.

Joan answers Rick's specific question only by giving a more
or less obvious indication of her age. Joan's response can also
be seen as triggering an implication that would include both an
indication of age and an indication of unwillingness to be more
specific. Joan's intention to be evasive is a clue to Rick not to
pursue the question of her age. By manipulating the focus of the
question, the speaker answers a question different from the one
asked, making sure thereby that he or she has control over how
the exchange develops.

A fascinating example of how evasion is not just optional, but
a necessary part of what speakers must sometimes say, is seen
in the following real-life case. When he was preparing for his
Senate confirmation hearings, future secretary of labor Robert
Reich practiced answering questions about his credentials with
various Democratic staffers who played the parts of senators on
the committee. Reich recalls that he was peppered with many
questions that he found difficult to answer. But when he was
asked a question for which he felt he had something intelligent to
say, he often gave a long and complicated answer. At this point,
as Reich tells the reader, his chief interrogator, a rotund, middle-
aged staffer with decades of experience at this sort of thing, cried
out:

"Time out, let's stop here and critique your performance so far."
"Look," he says, stepping out from behind the table that serves

as a mock committee rostrum. "This hearing isn't designed to test your knowledge. It's purpose is to test your respect for them."

I'm confused and hurt. I feel as though I've failed an exam. He senses it.

"You don't have to come up with the right answer," he continues, pacing round the room. "You've got a big handicap. Your whole life you've been trying to show people how smart you are. That's not what you should do on Thursday. You try to show them how smart you are, you're in trouble."

"But I have to answer their questions, don't I?"

"Yes and no." he says. "You have to respond to their questions. But you don't have to answer them. You shouldn't answer them. You're not expected to answer them."

The others laugh. I'm bewildered. "What's the difference between answering and responding?" I ask.

"Respect! Respect!" my chief interrogator shouts. He walks over to me and leans down so that his face is close to mine. "This is all about respect," he says. "Your respect for them. The President's respect for them. The executive branch's respect for the legislative branch. Look, the President has nominated you to be a Cabinet secretary. They have to consent to the nomination. Barring an unforeseen scandal, they will. But first you have to genuflect." He gets on his knees, grabs my hand, and kisses it. The others roar. "You let them know you respect their power and you'll continue to do so for as long as you hold office." He sits down again. He lowers his voice. The others in the room are enjoying the spectacle. "If you lecture them, they don't feel you respect them. But if you respond to their questions with utter humility, they will feel you do."[49]

Reich's conversation shows that in some circumstances, honestly answering a question is the last thing a person should try to do. Of course, when speakers equivocate too much in particular contexts, severe problems can arise. For example, excessive mitigation in speech has been shown to be a significant factor in airline accidents. Consider the following real-life scenario, which involves a great deal of mitigation in the form of speech act indirection.[50] The conversation is between a pilot and copilot on an Allegheny Airline flight to Rochester, New York, as it approaches the runway:[51]

Captain:	Yeah, it looks like you got a tailwind here.
Copilot:	Yeah.
Captain or Copilot:	Yeah moves awfully # slow.
Copilot:	Yeah the # flaps are slower than a #.
Pilot:	We'll make it, gonna have to add power.
Copilot:	I know.[52]

The aircraft then overran the runway by 728 feet during land-ing. The likely reason was that the aircraft was going consider-ably faster than the recommended speed. As the crew and pas-sengers all survived the accident, the National Transportation Safety Board was able to interview the crew about their actions. The captain reported that he did not remember being over the recommended airspeed and had no explanation either for flying at excessive airspeed or for not noticing it. The interesting point was that the copilot mentioned in his interview that he tried to warn the captain in subtle ways, like mentioning the possibility of a tailwind and the slow flap extension. The copilot said that he thought that the captain understood the meaning of these remarks and would take the appropriate action. But the captain later re-ported that he didn't interpret the copilot's remarks to mean that they were going too fast. This example demonstrates some of the real-world dangers of excessive mitigation in expressing one's communicative intentions to others.

SPEAKING OFF-RECORD

Speakers mostly attempt to communicate "off-record" when faced with different communicative dilemmas. An "off-record" mes-sage is one where it is not possible to attribute only one clear communicative intention to what the speaker says. Thus, if a speaker wants to criticize someone (i.e., a "face threatening" act) but wants to avoid the responsibility for doing so, he or she can speak off-record and leave it up to the addressee to interpret the remarks. Off-record utterances usually say something more general or actually different from what a speaker actually intends to be understood. In either case, listeners must draw some inference to recover what the speaker intended. The basic way of doing this is to invite conversational implicatures based on what seems most relevant given the context.

There are a variety of linguistic strategies that speakers can use in context to communicate off-record. Many of these strategies use metaphor, irony, understatement, rhetorical questions, and so on, which are actually "on-record" when the speaker and listener share enough common ground information so that only one interpretation is defeasible. A speaker conveys a message "off-record" when he or she can deny having that intention and can articulate a different intention that still reasonably fits with what was said. Presented below are several ways that speakers communicate "off-record."[53]

- Give hints: Sally says to Peter *It's cold in here* to get him to close the window, or Jane says to Paul *The soup's a bit bland* to get him to pass the salt. Both utterances indirectly convey what the speaker desires without having to directly impose on the addressee.
- Give association cues: Larry says to David *Oh God, I've got a headache again* as a request to borrow David's swimming suit if both Larry and David know they share an association between Larry's having a headache and his wanting to borrow David's swimsuit in order to swim off the headache.
- Presuppose: Beth says to Carol *John's on the phone yet again*, which includes the word *yet* to prompt Carol to search for the intended relevance of the presupposed prior event and thus indirectly implies a criticism of John's constant use of the phone.
- Understatements are a way of generating implicatures by saying less than is required and providing less information than is required. The speaker thus invites the listener to consider the reason why he or she is providing insufficient information. For instance, Rick and Stacey are looking at a house they are considering buying and Rick says *It needs a touch of paint* when both can obviously see that the house is in poor shape. By stating less than

is obviously the case, Rick conveys what he really feels without unduly criticizing the house or the person selling it.

• Overstatements, or hyperbole, involve a speaker's saying more than is necessary. By exaggerating beyond the actual state of affairs, the speaker implicates something beyond what is said. For instance, Greg says to Martha *There were a million people in the co-op tonight* as an excuse for his being late getting home. To take another case, Steve might say to a customer in his store, *Oh no, Mr. Smith, we never meant to cause you any trouble. Nothing could have been further from our minds. I can't imagine how you could come to that conclusion. It's out of the question.* Speaking this way indirectly conveys sarcasm, a message that might be understood by Steve and his coworkers but not by the addressee, Mr. Smith.

• Use tautologies: By uttering a tautology, a speaker encourages others to look for an interpretation of the noninformative, patently true, utterance. These may take the form of excuses such as *War is war* or *Boys will be boys*, or as a criticism as in *Your clothes belong where your clothes belong, my clothes belong where my clothes belong*.

• Use contradiction. By stating responses that contradict each other, speakers make it appear that they cannot be telling the truth. Speakers thereby encourage listeners to look for interpretations that reconcile the two contradictory propositions. For instance, Chris says to Arthur *Are you upset about that?* Arthur replies *Well, I am and I'm not* and thus conveys his ambivalence. Contradictions may convey criticism; for instance, Kerry might say of a drunken friend to a telephone caller *Well, John is here and he isn't here.*

• Be ironic: Speakers can convey something indirectly by saying something that appears to contradict what is really meant. *John's a real genius* (after John has done many stupid things in a row), *Lovely neighborhood* (in a slum), and *Beautiful weather, isn't it?* (to a postman drenched in a rainstorm).

• Use metaphor. The meanings of metaphorical statements are usually on the record, but exactly which meanings the speaker intends may be off the record. For instance, when Tom says to Richard *Harry's a real fish*, Tom may convey any one of a number of ideas about Harry that Richard is free to choose from and which, if confronted with, Tom may deny as part of his meaning (e.g., that Harry swims, drinks, is slimy, or cold-blooded like a fish).

- Use rhetorical questions: Speakers may ask questions that leave their answers hanging while implying various meanings, such as *How was I to know?* (an excuse) or *How many times do I have to tell you...?* (a criticism).
- Be vague: Jonathan says to Melissa *I'm going you-know-where* or *I'm going down the road for a bit* to imply that he's going to the local pub.

These various off-record strategies allow speakers to deny their covert communicative intentions if questioned by someone else.

One final, interesting way for speakers to convey their communicative intentions "off-record" is to use innuendo. Innuendos are one type of collateral act where a speaker's intention may or may not be intended to be recognized.[54] Covert collateral acts are specifically performed with intentions that are intended not to be recognized. The idea is to get someone to think you think something without recognizing that's what you want him to do. Communicative intentions can be said to be overt when the speaker intends for his or her intent to be recognized, while at the same time the listener assumes that the speaker intends for her intent to be recognized. In such cases, the speaker's intent is "mutually manifest." Most indirect acts, for instance, are performed with an intention that can be reasonably expected to be recognized (on the basis of the utterance and context), so that the speaker cannot, if challenged, plausibly deny that he intended the listener to infer his intentions. Although I may indirectly comment on the chilliness of the room, I'm not necessarily trying to get someone to recognize that my communicative intent is to get you to shut the window.[55] The key to innuendo is deniability. Speakers know that in choosing their words they bear no responsibility for the inference they covertly intend for their listeners to draw.

A classic example of innuendo concerns the story of a sea captain and his first mate.[56] The captain, incensed by his first mate's drunkenness, wrote in the ship's log *The first mate was drunk all day.* The first mate read this and confronted the captain, who then replied, *Well, it was true, wasn't it?* The following day, the first mate, whose normal duties included writing up the ship's log, got his revenge. He wrote in the ship's log, *The captain was sober all day.* When the captain read the log he became angry at the implication he was not normally sober. When confronted by the captain, the first mate replied, *Well, it was true, wasn't it?*

In fact, innuendoes like the above only succeed if their intent is not recognized. For the most part, however, innuendos succeed only if the intent is recognized, or rather suspected. As the philosopher Peter Strawson once put it: "The whole point of insinuating is that the audience is to suspect but no more than suspect, the intention, for example, to induce or disclose a certain belief. The intention one has in insinuating is essentially non-avoidable."[57]

The covert message in an innuendo can be made more explicit by an act of apparent contradiction. A great instance of this occurred during the 1992 presidential campaign when President Bush's deputy press officer Mary Matalin was criticized for putting out what was described as a "snarling" press release attacking Bill Clinton. In an interview with the press, Matalin defended herself against accusations of peddling sleaze when she said *We never said to the press that he's a philandering pot smoking draft dodger.*[58] By contradicting the innuendo, Matalin found a clever way to reinforce to the press the communicative intention of her original comment.

A CASE STUDY IN INDIRECT COMMUNICATION

Attributing intention to others to create publicly recognized meanings is a necessary, but potentially risky, process. When disputes arise between people, interpreting what other people intend by what they say can often lead to terrible misunderstandings. In many cases, people will speak indirectly to convey what they mean without directly meaning what they say so as to minimize the risk of offending others.

Consider the following example of people speaking indirectly through metaphor and allegory to resolve a dispute in a non-Western culture.[59] The Managalese of Papua New Guinea avoid open displays or discussion of individuals' supposed intentions. People privately gossip about others' actions, but they don't assign intentions and prefer to elicit responses from others through metaphor, discussions of illness, and dreams. The Managalese preference for indirect forms of communication over open negotiation reflects their ambivalence toward public displays of power and coercion.

The conflict discussed here arose when Baho discovered that his brother's daughter, whom he was responsible for, had eloped with a boy visiting some nearby relatives. After learning this, Baho went to the house of the boy's guardian, Nevil, and addressed him and several others. In his allegorical speech, Baho employs two related metaphors: dogs and the scenario of following a path (blocked by a felled tree). Talking about dogs invokes the idea of loss or theft (the elopement of Baho's daughter), as dogs are often viewed as promiscuous thieves who steal even from their masters. The discussion of following a path signified a possible, but obstructed, reconciliation with kinsmen.

Baho stands in front of his audience, who are mostly sitting by the door of Nevil's house. He begins:

> Before, I raised many dogs when I lived in Jinebuina. I raised many dogs, went up to the mountains, caught game, brought it back, and ate it. Then, a little while ago, we fought; went down there to Kavan and my dogs died. Because I was living down there, I didn't see that a big wind came and blew a tree over. So, I thought, I might go and get some black cane (for a weaving belt), prepare it, and maybe catch some game or pull out some yellow cane (to weave a design in the belt). I thought I would go up (to my usual place) look up and see the cane standing there. I would climb up and get the cane and prepare it. I would go up, see the game, get some black and yellow cane, prepare them and go home, so I went up the path but the path was blocked (by a fallen tree) so I stopped, thought I would prepare the black cane, get some game to eat and leave (without the yellow cane). I went back (home), found (another kind of yellow cane), prepared it, used it in my weaving and came up here. I am finished.

Immediately afterwards, one of the audience replies:

Baho told you a story. Did you understand it? Baho left something
of his here. You stole it, so he has to come up here to look for it,
and he has asked that whoever has seen it not wrap it up and put it
away, but let him see it. If something of yours dropped, we would
bring it here, put it down, and ask who it belongs to and give it to
you. We should help him by bringing it out (the thing that he lost)
and putting it here....

At this point, Nevil, still seated, responds:

I haven't seen one of my dogs and am looking for it. I was looking
for it when Roti (Baho's wife) came here chasing it. I was looking
when Roti came up to speak to me. "Your dog is staying down
there (near Kavan). Isn't that why you are looking around?" she
asked. That is what I heard and (why I have spoken). Now, perhaps
(the story) is finished.

Following Nevil, another audience member provided an interpretation for everyone (including the anthropologist recording
the event):

Nevil told a story. I will explain it. I will explain. A dog that he
fed did something, so he has told an allegory about it. He thought
about the story and then spoke. A boy from here went down and
got a wife, and we didn't see what happened, so (Baho) came up
here and told us the story we have just heard. Baho came up here
looking for the dog that he had fed game. He wants his brothers
and cousins to chase it with him. So, Nevil spoke, we heard him
and I have explained what he was thinking when he spoke. It was a
dog of Nevil's; one that he had fed. Nevil had raised the dog, and
they went around together. He went around and with it, but the
dog stayed down there with relatives when he came back. That
person went there; stayed with them and ate. They gave him food
and game. These people who are looking for them gave food and
game to eat. The dog stayed and ate and thought "They will go."
They went looking (for him), but the dog stayed there. "Your dog
went down there and stayed with us," they said. They thought,
"Who gave the dog scraps of food to eat? What did it smell?" They
went looking, and I stayed here looking and have now found it.
This (interchange) is finished now.

Finally, Dajahare turned to Baho, who replies: *I got what I was looking for.*

Metaphorical forms of talk like the one examined here help to maintain personal autonomy while sustaining polite interactions among equals. Nonetheless, indirect discourse is also potentially threatening, particularly if the speaker addresses the allegory to a specific individual, as Baho does to Nevil, and then requests an interpretation. In cases like this, a reply is offered without certain knowledge of the original speaker's communicative intentions, but is constructed to advance a jointly constructed statement of their mutual intentions. Men and women among the Managalese report instances of being "tricked" into agreeing to some jointly constructed meaning, because they did not recognize an allegory. Allegorical talk allows speakers to express overt intentions without directly revealing their covert beliefs and intentions. Through continued discourse, speakers and listeners can achieve a mutually satisfying understanding, sufficient for the specific social context.

As suggested in Chapter 5, adopting a cross-cultural perspective on ordinary forms of talk provides several interesting challenges to traditional views of intentional communication. The strong possibility remains, though, that non-Western speakers still seek to understand the communicative intentions of others in saying what they do, even if their intentions are expressed quite indirectly and do not limit how others will respond.

CONCLUSIONS

People frequently say things that don't directly express their beliefs or thoughts. When speaking figuratively or indirectly, people rely on listeners to infer different aspects of their communicative intentions, even in cases where speakers wish to avoid responsibility for the meanings that listeners understand. Listeners often recognize speakers' communicative intentions quite quickly (as part of early comprehension processes) without necessarily having to analyze the literal meaning of speakers' utterances. This fact again drives home the important point that conversational participants are strongly disposed to infer the communicative intentions of others. People don't ground their interpretations of meaning in what the words or utterances literally say, nor do they just figure out the meanings of words and utterances in context but apart from making strong inferences about what speakers intend to communicate. Understanding what people mean when they speak indirectly or figuratively also illustrates how conversational participants readily coordinate their mutual beliefs for the purpose of creating joint interpretations of what they mean. This coordination points, once more, to the significance of a dialogic view of communication in explaining people's experience of meaning in ordinary conversation.

Chapter 7

Writing and Reading

Most people aren't terribly surprised to learn that speakers' intentions are critical to listeners' understanding of spoken language. After all, the close physical proximity between speaker and addressee – the person to whom the speaker directs his or her utterance – forces people to seek out a speaker's communicative intentions. Much of the evidence discussed in the previous chapters lends credence to the idea that speakers' intentions are essential to spoken language interpretation. But does this conclusion hold true for how people interpret written language?

Understanding written language presumably differs from comprehension of verbal speech, because written language tends to be more "decontextualized," with far fewer cues available about an author's possible communicative intentions.[1] Writers, unlike speakers, do not produce language in the company of someone else who is the intended audience for what is written. For this reason, a written text, unlike spoken communication, must function apart from the context of its production.[2] Philosophers back up this assertion by having us consider situations like the following.[3] Imagine that you are blindfolded and brought into a room in which sits a table. On the table is a single piece of paper with the following text:

Whales eat plankton.

How might you make sense of what this text means? In this situation, you have no knowledge of who wrote the text, the conditions under which the text was composed and transcribed onto the piece of paper before you, or the possible context from which the text was taken. All you have is what is presented on this single piece of paper. The fact that readers can make sense of the text suggests to many scholars that people are able to form reasonable interpretations of what texts mean without any regard to the person(s) who created the text or their possible intentions in doing so.

This traditional view about the the difference between spoken and written language remains firmly embedded in most discussions about the role of intentions in theories of language interpretation. Finding the meaning in a text cannot depend on recovering anything about an author's intentions because there is little common ground between author and reader, especially in a case where a reader has no knowledge of whom an author is, or why he or she has written a particular text. This problem is seen in the extreme in the case of authors who are dead and no longer able to offer explanations of their communicative intentions.

My aim in this chapter is to suggest that this traditional view of writing and reading is wrong. Although different in many respects, writing and reading, like speaking and listening, are social transactions that require cooperation and coordination on the part of writers and readers. A central aspect of producing written language, and understanding it, is the specific attempt to achieve successful communication of intentional meanings. I argue that readers who are aware of who an author is, and what that person's status might be, are much better able to understand and evaluate expository and literary texts. I also suggest that acknowledging the time-course of understanding will clarify some of the debates over intentions in writing and reading.

THE TRADITIONAL VIEW
OF WRITTEN LANGUAGE

Let's begin by examining in slightly more detail some of the traditional assumptions about the processes and products of writing and reading. According to the traditional view, written language differs from spoken discourse in several notable ways. First, oral discourse allows speakers to gauge the clarity and effectiveness

177

of a message as they present it. Speakers can modify the explicitness, form, and tone of their discourse "on-line," and negotiate with their audience to overcome misunderstandings as they occur. With writing, on the other hand, any feedback received is often greatly displaced by time. Writers must learn to anticipate the needs, interpretations, and reactions of their readers. They can aim their message at a particular audience to be sure, but they rarely share the background knowledge and sociohistorical location of all their potential readers, and they seldom know whether their message has reached its target to be understood as intended.[4]

Writing and speaking are also assumed to differ in terms of the flexibility and abstractability of the resulting discourse. Speech is more context-sensitive than writing because of the proximity of speaker and addressee. If a particular message is not "finding its mark," it can be immediately redesigned. On the other hand, written discourse is less context-dependent and more abstractable than speech. Many writing instructors encourage their pupils to produce texts that can be appreciated and understood regardless of who reads them and when. Writers, unlike speakers, are obligated to be explicit, to represent fully what they mean to say in texts.

Finally, writing and speaking differ in the burden placed on readers and listeners. In spoken discourse, the burden of organizing the discourse is shared between speaker and listener. Writers, by contrast, work independently of their eventual readers and must assume a greater burden for structuring their texts. With written texts, the author's relative isolation keeps the message more focused and prevents outside voices from interfering with authorial intentions.

These traditional ideas about the differences between spoken and written language have been elaborated upon in recent decades by psychologists and educators interested in the relationship between thought and language. Writing is seen as fostering critical reasoning skills by requiring students to master the logical or ideational functions of language, and to distinguish these from the interpersonal properties of spoken language. Because written texts are biased in favor of fuller semantic representation than spoken utterances, learning to write and read enhances thinking as well as language skills. Learning to read school texts specifically requires coping with the demands of an objective, universal, and analytic medium.

Several psychologists argued that basic cognitive processes of abstraction, generalization and inference are encouraged by the propensity of written language for reflection and analysis. Schooling and literacy are the primary factors involved in the development of context-free abstract thought, mainly because of the impact of written language on cognitive processes. By learning to write, students learn skills of critical analysis because of the requirements of written language for autonomous texts. Language development, in this view, is the progressive separation of speech from dependence on context for meaning. Language starts as telegraphic and context-embedded and becomes elaborated and explicit.[5]

PROBLEMS WITH THE TRADITIONAL VIEW

There are several problems with the traditional view of written language, each of which bears directly on the possible role of authorial intentions in text understanding. First, it is difficult to maintain a principled distinction between what goes on in understanding spoken and written language. Although certain kinds of written language, such as formal speeches, lectures and seminar discussions, appear to be rather autonomous and decontextualized, many other forms of written text, such as public signs, personal letters, kit instructions, and notes left on refrigerator doors, reflect the qualities of spoken discourse. Many forms of written discourse, such as private letters, presume a rich common ground between author and reader.

Scholars who make arguments about the lack of author-reader interaction misunderstand the extent to which readers of literary texts presuppose information about what authors are trying to do or communicate. All writing presupposes a certain class of readers. Victor Hugo presupposed nineteenth-century French readers; journalists writing in the *Santa Cruz Sentinel* presuppose

American English readers knowledgeable about people, places, and current events in Santa Cruz, California; authors of the textbook *Advanced Psychological Statistics* presuppose readers familiar with the materials in *Introductory Psychological Statistics*. Readers may assume a great deal about what even unidentified authors know, and what these authors may assume about them as readers. These assumptions range from recognition of the mutual belief that author and reader are reasonably competent speakers of the same language, up to very specific mutual assumptions about particular linguistic and conceptual knowledge from which readers can draw inferences about what authors intend to communicate.

Part of the reason why the traditional view of written texts is so firmly embraced by many scholars is that most comparisons of spoken and written language analyze completely different genres. Researchers typically compare casual conversation with expository prose and attempt to generalize their findings to all aspects of spoken and written language. For example, one study, which noted important differences in the functions of spoken and written language, compared transcripts of television talk shows with published newspaper columns.[6] The spoken data were relatively informal, and interactive, rather than content-focused, whereas the written data were relatively formal and content-focused. No wonder people assume that spoken and written language fundamentally differ! Yet a better test of differences between speech and writing would contrast casual speech (e.g., conversation between friends) against casual writing that is highly interactive (e.g., letters to friends), and formal speech (e.g., lectures) against formal writing that is highly content-based (e.g., expository texts). One analysis did precisely this by comparing interviews with university students about high school and university life with written data in the form of university students' "life-forecast essays" about their lives from graduation to retirement. The results showed that spoken language actually contained *more* "structural complexity" than did written discourse.[7]

Many linguists now argue that rather than drawing a rigid distinction between spoken and written language, it makes better sense to differentiate between four kinds of discourse: unplanned spoken, unplanned written, planned spoken, and planned written.[8] In any culture, spoken and written language crossfertilize each other so the particular features which distinguish each are constantly changing.[9] For example, at the same time that writers of fiction have increasingly used quotation marks to personalize their writing and bring an emotional directness to their prose, many speakers have learned to indicate quotation marks with their fingers as a para-linguistic gesture. Moreover, one examination of short stories written by a novice writer showed that they were not decontextualized but instead were highly contextualized, requiring significant "filling-in" inferences to be understood.[10] An important constraint on the "filling-in" process is the search for what writers most likely intend to communicate via their work.

Numerous think-aloud studies have shown that writers tend to make many assumptions about what readers already know, and what they will want to gain from reading text.[11] Writers must make many assumptions about their present and future readers. What do readers know? What do readers expect from a text? What might be most relevant to the readers' discourse goals? How does a particular text make readers feel? What sort of an authorial persona do readers expect? These assumptions influence how writers craft their texts. In cases where there are multiple readers, some of these assumptions might be more applicable to some readers than to others.

Writers must also be authorities about the topics they discuss, as well as authors of the texts they write. This implies that writers often have to learn what their audience already knows (and what they do not know) in regard to the topic of the text. Writers may have to be more familiar with texts that members of their targeted audience have read, or perhaps even texts that members of their audience have written.[12] Finally, reading one's own writing is a critical part of the constructive process of writing. Empirical studies demonstrate that people frequently pause to review what they have written. People experience significant problems maintaining continuity in their writing if they are prevented from reading what they have already written.[13] Reading and writing blend together, and a person is often in two roles concurrently –

the role of reader who builds meaning *from* a text, and the role of writer who builds meaning *for* a text.[14]

The most important thing about written texts, especially expository prose, is not that the writer's meaning is clear, because it is fully represented and decontextualized in autonomous text. Rather, it is the features of the expository genre (e.g., tone, organization, patterns of organization, the titles) that prompt readers to interpret what is said as indeed part of what a writer intended to communicate. As educational psychologist Martin Nystrand put it, "The salient features of clear, written communication lie not in the interaction of reader and text but rather in the interaction between reader and writer by way of the text."[15] Texts work most effectively when they establish and maintain shared perspectives between writers and readers. Texts are most readable when writers elaborate their meanings precisely in those places where reciprocity between authors and readers is threatened.

AUTHORIAL INTENTIONS IN WRITING

It may seem obvious to almost everyone that authors must have intentions that drive them to write, and to write in the particular ways that they do. But is it possible to think about writing, and conversely about reading, as authorless activity? For instance, one might imagine that given enough knowledge of the world and the conventions of language that a computer program could be created to compose reasonable stories. But this turns out to be much harder to do than one might think, unless the computer has some sense of itself as an author with particular intentions "in mind."

A variety of computer programs have been created that can compose stories. One early program, called TALESPIN, had knowledge about the likely goals and plans of a cast of simple woodland creatures. To tell a story, TALESPIN generated some likely goals for these creatures and then simulated their attempts to achieve these goals:

> John Bear is somewhat hungry. John Bear wants to get some berries.
> John Bear wants to get near the blueberries. John Bear walks from

cave entrance to the bush by going through a pass through a valley through a meadow. John Bear takes the blueberries. John Bear eats the blueberries. The blueberries are gone. John Bear is not very hungry.

As this example illustrates, TALESPIN often told stories that lacked purpose. The characters act in reasonable ways, and the story world is consistent and detailed, but the stories have no point or purpose. TALESPIN's stories don't read like stories. TALESPIN knows about the characters in its story world, about the kinds of things that they can do and the kinds of goals they can have, but TALESPIN lacks any knowledge about itself as an author. TALESPIN does not know why it tells stories.

Clearly, storytelling is more than creating plausible accounts of how characters might achieve their goals. Authors are not purely simulators of reality; they have purpose and intention in their writing. The events of a story are crafted to fulfill goals other than a mere slavish consistency with real life. To be cognitively plausible, and to create stories with purpose and direction, a model of storytelling must explicitly represent the author's goals and the process of achieving those goals.

Although researchers may not understand everything about why authors write, a great deal has been learned about how good authors write. This approach has led computer scientist Scott Turner to create MINSTREL, a computer program that tells short, theme-based stories about King Arthur and his knights of the round table.[16] Narrowing the range of storytelling to a specific style, a specific length, and specific milieu makes the storytelling manageable and permits MINSTREL to focus on the process of storytelling. MINSTREL selects a single, primary author goal, for instance, to tell a story that illustrates a particular theme. Limiting MINSTREL to spinning short, theme-based stories about King Arthur revealed four important classes of author-based goals: (1) thematic goals, (2) drama goals, (3) consistency goals, and (4) presentation goals. Thematic goals are concerned with the selection and development of a story's theme. Drama goals are concerned with the use of dramatic writing techniques to improve the artistic quality of a story. Consistency goals focus on creating a story that is plausible and believable. And presentation goals are concerned with how a story is presented to the reader. Here is one story from MINSTREL titled "Richard and Lancelot":

It was the spring of 1089, and a knight named Lancelot returned to Camelot from elsewhere. Lancelot was hot tempered. Once, Lancelot lost a joust. Because he was hot tempered, Lancelot wanted to destroy his sword. Lancelot struck his sword. His sword was destroyed.

One day, a lady of the court named Andrea wanted to have some berries. Andrea went to the woods. Andrea had some berries because Andrea picked some berries. At the same time, Lancelot's horse moved Lancelot to the woods. This unexpectedly caused him to be near Andrea. Because Lancelot was near Andrea, Lancelot saw Andrea. Lancelot loved Andrea.

Some time later, Lancelot's horse moved Lancelot to the woods unintentionally, again causing him to be near Andrea. Lancelot knew that Andrea kissed with a knight named Fredrick because Lancelot saw that Andrea kissed with Frederick. Lancelot believed that Andrea loved Frederick. Lancelot loved Andrea. Because Lancelot loved Andrea, Lancelot wanted to be the love of Andrea. But he could not because Andrea loved Frederick. Lancelot hated Frederick. Because Lancelot was hot tempered, Lancelot wanted to kill Frederick. Lancelot went to Frederick. Lancelot fought with Frederick. Frederick was dead.

Andrea went to Frederick. Andrea told Lancelot that Andrea was siblings with Frederick. Lancelot believed that Andrea was siblings with Frederick. Lancelot wanted to take back that he wanted to kill Frederick, but he could not because Frederick was dead. Lancelot hated himself. Lancelot became a hermit. Frederick was buried in the woods. Andrea became a nun.

This story illustrates how the inclusion of some sense of itself as an author with particular intentional goals allows MINSTREL to create reasonably straightforward stories. MINSTREL composes stories that are more purposeful, organized, and recognizable (as stories) than earlier computer models of story generation, because it has purposeful goals, and knowledge of those goals, just like a human author. Of course, this brief demonstration of a complex computer model doesn't approach the sophistication or creativity of real human authorship. But the development of MINSTREL shows that authorial intentions are essential for establishing meaningful coherency in narratives.

ASSUMPTIONS ABOUT AUTHORS IN READING

Does knowing who the author is matter to what texts people read and how they read them? A reader can obviously read without consciously thinking about the author. I can immerse myself in reading a novel, focusing entirely on the characters and story line, or I can read a feature in the newspaper, with no consideration of who wrote the text in either case. Of course, if I read in this way, I might not fully grasp the significance of the novel or appreciate its art, or gain a feeling of social connection through the author's voice. Authorship does not matter equally in all types of reading. Some texts are even produced to appear as if there were no authors at all, such as in catalogues, many historical texts, technical material, laws, and so forth.[17]

But these texts may not be as authorless as they first appear. Many compendiums certainly provide a very personal sense of authorship (such as Julia Child or the *Frugal Gourmet* cookbooks).[18] When I want to follow a recipe or place an order, I care very little about authorship, and I certainly do not use it for interpretive purposes (although, by this point, I have accepted or taken for granted the author's accuracy and authority). My mother, on the other hand, reads cookbooks for the pure pleasure of seeing the author's sense of accomplishment and individual style. In general, the ways in which author awareness is used will vary according to circumstances depending on, among other things, the type of text read and the reader's individual purposes.

The specific information readers have about an author's background, his other works, his general stance in civic life and so on, can, and in many cases should, influence how people construe some discourse. Consider the judgment that a particular newspaper column is, or is not, sexist, ageist, or racist. Readers do not make judgments like this based on the text alone, but usually consider the gender, age, and ethnic identity of the author, her particular personae, her previous writings, and any other peculiar beliefs that form part of the author's recognized worldview. Well-known authors, such as popular newspaper columnists, expect readers to take this understanding into account when evaluating what is stated. When the conservative political columnist Pat Buchanan writes a newspaper or magazine piece, readers may take it to mean something quite different than they would if someone else said the same thing at the same time, because of what readers know about Buchanan and his political views. The common ground that accumulates between author and reader constrains people's understanding of an author's text. None of this dictates that readers *must* know something about the author's actual mental state or attitudes at the time a written text was composed. Instead, readers knowing something about an author, and their assumption that the author believes people bring this information into the act of reading, influences how readers interpret what is written.

Readers want to know who an author is and seek out specific authors as they would old friends, precisely because of the feeling that reading familiar authors is like entering into conversation with an old friend. A concrete example of how my knowledge about an author influenced my interpretation of a text came to light when I read the following opening paragraph from a story by John Cheever.[19]

> I am keeping this journal because I believe myself to be in some danger and because I have no other way of recording my fears. I cannot report them to the police, as you will see, and I cannot confide in my friends. The losses I have recently suffered in self-esteem, reasonableness, and charity are conspicuous, but there is always some painful ambiguity about who is to blame. I might be to blame myself. Let me give you an example. Last night I sat down to dinner with Cora, my wife, at half past six. Our only daughter has left home, and we eat these days, in the kitchen, off a table ornamented with a goldfish bowl. The meal was cold ham, salad, and potatoes. When I took a mouthful of salad I had

to spit it out. "Ah, yes," my wife said. "I was afraid that would happen. You left your lighter fluid in the pantry and I mistook it for vinegar."

There are many reactions readers might have to this text. For instance, a reader might simply conclude that this story is about a man who thinks his wife might be trying to kill him. But when I first read this passage, I immediately took great delight in seeing how John Cheever, once again, grabbed my attention with one of his classic opening paragraphs. I didn't think that the main character was in real danger from his wife. Yet the scene presented here makes me want to read more, to figure out what exactly is going on within this narrative world that Cheever created for me and others to take pleasure in. When reading this passage, and the rest of the story, I felt that I was entering into conversation with an old friend, John Cheever, a feeling I often experience when reading texts of essayists, poets, and novelists whose work I have read before.

Although some scholars may reject the notion that readers should seek the real author's private psyche through the text, it seems essential that readers somehow consider the author's presence in their reading. "We can experience the ebb and flow of a text – its resolutions and surprises, its climaxes and anticlimaxes – only if we assume while reading that the author has control over its shape."[20] A sense of the author, real and implied, permits the reader to analyze how a text is exerting its influence. Readers who recognize a text as a set of author's choices are more likely to appreciate the craft of the story. Readers who can effectively distinguish author, narrator, and characters are more likely to be aware of stance and tone and to recognize irony and other literary devices that authors use to convey what they mean. Readers who are aware of the author's position and the sources of the author's information (e.g., interior views of characters, information from omniscient sources) are better able to evaluate the qualities of characters and to appreciate the twists of a story's plot.

Some authors, in part reacting to the postmodern fiat about the "death of the author," insist on their right to be identified. For instance, in the bibliographical information prefacing her novel *Mary Swann*, Carol Shields includes the statement, "The Author asserts the moral right to be identified as the author of this work."[21] Shields's assertion of her own identity is a bit unusual in that many fiction writers have attempted over the last century to obscure their appearances in their work.[22] As psychologist Richard Gerrig has demonstrated, reading has become an act of entering into a world that seems to offer direct experiences without noticeable author intervention.[23] However, as literary theorist and critic Wayne Booth points out, an "author cannot choose to avoid rhetoric; he can choose only the kind of rhetoric he will employ."[24] Authors may be less likely to pose themselves as narrators, and may be unwilling to provide direct commentary on what they are doing in their texts, but often still use various "author-revealing" devices for communicating voice, tone, and point of view.

People find it hard to ignore the presence of a real-life author in many, but not all, texts. For instance, academic texts are often presumed to be highly decontextualized and fully explicit. Editors of academic journals often ask that authors remove all evidence of who they are from their manuscripts so that critics can objectively evaluate whether the work is suitable for publication. After all, authors rarely surface in most textbooks, where the goal is to present objective facts and well-reasoned arguments. Asking authors to remove their presence from texts should, so the argument goes, allow readers to assess the scientific or scholarly merits of a text apart from who wrote it (or what affiliation the author has). Some academic authors argue that their manuscripts are rejected more on the basis of the reviewer's subjective biases (such as the prestige of the author's affiliation) than on the basis of overall scientific or scholarly merit.[25] But many scholars respond that attempts to make the author anonymous fail because reviewers feel they can identify the authors of many articles (based on citations, previous work, and so on). Moreover, is it really unfair to include knowledge of the author's reputation in one's judgment of suitability for publication? Just as statistical tests address the question of reliability of findings, so too the reputation of the author may provide indirect, supplementary information about the reliability of the findings. Asking authors to remove all identifying information in the peer review of grants would minimize or eliminate the important role of the author's research "track record" in deciding the merits of the proposed research.

A compelling analysis of how background assumptions about authors inform readers' interpretations of author-intended meaning is found in an examination of Watson and Crick's famous 1953 article in which they announced the double-helix structure of DNA.[26] Early in their short article, Watson and Crick commented on some previous ideas by Pauling and Cory, saying, "Their model consists of three intertwined chains, with the phosphates near the fibre axis, and the bases on the outside."[27] The word "model" is ambiguous. Some of its potential meanings appear to be ruled out by clues in the text itself. But, it seems, this is not true for the two meanings of "model" from which the reader must choose: (a) a physical representation that shows what an object looks like; and (b) a theoretical description. How are readers to know that Watson and Crick are using the term "model" in the latter sense? Background knowledge about the nature of the scientific enterprise seems to be involved here. Readers with no understanding of the role of theoretical descriptions in science will not be sure how to interpret the ambiguous term "model." Thus, assumptions about the nature of the scientific enterprise constrain the meaning of utterances in the texts. This is one respect in which Watson and Crick's text is not fully explicit.

Watson and Crick's text at one point says, "We believe that the model which gives the X-ray diagram is the salt, not the free acid." Identifying the referents of this expression is required to understand Watson and Crick's general argument, especially in terms of understanding the referent of X-ray diagram. A reader who does not know what diagram Watson and Crick are referring to cannot claim a full understanding of this text. But how do readers know what X-ray diagram the authors are referring to? There is no reference to X-ray diagrams earlier in the text. Watson and Crick assumed that the reader will be able to identify the X-ray diagram referred to on the basis of their specialized background knowledge of biochemistry, as it was understood in 1953, particularly the work on the X-ray structure of various molecules.

Finally, coherence is not merely a text-based property but crucially depends on background assumptions brought to the interpretation of the text by the reader. Consider these lines from Watson and Crick's text: "A structure for nucleic acid has already been proposed by Pauling and Cory. They kindly made their manuscript available to us in advance of publication. Their model consists of three intertwined chains, with the phosphates near the fibre axis, and the bases on the outside." Determining a coherent interpretation of these sentences requires readers to reconstruct the relationships among Pauling and Cory's proposal, their manuscript, and their model. In particular, a coherent interpretation of these lines requires that the reader identify the manuscript in the second sentence as the manuscript in which Pauling and Cory set out their proposal referred to in the first line, and identify the model referred to in the last line as Pauling and Cory's proposed structure for nucleic acid. Background knowledge about the role of proposals and numbers in science and about the conventions of publication in science is involved here. It is safe to say that a reader with no background knowledge of this material will find it very difficult to construct a coherent interpretation of these few lines. Context, in the sense of assumptions selected from the cognitive environment of the readers, thus also plays a role in enabling the reader to construct a coherent interpretation for the text.

These few examples of the role of background assumptions in the interpretation of Watson and Crick's article illustrate that expository texts are not decontextualized and fully explicit, and that contextual assumptions supplied by the reader, especially what readers assume about authors and what they know, play an integral and essential role in the interpretation of texts.

Scientists bring their own assumptions about what other scientists may really intend to communicate in expository texts. One well-known study of scientific disputes demonstrates that scientists, when talking about colleagues' data that support a competing theory, do not explain them as a mere reflection of factual reality (empirical data) but attribute to them a rhetorical intention.[28] For instance, consider the following statement from a biochemist in regard to a debate in the literature in which he was engaged with another scientist:[29]

> I think that there was just a tendency for people to try to give the impression that they were right. And a lot of us found that they were betraying us, you know, that they were really being very dogmatic about their views and they had very strong personalities and they were wrong. I think that that's one of the things that I probably discovered at an early enough age to where I could reorient my way of approaching things and not worry about what these people were saying and in fact attack them every chance I got and really to try to cut them to pieces to make them get down to just how you can say such and such. Where is the data for this? How can you exclude this? And then you found out that some of them had a hearing problem. Perry could never hear what I had to say. He always had a hearing problem every time I asked him a question at the meetings.

Note how the speaker's own view is taken to be synonymous with the correct scientific view, as if his theoretical position represents an "unmediated expression of the natural world."[30] As another scientist commented in regard to the same debate: "I have no axe to grind ... it's very easy to go the way the evidence seems to point."[31] But the scientists who are viewed as being in error are seen as "strong individuals who want to interpret everything in terms of their theories." Thus, the false claims are understandable in terms of various human attributes, such as the scientists' personalities and their possible rhetorical intentions in crafting research publications. The irony, of course, is that scientists view their own writings as if they are free of rhetorical intentionality and simply reflect empirical facts uncovered from their scientific work.

Understanding expository texts, such as scientific articles, differs in detail but not in substance from the interpretation of literature. Readers look to authors when reading expository texts in different ways, and for somewhat different purposes, than they do when reading literary texts. For instance, when reading factual material in a newspaper article or a research journal, it is important to consider whether the implied authority is appropriate, or whether it is a mask used to hide ignorance or bias. Authors of expository narratives do not mask their own personas, they simply attempt to blend into the text in a way that makes the author's voice appear beyond question. Obviously, effective readers of the columns that appear on the op-ed page of the *New York Times* carefully consider, for instance, whether an author is a liberal or conservative, a Democrat or a Republican, a representative of a special interest group, a member of a particular nationality or ethnic group, or even, a man or woman. In such cases, readers are trying to understand why the author is taking a particular position in the editorial. However, good readers must consider who the author is when reading news stories as well. Although news stories might attempt to be accurate representations of "facts," the facts that are used and how they are assembled are shaped by the author's biases and beliefs. For example, many people assess the accuracy and significance of news stories in the *National Enquirer* differently than they do stories published in the *New York Times* or the *Wall Street Journal*.

There are several empirical studies demonstrating the importance for readers of knowing something about the author. Some evidence suggests that such knowledge and awareness of the author's possible psychological states is used by readers when thinking about authors. Skilled readers, because of their knowledge of personality traits, often come to highly similar interpretations of who wrote the text and the personality that was communicated.[32] As young readers mature, they learn more reasons for authorship and develop more complete conceptions of authors' intentions to communicate social information.[33] One study in which fourth-grade students were taught to "question the author" showed concrete effects of students interpreting expository and literary texts in terms of what authors might be trying to accomplish. When students commented on the reading they did they often noted their difficulty in reading texts when authors did not express ideas clearly. For example, students stated in regard to the author's fallibility:[34]

> [Questioning the author] is good because some things the author don't say in a clear way. He's just bursting them out and he don't tell you what they really mean.

What you do is you learn more about what's written down than just what's written down. You explore more into it.

You need to figure out and put the clues together, but you don't have all the clues.

These students appear to have acquired confidence to challenge the authors of the texts they read. Researchers argue that one of the aims of programs to help students understand ideas in texts through dialogue with authors is to "depose the authority of texts by actualizing the presence of an author as a fallible human being."[35]

A different study of high-school seniors, identified as good readers, found that making connections with authors was a major part of how the students responded to texts.[36] In this study, the students read two texts and engaged in a think-aloud activity during their reading/comprehending. These students not only voiced connections with the authors and the authors' intentions, but they used this "author-based" strategy more frequently than they did some other recommended comprehension strategies (i.e., questioning). In a similar study with adult proficient readers, this tendency to strategically infer something about authors and their possible intentions was even more marked.[37] These strategic behaviors, called "rhetorical inferences," were made 60 percent of the time in order to resolve difficulties of interpretation. That is, when students were having trouble making sense of a text, they were more likely to consider who the authors were and what they might be attempting to communicate. Students consciously inferred something about the authors of the text more frequently when they were reading abstract, difficult to understand texts than when reading easier ones.

Another study showed that children who were enrolled in classes that emphasized author awareness had higher recall of text information, but were also more critical of the logic and clarity of what they read.[38] One analysis of different statistics texts even showed that readers have an easier time understanding the material when the author is visible in the text to help personally guide them through potentially difficult discussion.[39] A different study found that high school students reading a history textbook written by a "visible author" leads students to a closer association with the material, for example, giving ten times more personal thought to the historical information described in the text.[40] Students reading the same material, but written in a more anonymous style, responded much more passively, and often commented on the tedious nature of the material. A visible author engaged students in a dialogue. For instance, one student, Tom, read the following visible text:[41] "I like to think of Egypt as a natural fortress. You see, the country was surrounded on all sides by imposing natural barriers.... So unlike the often-invaded people of Mesopotamia, Egyptians were secure in their homeland."

Tom's response to this segment in the visible text was "So, she's coming from her point of view. The author's point of view. She thinks Egypt was a natural fortress because, um, the Mediterranean and people couldn't come in because of the cataracts and stuff. And, um, and I think, she's wanting the reader to figure it out why it was a natural fortress; so you want to read why she thought it was a natural fortress."

Tom goes beyond the information simply presented on the page and reads for the author's intentions and purposes (and judges the author to be a woman). Interestingly, when students reading the visible-author texts were asked to give their impressions of the authors, they described the implied author as younger, likely to be either male or female (as opposed to only male), dressed more casually, and probably be a better classroom instructor than was the case for "invisible authors." The success of any textbook depends on how its author presents him or herself as a visible presence in a conversation with the reader.

University students frequently fail to consider how a text could be understood or misunderstood by readers other than themselves. For instance, college students were quite good at paraphrasing and summarizing historical texts, but they were limited in their ability to analyze and criticize these texts.[42] Professional historians, on the other hand, reading the same text were much more concerned with authorial intention and rhetorical form than were college students. Historians actively distinguished what an author was attempting to get some reader to believe from what they themselves were in fact willing to believe. Some research shows that professional historians hold complex mental conversations involving the hypothesized authors of texts, the imagined readers, and the "I" who is the actual reader.[43]

One study analyzed college students' journals created while reading several literary texts.[44] The students were told to simply write down their reactions to the texts, their questions, their reactions to classroom discussions, and their views of literature and writing. An analysis of these journals revealed several interesting points about students' perceptions of authorial intent. First, students who performed better in the course tended to spend more time in their journals talking about authors' varying purposes and intentions in crafting their texts. Second, better students tended to speculate more about the personalities of the authors, as revealed by the characters and events portrayed in their texts. Highly visible authors establish a close relationship with the information in the text, thereby conveying a sense of immediacy and vitality to readers.

Poorer readers sometimes fail to ask themselves: (a) Why is the author saying this? (b) What assumptions is the author making about the audience? (c) What does the author want the reader to think? (d) What does the author think of the protagonist or subject matter? (e) What is the author's attitude toward me? and, (f) Why is the author writing in this manner and not in some other way?[45]

Consider how one excellent student provides a good example of sophisticated use of author's aim and the literary devices used to effect this aim. She discusses the aim of Boccaccio in the *Decameron*, specifically in "the way the author invents lies." She goes on to talk about lying as a theme in the story: "Each story in the *Decameron* incorporates a lie which gets the main character out of trouble. Meant to be amusing to the reader, the lies seem to relate the irony of life as we see it. In the story of Sir Cepparello we see a character who lies continually throughout his entire life, and who on his deathbed still lies."[46]

Although this excerpt focuses on the character of Sir Cepparello and his intentions in lying, the student discusses Sir Cepparello to make a broader point about the theme of lying. But now, the student goes on to discuss the author's purpose in using irony: "All of the lies that Boccaccio writes in his "Decameron" are very interesting because of the twists on human nature. The fact that Alatiel tells her father that she had been a nun in the time that she was way from him and the fact that he believed her seems so ironic. She could have made up any kind of story, but by telling him the exact opposite truth gives an added turn of the knife... Boccaccio uses lies in a way that the readers finds liars amusing rather than looking at the characters with a bad intent."[47] The *Decameron* is a complex tale, and the student's attempt to untangle some of its mysteries demands that she hypothesize about what the author is doing and what he specifically intended for readers to infer as part of their understanding of the text.

Most psychological studies of text interpretation suggest that the main aim of discourse, and implicitly that of authors, is to convey new information. But the psychologist William Brewer suggests that there are at least four types of discourse intentions: to inform (i.e., the author's intent is to provide new information); to entertain (i.e., the author's intent is to amuse, frighten, excite), to persuade (i.e., the author's intent is to persuade or convince); and to express literary or aesthetic statements (i.e., the author's intent is to provide an aesthetic experience for the reader).[48] For instance, in the following statement, it appears that the author's intent is to inform: *Thousands of miles of scenic America separate the Atlantic coast from the Pacific coast.* In contrast, the author's intent in the following statement is to entertain: *Bumping along the interstate highways with two small restless children and one large restless dog, we tried in vain to take in America's natural wonders.*

Of course, any individual statement or text may reflect several different authorial intentions at the same time. Thus, a biography can both inform and entertain, and in some cases may even have unusual literary and aesthetic dimensions (e.g., works by the historians Simon Schama or Richard Holmes). People may experience aesthetic pleasure when reading, even if this was not part of the author's specific communicative or expressive intention. Someone reading a government document, for instance, may take pleasure from the convoluted syntax and semantics, although the reader knows that the text was not written with this intention in mind.[49] In general, writing and reading are social events involving transactions similar to those that occur in the context of negotiations between people during conversation. Texts are part of an ongoing conversation within a discourse community.[50]

Psychologists have provided much evidence in support of the idea that the construction of a coherent mental representation of a text is critical for successful interpretation of both literary and nonliterary texts.[51] This view of reading implies that textual properties, readers' cognitive processes, and authorial intent all interact in significant, complex ways. For instance, the causal properties of a text and the ensuing inferential processes engaged in by the reader allows authors to create a wide variety of experiences (or "narrative world") in their texts.[52]

To give a specific instance of how readers' perceptions of authorial intent combines with other aspects of a reader's cognitive processes, as well as with the properties of the text itself, consider the following story by Ambrose Bierce, entitled "How Leisure Came."[53]

> A Man to Whom Time Was Money, and who was bolting his breakfast in order to catch a train, had leaned his newspaper against the sugarbowl and was reading as he ate. In his haste and abstraction he stuck a pickle-fork into his right eye, and on removing the fork the eye came with it. In buying spectacles the needless outlay for the right lens soon reduced him to poverty, and the Man to Whom Time Was Money had to sustain life by fishing from the end of a wharf.

The psychologists Joe Magliano and Arthur Graesser propose that readers generate a wide variety of inferences when they comprehend a text like the above.[54] The most central inferences include the following:

1. Referential (e.g., the text *on removing the fork the eye came with it* gives rise to the inference that that *fork* is the referent of *it*).
2. Causal antecedent (e.g., the text *In his haste and abstraction he stuck a pickle fork into his right eye* gives rise to the inference that the man mis-aimed his fork).

3. Causal consequences (e.g., the text *on removing the fork the eye came with it* prompts the inference that the man will be blind in his right eye).

4. Superordinate goal (e.g., the text *A Man to Whom Time Was Money, and who was bolting his breakfast in order to catch a train* prompts the inference that the man wanted to get to work).

5. Superordinate goals/actions (e.g., the text *who was bolting his breakfast* gives rise to the inference that the man grasped his fork and moved it toward his mouth).

6. Instrument (e.g., the text *the Man to Whom Time Was Money has to sustain life by fishing from the end of a wharf* prompts the inference that the man uses line and a hook to fish).

7. Instantiation of a noun category (e.g., the text *breakfast* prompts the inference of some specific food being eaten like bacon and eggs).

8. State (e.g., the text *the Man to Whom Time Was Money had to sustain life by fishing from the end of a wharf* gives rise to the inference that fishermen are poor).

9. Theme (e.g., the entire passage prompts the inference that the man's situation was made worse by his haste).

10. Author's intent (e.g., the entire passage suggests that Bierce wants to lambast workaholics).

11. Reader emotion (e.g., the text *on removing the fork the eye came with it* prompts the reader to feel disgusted).

Cognitive psychologists have debated whether any, some, or all of these inferences are automatically drawn by readers (i.e., as part of readers' immediate comprehension of texts).[55] One possibility is that many low-level text-based inferences are always automatically inferred (e.g., referential, subordinate goals/actions), while others are generated optionally (i.e., as part of interpretation processes) only under special circumstances (e.g., theme and author's intent). Unfortunately, there has been little empirical research on whether author intent inferences are automatically, and effortlessly, generated during normal reading. But a reader's construal of an author's intent may be more extensive than indicated by the above scheme. Rather than constituting only the highest level of meaning for an entire passage, authorial intentions might also influence readers' interpretations of smaller text segments and the interrelationship among them. For example, readers may immediately (as part of comprehension processes) draw many low-level inferences (e.g., causal consequences, superordinate goals) because they assume authors intend for them to construct these types of meanings. Readers may also recognize that the theme and emotions evoked by the text are critically influenced by what the author does in the text and how the author, at some points, explicitly wants readers to recognize that this is what is happening.[56] This point-driven reading strategy assumes that a text contains many valid, pragmatic points that the author wishes readers to infer.

One study that looked at readers' complex interpretations of an author's intentions explored college students' understandings of satirical texts. In his *Politically Correct Bedtime Stories*, James Garner satirizes political correctness with his tongue-in-cheek versions of classic fairy tales. For example, he writes in "The Three Little Pigs":[57]

> Once there were three little pigs who lived together in mutual respect and in harmony with their environment. Using materials that were indigenous to the area, they each built a beautiful house. One pig built a house of straw, one a house of sticks, and one a house of dung, clay, and creeper vines shaped into bricks and baked in a small kiln. When they were finished, the pigs were satisfied with their work and settled back to live in peace and self-determination.
>
> But their idyll was soon shattered. One day, along came a big, bad wolf with expansionist ideas. He saw the pigs and grew very hungry, in both a physical and an ideological sense. When the pigs saw the wolf, they ran into the house of straw. The wolf ran up to the house and banged on the door, shouting, "Little pigs, little pigs, let me in!"
>
> The pigs shouted back, "Your gunboat tactics hold no fear for pigs defending their homes and culture."
>
> But the wolf wasn't to be denied what he thought was his manifest destiny. So he huffed and puffed and blew down the house of straw. The frightened pigs ran to the house of sticks, with the wolf in hot pursuit. Where the house of straw had stood, other wolves bought up the land and started a banana plantation.

In other stories, a feminist princess kills a greedy frog/land developer, and multicultural bears defend their home and freedom against an invasive biologist. Through liberal use of politically correct terminology and revised plot lines, Garner pokes fun at an ideology that has (to some observers) gone out of control. Even his elves are "vertically challenged."

How do readers interpret *Politically Correct Bedtime Stories*? How would someone come to the conclusion that these stories are satirical? What role do the author's communicative intentions play in the interpretation of satirical narratives? Kerry Pfaff and I have attempted to answer these questions by conducting a series of studies looking at college students' interpretations of different politically correct bedtime stories.[58] We specifically asked participants to write down their interpretations of these stories as they read each one line by line. The results of several studies showed that readers construct a consistent picture of the author and what he intends when they read these satirical stories. The points that people wrote down, the questions that they asked, and their perceptions of the author agree with each other, even if they do not necessarily reflect the author's expressed intentions and actual characteristics. Specifically, when participants said that the point of a story was to satirize political correctness, they also described the author as not being politically correct. But when they believed that the point was to criticize imperialism or to provide hope for the downtrodden, the participants described the author as politically correct and anti-imperialist. At the very least, this shows that readers considered the author when they read satire, and that they feel free to speculate about what kind of person the author might be and about her motivations in writing the stories.

In a different study, Pfaff and I varied readers' information about the author's opinions and attitudes. For instance, we told participants that the author of the politically correct tales held conservative or liberal political views, or the readers were given no information about the author's presumed beliefs. Not surprisingly, readers' interpretations of the satirical stories differed depending on what they were told about the author. As expected, a conservative author was matched with more stereotypically conservative interpretations, whereas a liberal author was matched with liberal interpretations. However, the idea that the author's aim was to make fun of political correctness was not considered to be unlikely even for a liberal author, though it was significantly less likely than for a conservative author. This study showed that readers use information about the author's attitudes and opinions in order to interpret the stories, but that readers do not necessarily believe that the satirist is antagonistic toward the object of the satire. Overall, readers matched what they know about the author to their interpretations of the text, but also realize that very different authors may intend to satirize the same object.

The evidence from these studies is sufficient to dismiss the idea that readers do not search for authorial intentions when interpreting literary texts. Although this conclusion does not bear on the question of whether attention to an author's possible intentions should in any way constrain critical readings of narrative, it is more than evident that readers often make inferences about an author's intentions when reading, at the very least, satirical stories. Readers do not necessarily draw inferences automatically about authorial intentions, at least based on the Pfaff and Gibbs evidence. Our studies only probed readers' conscious understandings of what they read. The most cautious conclusion, at this point, is that readers will frequently attempt to construct a mental model of the author (the "implied author") that is consistent with what they believe to be the points of a satirical story.[59]

CONCLUSIONS

The traditional view that reading doesn't require any inferences about a writer's communicative intentions fails to account for a variety of empirical evidence. Readers who are aware of who an author is, and know something about the author's status and point of view, are especially capable of interpreting and evaluating expository arguments and the aesthetic aims of literary texts. None of this implies that people *only* seek to infer something about a writer's possible communicative intentions. Once again, there may be instances when readers expand upon what an author intended to communicate and thereby discover different implications for what is written. People are most likely to do this at later temporal moments of linguistic understanding, perhaps when they are reflecting upon an author's meaning or contrasting the ideas presented in one text with those in another. I'll consider this idea in more detail in Chapter 9. Yet it is clearly the case that people's ordinary disposition to make assumptions about authorial intentions plays a critical, and essential, role in our meaningful experience of interpreting written texts.

Part IV

Intentions in Criticism

Part IV examines some of the difficulties for any theory that people always, or only, infer authorial intentions in the interpretation of literature, legal texts, and artworks. Many scholars maintain that trying to ground interpretation in authorial intentions is both fruitless and excessively limiting. I argue that critics of intentionalism cannot ignore fundamental cognitive processes by which people, including scholars, construct such interpretations. I describe some of the complexities for the concept of authorship and how these problems alter, to some degree, any comprehensive view of intentional meaning. I specifically suggest that criticism need not be limited by the search for authorial intentions, but that our often tacit recognition of intentionality plays a role in the creation of both intentional and unintentional meaning. Once again, acknowledging the diversity of meaningful experiences provides a framework for understanding the place of intentions in the interpretation and evaluation of literature, legal texts, and artworks.

Chapter 8

Questions of Authorship

Knowing who an author is and what his or her likely intentions are in creating a text or artwork is tremendously important to most of us. Not knowing who wrote, or created, some artwork is often very frustrating. Our culture places great worth on the identity of speakers, writers, and artists. Perhaps the single most important aspect of "authorship" is the vaguely apprehended presence of human creativity, personality, and authority that nominal authorship seems to provide. It is almost unthinkable for a visitor to an art museum to admire a roomful of paintings without knowing the names of the individual painters, for a concertgoer to sit through a program of symphonies and concertos without knowing the names of the individual composers, or for a reader not to know who the writer is of the novel she is reading.[1] Publishers proudly display authors' names on the jackets, spines, and title pages of their books. Book advertisements in the *New York Review of Books* and the *New York Times Book Review* regularly include pictures of authors and quote authors as they talk about their work, both of which show that our interest is as much in authors as in their books.[2]

Despite our admiration of individual writers, there remain many questions about authorship that pose significant problems for intentionalist views of meaningful experience. If we don't know who wrote something, or mistakenly assume that someone wrote something when in fact he or she didn't, or if an author secretly, or even publicly, collaborated with others in writing something, can we ever claim that "authorship" constrains interpretation? The aim of this chapter is to explore some of the complexities about authorship. I will advance the idea that the multifaceted nature of authorship complicates any simple view of intentionalism. Yet these complications don't eliminate the cognitive unconscious drive toward inferring something about both real and hypothetical authors'/artists' communicative intentions.

THE AUTHENTICITY OF INTENTIONS

Academic scholars have struggled in many public debates over the identities of classic authors.[3] The best example of this is seen in the fight over whether William Shakespeare, the bard of Stratford-on-Avon, wrote the plays, sonnets, and poems that Western civilization has grown to cherish. Many people argue that the man from Stratford could not have possibly written these classic works, but that Edward de Vere, the eleventh earl of Oxford (1550–1604), wrote and published the work under the pseudonym William Shake-Spear.[4] Edward de Vere was a highly erudite, educated man whose royal court experience gave him an appropriate background to be the author of the complex literary, historical, and political allusions found in Shakespeare's thirty-eight plays. A few Shakespeare enthusiasts argue that it matters little who actually penned the work we now think of as Shakespeare's. But some literary critics contend that if it were authenticated that the work is that of the earl of Oxford, then the plays would be understood in a different historical context. In many cases, for instance, readers would interpret the plays as expressing greater parody and satire of specific people and events, given that de Vere actually knew, interacted with and had his own struggles with, some of the characters represented in the plays. As one critic noted in a recent discussion about the true author of Shakespeare's plays: "I have a passionate love for the plays and I find that the plays for me are enhanced by having a real life to put behind them."[5]

Another effort to find the "real" author of a literary work recently surfaced in the public mind with the 1996 publication of *Primary Colors*, a thinly veiled novelistic account of Bill Clinton's 1992 presidential campaign. When the novel was published with "Anonymous" as the author, the media quickly tried to track down the person who wrote the book. Various people were questioned and a computer analysis of Anonymous's writing style was conducted and compared to the writings of journalists who covered the 1992 Clinton campaign and presumably had behind-the-scenes knowledge of the people close to the campaign. Later on, one handwriting expert pointed to the journalist Joe Klein of *Newsweek* and *CBS News* (and the person originally identified as the culprit by a computer analysis of the *Primary Colors* text). Given the overwhelming evidence against him, Joe Klein finally admitted that he was the author of *Primary Colors*. After this revelation, Klein was widely criticized for his earlier denials that he was the author. Klein argued that he thought it important to distinguish Joe Klein the journalist from Anonymous, the author of *Primary Colors*, and complained that he felt tremendous pressure living under these two personas. Klein was soon fired from *CBS News* and was suspended as a columnist for *Newsweek* because his denials were seen as compromising his ethical responsibility to tell the truth as a journalist. Of course, Klein still earned over six million dollars in royalties for his "anonymous" authorship of *Primary Colors*.

There are several wonderful, but nonetheless shocking, stories that illustrate how people's assumptions about the authenticity of an author's intentions affect their critical assessments of artwork. Consider the case of the Ern Malley affair. One day in late 1943, a young Australian literary editor named Max Harris received an unsolicited manuscript in the mail from a woman, Ethel Malley, that contained a series of poems written by her recently deceased brother, Ern Malley. Ethel Malley had unexpectedly discovered her brother's poems and wondered if Harris thought they had any literary merit.

Harris was immediately entranced by the poems of this mysterious, and now dead, author, and soon decided to publish several of the pieces in the literary journal he edited, *Angry Penguins*. The special issue of the journal received great critical acclaim when it appeared in the autumn of 1944. Few poets, and certainly no young Australian poet, had ever had a more auspicious launch for his work. Consider one of Ern Malley's more notable poems entitled "Durer: Innsbruck, 1495":

I had often, cowled in the slumberous heavy air,
Closed my inanimate lids to find it real,
As I knew it would be, the colourful spires
And painted roofs, the high snows glimpsed at the back,
All reversed in the quiet reflecting waters –
Not knowing then that Durer perceived it too.
Now I find that once more I have shrunk
To an interloper, robber of dead men's dream,
I had read in books that art is not easy
But no one warned that the mind repeats
In its ignorance the vision of others. I am still
The black swan of trespass on alien waters.[6]

Max Harris wrote of Ern Malley in his preface to the special issue of *Angry Penguins*: "I was immediately impressed that here was a poet of tremendous power, working through a disciplined and restrained kind of statement into the deepest wells of human experience. A poet, moreover, with cool, strong, sinuous feeling for language."[7] What a tragedy to lose such a gifted poet to an early death!

It soon became apparent, though, that the real tragedy of Ern Malley was not that this gifted poet died young and unrecognized, but that he had never lived. Both Ern Malley and his entire body of work had been created over the course of a single afternoon in a military barracks in Melbourne by two young poets, Corporal Harold Stewart and Lieutenant James McAuley. Stewart and McAuley were disenchanted with contemporary literary trends and created Malley and the poetry as a protest against the pretentiousness of Harris and other members of the literary establishment in Australia in the 1940s.

The Ern Malley affair, as it was quickly called, raises several questions about the role of authorial intentions in how people read and critically evaluate literary works. Why do readers think differently about a text upon discovery that it was written by someone other than was originally thought? If the "real" meaning of a text is what is presented *in the text itself* apart from whatever its author(s) intended to communicate, why should it matter whether a poem such as "Durer: Innsbruck, 1495," was written by a tragic individual or by two smart-aleck soldiers trying to pull the wool over everyone's eyes? Do readers, for example, interpret the expression *I am still/ The black swan of trespass on alien waters* according to different cognitive criteria if they know that this line was created as part of a hoax?

The more recent case of Forrest Carter, the author of the best-selling *Education of Little Tree*, provides another occasion to reflect on the troublesome role of authenticity of intentions in text interpretation.[8] Carter's book presents the autobiography of Little Tree, orphaned at the age of ten, who learns the ways of Indians from his Cherokee grandparents in Tennessee. The book received great critical acclaim when it was published in 1976. One poet and storyteller of Abnaki descent hailed it as a masterpiece – "one of the finest American autobiographies ever written" – that captured a major vision of Native American culture.[9] The book has sold over 600,000 copies, was displayed on the gift tables of Indian reservations, and assigned as required reading in many Native American literature courses on high school and college campuses.

To almost everyone's complete surprise, the name on the cover of *Education of Little Tree*, Forrest Carter, was later revealed to be a pseudonym for the late Asa Earl Carter, a Ku Klux Klan terrorist, right-wing anti-Semite, and secret author of the famous 1963 speech by Governor George Wallace of Alabama: "Segregation now ... segregation tomorrow ... segregation forever."[10] The revelation about the "true" identity of the author of *Education of Little Tree* was a tremendous embarrassment to those critics who embraced the book as authentic testimony to the Native American experience. For many critics, the *Education of Little Tree* no longer had the same critical and cultural merit it previously did because of the now-different assumptions about the book's author and his possible communicative intentions in creating the work.

Our assumptions about who created some artwork also influence our interpretation and appreciation of that work. Recently in Australia, a highly promising Aboriginal painter named Eddie Burrup, noted for his landscapes, using dot-style techniques and incorporating Aboriginal symbols, was shown to be an eighty-two-year-old woman of Irish descent named Elizabeth Durrack. Art dealers and Aboriginal artists were outraged by this revelation. One curator who had exhibited some of Burrup's paintings commented, "How dare anyone appropriate a culture like that. Nothing justifies inventing an Aboriginal person ... It's a massive fraud." But another curator, who was a judge for a prestigious prize that Burrup's work was being considered for, said, "I don't give a hoot who painted it. We're not judging the artist. We're judging the work of art. So really what name is appended to it I don't think matters a great deal." The actual artist, Elizabeth Durack, said that she created Burrup as a composite of old men she had met growing up. She noted "Eddie Burrup is very alive to me." When asked whether she invented the artist, Durack responded, "That's a hard one to answer. Maybe he's a figure of my persona."[11]

Establishing the authenticity of an artwork is of great concern for curators and collectors, who are on constant watch for forgeries. Despite the significant amount of time and money often spent in determining which particular art objects are genuine, art forgeries have often infiltrated art museums and collections of private works. Just how important questions about authenticity remain for contemporary culture was nicely illustrated in an exhibition at the Metropolitan Museum of Art in New York City during the fall of 1995.

This exhibit, titled *Rembrandt – Not Rembrandt*, tackled the question of whether thirty-seven paintings on canvas, once attributed by curators at the Met to Rembrandt himself, were authentic, as opposed to having been painted by students or followers of Rembrandt in Holland during the seventeenth century. The exhibit focused specifically on various scientific methods of examination, including "X radiography," neutron activation autoradiography, and microscopic analysis, used to determine whether parts of the thirty-seven paintings were actually painted in the classic style of Rembrandt during his lifetime, or were painted by others both during his lifetime and after. The museum's painting curators explicitly maintained that connoisseurship was the ability to detect and appreciate artworks created by specific individuals (and not others). Clearly, artworks created by lesser known students or followers of famous artists like Rembrandt are viewed as having diminished aesthetic merit, despite strong similarity to any of the well-documented original works by Rembrandt. The approach taken for the Rembrandt exhibit by museum curators, and by scientists from the chemistry department of Brookhaven National Laboratory in New York, demonstrates the extent to which authenticity, and authentic artistic intentions, is seen as a mark of great artworks.

What makes the forgery of a painting, which to the naked eye is indistinguishable from the original, less valuable than the original? Many critics have reluctantly reached the conclusion that there is no difference. The philosopher Nelson Goodman once asked us to consider the following problem. Suppose we have before us Rembrandt's original painting *Lucretia* and right beside it a perfect imitation of the same painting. We know from various sources that the painting on the left is indeed Rembrandt's original work, and that through X-ray photography and chemical analysis that the painting on the right is a false painting, only recently created. But despite our knowledge that there is a difference between the two works, other viewers cannot see any difference between them. If the two pictures are switched while our eyes are closed, spectators will not be able to decide which painting is which, merely by observing them. Is there any aesthetic difference between the two pictures?[12] As Goodman put it, "The more pertinent question is whether there can be any aesthetic difference if nobody, not even the most skilled individual, can even tell the pictures apart by merely looking at them."[13] For the present purposes, people can ask whether they have a different aesthetic experience in looking at a painting or any other artwork by merely knowing that a particular individual, for example, Rembrandt, created a work with a particular set of intentions for them to recognize.[14] The philosopher Monroe Beardsley argued that if a forgery is indistinguishable from an original, it will have the same aesthetic value as the original.[15] Forgeries may be morally wrong, but their value may be as great as any other aesthetic object.

Yet the philosopher Peter Unger has forcefully attacked this idea of faithful representations by asking us to imagine the following thought experiment.[16] He asks us to think about human, instead of artistic, forgeries. Imagine a machine that is capable of cloning adult human beings to create perfect duplicates both physically and psychologically, which possess not only all of the original's personality traits but her memories as well. Now imagine that someone has used this machine to clone an exact duplicate of your daughter and confronts you with a choice between two options:

> On the first option, your daughter will live and continue to occupy the same place in your family, while the duplicate is destroyed. Further, on this option, after the duplicate is killed, you will suffer some considerable painful experience, produced by some electric shocks and, except for the stipulated fact regarding your daughter, you will get no rewards. On the second option, the duplicate lives and occupies that role, while your daughter is destroyed. Further, after the switch you will suffer no painful electric shock and will get a large reward. For example, in some apparently plausible way, such as the inheritance from your cousin of a patent that becomes very valuable only later, you will acquire a hundred million dollars.[17]

In other words, you can trade your daughter for a perfect duplicate and in return save yourself a lot of physical pain and make a lot of money to boot. Would you do it? The answer is, of course not. We make this choice not because the clone lacks any physical or psychological attribute that your original daughter possessed, but just because it isn't your original daughter. The clone does not have the same historical origin as does your daughter. Many critics and observers make the parallel claim for works of art.

Of course, imitations flourish now in the art world. I personally take great pleasure in the playful spirit of works that raise provocative questions about authorship and the role of original intentions in the interpretation and appreciation of artworks. Forgers have their own aesthetic and communicative intentions motivating their work. One of the most famous "art fakers" in the twentieth century was Han van Meegeren, a Dutchman who started forging paintings in the 1930s, most notably those claimed to be done by Johannes Vermeer. Upon discovery, van Meegeren claimed that he started faking to revenge himself on hostile critics of his own artwork.

In the music world, John Shmarb, an American composer, cleverly arranged to have one of his compositions be discovered and attributed to the nineteenth-century composer Johannes Brahms. The piece, supposedly Brahms's Fifth Symphony completed just prior to the composer's death in 1897, was performed once to tremendous acclaim, including one review that stated, "The four extended movements of the Symphony are each of the highest order and exemplify many of the composer's finest traits."[18] Soon Shmarb announced his achievement to the world. When asked why he created the hoax, Shmarb replied,

> For the last ten years publishers and critics and musicologists have been dismissing my work as inconsequential because they claimed all I did was copy nineteenth-century music. Well, I finally got fed up. They weren't being fair to my music. Now that the world has judged my work as it would judge of any nineteenth-century composer, my genius has been acknowledged. I am not imitating Brahms. I am simply composing as a contemporary of Brahms might have. I find it natural to write in the Romantic vein and want to continue to do so. A great work is a great work, whether composed by Brahms or Shmarb.[19]

Some people believe that Shmarb makes a very good point. But for many observers, knowing who really created an artwork is fundamentally important. Even if we are able to create perfect recreations of artworks, these new works would have much less value for us than the originals because they lacked the motivating agency of an author or artist. Of course, some reproductions are perfectly acceptable to us. Few people especially care when reading Shakespeare or Chaucer whether the text is presented in the original typography. Although some collectors clearly value first editions of great books, we recognize that there is little to be gained for us, in recovering these writers' communicative intentions, from reading these books in their original published forms. But we clearly value seeing the exact colors Rembrandt employed as he looked in the light of his studio or the colors Michelangelo saw as he gazed up at the Sistine ceiling.

But consider some of the new work on creating music by computer. Musicologist David Cope has developed several computer programs that compose "new" works by artists from Bach and Mozart to Prokofiev and Scott Joplin.[20] Cope's programs create in the style of these composers by basic principles of analysis, pattern matching, object orientation, and natural language processing. I have heard several of these "experiments in musical intelligence" and find them aesthetically pleasing. Of course, some critics object that these new compositions do not possess the same aesthetic level as those by the original composer (a point that Cope agrees with). As one critic noted: "The question is, is it even theoretically possible for a computer program, no matter how sophisticated, to produce good Mozart? I claim that it's not. The reason is because Mozart – the real Mozart – was a holistic analog phenomenon, not a reductionist digital phenomenon. The real Mozart had unconscious drives, turbulent flashes of emotion, and a sly sense of humor."[21]

Cope has a different perspective on creating new compositions by old masters. He wrote:

> Interestingly, when the output from a computer program is deemed good – so good that even informed critics acknowledge it – credit is often given to performers rather than the programmer. Although it is true that a good performance can greatly enhance the perceived quality of a work, especially when combined with the appropriate performance practice, good performance cannot save weak or unmusical work. Music is great because the proportions of that music match those propositions we deem artistically genuine. Whether those proportions exist because a human or a machine created or performed them is irrelevant.[22]

Adam Gopnik takes off on this point of view in an article on questions regarding the authenticity of several of van Gogh's paintings:[23]

> A great artist is not, as a lot of people seem to think, a kind of burglar, who leaves his fingerprints on luxury goods, but a poet, who creates a style so distinctive that poems in the style are his even when they're not. "The Polish Rider" is obviously a Rembrandt, no matter what apprentice touched it, in the same way that, say, the Washington Square Arch is by Stanford White no matter who put the trowel to the cement. Even if the van Gogh "Sunflowers"

turns out to be a Schuffenecker (one of van Gogh's contemporaries) "Sunflowers," the Japanese [who purchased "Sunflowers" in 1987 for forty million dollars] were still getting value for their money. What they were buying was a little piece of the van Gogh romance, the van Gogh mystique, and what they got, if it wasn't van Gogh, is a much purer expression of their own van Goghism than honest-to-God van Gogh might be.

But do you think that the Japanese businessman who purchased *Sunflowers* for forty million dollars sees the matter in the same way?

THE MULTIPLICITY OF AUTHORS

Most of the debate over whether authorial intentions play a role, or constrain in significant ways, the interpretation of meaning generally assumes the concept of solitary authorship. Under this idea, the text arises from the creative efforts of a single individual. But historical studies of writing practices suggest that the modern view of the author as a single creative force in the production of literature, far from being timeless and universal, is a relatively recent formation.[24] Our common conception of solitary authorship is the result of a quite radical reconceptualization of the creative process that culminated less than 200 years ago in the heroic self-presentation of Romantic poets.

Up until the Renaissance, most texts circulated freely without established links to their creators. The term *author* was "an accolade" given to any popular writer whose work was studied, lectured on, and frequently quoted by scholars. But for many centuries there was much borrowing and imitations of texts, with authors rarely either getting credit for their creative work or having any ownership rights over it . As late as 1750 in Germany, the writer was still being represented as just one of numerous craftsmen involved in the production of a book, not superior to but on a par with other craftsmen. What we now call literary texts, for example, were accepted and validated without any question about the identity of the author. Literary texts were predominantly guaranteed their authenticity by their age alone. Scientific texts, on the other hand, were only considered authentic during the Middle Ages when the author was clearly identified. During the seventeenth and eighteenth centuries, these roles reversed; literary texts required an author's name, and scientific works came to be understood and accepted on their own merits.

In this same period of time, the Romantic poets claimed that genuine authorship is originary in the sense that it results not in a variation, an imitation or an adaptation, but in an utterly new, unique, original work. Creative writing was conceived as occurring at a single, inspirational moment when the work "rose spontaneously from the vital root of genius; it grows, it is not made."[25] Poets referred to the process of writing as "spontaneous overflow" (Wordsworth), "unprecedented torrent" (De Quincy), "something separable from the volition" and the "undisciplined overflowing of the soul" (Shelley).[26] As John Keats noted: "If poetry comes not as naturally as the Leaves to a tree, it had better not come at all."[27]

These Romantic attitudes form part of the foundation for the widespread contemporary belief that authors are solitary, inspired, creative geniuses. Yet the concept of solitary authorship, and its allied belief in the authority of individual intentions in the experience of meaning, can be criticized on various grounds. Among the problems associated with constructing the author as a single individual embodying a unified mind and personality, is that many texts are composed by more than one writer. Multiple authorship takes many different forms. A work might be a collaborative product of the nominal author, a friend, a spouse, a ghostwriter, an agent, an editor, a publisher, a censor, or a printer. In most cases, a work is the result of several people acting together or in succession.

To take one kind of example, consider academic journal articles published in the natural sciences.[28] Over the past forty years, the average number of authors of scientific papers has steadily increased, doubling from 1.8 per paper in 1955 to 3.5 today. In physics, the average number of coauthors has risen dramatically. For instance, the number of coauthors of papers published in the distinguished journal *Physical Review Letters* has grown from 5.6 in 1989 to 7.2 in 1995. Many papers have upwards of several hundred authors. When two competing teams of physicists published separate papers in April 1995 in *Physical Review Letters* announcing the discovery of the top quark, one paper listed the names of 437 authors and their 35 institutions, while a second paper in the same issue listed 403 authors and their 42 institutions.

One analysis of 4,000 scientific journals conducted by the Institute for Scientific Information in Philadelphia and published in *Science Watch*, found that the number of papers with more than 50 authors grew from 49 in 1981 to 407 in 1994. Articles with more than 100 authors grew from 1 to 182 over the same period, while those with more than 200 authors rose from 1 in 1988 to 98 in 1994. Papers with more than 500 authors, nonexistent until 1989, exhibited the same trend, rising from 1 in 1989 to 18 in 1994.[29]

How does a reader infer authorial intentions for a text with over 200 authors? One might argue that scientific papers are less prone to problems of interpretation given their factual nature. A great deal of the debate in science focuses on what certain scientists (individuals and collaborative groups) intended to communicate by the facts and ideas they present in their scientific writings. It is unlikely that the 437 authors of a single physics article actively participated in the writing of one text. Although coauthored texts are mostly viewed as having meaning that arises through some process of negotiation among the authors, there is usually a great diversity of views held by the many authors of a single text. Scientists exchange a great deal of information about each other's ideas that never becomes part of a text, but which is nevertheless indispensable for interpreting scientific papers.[30] Thus, many texts do not come close to accurately portraying the authorial intentions, or at least the individual beliefs of the authors. How can readers assume anything about authorial intentions under such circumstances?

Many of the cherished literary works in our culture were written as collaborations, despite the claims that a single individual composed the texts and thus deserves all the fame associated with a particular book's celebrity. Some well-known novels and poems for which there appears to be ample evidence of joint authorship are Coleridge's *Ancient Mariner*, Mary Shelley's *Frankenstein*, D. H. Lawrence's *Women in Love*, Sylvia Plath's later poems in

Ariel, and James Jones' *From Here to Eternity*. In addition, many of James Michener's novels, a recent example of which is *Texas*, were written in part by a research team; and recent revelations suggest that many of Jerzy Kosinski's novels were coauthored with various editors and assistants.[31] In some notable instances, texts were written by a team of writers but published under the name of an author who was dead, such as later novels in the James Bond series.

The editors who reshaped and rewrote two of the largest-selling novels ever published, *Peyton Place* by Grace Metalius and *Valley of the Dolls* by Jacqueline Susann, operated in a well-established tradition, all the while professing to be no more than a practical mechanism serving to realize the author's intentions. Maxwell Perkins, editor to F. Scott Fitzgerald, Ernest Hemingway, and Thomas Wolfe, among a long list of notable authors, was the best-known editor who worked in this tradition.[32] A recent study of the German playwright Bertolt Brecht suggests that Brecht's sometime mistress and longtime collaborator, Elizabeth Hauptmann, wrote "at least 80 percent" of *The Threepenny Opera* and created many of Brecht's feminist heroines. Other of Brecht's lovers are now supposed to also have made significant contributions to Brecht's work. As one Brecht scholar has noted, Brecht was not a genius in his own right, but "a place where genius gathered."[33]

T. S. Eliot's famous poem *The Waste Land* stands as a notable instance of a coauthored poem that is consistently attributed to one author alone. There is documentary evidence from Eliot's manuscript that Ezra Pound contributed substantially to the published poem. Pound helped carve out the 434 lines of *The Waste Land* from the 1,000 lines of the first draft, in addition to making major alterations to many other aspects of the poem before it was published. Eliot always acknowledged Pound's significant contribution. As he put it in 1938, Pound "turned a jumble of good and bad passages into a poem."[34] But a large contingent of Eliot scholars have insisted on minimizing Pound's contribution despite this and other evidence to the contrary. The obvious implication of the denial of Pound's contribution to Eliot's writing of *The Waste Land* is that the poem would somehow be perceived as a lesser work than it is now taken to be.[35]

Most critical appreciation of literature require that a text be the product of a single, originary mind. But authors, editors, publishers, critics, and reviewers are in a dynamic social system, in which the roles of production, distribution, reception, and postprocessing of literature seem to be blended together. Some authors/researchers voice great concern about the increasingly collaborative nature of writing. As one academic psychologist recently wrote:

> Although this comingling of the legitimate roles of author, editor, and reviewer is troublesome, what is even more disturbing is the final product: a manuscript that its author may not have intended to write, which expresses in someone else's language thoughts the author may not have intended to convey, under a title the author may not have selected. Such situations turn editors and reviewers into ghostwriters, thus blurring the responsibility for a manuscript's content and raising the question of legitimate authorship.[36]

Little of what appears in daily newspapers and televised newscasts follows principles of attribution held so dear in academic contexts.[37] Many stories, ostensibly written by local journalists, consist largely of material they have rewritten (often only lightly) from press releases issued by newsmaking organizations. A large proportion of news which appears to be produced by local reporters is primarily the work of press officers working for companies, government departments, and other organizations.

A related problem for the traditional concept of authorship is seen in cases where the "author" of a text has no historical connection with the writer, such that the author's intentions do not depend on what the writer could have meant. Consider the case of a loving husband who writes the words *I love you* on a small piece of paper and leaves it on his wife's pillow for her to find.[38] Suppose that the husband finds the same piece of paper on his pillow later that night. In this case, the meaning of the text that his wife loves him is unambiguous. Yet the author here (the wife) will not be historically connected to the actual writer of the note (the husband), nor will the wife's intentions be dependent upon what the writer (the husband) could have meant by the expression

I love you. After all, the husband could only have meant that he loves his wife, not that his wife loves him as well.

This example also illustrates how a single text can fulfill several different intentions. Not only does the husband's note convey his own intentions to his wife, it can also be used to convey the wife's feelings toward the husband. This same note could even serve the intentions of the husband's bowling buddy if he borrowed the note to put on his wife's pillow. Even the wife's secret lover could take the same note and leave it for the wife to express his own intentions, which are in direct conflict with those of the unknowing husband. I might even purchase a birthday card from a local store, present this to a friend, and claim authorship of the sentiments expressed in the card simply because I signed and sent the card to a particular person, even if as "author" I am not historically connected to the person who wrote the text.

Separating writers from their texts does not imply that readers are indifferent to who has written a text any more than the idea of a writer being the origin of a work must imply that he or she should control its meaning. We need to acknowledge the importance of both the writer (the creative author) and the author (the created author) to understand the range of possible meanings a text conveys.

The demise of the illusion that authorship is a solitary and originary activity has been greatly hastened by the rise of electronic technology. A great example of this is found in ongoing discussions that are being conducted in so-called "news groups" on computers. As James Bolter said,

> When one subscriber in a news group publishes a message it travels to all the dozens or hundreds of others who belong to that group. The message may elicit responses which in turn travel back and forth and spawn further responses. The prose of these messages is almost as casual as conversation precisely because publication in this medium is both easy and almost unrestricted. The transition from reader to writer is completely natural. The reader of one message can with a few keystrokes send off a reply. Readers may even incorporate part of the original message in the reply, blurring the distinction between their own text and the text

to which they are responding. There is also little respect for the conventions of the prior medium of print. Subscribers often type newspaper articles or excerpts from books into their replies without concern for copyright. The notion of copyright seems faintly absurd since their messages are copied and relayed automatically hundreds of times in a matter of hours.[39]

The myth of solitary authorship has been damaged even more with the development of "hypertext" technology. The term "hypertext" refers to a principle for creating conceptually useful links between different texts or portions of texts. Compositional hypertext creates a "network of alternative routes (as opposed to print's fixed unidirectional page-turning)... in which reader and writer become co-learners or co-writers."[40] In this nonsequential mode of writing, multiple people interactively choose branches of a story (or poem) to develop, creating a multiauthored document that is still open to subsequent change.[41] Software tools such as *Storyspace* and *Intermedia* offer writers (and students of writing) the ability to create and navigate within the space of such nonlinear composition. Many hypertexts now circulate in computer networks that invite readers to modify the text as they think best. It is conceivable that in some cases only a small fraction of the material seen on computers emerges from the original writer's keyboard. For instance, the performance artist Douglas Davis has inaugurated a Web site with the title *The World's First (and probably longest) Collaborative Sentence*. As of September 1995, more than 50,000 collaborators had left their mark on this text.[42]

The rise of compositional hypertext destroys various cherished literary notions such as that authors can be distinguished from readers, that a text is the property of its author, that a text should speak with a single, clear voice, that a text should be fixed, unchanging, unified, and coherent, and generally speaking, that an author writes by herself, and a reader reads by herself.[43] Many writers have now argued that electronic discourse provides a compelling reason to abandon the traditional concept of authorship.[44]

What are the guidelines for claiming authorship or giving a colleague co-authorship when the exchange of ideas is diverse and extensive, multiple levels of feedback have been utilized, and cross-fertilization abounds? How do we know who said what, who said it first, and how much one has to say before it counts? Problems of multiple authorship are especially dramatic in film and theater. Not only does it take an enormous number of people to create plays and films (agents, studio executives, producers, directors, writers, actors, designers, technicians, editors), there are also potential conflicts of interest and authority among them at every crucial moment of production.[45] The "author" of a play is still connected to the nominal writer of the work (e.g., Arthur Miller, Tennessee Williams), just as with poems, autobiographies, and novels. The screenwriter has been, and to some extent continues to be, a largely unrecognized contributor to the process of filmmaking. Several writers will often have taken part in a film project before completion of the shooting script, one of whom specializes in the basic plot (or treatment), another in the screenplays, another in dialogue, and so on. If a project succeeds to the point of actual filming, there follows a continual process of rewriting which involves specialists labeled continuity writers, troubleshooters, gag writers, dialogue doctors, and script doctors – never mind the active contributions of producers, directors, and actors.

Film critics have experienced great difficulty talking about authorship in film because of the problem of attributing a film to a single person or even connecting specific parts of films to specific writers. As a solution to this problem, the *auteur* theory was invented by François Truffaut in the 1950s in France and by other "New Wave" writers in *Cahiers du cinema*. The idea was popularized in the United States about the same time by Adam Sarris and Elgin Archer in the journal *Film Culture*. The *auteur* of any film is the director, who more than any writer becomes the motivated creator of a film, the most conspicuous single identifiable person associated with the work. For instance, Orson Wells, Alfred Hitchcock, John Ford, and François Truffaut have been routinely treated as the *auteurs* of their films because of the distinctive themes and techniques found in their respective works.

But the idea of director as sole author will not hold up under scrutiny. It is simply not possible for one person to provide the entire creative force behind so complex a work as a modern film. Even combined screenwriters, directors and actors, such as Charlie Chaplin, Orson Wells, and Woody Allen, have been influenced by and immediately assisted by others in close collaboration (including all the people responsible for various post-production operations, such as special effects, sound rerecording, composing, orchestration, film editing, etc.). In general, there are problems inherent in attributing sole responsibility for a film to the director (or to any individual, whether producer, screenwriter, or actor). The circumstances of film and stage production are too complicated, requiring too many specialized individuals, to be seen as the product of a single person or entity.

A further challenge to the myth of single authorship comes from studies on the concept of copyright. Questions about authorship were instrumental in development of eighteenth-, nineteenth-, and twentieth- century Anglo-American copyright doctrine. Since the French copyright law of 1793, authors have retained property rights over the fruits of their labor even after the work is sold to someone else. Being an author, as opposed to a laborer, is justified by the presence of human intelligence and imagination that are legible in the work, with that work being seen as containing the reflection of the author's personality.[46] In recent years, lawyers and judges have invoked the concept of the Romantic "author-genius" in rationalizing the extension of copyright protection to computer software. Computer programs are seen as no less inspired than traditional literary works, and the imaginative processes of the programmer are analogous to those of the literary author. Several court rulings illustrate the Romantic idea of the author as a solitary genius. In *Feist Publishers Incorporated v. Rural Telephone Service* the Supreme Court ruled that a company could copy the Rural Telephone Services white pages directly because copyright requires "some minimal degree of creativity," something that the Rural Telephone Service had not demonstrated despite the significant effort that went into creating the white pages directory.[47] This court decision shows how the Romantic idealization of authorship is alive and well in the late twentieth-century American legal culture.

But there remain perplexing cases in which it is difficult to determine who should receive credit for authorship. This is especially problematic in situations where one person borrows, or samples, ideas or material from another source. Consider the famous case of artist Jeff Koons's sculpture *Puppies*. The idea for Koons's sculpture comes from a photograph, originally taken by a Mr. Rogers, depicting a middle-aged couple holding a litter of German shepherd puppies. The black-and-white image first appeared in Rogers's newspaper photography column. Jeff Koons took this image as the basis for a larger three-dimensional wood sculpture with a nonnaturalistic color scheme. Koons argued that his choice of the image was quite deliberate, because the theme of the exhibition in which the sculpture was displayed (the exhibit was called *Banality*) demanded the borrowing of preexisting images.

Rogers later sued Koons for copyright infraction. Both the district court and the court of appeals granted summary judgment for the plaintiff and against Koons. In each decision the court opinion reflects a faith in the ideology of romantic authorship. One judge wrote: "The copying was so deliberate as to suggest that defendants resolved so long as they were significant players in the art business, and the copies they produced bettered the price of the copied work by a thousand to one, their piracy of a less-well-known artist's work would escape being sullied by an accusation of plagiarism."[48]

This argument shows that the conflict between Koons and Rogers is not between the competing classes of two cultural workers pursuing different objectives in different mediums, but between a "pure" artist on the one hand and corrupt "players" in the art business on the other. The judge's decision concluded by questioning a newspaper critic's assessment that "Koons is pushing the relationship between art and money so far that everyone involved comes out looking slightly absurd."[49] The judge also questioned the way Koons does his work: "While Rogers is a complete artist who makes his living by creating, exhibiting, publishing, and otherwise making use of his right in his photographic works, Koons does not personally execute his projects, but directs many other artists and craftsmen, often from a distance, in the creation of his sculptures."[50]

The judge certainly considered Koons's defense that the sculpture was a satire or parody, qualifying as privileged, fair use. But he noted that the fair use doctrine applies only when "the copied work itself is at least in part an object of the parody."[51] Thus, there must be public awareness of the original work in cases of fair use parody. "By requiring that the copied work be an object of the parody, we merely insist that the audience be aware that understanding the parody is an original and separate expression, attributable to a different artist."[52]

What's interesting about the case of Koons's *Puppies* for the debate over intentionalism is that copyright laws have failed to comprehend collective creativity. The court maintained a strong allegiance to the ideology of Romantic authorship and refused to acknowledge the complexity of artworks where the intentions of the artist are to comment on, or parody, some other artistic idea or material. Opponents of intentionalism see examples such as Koons's work in *Puppies* as illustrating the problem of assuming that there must be a single creative author behind any artwork. It makes little sense under these circumstances, many claim, to argue that our appreciation and critical interpretation of Koons's artwork depends on our recovery of his communicative intentions.

My view, however, is that what makes Koons's *Puppies* so interesting is precisely that he expresses his own particular communicative intentions about a work originally created, in a different medium, by another artist. The interplay of authorial intentions, both those of Koons and the photographer who took the picture on which Koons's work is based, complicates the idea that our aesthetic experience in viewing *Puppies* is grounded in understanding the intentions of a single creative author/artist. Nonetheless, my appreciation of this work partly stems from the attempt to understand the interplay of the different intentions of each "voice" motivating the artwork. Rather than abandon intentionalism in cases like this, we need to embrace the mosaic of intentions for a fuller understanding of particular works of art.

ONE PERSON AS SEVERAL AUTHORS

Fernando Pessoa (1888–1935) was a Portuguese poet who wrote under numerous "heteronyms" or literary alter egos. Unlike many other early twentieth-century writers (Pound, Rilke, Valery) who used alter egos in their writing, Pessoa devoted his life to conferring substance to each alter ego, giving each a personal biography, psychology, politics, aesthetics, religion, and physique. Albert Caeiro was an "ingenious, unlettered man who lived in the country and had no profession. Richard Reis was a doctor and classicist who wrote odes in the style of Horace. Alvardo de Campos, a naval engineer, started out as an exuberant futurist with a Walt Whitmanesque voice, but over time he came to sound more like a mopey existentialist."[53] Pessoa also developed several other "semiheteronyms," most notably Bernardo Soares, whose well-known fictional diary was entitled *The Book of Disquietude*. As many as seventy-two names besides Fernando Pessoa were "responsible" for the thousands of pages of texts and poems discovered in Pessoa's possession when he died. These "authors" did not act or write alone, but collaborated, critiqued, and translated one another.

Pessoa and his "heteronyms" and their constant striving toward fragmentation of the self, in part to espouse skepticism toward the belief in "essences," throws into chaos any firm belief that authorial intentions arise from unified minds. As Bernardo Soares wrote in *The Book of Disquietude*:[54]

> I am, in large measure, the selfsame prose I write. I unroll myself in periods and paragraphs, I make myself punctuation marks; in my unbridled allocation of images I'm like a child using newspaper to dress up as a king.... I've made myself into the character of a book, a life one reads. Whatever I feel is felt (against my will) so that I can write that I felt it. Whatever I think instantly takes shape in words, mixed with images that undo it, opening it into rhythms that are something else altogether. From so much self-modeling, I've destroyed myself. From so much self-thinking, I've now my thoughts and not I.... And so, describing myself in image after image – not without truth, but also with lies – I end up more in the

images than in me, stating myself until I no longer exist, writing with my soul for ink, useful for nothing except writing.

Some critics might argue that cases like Pessoa's are damaging to the traditional belief that reading necessarily centers on the authorial intentions of a single coherent mind. I agree with this assessment. Yet reading Pessoa and his associates in light of what is known about Pessoa's life evokes the question "who is writing?" Even if we disregard Pessoa's conscious attempt to dissolve himself into "nothing except writing," our understanding of the plurality of meanings in Pessoa's work crystallizes our surrendering to Pessoa's complex authorial intentions.[55]

ONE AUTHOR WITH CONFLICTING INTENTIONS

A different problem with the concept of authorship arises when examining cases of a single author with multiple, conflicting intentions. Just as a single speaker may have multiple goals, so too do authors of written texts pursue multiple goals, sometimes reflecting their different personas as animator, author, and principal. One excellent example of this has been shown by literary theorist Paisley Livingston in his analysis of one set of texts by Edgar Allan Poe.[56] In 1844, Edgar Allan Poe published the story "Mesmeric Revelation" that introduced the so-called facts about mesmerism and suggests that a mesmerized person can converse with others long after his death. Poe later elaborated on this theme in another published story, "The Facts in the Case of M. Valdemar." This story describes a putative factual case history, as the story's narrator criticizes people who doubt the existence of mesmerism. The narrator describes how he frequently mesmerized a Mr. Vankirk, who called on the narrator for medical attention on many occasions. Much of Poe's story presents a transcription of the narrator's last conversation with Vankirk who, under mesmeric influence, recounts "a metaphysical revelation in which the dualism of mind and matter is resolved."[57]

The publication of Poe's stories prompted a slew of varying responses from readers and critics. For some readers the texts were understood as simple fact, for others the story was pure fiction, while for a third group of readers, the stories were unsuccessful hoaxes. The texts were reprinted in America and England several times in the months immediately following their first publication. Several editors prefaced the texts with statements informing readers that the stories were true accounts of people's experiences. Other editors suggested that the texts might be fictional. As one editor wrote: "We do not take the following articles as an historical account, nor, as a burlesque on mesmerism; but, as a presentation of the writer's philosophical theory, which he wished to commend to the attention of his readers."[58]

What were Poe's intentions in writing these stories about mesmerism? Was his aim to convince readers that his stories were fiction? Did he want to deceive naive readers that mesmerism actually existed? Might Poe have even believed mesmerism to be literal fact? Or did perhaps Poe have multiple, conflicting intentions making it impossible to make sense of the text by recovering what Poe, as a single individual, intended to communicate?

As Livingston makes clear, a close examination of the historical circumstances surrounding publication of Poe's stories does not provide any easy answers to these questions. Soon after publication of an earlier mesmeric piece, Poe revealed in two letters that the case of M. Valdemar was a hoax. But when Poe published another story after "Mesmeric Revelation" had appeared, he did nothing to insure that readers would not believe the next text as another truthful story. In fact, when he reprinted the Valdemar story, he prefaced it with the following introduction: "An article of ours, thus entitled, was published in the last number of Mr. Colton's "American Review," and has given rise to some discussion – especially in regard to the truth or falsity of the statements made. It does not become us, of course, to offer one word on the point at issue. We have been requested to reprint the article, and do so with pleasure. We leave it to speak for itself. We may observe, however, that there are a certain class of people who pride themselves upon Doubt, as a profession."[59] Poe was deliberately ambiguous in this statement. Nothing he said was untruthful, but he clearly wished to encourage some readers to believe in the truthfulness of his stories. Poe later wrote that he found it "unsurpassably funny" that some readers actually believed his mesmeric tales to be factual. Yet this point does not directly imply that Poe specifically intended for readers to recognize the pretense in his stories. In one letter to an editor, Poe actually defended some of his more gullible readers: "Why can't a man's death be postponed indefinitely by Mesmerism? Why cannot a man talk after he is dead? Why? – why? that is the question; and as soon as the Tribune has answered it to our satisfaction we will talk to it farther."[60] Again, Poe attempts to keep alive the possibility that the events described in his tales might be true. Poe clearly would have been disappointed had none of his readers believed in the story's truth. Poe must have known that mesmerism was widely discussed in the 1840s and that many people surely were more than likely to believe in the fictional events he described in his stories.

If Poe really intended for his mesmeric texts to be read as fictional stories, he certainly might have tried to manifest his intentions more clearly in the texts. Instead, as the above letter shows, Poe challenged skeptics to prove that the events in his stories could not have actually happened. Some people might interpret this challenge as a publicity stunt to sustain the controversy regarding his work. Some critics, in fact, have denied that Poe believed in any of his mystical writings, while other critics suggest that Poe was being ironic and intended to mock believers of his mesmeric stories. Nonetheless, several of Poe's letters indicate his intense curiosity over whether his fiction, and the metaphysical ideas described in it, might indeed have some authenticity. He sent a copy of "Mesmeric Revelation" to a university professor and said in his letter: "You will, of course, understand that the article is purely fiction; but I have embodied in it some thoughts which are original with myself and I am exceedingly anxious to learn if they will strike you as well based."[61] We might even suppose that Poe might have had no particular convictions about the truthfulness of his stories.

Literary critic Paisley Livingston concludes from his analysis of the evidence on Poe's authorship of the mesmeric texts that some hypotheses about Poe's intention can be supported, but not others. The historical evidence is consistent with the claim that Poe specifically intended his stories to be read as pure fiction. Livingston prefers the idea that Poe was a highly strategic writer with multiple intentions, which were oriented in relation to not only several different audiences, but to several different stages in the reception of his work. Given Poe's multiple intentions, it makes little sense to assume that Poe had only a single, definitive intention to convey with his mesmeric fiction. This discussion of Poe's authorship of one set of stories reveals just one of the difficulties in assuming that authors have firm, consistent intentions motivating their work. Nevertheless, readers still assume that authors possess a certain degree of rationality that constrains the creation of their texts and how people should make sense of what they are reading.

A NEW VIEW OF AUTHORSHIP

Many scholars now argue that an author is whoever can be understood to have produced a specific text as we interpret it. Authors should not be recognized as "genuine" but as "idealized product(s)."[62] The philosopher Michel Foucault emphasized that authorship is a socially constructed concept: "The coming into being of the notion of 'author' constitutes the privileged moment of individualization in the history of ideas, knowledge, literature, philosophy, and the sciences. Even today, when we recognize the history of a concept, literary genres, or schools of philosophies, these categories seem reliably weak, secondary, and superimposed scansions in comparison with the solid and fundamental unit of the author and the work."[63] Authors are not real individuals, but characters made manifest by our own interpretation of texts.[64] Readers postulate the existence of an author to help them account for a text's functions. In general, writers produce texts. Some texts are subject to critical interpretation that requires that they be recognized as the products of idiosyncratic agents. Interpreting texts in this way implies that we regard texts as literary works. And, finally, works generate the figure of the author. As literary critic and author Jay Parini has noted, "I want to believe that my voice is unique and that my contribution stands alone. I doubt there is a writer alive who doesn't think the same way. Nevertheless, Foucault's point is useful in modifying the naive pretension, and occlusions, of the old genius theory of creative writing."[65]

The idea that the writer (the person or persons who actually composed a work) might differ from the author of a work greatly complicates the search for authorial intentions. Whose intentions are readers actually seeking? Literary theorist Wayne Booth has suggested that four important personages are involved in the creation and interpretation of any literary text: the author, the implied author, the reader, and the implied reader.[66] The author is the real flesh-and-bones person who composed the story. The implied author refers to the writer's persona that is created and communicated in the story. The reader is a real person, whereas the implied reader is the audience that must have been assumed by the writer in laying out the tale. The author and reader are real, and the implied author and reader are fictions created to communicate a story effectively.

Booth argues that the reader must be positively inclined toward the implied author if the text is to be viewed positively or sympathetically. According to this view, one of the reader's most central responsibilities is to recognize the implied author and his or her point of view, attitudes, and biases. Readers need not always consider the actual author (although, at least in some cases, this may be necessary), but to understand the art of the story fully the reader must develop some sense of the relationship between the real and implied authors, that is, the reader should try to understand how the implied author is having an effect on the readers. According to one commentary on this point: "As we read any literary work, we necessarily create a fiction or metaphor of its author. The author is perhaps our myth, but the experience of literature partly depends on that myth."[67]

I agree wholeheartedly with this critical statement. For others, including many notable writers, the entire question of who one is when writing remains mysterious and undecidable. A wonderful illustration of this is given in the essay "Borges and I" written by Jorge Luis Borges.[68]

It is to my other self, to Borges, that things happen. I walk about Buenos Aires and I pause, almost mechanically, to contemplate the arch of an entry or the portal of a church; the news of Borges comes to me in the mail, and I see his name on some list of professors or in a biographical dictionary. I am fond of hourglasses, maps, eighteenth-century typography, the etymology of words, the tang of coffee, and the prose of Stevenson; the other shares these enthusiasms, but in a rather vain, theatrical way. It would be an exaggeration to call our relationship hostile. I live, I agree to go on living, so that Borges may fashion his literature; that literature justifies me. I do not mind admitting that he has managed to write a few worthwhile pages, but these pages cannot save me, perhaps because good writing belongs to nobody, not even to my other, but rather to language itself, to the tradition. Beyond that, I am doomed to oblivion, utterly doomed, and no more than certain flashes of my existence can survive in the work of my other. Little by little I am surrendering everything to him, although I am well aware of his perverse habit of falsifying and exaggerating. Spinoza understood that everything wishes to continue in its own being: A stone wishes to be a stone, eternally, a tiger a tiger. I must go on in Borges, not in myself (if I am anyone at all). But I recognize myself much less in the books he writes than in many others or in the clumsy plucking of a guitar. Years ago I tried to cut free from him and went from myths of suburban life to games with time and infinity; but those games belong to Borges now and I will have come up with something else. And so my life leaks away and I lose everything, and everything passes into oblivion, or to my other.

... I cannot tell which one of us is writing this page.

Borges is right to suggest that each writer has many different selves. Yet this complication doesn't eliminate the importance of inferring something about what an author, even with multiple selves, intends to express by his writing.

CONCLUSION

The fragmentation of authorship in the twentieth century clearly challenges any simple view of intentionalism. Our experience of meaning when reading texts, watching plays or films, or observing artworks cannot rest solely on the recovery of a well-articulated set of ideas from a single author/artist possessing a unified mind or sense of self. But this glaring fact does not imply that people never, or even rarely, make assumptions about authorship in making sense of language or art. People will often assume, perhaps incorrectly, that what they read or see arose from a single, unified mind. This might occur especially during some of the earliest temporal moments of understanding when people quickly, unconsciously comprehend by assuming that *some* intentional agent(s) produced a specific artifact. Yet at later phenomenological moments, such as when someone closely studies a poem or play, people may become aware of the presence of multiple voices, both within and across individuals, underlying a human artifact. The cacophony of voices motivating any linguistic or artistic work provides for a richer set of weak implicatures and other meaningful interpretations that cannot be linked to the minds of the original creators of these works. Once more, it would be a mistake to claim that this kind of meaningful experience is completely divorced from any consideration of authorial intentions.

Chapter 9

Literary Interpretation and Criticism

What must it be like to write a novel, poem, or play that people don't seem to understand? Several famous novelists have experienced bewilderment over how their works have been misinterpreted, or overinterpreted, and their communicative intentions distorted or completely ignored. In the introduction to the 1973 edition of her classic novel *The Golden Notebook*, Doris Lessing reflects on her own situation:[1]

> Ten years after I wrote it, I can get, in one week, three letters about it, from three intelligent, well-informed people, who have taken the trouble to sit down and write to me. One might be in Johannesburg, one in San Francisco, one in Budapest. And here I sit in London, reading them at the same time, or one after another – as always grateful to the writers, and delighted that what I've written can stimulate, illuminate – or even annoy. But one letter is entirely about the sex war, about man's inhumanity to woman, and woman's inhumanity to man, and the writer has produced pages and pages all about nothing else, for she – but not always a she – can't see anything else from the book.
>
> The second is about politics, probably from an old Red like myself, and he or she writes many pages about politics, and never mentions any other theme.
>
> These two letters used, when the book was as it were young, to be the most common.
>
> The third letter, once rare but now catching up on the others, is written by a man or a woman who can see nothing in it but the theme of mental illness.
>
> But it is the same book.

And naturally these incidents bring up again questions of what people see when they read a book, and why one person sees one pattern and nothing at all of another pattern, and how odd it is to have, as author, such a clear picture of a book, that is seen differently by its readers.

One might simply suggest that the problem with Lessing's readers is less with them than with Lessing herself having failed adequately to express her communicative intentions in her writing of *The Golden Notebook*. Of course, readers and critics have debated the meanings of many classic novels for decades, even centuries, and will likely continue to do so. Yet the fact that readers disagree with an author, or that readers disagree among themselves, as to what a literary work means, doesn't at all imply that readers ignore authorial intentions or don't at some point consider what an author might have intended to communicate in a text.

Much of the focus in literary theory over the past fifty years has centered on the issue of whether recovery of an author's intentions can, or should, play a role in literary interpretation and criticism. My aim in this chapter is to explore some of the major literary approaches to this issue in light of the ideas and research from cognitive science on people's interpretation of written language. I argue that many literary theories focus exclusively on some aspects of interpretation, failing to acknowledge, in part, important cognitive factors in people's experience of meaning. Taking the cognitive intentionalist approach shows, at the very least, how assumptions about authorial intentions play a critical role in reading and criticizing literature. Nevertheless, readers/critics may reach beyond authorial intentions in inferring complex patterns related to a whole host of cultural, historical, and personal factors. Yet departing from what authors intend may, in many instances, be tightly linked to authorial intentions.

AUTHORS MISINTERPRETED?

Doris Lessing's questioning of how readers view her novel *The Golden Notebook* reflects an enduring struggle between writers and readers over who has the right, and is in the best position, to define literary meaning. Consider what the novelist Amy Tam has discovered since her first novel, *The Joy Luck Club*, was published to great acclaim in 1989. This book tells the tale of a young Asian American woman and her extended family. Tam later commented on the considerable and sometimes outrageous speculation from students and professors about the book's literary significance, its symbolism and authorial intentions.[2] Unlike authors such as Henry James, who are long dead and unable to respond to critical perceptions of their work, Tam noted: "I, however, have the distinct pleasure of knowing, while still alive, what I meant when writing *The Joy Luck Club.*"

Tam goes on to discuss some of the notable responses to her work. "One student discovered that *The Joy Luck Club* is structured to the four movements of a sonata. The proof lay in the fact that my parents wanted me to become a concert pianist, as mentioned in my author's bio and book jacket."

On another occasion, Tam read

a master's thesis on feminist writings, which included examples from *The Joy Luck Club*. The student noted I had often used the number four, something on the order of 32 or 36 times, in any case a number divisible by four. Accordingly, she pointed out, there were four mothers, four daughters, four sections of the book, four stories per section. Furthermore, there were four sides to a mahjong table, four directions of the wind, the four players. More importantly, she postulated, my use of the number four was a symbol for the four stages of psychological development which corresponded in uncanny ways with the four stages of some kind of Buddhist philosophy I have never heard of before.

The student recalled that the story contained a character called Fourth Wife, symbolizing death, and a four-year-old girl with a feisty spirit, symbolizing regeneration. And there was a four-year-old boy who drowns and, perhaps because his parents were Baptist, he symbolized rebirth through death. There was also a little girl who receives a scar on her neck at the age of four, who then loses her mother and her sense of self. She symbolized crisis.

Tam continued in her response to the student's analysis of the book:

In short, her literary sleuthing went on to reveal a mystical and rather byzantine puzzle, which once explained proved to be completely brilliant and precisely logical. The student later wrote me to ask what I thought. The truth is, I do indeed include images in my work, but I don't think of them as symbols, not in the Jungian sense. They are Freudian, only in the sense that what I intended and what I wrote are not what someone else says I meant. I don't intend to hide symbols at regular plot points. If there were symbols in my work, they exist largely by accident, or in someone else's interpretive design.

Tam went on to say:

I don't claim my use of the number four to be a brilliant symbolic device. In fact now that it's been pointed out to me in rather astonishing ways, I consider my overuse of the number four to be a flaw.

Reviewers and students have enlightened me, not only about how I write, but about why I write. Accordingly, I am driven to capture the immigrant experience, to demystify Chinese culture, to point out the difference between Chinese and American culture, even to pave the way for other Asian American writers. I am not that noble. The truth is I write for myself. I write because I enjoy stories and make-believe, the power of words and the lovely peculiarities of language. I write because there is a lot I don't understand about life and death, myself and the world, and the great in-between.

The Joy Luck Club is now required reading in many high-school and college courses in ethnic studies, Asian American studies, Asian American literature, Asian American history, women's literature, feminist studies, and courses on feminist writers of color. In response to all the arguments from teachers and critics that Tam's book expresses her responsibilities to advance multiculturalism, and the voice of ethnic women, Tam responded:

Until recently, I did not think it important for writers to express their private intentions in order for their work to be appreciated. My domain is fiction and I believe that the analysis of my intentions was the domain of literature classes. But I have realized that their study of literature does have its effect on how books are being read and thus what might be read, published, and written in the future. For that reason I do believe writers today must talk about their intentions, if anything, to serve as an antidote to what others define as to what our intentions should be.

Tam's plea for authors to take greater responsibility in clarifying their intentions stands in marked contrast with the long tradition in literary and aesthetic theory that explicitly denies the individual author any rights in defining her artistic meaning. Tam's plea, ironically, also conflicts with the claims of contemporary feminists and others who argue that their positions as women or as members of certain races and ethnicities, should help define how their works are to be interpreted. Yet Tam's statements clearly show how important it is for some authors to have their communicative intentions recognized and appreciated.

Perhaps the most famous case in recent history of how an author's presumed intentions were possibly misinterpreted, at great personal cost to the author, is found in the 1988 publication of Salman Rushdie's book *The Satanic Verses*.[3] This novel is about the problems of third-world immigrants in present-day England. The story, which has an extremely complex set of plots, switches back and forth between London and Bombay and between the present day and seventh-century Arabia. Several chapters of the book contain remarks that even moderate Muslims, let alone fundamentalists, regard as blasphemous. For instance, Rushdie dubs Mohammad "Mahound," a name used by Islam-hating Christians to refer to Islam's holiest figure as a false prophet and an agent of the devil – if not Satan himself. Rushdie calls the holy city of Mecca "Jahilia," which means "darkness" or "ignorance." He depicts twelve prostitutes as taking the names and personalities of Mohammad's twelve wives. Worse yet, Rushdie offers several remarks offensive to the Koran.

The publication of Rushdie's book provoked an international debate on the nature of artistic license. Ayatollah Khomeini issued a *fatwa*, a religious edict, against Rushdie in 1989, in which he called on all zealous Muslims to go forward and kill Rushdie for his insults to Islam. The death sentence stirred trouble throughout the world. Many countries recalled their ambassadors from

Tehran, citing the *fatwa* as a fundamental breach of international law and practice. Bookstores in London, Oslo, and Berkeley were firebombed. Five people were killed and a hundred wounded when demonstrators attacked the U.S. embassy in Islamabad. Twelve rioters were shot dead in Bombay. One translator of *The Satanic Verses* was stabbed to death, while another was stabbed and wounded. Several bookstore chains in the United States refused to sell the book. Although Rushdie has become a more visible public figure over the last few years, he is still surrounded by bodyguards wherever he travels.

The Rushdie affair highlights the horrible consequences that our presumption of authorial intentions can have in our interpretation of meaning. Rushdie defended himself in several, sometimes contradictory, ways, arguing that his intentions in writing *The Satanic Verses* were not to defame Islam. Yet many readers and critics found Rushdie's explanations unconvincing. Some readers stressed the importance of the author's presumed intentions and constructed their interpretations of the book on the basis of Rushdie's ascribed status as one familiar with Islam. For instance, in an open letter to Rushdie, S. Nomanul Haq accused him of deliberately mutilating history: "Most of your Western readers are unable to gauge the acuteness of your blow to the very core of the Indian subcontinental culture. They cannot estimate the seriousness of the injury because they do not know the history of the aggrieved. You do know it and therefore one feels that you foresaw, at least to some extent, the consequences."[4]

Another critic observed that it was surprising that Rushdie himself should foresake the textual subtleties of his book and fall back on the idea that his meaning was misappropriated: "Rushdie suddenly rediscovers a naive faith in the conscious intentions of the artist and appears to believe that if he proclaims his own holy intentions loudly enough the unholy results of the publication of the Satanic Verses will be annihilated, or neutralized."[5]

It could be argued, however, that the one person who has the right to claim knowledge of his conscious intentions is the author himself, even though his text might betray or transcend them.[6] But Rushdie is caught in a terrible paradox. His stated intentions are not considered relevant to a reading of his work, but the text is used to ascribe intention, desires, and concerns to Rushdie as author. Feroza Jussawalla noted that "Rushdie has become a victim not of the Muslim mind so much as of the indeterminacy, which is the condition of postmodernism, whereby authority has been completely wrested from the author and in his absence has been placed in the warring factions of readers."[7] As Rushdie himself has argued, as a postcolonial author he is not permitted the attribute of indeterminacy, which is only afforded to his text.

The traditional view of literary theory is that the task of interpretation is to explicate what a literary work means. It is now a central theme of much modern criticism that a literary text is a complex entity composed of different meanings, presented not as alternatives and not successively, but as mutually interacting and simultaneous. Disagreement among critics is necessary because of the indeterminacy or lack of stable meaning of texts and because texts underdetermine what they actually are intended to communicate.[8] Far from being a defect, the ambiguity of texts is really a distinguishing mark of literary works, such as those authored by Lessing, Tam, and Rushdie.

My discussion of how several contemporary novelists respond to public readings of their work illustrates some of the struggles associated with intentional meaning in the experience of literature. Many literary theorists aim not only to describe how literary interpretation takes place, but to prescribe specific guidelines for finding correct interpretations or readings of texts. In many cases, scholars have butted heads with authors, such as Lessing, Tam, and Rushdie, who adhere to the more traditional belief that what an author intends to communicate in a literary work should matter, or at least be considered, when a text is read and criticized. Let's consider some of the approaches to literary interpretation in order to explore the extent to which literary criticism places different emphases on authorial intentions.

SUBJECTIVE INTENTIONALISM

Subjective intentionalism is a long-standing approach to literary interpretation that often focuses on the biographies of authors who create literary works. This view maintains that an author's successfully realized intentions determine a text's meaning. Authorial intentions, if successfully executed, are publicly manifest in the work. The meaning of a literary work can be ambiguous or multilayered, but this is usually because the author purposefully intended the text to be read in this way. The intentions behind a literary work need not have been consciously present in the author's mind when he or she wrote the text. Moreover, an author might have difficulty articulating a work's main intentions, if asked, just as people often have difficulty in describing what they did in performing a familiar, yet complex, action.

Many literary critics seek to recover, explain, and clarify something about the author's intentions in literary texts. Critics often focus directly on investigating how the author wrote and revised a work, the circumstances under which a text was published and initially received by critics and readers, the author's reading and education relevant to a work, comments the author has made about a work (i.e., letters, journals, diaries, recorded conversations), relationships between aspects of a work and details of the author's life, relationships between aspects of a work and the author's other work, and the historical, political, social, and cultural contexts that, although beyond the author's control, are channeled through the author into a work. All these factors fall under the general heading of a concern with authors and their subjective, communicative intentions.

A good example of how concern with an author's biography, and possible subjective intentions, might influence literary interpretation is seen in one examination of part of a poem by the eighteenth-century poet John Keats.[9] Consider the final lines of Keats's "Ode on a Grecian Urn":

> "Beauty is truth, truth beauty," that is all
> Ye know on earth, and all ye need to know.

Critics have sought to explicate how these lines reflect Keat's philosophy about the relationship between beauty and truth, and more generally the equation of art with life. But literary theorist John Stillinger suggests that Keats may have not had any particular philosophical idea when he penned these lines. Keats wrote very extemporaneously. As Keats once wrote: "If poetry comes not naturally as the Leaves to a tree, it had better not come at all."[10] In this light, Stillinger argues that it makes little sense to assume that Keats had some deeper philosophical intention motivating this, and many other, poems. This doesn't imply that Keats has no intentions in writing these lines, only that his spontaneous working style, as evident from biographical sources, precludes the possibility that his poem was the product of serious philosophical thought. The poet Samuel Coleridge, who wrote great works such as *The Rime of the Ancient Mariner*, on the other hand, often composed many drafts of each poem, with each draft revealing quite specific, and different, authorial intentions. The final draft of Coleridge's poems are not necessarily the only versions that require our critical attention.

Consider now a different example of how knowing something about an author informs readers' understanding of literature. Anne Sexton became a poet in the early 1960s after having experienced the traditional woman's roles of wife, mother, and housewife. After a psychotic breakdown, Sexton's psychotherapist encouraged her to write. Sexton remembered: "Don't kill yourself," he said. "Your poems might mean something to someone else someday." "That gave me a feeling of purpose, a little cause, something to do with my life, no matter how rotten I was." As Sexton became a well-known poet, one of her therapists criticized her for putting her poetry before her daughter. Sexton responded: "The writing comes first. This is my way of mastering experience."[11]

Most of Sexton's work directly reflected her varied experiences as a woman. For instance, the poem "Live," from her third book, *Live or Die*, shows Sexton trying to locate the source and reason for life given her situation, experience, and identity. Here are the opening lines from that poem:[12]

> Today life opened inside me like an egg
> and there inside
> after considerable digging
> I found the answer.
> What a bargain!

> There was the sun,
> her yolk moving feverishly,
> tumbling her prize –
> and you realize that she does this daily!
> I'd known she was a purifier
> but I hadn't thought
> she was solid,
> hadn't known she was an answer.

Sexton's words illustrate how life materializes from inside herself, spiritually as well as physically. The *sun* inside her is what she must deliver, give birth to, and make an extension of her very body. Sexton continues in the poem:

> So I won't hang around in my hospital shift,
> repeating the Black Mass and all of it.
> I say Live, Live because of the sun,
> the dream, the excitable gift.

Sexton's *excitable gift* is her poetry, and the act of writing allows her to understand her experience. Sexton's intention in this poem seems evident. Unlike most male "confessional" poets, who tend to abstract or generalize upon their experiences, and for whom the idea of "persona" in their work separates the poet from the speaker of a poem, Sexton wrote to bridge the gap between the poet and the narrator of her poetry. Reading Sexton's work gives an intimate portrait of how her own identity, her particular communicative intentions as a real person, Anne Sexton, became part of her poetical meaning. Knowing something about Sexton the person defines our experience of Sexton the writer.

Of course, there are always problems associated with judging people from the work they do. Even though people like Anne Sexton may try to express themselves through their writing, music, acting, or art, their works must largely stand on their own. An insensitive, immature person may produce a magnificent novel. An otherwise sensitive, mature person may create trite poetry. A philosopher or poet may celebrate humanity in his or her work yet appear to all the world as a misanthrope. Anne Sexton certainly gave direct evidence of herself in her poetry, and to some, including Sexton herself, the poetry provides the most accurate image of the "real" Anne Sexton. But as psychiatrist Arnold M. Ludwig asks: "Who is to say that Anne Sexton, the housewife and mother, is any less real than Anne Sexton, the poet, just because she believes herself to be and doesn't feel completely comfortable in those roles?"[13]

Despite the appeal to authors and their biographies in asking and answering many questions about literary interpretation, scholars must be especially careful not to confuse the idea that all textual meaning reflects something about an author's beliefs and intentions, with the more dubious claim that the meaning of a text is identical with the author's conscious or communicative intentions. An author's writing might very well fail to express what the author intended it to mean. It is almost impossible for authors to write in such a way that all of their intentions will be transparent to all readers. At the same time, authors don't necessarily intend to communicate only unambiguous meanings in their texts. Many authors also intend to achieve various aesthetic goals some of which are best met by leaving certain messages unclear. For instance, consider the enduring controversies surrounding the meaning of Henry James's *The Turn of the Screw*. Two interpretations have now become standard. One suggests that the story's protagonist, the governess, sees and engages in battle with real ghosts. A second reading is that the "ghosts" are only projections of the governess's mind. Are these two interpretation incompatible? One possibility is that it was James's particular intention to show the multitude of interpretations that any text, even in any individual speech act, can be given.[14] Moreover, it is not always reasonable to ascribe a single intention to the author of a literary work. Literary works are generally produced over a period of time, and it is unlikely that the complex structure of goals and intentions that motivate the final text remain perfectly consistent throughout the writing process. This is similar to how speaker's intentions may change in the course of a conversation (see Chapters 3 and 5).

Subjective intentionalism is closest in spirit to the traditional view in cognitive science that linguistic understanding is ultimately aimed at recovering what a speaker or writer intended to communicate. None of this implies in the case of literary criticism that readers should always defer to the author's subjective intentions, or to what authors say about their works, in determining the ultimate value of a literary text. What an author intends to communicate may only provide a springboard for the potentially endless future interpretations of a literary work. Just as in the case of interpreting spoken language and expository texts, people may infer meanings that are only weakly tied to an author's communicative intentions. Yet the most interesting cases of readers inferring meanings that differ from what authors intend may arise precisely when an author has complex, sophisticated communicative intentions. For instance, folks tales and romance novels may evoke a range of interpretations. But these forms of literature don't express the range of meanings found in a Shakespeare or an Ionesco play, in Eliot's *The Waste Land*, or in a Henry James novel. The author's intentional purpose to design a text in particular ways so as to create complex meanings is exactly what readers exploit in constructing their own interpretations of what is written. Thus, readers' reactions to literary texts are still in significant ways rooted in their understandings of authorial meanings.[15]

NEW CRITICISM

The idea that literary criticism should take place apart from reference to authors' lives and subjective intentions has a long history. Back in 1869, fifty years before the open debates between biographical or historical scholars and explicative critics, the critic Alexander Bain complained in *The Fortnightly Review*: "But when a man gets into literary criticism at large, the temptation to deviate into matters that have no value for the predominating end of a teacher of English, is far beyond the lure of alcohol, tobacco, or any sensual stimulation. He runs into digressions on the life, the character, the likings and dislikings, the quarrels and friendships of his authors..."[16]

The New Critics in the 1930s through 1950s revived this idea and argued for a fundamental separation of subject and object (reader and text), rendering the literary text separate from both its historical context and its readers. New Criticism reached its zenith with the publication in 1946 of W. Wimsatt and Monroe Beardsley's famous essay on the "Intentional Fallacy."[17] The fallacy was usually taken to suggest that the original "design or intention of the author" is not the appropriate standard for either judging the literary merit of a text or determining anything about the formal characteristics of a work.

What anti-intentionalists, like the New Critics, disputed is the specific idea that intentions are a necessary or even a relevant aspect of the context of production in which a text may justifiably be situated. Intentions may be relevant to what an artist was trying to do, but they are not always indicative of what the artist has actually done in making a work. Once completed, literary works have a life independent of their authors. Authorial pronouncements are interesting, but authors can be mistaken in the interpretations they offer, and they may have more difficulty in reporting their intentions clearly than they had expressing their intentions in the work. In the twentieth century, many writers and critics have urged that textual criticism be insulated from the study of authors' lives. As the poet T. S. Eliot commented: "The method is to take well-known poems ... without reference to the author or to his other works, analyze it stanza by stanza and line by line, and extract, squeeze, tease, press every drop of meaning out of it that one can. It might be called the lemon-squeezer school of criticism."[18]

The literary critic Jane Thompkins recently described her graduate school years at Yale, a bastion for New Criticism in the 1950s, in terms of the limits New Criticism placed on her scholarly work:

> My dissertation, on Melville's prose style, exemplified a kind of work we did. A chapter would begin with a long quotation from one of Melville's novels and, through painstaking analysis of its word choice and sentence structure, would derive the author's worldview at the time he wrote it. I couldn't say "the author" or "Melville"; I had to say "the narrator," because equating the author with anything he wrote was considered naive, an example of "the genetic fallacy," which reduced a literary work to its conditions

of origin. Nor could I ever say anything about how the language made me feel (though that was my whole reason for writing on the topic), because that would have been to commit "the affective fallacy," confusing a literary work with its effects.[19]

What an author, like Melville, actually intended in creating a piece of literature was clearly not worthy of scholarly consideration unless one was interested in inferring something about the author of a text. But as New Critical theorists have always maintained, biography is not equivalent to literary interpretation, which should always focus on the meanings of texts, not on the people who wrote them.

A full reading of the New Critical ideology in the 1940s and 1950s reveals that New Critics denied neither that texts have authors, that authors have intentions, nor that readers should be interested in those intentions. New Critics only demanded that whatever an author's announced intent, or presumed attitude at the time of writing the text, that readers and critics should not confuse the author's subjective intent with the intent actually expressed by a text. Wimsatt wrote in 1968 that "What we meant in 1945, and what in effect I think we managed to say, was that the closest one could ever get to the artist's intending or meaning mind, outside his work, would still be short of his effective intention or operative mind as it appears in the work itself and can be read from the work."[20]

The construction of the *effective intention* or verifiable intent of authors was the goal of interpretation, not the reconstruction of what actually had been in the author's mind at the time he or she composed the text. This denial of an author's subjective intentions received the official support of the Modern Language Association in 1963 when the eminent literary critic Northrup Frye repeated in an MLA-sponsored essay:

> We have to avoid the blunder that is called the intentional fallacy in criticism. The question "what did the author mean by this?" is always illegitimate. First, we can never know; second, there is no reason to suppose that the author knew; third, the question confuses imaginative with discursive writing. The legitimate form of the question is "what does the text say?"[21]

New Critics often worry that allowing extratextual material about an author's intention into the task of interpretation will make literature less important than the other material, such as information about the lives of authors like John Keats and Anne Sexton. But why should evidence from external sources, such as the author's biography or what the author says about a work, be excluded from consideration in literary interpretation? If critics can rely on an author's other literary texts in interpreting a single piece of artwork, why can't other texts assist literary interpretation, such as an author's nonfiction work, autobiographical material, or any other statement by an author about the purpose of his or her writing? For instance, why can't Henry James's nonfiction work *English Hours* be used to interpret his novel *The Turn of the Screw*? Why can't biographical material about Anne Sexton be recognized as part of the context for interpreting aspects of her poetry? Why can't Amy Tam's statements about her intentions in writing *The Joy Luck Club* at least be considered in thinking about her novel?

Denying these possibilities goes against people's fundamental disposition to use their knowledge of a speaker or author in immediately drawing certain inferences about the meaning of an utterance or text. New Critics may deny the importance of biographical material in literary criticism, but they can't ignore the constraining presence of fundamental cognitive processes aimed at – momentarily, at any rate – constructing interpretations based on what some intentional agent might have intended when creating a literary work. Again, none of this implies that a text's only meaning is connected with what an author had in mind when producing the text. The cognitive intentionalist premise only suggests that appeal to an author's possible communicative intentions is part of what happens when anyone attempts to make sense of human language.

Another way that New Critics, and others, argue against intentionalism is by saying that readers can easily comprehend what an utterance means simply by appealing to the context in which that utterance appears. Yet our understanding of context itself requires some understanding of the author's intention. Context is not something that is simply there in any objective sense, apart from some determining action on the part of the author or the reader. Readers must infer something about what an author intends to communicate more generally in a text as part of interpreting what any single utterance in the text might mean.

THE INTENTIONALIST BACKLASH

In the 1960s a significant backlash emerged against the strict views of New Criticism and its advocacy of the intentionalist fallacy. This movement arose partly because of the influence of analytic philosophers' theories of meaning in terms of intentions and speech acts.[22] The literary theorist and critic E. D. Hirsch argued that a text has to represent someone's meaning and that no adequate proposal exists for judging the validity of an interpretation unless the author's literary intentions are taken into account. Even without independent evidence of authorial meaning, such as from biographical material, the proper task of literary interpretation is to analyze textual meaning, not for its own sake, but for the authorial meaning it discloses. A word sequence means nothing in particular unless either somebody means something by it, or someone understands something.

Hirsch acknowledged that in searching for authorial intentions, readers should not seek the actual explicit thoughts of the real author while composing the text. Authorial intentions must be tied to public, shareable meanings as evident in the text itself. Seeking authors' intentions in this way places important limitations on the scholarly practice of literary interpretation. Authorial intentions provide the main criterion for textual interpretation that enables literary analysis to be objective. Readers should begin by positing a genre for a particular work (e.g., scientific prose, lyric poetry, a novel, an epic play) and use this as a general framework for interpreting the author's typical meanings. Even though authorial intentions are not the only possible norm of interpretation, they provide the only practical norm for a cognitive discipline of interpretation. Without consideration of authorial intentions, there is simply too much indeterminacy and instability in the public linguistic conventions governing meaning and no stable object for literary study and criticism.[23]

Philosopher P. Juhl went further than Hirsch by insisting that all interpretation logically implies authorial meaning.

> In speaking of what an author intended to convey by his work, I do not mean what he planned to write or convey. Nor am I using the term 'intention' in the broader sense of 'motive' in which it may include, for example, his desire to achieve fame or other causal factors.... Rather I am using the term in the sense of an author's intention in writing a certain sequence of words – in the sense, that is, of what he meant by the words he used.[24]

More recently, literary and cultural scholars have restored the critical dimension of the author to interpretive practice in a different way by embracing historicist, Marxist, Frankfurt school, feminist, and postcolonial frameworks.[25] These critics view an author's work in relation to the social, economic, political, and gendered contexts in which the literary text was written. For instance, one critic introduced new historicism in the following manner: "The writing and reading of texts, as well as the processes by which they are circulated and categorized, analyzed and taught, are now being construed as historically determined and determining modes of work. What have often been taken to be self-contained aesthetic and academic issues are now seen as inextricably linked to other social discourses, practices, and institutions ..."[26] For instance, Stephen Greenblatt, an influential literary critic, says of Shakespeare: "Shakespeare became the presiding genius of a popular, urban art form with the capacity to foster psychic mobility in the service of Elizabethan power.... [he] approaches his culture not, like Marlowe, as rebel and blasphemer, but rather as dutiful servant." Greenblatt also writes about Spenser: "Spenser worships power.... [and] is our preeminent poet of empire," and his writings are "not achieved in spite of what is for us a repellent political ideology – the passionate worship of imperialism – but are inseparably linked to that ideology."[27]

Feminist literary critics have engaged in similar kinds of explorations about the social and political contexts for women's writings. Sandra Gilbert and Susan Gubar's *The Madwoman in the Attic*, for example, describes how great nineteenth-century writers, such as Jane Austen, the Brontes, George Eliot, Mary Shelley, and others, had to struggle against "patriarchal poetics" and "patriarchal poetry" in their writing.[28] Gilbert has commented about feminist criticism, "Most feminist critics speak...like people who must bear witness, people who must enact and express in their own lives and words the revisionary discovery that the experiences of women in and with literature are different from those of men."[29] Who the author is, what she has experienced and brought to her writing, is a central part of feminist reading and criticism.

Unlike the New Critic's approach, feminist, ethnic, and historicist scholars maintain that literary criticism takes place at the moment readers become critically aware of the social, psychological, and political forces that influence authors, the texts they write, and what these texts signify in broader sociopolitical contexts.

The intentionalist backlash correctly reestablishes a role for authorial intentions in the interpretation of literature. Recent advances in literary and cultural studies, mentioned above, also note the clear significance of social, political, and gender contexts in understanding what is important about textual meaning. In both ways, the intentionalist backlash has links to the cognitive science research discussed in Parts II and III. Nonetheless, devoted intentionalists, like Hirsch and Juhl, mistakenly adhere to the idea of objective interpretation through appeal to public, shareable conventions of meaning located in texts. These scholars underestimate the radical indeterminacy of linguistic conventions and fail to acknowledge the power that real authors have on contemporary reading practices. Advocates of feminist, historicist and postcolonial perspectives have provided some wonderful, although empirically speculative, ideas about how literary criticism can illuminate hidden forces at work in the creation of texts. Yet in some cases, these scholars don't demonstrate how these hidden forces might be tied to more fundamental cognitive processes that motivate authors' creating texts in the ways that they do. I'm not sure how feasible it is to expect such linkages to be established given the differing skills, and interests, of humanists and cognitive scientists. But one step is to explicitly acknowledge that a real author's conscious and unconscious mind constitutes an important guide force to the meanings attributed to literary texts.

POSTSTRUCTURALIST VIEWS

In the 1960s and 1970s several philosophers and literary critics declared their own interest in the intentional fallacy. Poststructuralists announced the "death of the author" as a precondition for the desired "birth of the reader" in literary criticism.[30] Roland Barthes dismissed the possible "presence" of the author in a text (the doctrine of the "death of the author"). Though authors may think they know what they intend, their thought and language are at the mercy of socioeconomic, psychological, and historical forces that cause them to mean something other than what they frequently intend. This blindness makes authors' intentions far less interesting than the operation of these external forces as revealed in their work.[31]

These poststructuralist arguments on the death of the author in literary criticism go beyond the hermeneutic claim that a text can acquire new meanings once it has been freed from authorial control. Poststructuralists, more specifically deconstructionists such as Jacques Derrida, argue that a text must from the very beginning be free from an author's intentions. Deconstruction doesn't demand a complete disregard for authorial intentions. For instance, in his reading of Rousseau's texts, Derrida appears to construct interpretations that Rousseau "himself could scarcely have been brought to entertain."[32]

Yet Derrida is not ignoring Rousseau's intentions as much as arguing that understanding of what a text can mean often requires seeing how it says something other than its specified intent. As evident in his infamous debates with John Searle, Derrida doesn't deny that language possesses intentional meaning. Instead, Derrida emphatically rejects the idea that philosophy can specify the rules for explaining how any text can mean. Theories of meaning, or of specific textual readings, must not not imply "either that I fully understand what the other says, writes, meant to say or write, or even that he intended to say or write in full what remains to be read, or above all that any adequation need obtain between what he consciously intended, what he did, and what I do while 'reading'."[33]

For deconstructionist critics, there is a break that "intervenes from the moment that there is a mark" on the paper, a mark that once there achieves meaning independent of authorial intentions through its "iterability," or its place in the web of all texts past and present. Conventions of meaning are irrelevant and attempts to determine an author's original intention are hopeless. As philosopher Michel Foucault maintained, authors should not be recognized as "genuine," but as "idealized product(s)."[34] Foucault promoted the idea of "anonymous discourse." He wrote: "Discourse is not the majestically unfolding manifestation of a thinking, knowing, speaking subject."[35] Furthermore, "The analysis of statements operates therefore without reference to a cognito. It does not pose the question of the speaking subject, who reveals or conceals himself in what he says, who, in speaking, exercises his sovereign freedom, or who, without realizing it, subjects himself to constraints of which he is only dimly aware. In fact, it is situated at the level of "it is said."[36] It is not accidental that current efforts to question the author have coincided with the collapse of the boundaries between criticism and literature. Formerly, when the author of a literary work was viewed as uniquely empowered and self-expressive, criticism and the critic could do no more than elucidate what some author intended. In a poststructuralist literary world, poems, literature *and* critical commentary share the same status as texts.

The possibility that there may be no legitimate, agreed-upon method for the critical interpretation of texts, and that every interpretation is itself a misinterpretation, has shaken the foundations of many humanistic disciplines. Many scholars who find poststructuralist theory unsatisfying have charged critics such as Barthes and Derrida with, consciously or unconsciously, attempting to dethrone the author. Descartes' notion of the self or subject as the source of knowledge and hence of broader social and cultural meanings, has been accepted in Western intellectual thought. It seems obvious that people are autonomous individuals, possessed of subjectivity or consciousness, which is the source of their beliefs and actions. However, scholars in many disciplines now question this assumption and have begun to raise fears about the impossibility of knowledge in the humanities and social sciences. In this way, the "author-be-damned" attitude of many poststructuralist literary critics and philosophers goes to the heart of what most positivist theorists hold dear when they make assertions about truth, meaning, and objective knowledge.

By subjecting a text (poem, play, or story) to detailed scrutiny, Barthes, for instance, "deconstructs" the world of a text, discovering a maze of endlessly shifting signs and signifiers, rather than viewing the text as a discrete and hermetically sealed object. In his book *S/Z*, for example, Barthes explores a simple story entitled "Sarrasine," by Balzac, with incredible attention to the multiplicity of meanings constituted by the text. For instance, consider Barthes's interpretation of two sentences presented near the beginning of the story:[37]

Midnight had just sounded from the clock of the Elysee-Bourbon. "A metonymy leads from the Elysee-Bourbon to the same *Wealth*, since the Faubourg Saint-Honore is a wealthy neighborhood. This wealth is itself connoted: a neighborhood of *nouveaux riches*, the Faubourg Saint-Honore refers by synecdoche to the Paris of the Bourbon Restoration, a mythic place of sudden fortunes whose origins are suspect; where gold is produced without an origin, diabolically (the symbolic definition of speculation)."

Seated in a window recess "The development of the antithesis normally includes the exposition of each of its parts (A, B). A third term is possible: a joint presentation. This term can be purely rhetorical, if we are concerned to *introduce* or *summarize* the antithesis; but it can also be literal; if we are concerned to denote the physical conjunction of antithetical sites: a function which here devolves upon *recess*, an intermediate place between garden and salon, death and life."

and hidden behind the sinuous folds of silk curtain "Hiding place: to be hidden."

I could contemplate at my leisure the garden of the mansion where I was spending the evening. "*I could contemplate* means I am going to describe. The first term of the antithesis (garden) is introduced here from a rhetorical viewpoint: there is a manipulation of the discourse, not of the story...We may note here, to return to it later, that *contemplation* a visual posture, the arbitrary delimitation of a field of observation (the *templun* of the augurs), relates the whole description to the model of painting."

Barthes continues on in this way to expound on the entire story in 561 numbered fragments, interspersed with 93 divagations, or meditations on Barthes's reading of the text, and on reading in general. As literary theorist Jay Parini describes it, according to the deconstructionists "meaning must be allowed to radiate in progressively widening circles like the concentric waves emanating from a stone tossed into the center of a pond. The deconstructionists seem to ride even the most distant waves without fear of losing sight of the original splash."[38]

Despite the forceful onslaught of these poststructuralist doctrines, many literary theorists are reluctant to completely abandon the idea that texts mean what authors intend for them to mean. Many philosophers and literary critics dismiss poststructuralist theory for its lack of seriousness, partly because of its advocates' playful, opaque style of argumentation.[39] Other literary scholars argue that a theory of interpretation must provide some basis for assessing what readings or interpretations of a text can be defeasible in principle. But as critic Michael Barnes notes: "if all meanings are equally useful, if all parts of the intertextual play of language are valid, then all interpretations are essentially indefeasible, none are false, none are true."[40] Even deconstructionist theorist Paul de Man recognizes that intentionalism is built into the very structure of language. He writes: "Even if we free ourselves of all false questions of intent and rightfully reduce the narrator to the status of a mere grammatical pronoun, without which the narration could not have come into being, the subject remains endowed with a function that is not grammatical but rhetorical."[41] DeMan admitted that the origins of texts reappear whenever a person reads and analyzes what texts could possibly mean.

A more serious problem for deconstructionist literary critics lies in their blindness to their own cognitive processes. When critics deconstruct a text, they start their analyses with some interpretation of what the text means before overturning, or dissembling, the possible ways that a text could have meaning. Part of the foundation for their initial analyses might very well be based on their tacit understandings of authorial intentions (as noted in Parts II and III). Cognitive science studies clearly demonstrate that people draw immediate inferences about authorial intentions in reading. These findings suggest that deconstructionist critics may very well be unconsciously analyzing something about authorial intentions as part of their immediate comprehension of textual meaning before engaging in more elaborate, conscious interpretation processes. Thus, authorial intentions play some role in how literary texts are understood and analyzed, even by critics who proclaim the "death of the author." Although certainty in recovering intentions may be unachievable, this does not mean, contrary to Derrida, that intentions are "in principle inaccessible."[42] Furthermore, intertextual considerations, which deconstructionists argue arise autonomously, might better be understood as built by readers given their own intertextual experiences (i.e., their reading of other texts). Meaningful experience is tied to the socially embedded cognitive reality of people writing, reading, and arguing about texts, not in some ethereal world of textuality apart from the people who create and use texts.

READER-RESPONSE CRITICISM

In the 1970s, a growing number of literary critics started acknowledging "the role of the reader" in text criticism.[43] Many of these scholars concluded that it is impossible to define "literariness" or "poeticity" solely on the basis of textual properties, or in terms of what authors specifically intend to express by their writings. Readers rarely limit themselves to understanding authorial meaning, so these theorists claim, nor should they. A text can never be said to have a single meaning: "The interpreter's task should be to elucidate the potential meanings of a text, and not to restrict himself to just one."[44] Readers respond to associations resulting from quite personal experiences; they compare fictional characters to people they know; they mentally file bits of information, phrasing, tropes, or arguments for future use in other contexts; they ask themselves, not about what authors may be expressing, but how the author could have held the worldview expressed in the text; and readers experience aesthetic or emotional pleasure (or the opposite) in the manner in which ideas are expressed in texts.

A good demonstration of reader-response criticism is given by the literary theorist and critic Stanley Fish in his essay "How to Recognize a Poem When You See One."[45] Fish presented a class of college students with a list of names (of linguistic and literary scholars) on the blackboard (left over from an assignment for a previous class), and told his students it was a religious poem which they should interpret. The students, who had been studying seventeenth-century religious English poetry for some time, started to note all sorts of structural and semantic regularities and began to generate biblical inferences in order to establish poetic coherence. According to Fish, this demonstrated that meaning and literariness are not textual properties, but interpretive constructions: "It is not that the presence of poetic qualities compels a certain kind of attention but that the paying of a certain kind of attention results in the emergence of poetic qualities."[46] Readers are socialized in certain interpretive communities in which certain conventions prevail (e.g., that a poem is a text containing repetitive patterns and hidden ambiguities).[47] Any social group may have in its own criteria for what counts as acceptable interpretations of text.[48] For instance, different religious communities have their own conventions for interpreting religious texts that constitute certain boundaries of acceptable meaning. Similarly, different schools of literary criticism adopt certain conventions for what they believe constitutes acceptable or intelligent interpretation. Yet what is most significant in how any text is to be interpreted, is not what the author demands, but what interpretive norms exist for a particular linguistic community at a particular moment of time.

Some empirical research has supported the claim that different communities embrace different interpretive strategies for literary texts. For example, readers' interpretation of the Hungarian novel *The Notebook* by Agota Kristof were similar for readers within a country, but different across countries.[49] French readers, who emphasize the psychology of characters, tended to see the novel's conclusion as representing people's maturation, their growing up, but German readers saw the story's ending in a more abstract fashion as representing the end of an epoch. These results are not surprising given that French and German readers belong to different "interpretive communities." Several other lines of experimental research also demonstrate how particular cultural and religious groups interpret texts differently according to culturally specific schemata (their particular knowledge and beliefs).[50]

From the cognitive intentionalist perspective, the reader-response view has much to offer. Readers are clearly influenced by existing community norms, just as authors are sensitive to these norms in creating expository and literary texts. Yet readers' sensitivity to social norms, and their recognition that authors also adhere to particular norms in different communities, is exactly why consideration of authorial intentions is a critical part of literary interpretation. Along with several other views discussed in this chapter, the reader-response view undervalues some of the greater complexities, including fundamental cognitive processes, involved in the creation and interpretation of literature.

THE INTENTIONS-ARE-EVERYTHING VIEW

After the prominent rise of deconstructionist and reader-response scholars of criticism, a radical defense of intentionalism was offered by literary scholars Steven Knapp and Walter Michaels.

They argued that literary meanings are always intentional and that "what a text means and what the author intends it to mean are identical."[51] This position "against theory" rejects the idea that the goal of literary theory is to provide an objectively valid method of literary interpretation. Instead of grounding the meaning of texts in authorial intentions, where intentions provide the hidden basis for meaning, the "against theory" view denies that there is any dualism between meaning and intention. There is no theoretical need for literary critics to "get back to" authorial intentions (the subjective intentionalism view) or to justify disregard for authorial intentions (the New Criticism and deconstructionist views), for the meanings of texts are and always will be identical to what authors intend.

The role that authorial intentions play (or don't play) in literary comprehension can be illustrated by the following scenario:[52] Imagine that you're walking along a deserted beach and you come upon a curious sequence of squiggles in the sand. You step back a few paces and notice that they spell out the following words: *The soul is a rope that binds heaven and earth.*

Most people recognize the squiggles as writing and understand what the words mean without knowing anything about the author or even without connecting the presence of the words to any notion of an author. The metaphorical comparison between *the soul* and *rope* makes sense without thinking of anyone's possible intention in writing this phrase. But now imagine that, as you are staring at this pattern in the sand, a wave washes up and recedes, leaving in its wake the following: *Ecstasy is a song-bird swarm beating its wings.*

It would be difficult to witness this event and still dismiss the question of intention. People feel compelled to explain what they have just seen. Are the marks in the sand produced by some mechanical device under the control of a poet hidden from the viewer; or are these squiggles in the sand mere accidents that can best be attributed to some unknown geological process of erosion produced by waves crashing on the shore? Consider the two possibilities. If the sand metaphors were written by some unknown person, then our reading of the metaphor might take into account the poet's literary intentions. On the other hand, if the metaphors were created by geological accident, our interpretations of these expressions might be quite different.[53]

This example might seem farfetched, if only because people seldom wonder whether the ocean is an intentional agent. But people also rarely acknowledge or question the presence of speakers' or writers' intentions in their understanding of metaphors like *The soul is a rope that binds heaven and earth*. Knapp and Michaels state that once it is recognized that the meaning of a text is simply identical to the author's intended meaning, the interpretive project of grounding meaning in intentions becomes incoherent. They argue that some scholars' desires to define textual meaning in terms of authorial intentions is misguided, because it assumes that looking for one thing (the authorial intentions) somehow provides objective criteria for seeking the other (the textual meaning). Yet this assumes that indeterminate textual meaning is recognized before our understanding of authorial intentions come into play to resolve this indeterminacy of meaning. But meaning and interpretation are inseparable – there is no meaning without interpretation. For instance, for people to recognize *My car ran out of gas* as a meaningful sentence, they must already have posited a speaker who has a specific intention. Determining the intention of any sentence does not require that readers add a speaker or author, but rather that they decide which person, among a range of possible ones, is speaking.

Despite their advocacy of intentionalism, Knapp and Michaels claim that intentionalism is methodologically useless because it gives scholars no help in deciding between competing interpretations of any text. Many anti-intentionalists, such as the New Critics and deconstructionists, confuse the activity of self-consciously arguing about intentions with the activity of assuming intentions – not a specific one, but just the unavoidable fact of one. This is a very important point. Too many debates about authorial intentions in literary criticism assume that consideration of a person's intentions is only a conscious activity. But critics of intentionalism ignore the possibility that readers tacitly assume that meaning is the product of an intentional agent, an assumption that shapes how texts are presumed to be understood and appreciated. Knapp and Michaels's thesis that interpretation always and necessarily involves the specification of intention does not grant priority and authority to the author, at least in terms of what the author says about his or her communicative intentions. Authors are in no more privileged relation to their own intentions than anyone else.

It is hard not to sympathize with the rehabilitation of intention as an inescapably relevant factor in literary interpretation. However, the "against theory" defense of intentionalism confuses the seemingly incontrovertible assertion that all linguistic or textual meaning is intentional with the very debatable assertion that the meaning of a text is identical to the author's intention or intended meaning. Simplistically conflating textual meaning with authorially intended meaning precludes the possibility that someone's speech or writing might *fail* to mean what it intended. Readers can still identify textual meaning with intention or intended meaning in the sense that there can be no linguistic meaning without a background of human intentionality, no "possibility of language prior to and independent of intention."[54] Scholars can even hold that every individual linguistic text requires some particular intention for its meaning. However, even if scholars deny that there can be intentionless meanings – that is, even if they accept the premise that texts regarded as intentionless are also meaningless – it still does not follow that "the meaning of the text is simply identical to the author's intended meaning."[55] All that follows is that the meaning of a text is inseparable from *some intention or another*.

Much of the research in Part III highlights the important possibility that readers (and listeners) often draw unauthorized inferences, meanings that go beyond what a writer (or speaker) intended to communicate. These inferences about unintentional meaning, in many cases, are linked to authorial intentions in significant ways. The intentions-are-everything view recognizes some of the cognitive nuances in how readers experience texts as meaningful, but fails to see that certain meaningful inferences clearly extend beyond what authors intended (or had explicitly in mind).

HYPOTHETICAL INTENTIONALISM

A recent proposal about intentions and literary interpretation is that a literary work does not mean (even in part) what an author specifically intended. What a work means is expressed by a *hypothetical intention* (i.e., a complex intention that a member of the intended or an ideal audience would be most justified in ascribing to the work).[56] The meaning of a text is generated by hypothesizing intentions authors might have had, given the context of creation, rather than relying on, or trying to seek out, the author's subjective intentions. Readers' interpretations of texts depend on their inferences about a hypothetical author founded in the linguistic conventions and artistic practices at the time the author wrote the work, as well as in publicly available knowledge of how the text was created. A work might display a multiplicity of meanings given the large set of intentions readers can hypothesize about an author and the conditions under which a work was written. This multiplicity of meanings is perfectly appropriate to propose even if the actual author intended only a single interpretation for a text.

A good illustration of the hypothetical-intentionalist perspective is provided by philosopher Jerrold Levinson in his discussion of Franz Kafka's "A Country Doctor."[57] Kafka's story describes a country doctor who is summoned in the middle of the night to care for a boy who has suffered a terrible wound. But the doctor leaves his house in a precarious situation as his servant, Rose, is now at the mercy of a menacing groom. Although the boy is beyond help, the doctor decides to attempt an unusual cure by getting into bed with the patient. As the doctor lies there, he finds it impossible to leave the boy despite his fears that his home might be destroyed by the servant and groom while he treats his patient.

Levinson suggests that background knowledge about Kafka is relevant to a reading of this story. Among the most important facts are the following: Kafka regularly worked at night; Kafka viewed his writing as "medicinal," "therapeutic," and "a calling"; Kafka did not separate his writing and his life; Kafka was familiar with Freud's classic book *Interpretation of Dreams*; and a later story by Kafka, "A Hunger Artist," is about a man who starves himself publically as both an artistic performance and an admission that ordinary food had no appeal for him.

With this background information, Levinson presented the following interpretation of Kafka's "A Country Doctor": The story is a dream report reflecting the conflict between ordinary, sensual life, as represented by the servant girl Rose and the doctor's comfortable home, and his calling to heal others through the practice of medicine. The doctor is actually an artist, something Kafka later wrote about more transparently in his story "A Hunger Artist." The doctor is in a bind, caught between the wounded boy and his domestic problems, just as Kafka was caught between his literary and domestic responsibilities. Finally, the sick boy is like the doctor's younger self; only through art can one first try to heal oneself, and only secondarily to heal others.

Levinson's brief interpretation provided his best informed reading of what Kafka was intending to communicate in writing "A Country Doctor." Even if someone later discovered from reading Kafka's secret diary, or from talking with some close friends of his, that Kafka's explicit intent in writing "A Country Doctor" was to criticize rural medical practices or to expose the ignorance of the Czech peasantry, these interpretations aren't supported by the text. A critical reading of what Kafka the writer was communicating in "A Country Doctor," given the available evidence, would not be superceeded by what Kafka the person might really have intended to mean when he composed the story.

There are several advantages that hypothetical intentionalism has over other intentionalist (subjective intentionalism and intentions-are-everything) and anti-intentionalist (New Critical and deconstructionist) views of literary interpretation. First, the idea of hypothesized authorial intentions can only be extended to take into account discoverable, unintended meanings that readers can reasonably ascribe to the author as a member of a class by virtue of his or her association with a particular literary tradition. Second, a broader concept of authors' hypothesized intended meanings can show how some meanings are justified with respect to a given historical period, because they are rooted abstractly in the consciousness of the historically constructed author, even if they may not be ascribable to the actual author. Most generally, understanding the meaning of a text especially in cases where several equally reasonable interpretations are available is not, and should not be, limited by what the author personally intended. But an audience can construct its best contextually informed hypothesis of authorial intentions for a given text in light of what is known about the author, the author's background, and the historical and cultural conditions under which the work was created.[58] Doing so puts readers in the best position to interpret any literary work in the context of the particular historically and culturally embedded author.[59]

DEPARTING FROM AUTHORIAL INTENTIONS

My review of several main trends in recent literary theory suggests that viewing literary interpretation as reconstruction of the author's subjective intentions does not prompt us to ask various questions about what a text does, how a text relates to other texts, how a text conceals and represses, how a text assumes and takes for granted certain ideas, and how a text advances or raises complications for long-standing assumptions about literature. It is exactly these sorts of questions that most modern critics find interesting. Some scholars, like Umberto Eco, want to find ways of limiting the range of admissible interpretations of texts so that some readings can be widely recognized, and rejected, as "overinterpretations."[60] For instance, is it possible to define which readings of Kafka's story "A Country Doctor" are implausible in almost any context?

Eco argued that debates in contemporary theory reflect familiar themes in Western intellectual history that express disdain for apparent meanings. People can often recognize overinterpretations of a text without necessarily being able to prove that one interpretation is the right one, or must be the only defeasible reading. Critics might say that any interpretation of a text is a bad one, because different public criteria can, and should, be brought to bear in making such a determination. According to Eco, the aim of a text must be to produce the "model reader"; that is, a reader who interprets a text as it was designed to be read (and this includes the possibility of the text being read with multiple interpretations). The "empirical reader" is a reader who makes conjectures about the kind of "model reader" postulated by the text. Readers interpreting empirical authors do not speculate about the author's intentions, but restrict their understandings to the text's intentions. Eco provides no specific rules for limiting interpretation, but he advances the idea that certain interpretations of texts prove themselves over time to the satisfaction of a relevant community.

Empirical authors may be able, at times, to rule out certain interpretations. Even Eco agreed that making an inference about the empirical author's intentions is essential. When I read a letter from a friend, I might later tell my friend how I interpreted some of the words or phrases and he may respond *No I didn't mean that*. It would be highly unusual for me to disregard the empirical author's real intentions in writing the letter. Extending this illustration, I might perhaps reinterpret my reading of what Doris Lessing, Amy Tam, or Anne Sexton wrote given information about their putative communicative intentions in writing their respective novels or poems. Still, Eco and others all agree that the empirical author cannot be the final arbitrator of textual meaning. If I were to apply my knowledge of Lessing's, Tam's, or Sexton's probable intentions in interpreting their works, I would do so not to validate one particular interpretation of a text, but to show possible links between an author's intentions and the text's intentions.

Eco suggested that when a critic uses biographical information about an author to do textual analysis, then that person is *using* and not *interpreting* text. Eco has no objections to critics using text for advancing the most daring deconstructive ideas, but "certain interpretations can be recognized as unsuccessful because they ... are not able to produce new interpretations or cannot be confronted with the traditions of the previous interpretations."[61]

The philosopher Richard Rorty takes issue with Eco's distinction between the interpretation of the text and its use. Rorty claims that readers can never discover what a text really means or is really like. Many readings of text may be so exciting and convincing that readers believe what a text is really about has been discovered. But what excites readers and convinces critics is more a function of the needs and purposes of these people who are excited and convinced than it is a matter of what a text is all about.[62]

Somewhat paradoxically, understanding when readings that diverge from an author's intentions might be permitted can best be examined by looking at the unintended consequences of an author's intentional activity. Talk of unintended consequences for a literary text, such as those that arise from overinterpretation, take shape against a background of understanding what an author really intended to communicate. The philosopher Noel Carroll provides a wonderful example of this link between intentional meanings with unintentional consequences in his analysis of Jules Verne's 1874 novel *The Mysterious Island*.[63] This novel belongs to a genre of literature, along with *Robinson Crusoe* and *The Swiss Family Robinson*, in which marooned wayfarers inhabit deserted islands and turn them into civilized villages. In Verne's *Mysterious Island*, a band of Union loyalists escaped from the Confederacy during the Civil War by hijacking a hot air balloon. The all-male company includes a journalist, an engineer, an educated middle-class adolescent, an ordinary sailor, a former slave, and a dog. Once aloft, the balloon is blown wildly off course and lands on a deserted Pacific island. Most of the novel focuses on how the group explores the island, employing their collective knowledge of advanced agricultural and industrial techniques to turn the island into a thriving, productive, modern village. But the marooned islanders are secretly aided by Captain Nemo, commander of the *Nautilus*. Nemo's interventions are revealed toward the end of the novel, which ends with a volcanic eruption from which the islanders are rescued in a narrow escape.

Verne's novel has always been read as pro-Union and pro-abolitionist. *The Mysterious Island* shows no sympathy for the Confederacy, nor for slavery, and praises Abraham Lincoln, even calling the settlement "Lincoln Island" in his honor. The Civil War is presented as a struggle to end slavery, and Verne strongly allies himself against racism in various ways throughout the novel. Despite these strong pro-abolitionist sentiments, readers of *The Mysterious Island* often detect a great deal of racism in the book. In particular, the former slave, Neb, is portrayed as superstitious, naive, docile, and childlike. He continues to call the engineer

"Master," and develops a special relationship with a monkey that the colonists domesticate. The monkey even performs some of Neb's kitchen duties.

Critics are often leery of drawing broad inferences from an author's depiction of a fictional character about the author's actual attitudes toward the social class from which the character comes. But as Carroll notes, it is difficult not to infer from Verne's characterization of Neb that African Americans are typically docile, childlike, naive, and close to lower animals. Even if Verne intended the portrayal of Neb paternalistically to enhance the humane treatment of African Americans, his characterization of Neb comes off as racist. This yields a contradictory conclusion that *Mysterious Island* is both antiracist and racist at the same time. The book appears antiracist when read in terms of Verne's intentional meanings, yet racist when read from a more contemporary viewpoint. Readers might argue that an analysis of Verne's book gives clear evidence of his racism, despite his antiracist intentions.

But as Noel Carroll makes clear in his discussion of Verne's novel, "the attribution of racism in this case – as with similar attributions of racism, sexism, classism, imperialism, and so on – actually requires that *Mysterious Island* be approached intentionalistically."[64] There is no problem in admitting that in doing something intentionally under one description (e.g., Verne intending his novel to portray African Americans in a positive light), one may be also doing something else under another description (e.g., Verne's novel having many racist elements). Thus, illuminating Verne's intentions does not preclude going on to say that he produced something that is racist, even if he did not know it. This is not terribly surprising given the dramatic changes in the nature of racism that have occurred since 1874. Carroll draws an analogy by asking us to assume that someone intentionally smoking cigarettes, say in 1930, might at the same time have been unintentionally incurring lung cancer. Indeed, many advertisements back then proclaimed smoking to be healthful, so that a person might have started smoking cigarettes with the intention of improving her health, while unknowingly harming it.[65]

Intentionalism in literary criticism does not mandate that if Verne's text is racist, then the author must be cognizant of that racism, that he must have intended it and perhaps be prepared to respond to accusations of racism. Identifying Verne's paternalist intentions is directly relevant to understanding and explaining his portrayal of Neb in *Mysterious Island*. The argument that authorial intentions are relevant to interpretation does not imply that literary interpretation is solely a matter of tracking authorial intentions. Everything a reader may want to say about the novel is not necessarily something that Verne consciously intended to say or to imply by means of *Mysterious Island*.

One mark of great literature is that it typically communicates a wide range of ideas simultaneously. Some of these ideas are those authors specifically wish to communicate; they want readers to recognize their intentions to communicate just these ideas. When a reader is reasonably certain that the author intended others to infer a particular meaning, this is often referred to as a *strong implicature*.[66] Yet, as we've seen in Carroll's discussion of Verne's *Mysterious Island*, as well as in other instances of literature and speech, readers often infer meanings that may not be part of what authors specifically intended to communicate. Many authors specifically intend for readers only to entertain the implicatures that were "manifest" in their writings (i.e., implicatures that modify the mutual cognitive environment of author and reader). When readers feel some encouragement to explore meanings that an author might not have explicitly wished for them to infer, the resulting meanings are *weak implicatures*.[67] The chapters in Parts II and III provide many examples of how people draw weak implicatures in conversation and reading. In both cases, these meaningful inferences are the listeners'/readers' responsibility and do not directly reflect what a speaker/writer had in mind or intended to communicate.

A wonderful place to see readers inferring many complex kinds of weak implicatures is in poetic metaphor. Consider the metaphor of "digging" used by Seamus Heaney in his poem "Digging":[68] The poem ends as follows:

> The cold smell of potato mould, the squelch and slap
> Of soggy peat, the curt cuts of an edge
> Through living roots awaken in my head.

> But I've no spade to follow men like them.
> Between my finger and my thumb
> The squat pen rests.
> I'll dig with it.

Heaney expresses the metaphorical idea that writing poetry is like digging, specifically like the digging of turf and potatoes. A whole range of inferences arise from people's reading of this poem, a very few of which can be loosely characterized as follows:

Digging is an activity with a long tradition in the community.
Writing poetry is an activity with connections to that tradition.
Digging is an activity which involves hard work.
Writing poetry is an activity which involves hard work.
Digging is an honorable activity.
Writing poetry is an honorable activity.
Digging involves intense concentration.
Writing poetry involves intense concentration.
Digging requires a great deal of self-absorption.
Writing poetry requires a great deal of self-absorption.

Readers of Heaney's poem, as of any literary work, are guided by the hypothesis of "thin authorial rationality." If an author intends to express an idea or attitude implicitly, the author will try to adopt expressive means that are likely to make these manifest to interpreters who are reasonably competent at assessing textual and contextual evidence.[69] The wider the range of potential meanings, and the greater the reader's responsibility for constructing them, the more literary the effect.

In reading "Digging," it isn't at all clear which, if any, of the above inferences Heaney wished for readers to draw. Most of the meanings inferred from reading this poem are weak implicatures that are difficult to paraphrase (or translate). People infer weak implicature by widely searching their knowledge of certain concepts, as well as their knowledge of specific authors and literary genres. Literary effects such as weak implicatures, again, are not specifically intended to be communicated by authors and understood as such by readers. Instead, weak implicatures are *manifest*.[70] An assumption is manifest to a person "if the environment provides sufficient evidence for its adoption."[71] Yet a meaning or implicature that is manifest is not actually mentally represented, because an assumption may be manifest without being consciously entertained. For instance, the fact that someone has spoken provides good evidence that he or she is indeed alive. But the inference that a speaker is alive need not be explicitly mentally represented. As Sperber and Wilson's relevance theory suggests, people are apt to infer more weak implicatures, and will actually maximize the number and kinds of these they can draw, while minimizing the processing effort needed to comprehend what the author has meant. When people read literature, they are not faced with the same time constraints encountered in conversational exchanges and can expend more cognitive effort inferring a wide range of weak, even very weak, implicatures.

This framework explains something about readers' psychological processes when interpreting poetic and literary meanings. Relevance theory recognizes that the responsibility for interpretations is shared by speakers/authors and listeners/readers, and that implicatures can vary in their strength. Different readers, for instance, will produce different readings, and the same reader will produce different readings on different occasions, because information in long-term memory varies with regard to what assumptions are attached to what information (e.g., concepts, beliefs, knowledge of the author), and how readily accessible they are at any moment in time.[72]

A final example of how relevance theory and its notion of weak implicature can be applied to literature is seen in one study that examined interpretation of Raymond Carver's story "Little Things."[73] This short tale describes a man about to leave his wife and their struggle over who shall take care of their baby. Readers' interpretations of one statement in particular illustrate the appeal of relevance theory. The story begins: "Early that day the weather turned and the snow was melting into dirty water. Streaks of it ran down from the little shoulder-high window that faced the backyard. Cars slushed by on the street outside, where it was getting dark. But it was getting dark on the inside too."

What did Carver intend to communicate by the last statement *But it was getting dark on the inside too*? Many student readers suggested that Carver referred to the psychological state of darkness as well as to the darkness of the physical environment inside. Metaphors like this are relatively common, and some readers will quickly infer this dual interpretation with little cognitive effort. Both meanings fit the story thus far, and are consistent with the rest of the story too. Yet which of these meanings might have Carver specifically intended readers to infer? Relevance theory states that an interpretation is consistent with the Principle of Relevance when it gives rise to adequate readings with no unjustifiable effort. Both the physical and psychological readings of *But it was getting dark on the inside too* seem quite adequate. When an utterance has two reasonable interpretations, relevance theory predicts that the first interpretation accessed and found to be consistent with the Principle of Relevance is the only appropriate interpretation.[74] If the physical reading of this statement involves less processing effort to construct, the psychological reading will be ruled out, and vice versa. But when both readings are equally easy to infer, then readers can suppose that both interpretations were authorially intended. This conclusion seems to hold true in this case, especially given that both interpretations fit the rest of the story, and that both meanings prompt weak implicatures as the story continues about the difficulties with human relationships. Of course, as readers spend more time with Carver's story and develop more extensive weak implicatures, additional readings of this line may emerge that might not be seen as specifically intended by Carver.[75]

Relevance theory does not provide an account of determining definitive readings of literary texts. Its primary aim is to show how ordinary readers and scholarly critics might engage in complex inferential processes, involving both the conscious and unconscious minds, when interpreting language. Note that the inferential processes described here are not special to literary language, but reflect general mental processes used in understanding any sort of language. Whatever we want to say about an artwork should be consistent with the ways in which we speak of intentional activity in general. This does not preclude discussion of the unintended consequences of the artist's activity. Nevertheless, even talk of unintended consequences needs to take shape against a background of understanding what was intended.

CONCLUSION

Contemporary theories of literary interpretation and criticism have something to offer in accounting for people's complex experience of meaning when reading and interpreting literature. My adoption of the cognitive intentionalist premise forces me to look more closely at the cognitive unconscious factors that shape various reading practices. I have expressed different reservations about each of the major literary theories discussed above, primarily criticizing these approaches for insufficient appreciation of ordinary readers' strong dispositions to attribute human intentionality to literature. Too many literary theories mistakenly banish assumptions about authorship from literary criticism, as if by mere authorial pronouncement fundamental cognitive processes could somehow be legislated away.

Literary criticism, nonetheless, has been particularly influential in highlighting the significance of unintended meaning in reading literature, something that many cognitive scientists have failed to appreciate. One approach to unintended meaning shows many similarities with the account of unauthorized inferences offered for spoken language comprehension. This view, adopted from relevance theory, recognizes some of the complexities in readers' interpretation of both intentional (i.e., strong implicatures) and less intentional (i.e., weak implicatures) as well as of clearly unauthorized (i.e., implications) meaning. An important part of this approach is the suggestion that some aspects of what readers infer arise from readers' understanding of authors' communicative intentions.

Chapter 10

Interpreting the Law

In January 1983, William W. Thompson, then a fifteen-year-old adolescent from Oklahoma, participated in the brutal murder of his sister's former husband. The victim was shot twice, his throat, chest, and abdomen were cut, his leg was broken, and his body was chained to a concrete block and thrown into a river, where it remained for almost four weeks. Thompson told others beforehand that he was going to help commit this murder, and afterwards bragged about his actions to friends and family. Although Thompson was a "child" as defined by Oklahoma law, he was tried as an adult, convicted of the murder, and sentenced to death by the trial judge. The Court of Criminal Appeals of Oklahoma upheld the verdict and the death sentence, and the case was then appealed to the U.S. Supreme Court in 1987. The main issue the Supreme Court considered in *Thompson v. Oklahoma* was whether it is constitutional to execute a person who was a "child" at the time he committed the offense. Thompson's attorneys argued that he should not be executed because this would violate Thompson's rights, as a "child," under the Eighth Amendment, which forbids "cruel and unusual punishment."

In June 1988 the U.S. Supreme Court ruled, in a majority decision, to vacate the order to execute Thompson.[1] The majority opinion by Justice John Paul Stevens noted that "evolving standards of decency that mark the progress of a maturing society" compelled the conclusion that it would be unconstitutional under the Eighth Amendment of the Constitution to execute a person for a crime committed as a fifteen-year-old.[2] Justice Antonin Scalia wrote a dissenting opinion in which he claimed that the Eighth

Amendment's ban on "cruel and unusual" punishment was not originally intended to forbid executions of juveniles. He argued:

> The age at which juveniles could be subjected to capital punishment was explicitly addressed in Blackstone's Commentaries on the Laws of England, published in 1769 and widely accepted at the time the Eighth Amendment was adopted as an accurate description of the common law. According to Blackstone, not only was 15 above the age (viz. 7) at which capital punishment could theoretically be imposed; it was even above the age (14) up to which there was a rebuttable presumption of incapacity to commit a capital (or any other) felony.[3]

Scalia's point was to suggest that there is no reason to prohibit execution of a person who committed a crime at age fifteen, because the Eighth Amendment's authors most likely did not intend for the law to be interpreted in this way.

William Thompson's case before the Supreme Court is at the heart of debates about how United States laws should be interpreted. What exactly does the Eighth Amendment mean by the phrase "cruel and unusual punishment"? How should judges and political officials determine what this phrase means in deciding cases such as *Thompson v. Oklahoma*? Constitutional scholars are deeply divided over how to answer these questions. Should judges be free to interpret the U.S. Constitution, according to contemporary or "evolving" standards, or must judges limit their readings of the law to how the framers of the Constitution specifically intended it to be interpreted at the time?[4] Justices Brennan's and Scalia's differing opinions on *Thompson v. Oklahoma* (1988) nicely demonstrate how competing views on the relevance of authorial intentions in constitutional interpretation can lead to different decisions regarding the life, or death, of American citizens.

Although some constitutional amendments are quite specific (e.g., Article 2 specifies that the president must be at least thirty-five years old), most amendments that address individual rights were drafted in exceedingly moral language. For instance, the First Amendment refers to the "right" of free speech, the Fifth Amendment to the legal process that is "due" to citizens, the Eighth Amendment to "cruel and unusual punishment," and the

Fourteenth Amendment to protection that is "equal." How must these and other amendments be interpreted, and what role do our understandings or assumptions about what the framers intended in writing these laws have in contemporary jurisprudence? My answers to these questions in this chapter will be that consideration of the framers' intentions is a crucial part of understanding what legal texts, such as the U.S. Constitution, *say*. But the original motivations for the framers' creation of the document demands consideration of something quite different – what the authors hoped to achieve by people's recognition of their communicative intentions.

THE DEBATE OVER ORIGINAL INTENT

Concern over whether judges will follow the specific intentions of the framers in judicial decision making has risen sharply over the past thirty years. Consider as two early examples, the following exchanges between U.S. senators and individuals nominated to serve on the Supreme Court. In 1967, Senator Sam Ervin questioned nominee Thurgood Marshall:[5]

> Sen. Ervin: I wish to repeat my question. Is not the role of the Supreme Court simply to ascertain and give effect to the intent of the framers of this Constitution and the people who ratified it?

> Mr. Marshall: Yes, Senator, with the understanding that the Constitution was meant to be a living document.

In 1971 Senator John McClellan asked a similar question of William Rehnquist during his confirmation hearing:[6]

> Sen. McClellan: Would you be willing, as a judge ... to disregard the intent of the framers in creating Constitution and change it to achieve a result that you thought might be desirable for society?

> Mr. Rehnquist: I do not believe I would Senator.

Both senators' questions point to the political reality that successful nominees to the Supreme Court must voice some adherence to the framers' intentions when interpreting the Constitution. Many citizens, scholars, and elected officials in contemporary life have criticized judges for ignoring original intentions in deciding court cases. When Richard Nixon was running for the presidency in 1968, he promised to appoint to the Supreme Court judges who were "strict constructionists," who saw their duty as simply to interpret existing laws, rather than to make new laws given their own judicial philosophies.[7] Judges should "interpret the Constitution strictly and fairly and objectively," and "not twist or bend" its words to advance their own social and political views.[8] This belief in judicial neutrality has been a favorite Republican dogma for decades. Presidents Nixon, Reagan, and Bush condemned liberal judges for "inventing" rights based on their own personal moral views, rather than interpreting the laws as they were intended to be understood by the framers. Jurists should only refer to "original intentions" in adjudicating constitutional cases.

During his 1985 confirmation hearings, Supreme Court nominee Robert Bork argued that if judges go beyond what the framers intended, they are then relying on "moral precepts" and "abstract philosophy," and therefore are acting as judicial tyrants, usurping authority that belongs to the people. This is exactly what the Supreme Court did, Bork claimed, when it handed down liberal decisions in the controversial abortion, death penalty, and affirmative action cases of the 1970s and 1980s. Bork's judicial philosophy embraces "originalism." According to "originalists" or "interpretivists," the proper aim of constitutional interpretation is to understand and deploy the intentions of the framers. As Robert Bork stated: "If the Constitution is law, then presumably its meaning, like that of all other law, is the meaning the lawmakers were understood to have intended."[9] Under this view, interpretation organizes textuality as the place where an author's intentions are represented in language and which posits interpretation as a process of deriving, according to the relevant aesthetic/political morality values, what that intention is, and hence, what the text "means." The originalists proposed the doctrine of "original intent" to promote judicial neutrality and fidelity to the Constitution.

On the other side of the debate on constitutional interpretation, "non-originalists" argue that to adapt the Constitution to changing conditions, the Supreme Court must go beyond the framers' specific intentions. To understand the true meaning of a legal text, jurists must not forget what has been learned from the events that transpired between the text's creation and the present.[10] As Justice Oliver Wendell Holmes argued in the late nineteenth century in reference to one case, it "must be considered in light of our whole experience and not merely in that of what was said a hundred years ago.... We must consider what the country has become in deciding what the Constitution means."[11]

How should these competing approaches be balanced in constitutional decision making? In *Thompson v. Oklahoma* (1988), jurists found the Eighth Amendment ambiguous in terms of what the text meant by the phrase "cruel and unusual punishment." Executing a person who was fifteen at the time of his crime would certainly be unusual. No person under the age of sixteen has been executed in the United States since 1948. Yet is executing a person who committed a crime at fifteen a "cruel" form of punishment? This question seems more debatable. The Eighth Amendment didn't, as Justice Scalia noted, reject the idea that a person who committed a crime at 15 could *not* be executed. But as Scalia also admitted, it is nearly impossible to determine the framers' specific view of "cruel and unusual punishment."

Debates over what the framers actually believed and intended are difficult to resolve. Whatever the hot issue in contemporary life (e.g., school prayer, balanced budgets, gun control, abortion rights, welfare policy), laypersons and legal scholars inevitably offer their own interpretations of what the framers of the Constitution must have originally intended back in the eighteenth century to reinforce their personal views. Consider the relations between church and state, especially over the question of whether prayer should be allowed in the public schools. Most efforts to determine the appropriate relationship between church and state have focused on interpreting the religion clause of the First Amendment: "Congress shall make no law respecting an establishment of religion, or prohibiting the free exercise thereof...."

Does this claim support or reject the idea that prayer should be allowed in the public schools? Answering this question is difficult, in part, because little agreement exists on the meaning of the actual words in the establishment clause. Some scholars and jurists read the establishment clause broadly, arguing that it removes the national government from any support or involvement with religion. Opponents of school prayer suggest that the framers intended to construct a high wall separating church and state. Other scholars and citizens interpret the establishment clause narrowly arguing that the First Amendment prohibits only a state supported church. Most recently, politicians such as Newt Gingrich and Pat Buchanan, along with right-wing Christian activists like Pat Robertson and Ralph Reed, have insisted that the framers wanted to establish a Christian government and would have been strongly in favor of prayer in the public schools. After all, Congress starts each session with a prayer, and the United States has as one of its mottos *In God We Trust*. Advocates of school prayer claim that the founders back in the eighteenth century did not specify the role of religion in the new national government, but instead wanted to leave it open to individual states to decide how to support religion. Determining which of these interpretations were the framers' actual intentions is almost impossible. What must a judge do in this situation?[12]

THE LETTER AND THE SPIRIT OF THE LAW

One popular approach to interpreting the Constitution that avoids problems of intentionalism is *textualism*.[13] Textualists hold that judges should stick closely to the literal meanings of legal text in adjudicating court cases. Adopting textualism is viewed as having several advantages.[14] First, textualism reduces the possibility that judges will read their personal opinions into laws, or make unwarranted inferences about the original intentions of a text's authors. Second, judges should find it easier to understand the plain, literal meaning of texts than to engage in arduous historical research about the intentions of individuals who lived as long as 200 years ago. Third, cementing constitutional adjudication in literal meaning promotes a more stable constitutional history by reducing the changing views of historians about the framers' original intentions. Finally, the text's literal meaning is really all that the ratifiers of the Constitution ever approved (i.e., they didn't ratify explicit statements of intentions).

There remains a strong belief in textualism among jurists and politicians, primarily because people assume that the meanings of most, if not all, laws seem so self-evident. But as the debate over the Eighth Amendment in *Thompson v. Oklahoma* indicates, what might be self-evident to one jurist is not at all obvious to another. Parts II and III described empirical research and theoretical ideas that raise serious questions about the assumption that the literal meaning of any word, statement, or text can be simply articulated. Listeners and readers do not interpret language according to its putative literal meanings (even as an initial stage of linguistic processing). This cognitive science research constitutes a serious obstacle to any interpretive theory that assumes literal meaning is primary, or can ever be readily determined.

Beyond this important point, there are additional reasons for abandoning textualism as a serious perspective on constitutional interpretation. The main problem is that most constitutional provisions were certainly not intended to be understood according to their literal meanings. As Supreme Court Justice Learned Hand once wrote: "There is no surer way to misread any document than to read it literally."[15]

There is a famous case, *Riggs v. Palmer* (1889), in which a man learned that he had been designated the heir under his grandfather's will, and so murdered the grandfather to collect the inheritance.[16] Should the man still collect the inheritance? The judges deciding this case disagreed over how to answer this question. Some judges argued that all one needs to do is to read the statute of wills and see what it says. Under this view of interpretation, the man who committed the murder, strictly speaking, should collect the inheritance even if he murdered his grandfather to get it. But other judges argued that laws must be read and interpreted against some general moral backgrounds, one of which is that people shouldn't profit through their own deliberate wrong. These judges prevailed in the case and the man was denied his inheritance.

Trying to interpret laws according to what they state literally will often undermine the very purpose for which these laws were adopted. The U.S. Constitution was drafted and ratified by people who strongly believed that the "spirit" of the law was as important as its "letter" in determining how that law was to be applied in governing the conduct of U.S. citizens.

INTENTIONALISM IN JURISPRUDENCE

How often do judges actually refer to the framers' original intentions in deciding court cases? One analysis of the 527 opinions given by Supreme Court Justices Brennan and Rehnquist over a ten-year period (1973–1982) looked at five types of constitutional arguments:[17] (1) *technical* arguments are characterized by an appeal to the "plain meaning of the words" of the Constitution, (2) *structural* arguments appeal to the larger framework of the Constitution as a whole and are not limited to "clause-based" interpretation of individual amendments, (3) *doctrinal* arguments focus on previous legal precedents that have arisen over 200 years of Supreme Court decisions, (4) *extrinsic* arguments appeal to contemporary values that are not specifically mentioned in the Constitution or any related doctrine, and (5) *historicist* or *intentionalist* arguments rely on the underlying intentions of the framers in enacting a particular law.

This analysis revealed that less than four percent of Brennan's and Rehnquist's decisions referred to historically based claims of the framers. As Justice Brennan noted, discussing the framers' intentions in constitutional issues is "little more than arrogance cloaked as humility."[18] The fact that Brennan and Rehnquist represented opposing, liberal and conservative, sides on most issues, suggests that there is little concrete evidence to support the widespread assumption that intentionalism is used to support primarily conservative political and legal agendas.[19]

Interestingly, Justices Brennan and Rehnquist both used extrinsic arguments in nineteen percent of their decisions. These arguments did not rely on the Constitution, the intent of the framers, or other doctrine, but were based on information not found in legal texts, such as changing social values. Even more interesting, though, is that when Justices Brennan and Rehnquist made intentionalist arguments, they did so with little evidence of the actual intentions of the framers. For instance, in his 1982 dissent in *Valley Forge Christian College v. Americans United* Brennan wrote that "the drafters of the Bill of Rights surely intended that the particular beneficiaries of their legacy should enjoy rights legally enforceable in courts of law," but he provided no specific historical data to back up his conclusion about what the framers "surely intended."[20]

In his book *The Language of Judges*, Lawrence Solon notes a paradoxical case in the Supreme Court where all nine justices agreed that the meaning of a provision was *plain*, but split five to four over what that provision meant.[21]

THE JUDGE'S TASK

What role should an author's intentions play in legal interpretation? The philosopher Ronald Dworkin has provided a complex answer to this question by asking us to consider the idea of writing a chain novel.[22] A chain novel is a text written by a group of people, rather than a single author, in which each writer in the group is responsible for one chapter of the book. One person writes a first chapter and sends it to the person who is to write the second chapter. This second writer reads the first chapter with its plot and themes and writes a new chapter, and then sends both chapters to a third person who reads them and writes a third chapter that further develops the story. The writing goes on in this way until each person in the group has written a chapter and the novel is completed.

The important similarity between this chain-novel exercise and the law, according to Dworkin, is that each author, after the first one, has the same two responsibilities as does a judge. Each author must create a new piece of work and develop or continue on the work of others just as each judge must both offer an opinion on a new case and adhere to the preexisting meaning of the relevant law. Each new chapter must be both a new creation and a further chapter in a single book, which means that each author must understand the meaning of the previous parts of the book so that new parts will serve to continue the same book that the first novelist began. Similarly, each judge must both decide a new case and decide it in a way consistent with the meaning established by existing law. How does a judge, or an author in a chain novel, accomplish this task?

Some might argue that a second writer of the chain novel (i.e., the author of the second chapter) must look for the first writer's intentions in producing the book's first chapter. With the first writer's intentions securely in mind, the second author writes a chapter that elaborates on the first author's intentions, so that a third writer can then discern the intentions of the first two authors and further carry out those intentions in the next chapter of the book. This process of discerning and carrying out the original intention would continue until the novel was finished, and the entire book should express a single literary intention. In the same way, a judge advances the rule of a specific law only by remaining consistent with the original intentions of the legislators who created the law. Judges further the law and carry it out only if they reiterate in their decisions the single intention behind the law's origin.

But Dworkin dismisses this account of a judge's task. He does not deny that ascertaining an author's or legislator's intentions must be an important part of legal interpretation, that the second author writing a chain novel might want to know what the first author intended to create, or even that a judge might be interested in a legislator's intentions with regard to the law. Dworkin dismisses the idea that attempts to understand original intentions somehow guarantee objectivity in legal interpretation. The inherent complexity of most intentions, especially in regard to individual rights, can conceivably be described in different ways. For instance, how might one describe the original intentions in creating the Fourteenth Amendment, especially in regard to the question of the constitutionality of the racial segregation of schoolchildren in the United States? Dworkin responds by asking us to consider the following:

Suppose a delegate to a constitutional convention votes for a clause guaranteeing equality of treatment, without regard to race, in matters touching people's fundamental interests; but he thinks that education is not a matter of fundamental interest and so does not believe that the clause makes racially segregated schools unconstitutional ... the delegate intends to prohibit discrimination in whatever in fact is of fundamental interest and also intends not to prohibit segregated schools.[23]

Which intention is seen as fundamental in this situation will be decisive for a judge's decision about the legality of segregated education. If a jurist assumes the first half of the intention is primary (i.e., that of guaranteeing equality of treatment in matters of fundamental importance), then segregated schools can rightfully be outlawed. If a jurist assumes the second half of the intention to be primary (i.e., that of intending not to prohibit segregated schools), then segregated schools cannot be viewed as constitutionally prohibited even if they preclude an equal treatment of blacks and whites. In both scenarios, the judge has interpreted the original framers' thoughts and intentions, but with significantly different outcomes. Dworkin denies that appeal to an "original" intention can provide the standard for interpretation of the law.

When legal scholars disagree about what the Constitution says about the Fourteenth Amendment, or any other amendment, the debate is not between intentional interpretations and some other kind of meaning, but between two specifications of the intentional conditions of the Constitution's production.[24] Bork's construal of the Constitution and its amendments assumes agents whose purpose was to limit future generations to the possibilities of actions conceivable back in 1787, or at the time any constitutional amendment was adopted. Bork imagined the framers saying something like "If we can't think of it now, we don't want anyone to think of it in the future." Bork conceded that present-day judges must exercise judgment in applying the framers' general principles to new circumstances, like electronic wiretapping. Yet as Bork argued, the framers misunderstood the force of their own principles in several instances.

A different view of the Constitution posits that the framers' purpose was to lay down general rules and standards which are rendered particular in the light of emerging information in changing circumstances. For instance, the framers stated that equality and liberty are important standards to promote in the United States, but whether or not a particular action affirms these values is something future generations must decide. Some historical evidence suggests that the framers clearly intended that their own interpretations of the abstract language they wrote should not be regarded as decisive in court.[25] This finding leads to the conclusion that originalism is a self-refuting idea. If judges are required to adhere to the framers' original intentions, yet the framers themselves intended their intentions not be binding, then originalism expresses an internally inconsistent thesis and makes no sense as a theory of constitutional adjudication.[26]

Perhaps the most famous case where the Supreme Court reinterpreted the Constitution in light of contemporary values was *Brown v. Board of Education* (1954).[27] Back in *Plessy v. Ferguson* (1896), the Supreme Court upheld a Louisiana law that required railroads to segregate passengers by race.[28] Horace Plessy was a black man who argued that Louisiana was not offering him equal protection of the law since enforced segregation certified the inferior status of blacks and gave that inferiority official standing. Instead of offering equal protection, Plessy argued, the law actually reconfirmed inequality. The Supreme Court rejected this argument, writing that the underlying fallacy of Plessy's argument was that the enforced separation of the two races straps the colored race with a badge of inferiority. If this is so, it is not because of anything found in the act, but solely because the colored race chooses to put that interpretation upon the law.

In 1954 in *Brown v. Board of Education*, Thurgood Marshall, arguing on behalf of Brown, offered evidence from social science research, especially from the studies of psychologist Kenneth Clark, that young children were psychologically stigmatized by state-imposed segregation. This finding of fact reflected a contemporary understanding of race relations. By considering "what the country has become in deciding what the Constitution means," the court decided to overturn *Plessy v. Ferguson* (1896).

The Supreme Court's 1954 ruling in *Brown v. Board of Education* demonstrated an application of the idea that what the framers of the Fourteenth Amendment concretely intended to accomplish might be ignored in light of a changed society. The historical record shows that the framers had clear expectations about the logical consequences of the Fourteenth Amendment. They expected it to end certain of the most egregious Jim Crow practices of the Reconstruction period. Yet they obviously did not expect it to outlaw official racial segregation in schools. The Congress that adopted the equal protection clause maintained segregation in the District of Columbia school system. But the Fourteenth Amendment did not *say* anything about Jim Crow laws or school segregation or homosexuality or gender equality, one way or the other. It contains only the famous clause "equal protection of the laws," which plainly describes a very general principle, not any concrete application of it. The framers intent, then, was to enact a general principle.

But if a text only means what its authors intend, aren't the authors of the Fourteenth Amendment the best authority as to what the equal protection clause prohibits and permits? Many scholars now argue that this is not necessarily so. The authors of the Fourteenth Amendment, or any law, might be mistaken about their own intentions, or they may have forgotten them, or never correctly understood them in the first place. More interestingly, the authors might be perfectly correct about their intentions and perfectly sincere in reporting their intentions, and still be mistaken as to what, in the case of the Fourteenth Amendment, the equal protection clause prohibits and permits.

A related way of talking about interpreting the Constitution, and other legal texts, in light of contemporary social circumstances is to recognize the allegorical (i.e., transhistorical) nature of linguistic interpretation.[29] Under this view, many terms in the law are uncertain and vague until a judge or scholar refers them, which is to say allegorizes them, to the realities of people's contemporary experience. For instance, one way to show how an author can understand a law without knowing exactly what the law prescribes is to consider the famous "no vehicles in the park" law. This law was originally enacted before the invention of the automobile. Must a judge now interpret this law, which had always been viewed as prohibiting bicycles and horse-driven carriages, as prohibiting people from driving their automobiles in parks? A judge may hold that the legislators cannot have believed that the law they enacted excluded automobiles, because they had no idea what automobiles were at the time they created the law. Nevertheless, the judge could decide that the law, when interpreted to mean what its authors generally intended it to mean, prohibits automobiles by assuming that automobiles were the kinds of objects that the legislators intended to include in the notion of vehicle. This allegorical view of legal interpretation was even more forcefully illustrated by *Brown v. Board of Education* (1954), where the equal protection clause was interpreted allegorically in light of the court's view of contemporary reality.

Not surprisingly, various judges and scholars have argued against allegorical legal interpretation. Justice Scalia maintained that questions about what constitutes a denial of equal protection must still be answered according to the time-dated meaning of equal protection in 1868, when the Fourteenth Amendment was originally enacted. Scalia asked whether segregated toilets in public buildings and forbidding women in combat denies equal protection on the basis of sex. Unisex toilets and "GI Janes" may be concepts the public is ready for, and something people are certainly free to require their legislatures to consider, but refusing to pass such laws does not violate the Fourteenth Amendment, because this is not what "equal protection of the law" ever meant.

Scalia took issue with allegorical legal interpretation in other situations as well. One example of how the Supreme Court interpreted a constitutional amendment in light of changing society is seen in a 1990 case where an adult was prosecuted for sexually abusing a young child.[30] The trial court ruled that the child should not be forced to testify in the presence of the defendant, and so, pursuant to state law, she was permitted to testify only with the prosecutor and defense counsel present, while the defendant, the judge, and the jury watched the testimony over closed-circuit television from another room. The Supreme Court upheld this ruling.

Scalia argued in his dissent that the Sixth Amendment provides that "in all criminal prosecutions the accused shall enjoy the right to be confronted with the witnesses against him." Scalia claimed that the framer's intention in saying that the defendant is allowed "to be confronted with the witnesses" means that the defendant must see the witness face to face, and not watch the witness on television from another room. The major purpose of this part of the amendment was to place pressure upon the witness given that it is difficult to accuse someone face to face when you are lying. Even if you are a little girl, and presumably would be frightened by having to testify face to face, the Sixth Amendment gives all accused persons the right to confront their witnesses.[31] Despite society's changing attitudes toward problems of child sexual abuse and toward little girls' fears in testifying against people who may have done them harm, it is wrong, so Scalia argues, to interpret the Sixth Amendment differently from what the law originally meant.

Dworkin agrees with Scalia that all jurists and lawmakers must search for what a text originally meant.[32] The moral reading view that Dworkin favors insists that the Constitution means what the framers intended to *say*. Originalism insists that it means what they expected the language to *do*. Constitutional law, as a matter of original meaning, sets out abstract principles rather than concrete or dated rules. "If so, then the application of these abstract principles to particular cases, which takes fresh judgment, must be continually reviewed, not in an attempt to find substitutes for what the Constitution says, but out of respect for what it says."[33] This view implies that the Supreme Court's *Brown v. Board of Education* (1954) decision correctly interprets what the Congress intended the Fourteenth Amendment to say, even though their ruling may very well defy what the amendment's authors and ratifiers expected the amendment to achieve.[34]

Most generally, appeals to the framers' original intentions decide nothing until choices are made about the right way to formulate their intentions in a particular legal context. If judges choose the most narrow, most concrete formulation of original intention, which fixes on the expressed opinions of the framers and ignores the more general moral vision they were trying to serve, then *Brown v. Board of Education* must be regarded as unfaithful to the framers' will. But if judges assign to the framers a principle that is sufficiently general not to seem arbitrary and ad hoc, like the principle that government must not discriminate on grounds of prejudice, then many of the decisions originalists castigate as illegitimate must be seen as good and proper.[35]

Few people who authored the equal protection clause thought that this would always forbid discrimination on grounds of age, property, sex, or even sexual inclination, or even that it made school segregation illegal. Interpreting the Constitution requires that jurists read it to say what their authors intended them to *say* rather than to deliver the consequences the ratifiers expected the Constitution to have. Judges must treat the Constitution as enacting abstract moral principles and should exercise moral judgment in deciding what they really require.

Of course, determining in a principled way what an amendment's author intended to *say* is not an easy matter.[36] Interpretive strategies, such as looking at the language used, or examining the historical record about what the authors might have meant, will themselves engage complex cognitive and rhetorical practices about which people often disagree.[37] Contrary to Dworkin and others, it isn't at all clear that the generality or abstraction with which a constitutional amendment is worded makes obviously transparent what its authors intended to say for all time. These interpretive strategies assume that the Constitution's, or any law's, meaning can be discovered as opposed to constructed. One must always argue why a particular interpretation should be accepted, both in light of the Constitution as a whole and the history of its interpretation. As legal theorist Lawrence Tribe has noted, there may not be any defensible set of rules for constitutional interpretation. "Insights and perspectives, yes; rules no."[38]

In conclusion, both sides of the originalist debate misconceive the role of the author's intention in textual interpretation by improperly conflating originalism (i.e., original intent) with intentionalism. To say that interpreting the Constitution requires the use of a conception of the author's intention does not privilege in advance any particular conception of that intention. Some legal theorists fear that adopting the intentionalist view would require them to accept the originalist conception of the author's intention.[39] The fear that every concrete intention attributable to the framers must be enforced in perpetuity drives "non-originalists" to divorce legal interpretation from any consideration of authorial intentions, saying that such intentions are always irrelevant.[40] But this position fails to recognize that textual interpretation partly involves the explication of an author's intention to mean something by what is said in the text.

A CASE STUDY OF LEGAL INTERPRETATION

Consider a different matter of legal interpretation that centered, in part, over what the authors of a text might have intended when they wrote it.[41] The 1972 U.S.-Soviet Union anti-ballistic missile (ABM) treaty outlined an argument for the reduction of ABMs in the United States and the Soviet Union. The most important provision in the treaty, Article 5, stated: "Each party undertakes not to develop, test, or develop ABM systems or components which are sea based, air based, space based, or mobile land based."[42]

Treaties are different from laws in that they are established as agreements between different parties and so the intentions of both parties are relevant. Until 1983 three different presidential administrations in the United States understood the 1972 ABM treaty, and especially the crucial provision in Article 5, as banning the militarization of space or even the development and testing of space-based ABM systems. But on March 23, 1983, President Ronald Reagan gave a televised address to the nation in which he revealed the administration's plan for the Strategic Defense Initiative (SDI), a research and development program designed to produce a space-based anti-ballistic missile system employing laser technology. President Reagan claimed that SDI was *consistent with our obligation* under the ABM Treaty.

As might be expected, several commentators quickly noted the contradiction between the 1972 ABM treaty and SDI. Nevertheless, from 1983 to 1985 the Reagan administration continued to maintain that the United States adhered to the traditional interpretation of Article 5. For instance, in late 1985 national security advisor Robert McFarland said, during an interview on "Meet the Press," that the ABM treaty "approved and authorized" development and testing of space-based ABM systems "involv-ing new physical concepts" such as laser or directed enemy tech-nology.[43] Soon afterward Secretary of State George Schultz expanded on the reasons for the new seemingly contradictory interpretation of the ABM treaty when he stated in a speech to the North Atlantic Assembly that "the treaty can be variously in-terpreted as to what kind of development and testing are permit-ted, particularly with respect to future systems and components based on new physical properties... it is our view, based on a care-ful analysis of the treaty text and in the negotiating record that a broader interpretation of our authority is fully justified."[44]

A great uproar arose in Congress in response to the Reagan administration's interpretation of Article 5. Congress held hear-ings in the House Subcommittee on Arms Control, International Security and Science to consider the "ABM treaty interpretation debate." One analysis of the record of this hearing reveals several interesting points about the arguments for and against the old and the new, or the "restrictive" and "broader," interpretations of Article 5. For instance, Leonard Meeker and Peter Didisheim from the Union of Concerned Scientists noted in their testimony to Congress that "the ordinary meaning of the treaty's terms are self-evident. The administration's argument that the treaty permits the development and the testing of space-based ABM weapons and components based on new physical principles cannot qualify as an interpretation in good faith."[45] Alexander Sufac, legal ad-visor to the secretary of state, countered that statement D of the agreement, negotiated at the time of the original treaty, implied that the Article 5 definition of ABM systems refers only to missile technology available in 1972 and that Article 5 did not limit de-velopment and testing of missile systems, such as SDI, developed after 1972.

What were the intentions of the participants who drafted the 1972 ABM treaty? Alexander Sufac commented in his testimony that because of the ambiguity in the treaty text, it was appropriate to consult the record of negotiations that took place at the time when the treaty was formulated to discover which interpretation of the treaty best reflects the participants' original intentions.[46] Of course, most discussions about what someone originally intended conflates what that person intended to communicate with what that person hoped to achieve as a result of others' reading of what is written. Not surprisingly, the original United States negotiators of the treaty disagreed in 1986 as to which interpretation was intended back in 1972 when they crafted the ABM treaty. Gerard Smith, the former chief of the U.S. delegation to the negotiations, disagreed with the Reagan administration's new interpretation of the treaty and testified that the negotiators' intentions supported the restrictive interpretation of Article 5. Yet Paul Nitze, a member of the original negotiating team, as well as President Reagan's special advisor on arms control, strongly endorsed the administration's new interpretation of the ABM treaty. Of course, it is always possible that the U.S. negotiators were in apparent agreement about their intentions back in 1972, but then shifted their views, either consciously or unconsciously, after the treaty was originally drafted. No resolution about the meaning of the ABM treaty emerged as a result of the 1988 congressional hearings. The Reagan and Bush administrations spent billions of dollars working on SDI, although the effort to develop space-based laser missile systems has now largely ceased.

The important lesson for the present discussion is that part of the battle over the meaning of the ABM treaty centered on what its authors might have intended to communicate in drafting the treaty. Appealing to what the actual authors – at least the American negotiators – might have intended did not provide a simple answer to the entire ABM treaty debate. Does this mean that we never, or should never, consider something about who wrote the treaty, why they wrote it, and why they employed the particular language they did, in our assessment of what the treaty means? Even though the search for original authorial intentions does not provide clear evidence on the interpretation of the ABM treaty, drawing inferences about authors' hypothetical intentions in regard to what they say is one major rhetorical strategy for structuring debate about what a text might mean. Although no one perspective on interpretation guarantees a single, unambiguous correct interpretation of a text, this doesn't mean that one can't vehemently argue for various interpretations based on a wide variety of evidence, such as the text, the history of its traditional readings, the authors' original intentions, and hypothetical intentions readers might infer regarding what authors have said (but not intended to achieve).

CONCLUSION

The debate over authorial intentions in interpreting law has often incorrectly assumed that what the framers of any law say must necessarily be similar to what they hoped to achieve as a result of instituting that law. But the moral character of many legal texts forces authors to craft their language to cover a wide range of social and legal situations. Consequently, even though the framers of any law perhaps desired to bring about a particular social outcome as a result of that law, interpreting their communicative intentions might lead in different contexts to different results. Under this view, recovery of an author's communicative intentions in designing some law is still seen as an integral part of understanding what the text says. This perspective on legal interpretation, which is consistent with the cognitive intentionalist premise, is related to the idea and evidence that people can distinguish between speaker's communicative intentions and meanings that are best characterized as implications of what someone said, yet are not specifically intended as part of what is said.

Chapter 11

Understanding Art

One of the most notorious artistic projects of the twentieth century began in New York City in 1917 when Marcel Duchamp, along with several companions, purchased a urinal from a plumbing manufacturer. Duchamp took the urinal back to his studio, turned it upside down, and printed the name *R. Mutt* and the date in large black letters on the lower left rim. He then submitted this object, entitled *Fountain*, to the 1917 *Independents* exhibition, along with a six-dollar membership fee and a fictitious Philadelphia address for Mr. Mutt.

The directors of the art exhibition declined to include Mr. Mutt's submission of *Fountain* in their show, responding that the object was "by no definition, a work of art." Marcel Duchamp soon published an unsigned editorial in a local magazine to describe Mr. Mutt's case, which read, in part: "Whether Mr. Mutt with his own hands made the fountain or not bears no importance. He CHOSE it. He took an ordinary article of life, placed it so that its useful significance disappeared with the new title and point of view – created a new thought for that object."[1]

Does present-day understanding and aesthetic appreciation of *Fountain* depend on, or demand, recovering something about Marcel Duchamp's communicative intentions in "creating" this piece of artwork? Duchamp and his friends clearly planned the entire event as a deliberate provocation of the New York art world in 1917. But *Fountain* was no mere joke, as it unquestionably expressed Duchamp's lifelong philosophy that artworks should be conceptual and not just retinal.

Simply calling something art does not necessarily make it art. For instance, on July 15, 1996, Jason Sprinkle, a Seattle artist, drove a pickup truck to the front of Seattle's busy Westlake Center mall. After parking the truck, he slashed the tires and walked away. The truck contained a huge red metal heart with the words *The Bomb* painted across the front. During a six-hour bomb detection operation, police evacuated the Westlake Center and a nine-block area surrounding the crowded shopping mall. Sprinkle, who insisted that the piece was a harmless artwork, was arrested. Bail was set at $100,000, and the artist now faces a possible five-year prison term and $10,000 fine.

To most observers, simply saying that *The Bomb* was artwork makes it no less of threatening as a real bomb. Then again, no matter what Duchamp's purpose was in "creating" *Fountain*, it remains, in some observers' minds, a urinal. Both these examples of conceptual art, divided by eighty years, show how an artist by intentional fiat can, at the very least, attempt to communicate artistic meanings. Duchamp's and Sprinke's works may, or may not, have failed to achieve their putative artistic aims, but in both cases, spectators must consider why some person created the artwork and ponder what meanings they are supposed to infer from observing the work. Many controversial incidents in art history drive home the point that how people interpret artistic artifacts depends crucially on our attributions of authorial intentions.

The aim of this chapter is to consider some of the critical debates over how best to characterize authorial intentions in art interpretation and appreciation. Questions about what artists (painters, sculptors, playwrights, composers) mean by their works have captured tremendous public attention in recent years. I will defend a view of artwork that places intentions at the center of ordinary and scholarly interpretive practice. However, the intentions spectators seek to recover are not necessarily those of the actual artist, but those of a hypothetical intentional agent, working in a particular historical context. More generally, understanding artwork is best described in terms of a dynamic relationship between the artist, the work, and spectators, which will sometimes lead spectators to draw meaningful inferences about a work that were not specifically in the artist's mind when the work was originally created.

ARTISTIC INTENTIONS

Shouldn't what artists say about their artwork influence how we interpret and critically evaluate their creations? Artists frequently publish manifestos explaining the motives and intentions for their work. An important part of such polemical writings is the firm belief that artists have something specific to communicate, and their primary function is to get others to understand, and eventually accept, these artistic intentions. For instance, over fifty years ago artistic authority could still be stated with confidence by practicing artists. Thus, the nonrepresentational painters Adolph Gottlieb and Mark Rothko wrote in 1943: "It is our function as artists to make the spectator see the world our way – not his way."[2] More than forty years later, though, the artist Keith Haring said:

> Often when I am drawing in the subway in New York City an observer will patiently stand by and watch until I have finished drawing and then, quickly, as I attempt to walk away, will shout out, "But what does it mean?" I usually answer "That's your part, I only do the drawings." I maintain that an artist is not the best spokesman for his work. For myself, I find that my attitude towards, and understanding of my work is in a constant state of flux. I am continually learning more of what my work is about from other people and other sources.[3]

Haring's comments reflect a widely held belief among artists that their own interpretations of their artworks are no more illuminating than are those offered by critics and viewers. Artists clearly revise their opinions of their artworks over time, a fact that makes artists' explanations of their work at any given moment somewhat suspect.

If artist's intentions do not *dictate* for all time what any artwork means, an enduring question remains as to what extent authorial intentions ever *constrain* the interpretation of meaning. There have been many notable public arguments about the meanings of artwork that focused on what an artist intended, or might have intended, to communicate. What is notable about many artistic controversies is just how insistent artists, and their supporters, are in defending artists' rights to have some say in how their art-works are interpreted (see Chapter 9 for a similar discussion on authors and literary interpretation).

For instance, Chris Burden attracted attention in the 1970s for his dangerous performances, including one where he allowed himself to be shot (the *Shoot* pieces). He commented that all people remembered about that work was "There's the guy who had himself shot! They don't go to the next step and wonder why I would want to do that, or what my reasons are."[4] He noted that people generally think he did the pieces for sensational reasons, or to get attention. Yet Burden protested that his intentions here have been wildly misunderstood:

> Those pieces were really private – often there were only two or three people there to see them, or maybe just the people who were there helping me ... It was more like a kind of mental experience for me – to see how I would deal with the mental aspect – like knowing that at 7:30 you're going to stand in a room and a guy's going to shoot you.... The violence part really wasn't that important, it was just a crux to make all the mental stuff happen.[5]

Burden, like many artists, wanted others to understand the motivation for his work, and for his artworks to be experienced in the intentional light in which they were created.

Recall the scandal back in 1987 in regard to some of Andrew Serrano's photographic work, especially the controversy that arose over his provocative piece entitled *Piss Christ*. The photograph was described in the *New York Times* as

> 60 inch by 40 inch and showing Jesus on the cross in a golden haze through a smattering of minute bubbles against a dark, blue-colored background. By slight twisting and considerable enlarge-ment, the image takes on a monumental appearance and the viewer would never guess that a small plastic crucifix was used. The work appears reverential, and it is only after reading the provocative and explicit title that one realizes the object has been immersed in urine.[6]

This photographic image provoked a national controversy when fundamentalist Christians objected to the work as blasphemous and criticized the National Endowment for the Arts (NEA) – which had contributed $15,000 – for spending tax dollars to support Serrano's art. Senator Al D'Amato of New York claimed, in a letter to the chairman of the NEA, that *Piss Christ* was "shocking, abhorant and completely undeserving of any recognition whatsoever. Millions of taxpayers are rightfully incensed that their hard-earned dollars were used to honor and support Serrano's work."[7] Senator Jesse Helms spoke out against Serrano as well in a speech on the floor of the Senate:

> What this Serrano fellow did to create this blasphemy was to fill a bottle with his own urine and then he stuck a crucifix – the Lord Jesus Christ on a cross – down in the urine, set the bottle on a table, and took a picture of it.... He is not an artist. He is a jerk. He is taunting a large segment of the American people, just as others are, about their Christian faith. I resent it, and I do not hesitate to say so.[8]

But many defenders of *Piss Christ* protested that critics completely misunderstood the communicative intentions Serrano wished for observers to recognize. Serrano wrote in a letter to the NEA in 1989:

> I am concerned over recent events regarding the misrepresentation of my work in Congress and consequent treatments in the media. The cavalier and blasphemous intentions ascribed to me on the Congressional floor bear little semblance to reality. I am disturbed that the rush to judgment by certain members of Congress has been particularly swift and vindictive. I am appalled by the claim of "anti-Christian bigotry" that has been attributed to my picture "Piss Christ." The photograph, and the title itself, are ambiguously provocative but certainly not blasphemous. Over the years, I have addressed religion regularly in my art. My Catholic upbringing informs this work which helps me to redefine and personalize my relationship with God. My use of such bodily fluids as blood and urine in this context is parallel to Catholicism's obsession with "the body and blood of Christ." It is precisely in the exploration and juxtaposition of these symbols from which Christianity draws

its strength. The photograph in question, like all my work, has multiple meanings and can be interpreted in various ways. So let us suppose that the picture is meant as a criticism of the billion dollar Christ-for-profit industry and the commercialization of spiritual values that permeates our society. That it is a condemnation of those who abuse the teachings of Christ for their own ignoble ends. Is the subject of religion so inviolate that it is not open to discussion? I think not.[9]

Not surprisingly, Serrano's statement about what he was trying to communicate with *Piss Christ* was not persuasive to critics of his work. To fundamentalist Christians, many members of Congress, and portions of the American public, it mattered little what Serrano thought he was doing by creating *Piss Christ*. All that counts for many people is their subjective impressions of the work.

Another case where an artist's intentions were publicly disputed is seen in a performance piece entitled *Victims*, created by the artist Karen Finley. In this work, Finley covered her naked body with melted chocolate and gave an impassioned speech about the plight of women in modern American life. Newspaper columnists Rowland Evans and Robert Novak complained that Finley's performance was "outrageous" and represented only a "chocolate-smeared young woman."[10] But Finley argued that her intention was to convey just the opposite: "My work is against violence, against rape, and degradation of women ... When I smear chocolate on my body it is a symbol of women being treated like dirt."[11]

Of course, just as might be the case with Serrano's *Piss Christ*, the fact that Finley's intentions were misinterpreted doesn't mean she was actually successful in communicating them in her artwork. Evans and Novak may have inferred something about Finley's intentions in creating *Victims* but misunderstood these intentions, either through their own fault, or because Finley didn't successfully realize her intentions in her creation. In both Finley's and Serrano's cases, we don't know whether the artist's intentions were considered and rejected, or never considered at all. Once again, determining what role intentions have in the experience of meaning requires that scholars consider the full range of understanding experiences, including those that lie outside of ordinary awareness.

The failure to acknowledge an artist's possible intentions in understanding and appreciating artwork is perhaps best illustrated, and most widely debated, in the case of photographer Robert Mapplethorpe's exhibit *The Perfect Moment*. Mapplethorpe's work is noted for images of flowers, self-portraits, and portraits of celebration. The exhibit included controversial images of interracial couplings, male frontal nudity, children in explicit poses, and sadomasochistic, homoerotic images. The Corcoran Museum in Washington, D.C., cancelled the planned showing of *The Perfect Moment* just before its scheduled opening in 1989 for fear of igniting additional controversy about NEA-funded artworks. In April 1990, the exhibit opened at the Contemporary Art Museum in Cincinatti, Ohio. Soon after the opening, the local police temporarily closed the exhibit in order to videotape its contents. Later, the city of Cincinnati brought suit against the Contemporary Arts Center and two curators for exhibiting *The Perfect Moment* on the grounds that some of the photographs (7 out of the 175 photographs exhibited) were obscene.

At the trial, the prosecution simply presented the "offending" photographs to the jury without any other evidence or testimony, saying that "each photograph speaks for itself and the jury will decide the merits."[12] The prosecution explicitly saw no need to inquire about Mapplethorpe's motives and intentions in creating his photographs in the belief that the obscenity of the pictures would be obvious to any ordinary citizen. The defense, on the other hand, introduced several expert witnesses (curators and art critics) who testified on the possible artistic meanings of the "offending" photographs. Although these witnesses varied considerably in their understandings of Mapplethorpe's intentions, the defense testimony highlighted the idea that artistic meaning, like all meaning, is a matter of interpretation, part of which focuses on what the artist might have intended to communicate by his or her artwork. The jury eventually acquitted the museum and the exhibit's two curators of the obscenity charges.

An interesting parallel between the Serrano exhibit, Finley's performance, and the Mapplethorpe trial is that the prima facie meaning of their respective artworks was deemed by critics to be obvious to any normal observer. What the artists may have intended to communicate apparently played no role in how these artworks were regarded. There was no sense that artistic meaning might in any way depend on people's assessments of what artists like Serrano, Finley, or Mapplethorpe intended to communicate by their artworks. However, it isn't clear whether observers and critics actually considered, and then rejected, what the artist in each case might be trying to communicate. All of the attention in these debates centered on people's final judgments, or products, of understanding, which tells us nothing about the various mental processes operating when people make immediate sense of artworks.

Another case where critics have gone beyond an artist's explicit intentions is found in the work of Cindy Sherman. In 1978, Cindy Sherman began to record her self-transformations photographically. She created numerous photographic series devoted to different themes, the first of which were black-and-white images imitative of film clips from the 1950s. Employing a wide variety of costumes and invented characters, Sherman developed a series of fictional visual personae, and later recreated visual representations of women in renowned paintings. Sherman's photographs of performative actions addressed a wide range of theoretical and social issues related to power, class, gender, sexuality, and increasingly forbidden territories of violence, decay, disfigurement, and violation that preoccupied the public in the early 1990s.

Sherman has always explicitly denied that her work addresses questions about women's identity and sexuality. For example, in a recent interview concerning her *Untitled Film Stills*, Sherman said: "I never thought of it as some sort of, oh, idea about the male gaze, you know," and "No, I have never been a fan of criticism or theories, so that actually none of that affected me and still doesn't" and "Many of my pieces are much more innocent than they are interpreted."[13]

Most observers happily seize on Sherman's work as pure masquerade and role playing, unrelated to the real Cindy Sherman. But as art critic Gen Deng made clear, what makes Sherman's work interesting, despite her protests to the contrary, is that people can see in her photographs a dialectical process working itself out through her approach to photographic images, from the black-and-white untitled film stills to the grotesque disintegration of the world portrayed by glossy color photography in the later eighties works.[14] This process did not really come about because of Sherman's theoretical understanding of subjectivity, the male gaze, or the crisis of capitalism. Sherman clearly never intended her photographs to be interpreted as conveying communicative intentions related to these issues. But people recognize how Sherman's artwork raises questions about women's identity and sexuality because of the historical and cultural contents in which her works are produced (and still exist). In a recent interview, Sherman commented, "Even though I've never thought of my work as feminist or as a political statement, certainly everything in it was drawn from my observations as a woman in this culture."[15] Sherman clearly recognizes, then, that readings of her work reflect meanings she didn't intend to communicate, but nevertheless have been manifest to viewers. These meanings may be seen in Sherman's work but have their roots in Sherman's own experiences as a woman. This process of discovering the meanings that were only "manifest" in her work can best be accounted for by relevance theory as described in Chapter 9.

One side effect of Sherman's decision not to use texts with her photographs, which reflects the explicit intention of making her artwork more ambiguous, was an increase in the diversity of meanings that others attributed to her works. Commenting on why she doesn't title her work, Sherman said:

> I want all the clues to what's going on in the pictures to be visual. I thought if I titled them, people would start to see what I was seeing in the picture. I like the idea that different people can see different things in the same image, even if that's not what I would want them to see. Especially with the Centerfold pictures. I got a lot of criticism from feminists who said I was promoting negative stereotypes of women as victims. Or with the one of the woman in black sheets lying in bed ["Untitled #93"], someone said it looked like it was from "True Detective" magazine, that it was trying

to make some woman who'd gotten raped look sexy. To me, the whole inspiration for the picture was somebody who'd been up all night drinking and partying and had just gone to sleep five minutes before the sun rose and woke her up. So it bothered me at first when people criticized the picture, seeing the side that I hadn't intended. I finally decided it was something I had to accept.[16]

In this way, Sherman has accepted how some understandings of her work are manifest in terms of a dynamic relationship between the artist, the work, and spectators, even if she did not specifically intend these meanings to be recognized by others.

WHAT COUNTS AS ART?

Consider the following argument by psychologist Paul Bloom.[17] Imagine that you are presented with a picture of a dog. When you look at the picture and categorize it as "a picture of a dog," what leads you to conclude that it was intended to represent a dog and not something else? Different clues could lead you to this conclusion. First, the artist could tell you something about her exact intention for creating a picture of a dog (e.g., the artist says to you *I painted a picture of a dog*). Or you might see that the title *My dog* was written under the picture, giving you a specific clue that the artist considered her work to be a picture of a dog.[18] You could also have seen the artist looking at a dog while she painted the "dog" picture. Perhaps the most important clue for you might be that by looking at the picture, you infer that the artist's intention was to present a picture of a dog. Something is a picture of a dog if what it represents looks like a dog.

People's judgments about which pictures look like which objects are not entirely based on what they see with their eyes alone. People's individual background knowledge about artistic conventions, or about the nature of representation in general, also plays some role. As Bloom argues, the logic behind an observer's interpretation of a picture is quite specific:[19] (a) a picture that looks like X is likely to have been created with the intention that it looks like X, (b) the usual reason that someone intends to make a picture that looks like X is because this is a good way to create something that will be recognized by others as representing X, and (c) the intention to create something that will be recognized by others as representing X is normally associated with the intention to represent X. Thus, a picture that looks like X is normally the result of the intention to represent X, and is normally a picture of X.

Some artists intend to create something that represents X, but do not wish others to infer, or at least to easily infer, that it is a representation of X. In fact, an artist may intentionally flout artistic conventions to make a statement about art itself. Modern art has many examples where a representation does not look like X, but which the artist still intends us to infer X. Jason Sprinkle's *The Bomb* comes to mind here. People's stereotypical image of a bomb is quite different from a large heart-shaped object sitting in the back of a pick-up truck. In general, visual representations are categorized in terms of people's inferences about artistic intentions. Taking this point of view, philosopher Richard Wolheim writes that to understand a painting, people must consider it "in the perspective of the artist," where this means "seeing the art and the artist's activity in the light of his intentions."[20]

Not all visual, or auditory, representations are the result of intentional psychological processes.[21] When a camera is pointed at Fred in good light and a rock hits it and the shutter snaps, the result is still a photograph of Fred, regardless of the lack of intention. Although the aesthetic qualities of photographs can be governed by intentions every bit as rich as those that underlie paintings, people tend to view their representational properties partly as the result of a nonintentional causal mechanism – a photograph represents whatever the camera is pointed at. Drawings, paintings, and sculptures, on the other hand, are created through purely intentional means, and our intuitions about these processes dictate how they are categorized, understood, and appreciated.

The philosopher Jerrold Levinson has a related position about what counts as art: "To be art is, roughly, to be an object connected in a particular manner, in the intention of a maker or profferer, with preceding art or art-regards."[22] Consider the example of Jaspers, who "directs our attention to a pile of wood shavings on the floor, a green 3 × 5 index card tacked to his wall, and the fact that Montgomery is the capital of Alabama. He names this set of things 'John.' He then says that this is his latest artwork."[23] Levinson argued that people are willing to accept Jasper's creation as an artwork only if they can be convinced that this collection of objects has been sincerely intended by Jaspers for others to regard in a certain way, one associated with how art is typically viewed.[24] This inference might be easier for people to understand in more traditional entities – for example, if Jaspers just put paint onto a canvas. But art has historically embraced a broader class of entities as artworks, and the status of creations by artists like Andy Warhol, Robert Rauschenberg, and Claes Oldenburg is hardly controversial anymore. Art critic Arthur Danto dubs this process of conceptualizing ordinary objects as artworks "transfiguration."[25] For instance, Duchamp's *Fountain* was originally a urinal. The act of transfiguring a urinal into a sculpture entitled *Fountain* is the result of an intentional act, not a physical one.

One criticism of this intentional-historical proposal about what counts as art is that intentions alone are not sufficient to cause people to view something as a member of an artifact kind. To take a simple case, imagine a madman who creates a tiny pile of dirt and states that this pile was successfully created with intention to be a chair. Most people would not view the pile of dirt as a chair, despite the maker's intentions. Or consider the artist Chris Burden, who in 1972 created a work titled *Deadman*, in which Burden had himself enclosed in a sack and placed in the middle of a California freeway. Burden, as well as critics like Danto, clearly viewed this performance piece as a work of art.[26] But many critics and observers disagreed. They didn't doubt the sincerity of someone who placed himself in the middle of traffic to make an aesthetic point. Yet critics argued that even if this object (i.e., a man in a sack on the highway) was created with the sincere intent to be a member of a certain kind (e.g., as an artwork), this is not always enough for others to believe that the object is in fact a member of that kind.

Despite this problem, the intentional-historical theory posits that people should infer a strong relationship between different artifacts and their makers' intentional states. Those instances in which there is an apparent intention to create an X without an X having actually been created might lead observers to wonder about the creator's state of mind and to doubt whether the right intention to create X actually existed. For instance, most people can't help wondering about Jasper's state of mind when he claims his pile of dirt was created to represent a chair.

Similar to the interpretation of literature, when viewers observe an artwork that evokes an emotion or idea, they do not automatically jump to the conclusion that the artist was in that state of mind when the work was created. Nor do people assume that the specific intentions emerged into the artist's consciousness when the work was completed. Nor do people assume that the artist intended for them to recognize that state of mind, if it did exist, as part of our understanding of the work. For instance, listeners must distinguish between calling a requiem "sad" and saying that its creator was sad when composing it. But when a critic calls a painting "pretentious," or Duchamp's *Fountain* "ironic," then a reference has been made to something that the creator displayed in the work itself.

Interpreting an artwork identifies the work's critical choice and explores how these decisions derive from a coherent design or plan. Philosopher Nan Stalnaker has outlined a theory that nicely expresses this point of view about art interpretation:[27] (1) Interpretation is a retrospective, idealized reconstruction of the artist's visually or formally expressed intentions. (2) An artwork's formal success – its performance in the present – provides primary evidence for a reconstruction of the artist's intentions. (3) While making no claims about the artist's conscious states, interpretation is credible only if the intentions attributed to the artist are consistent with all that is known about a work's creation. This account is similar to the idea of hypothetical intentionalism proposed in Chapter 8.

Contemporary artists are often quite specific about how their artworks are to be displayed precisely because they want tight control over spectators' inferences about their different intentional states. One of the most famous examples of an artist dictating how his or her work is exhibited is found in Marcel Duchamp's

Etant donnes at the Philadelphia Museum of Art. As one writer described the work:

> The viewer enters a small room and approaches an old wooden Spanish door, framed in a brick archway set within a plaster wall. He looks through the two holes set at eye-level in the door. The viewer, now voyeur, sees a brilliantly lit landscape in which a waterfall plays in the distance. A naked figure of a woman lies with her legs apart on a bed of brushwood holding in her left hand a dimly illuminated gas-lamp. The tableau is at once secret, shocking and enigmatic, with the face of the figure hidden from view by her flowing blond hair.[28]

Peeking into this scene, viewers experience a sense of intimate complicity between themselves and the artist, as if to ask themselves *What does Duchamp wish for me alone to notice*? Duchamp's carefully staged manipulation of the physical environment for his piece takes on primary importance in our psychological experience of the work.

A more immediate sense of the artist physically creating an artwork for a particular space is given by Richard Serra in his *Splashing* sculptures. Similar to the sweeping gestures that Jackson Pollack used in his "drip" paintings, Serra splashes lead at the edge where wall and floor meet. *Splashing* is successively realized in slightly different ways in each museum it is shown. Viewers of these exhibits are often provided with a narrative description of how Serra and his associates entered the museum in the middle of the night to create these sculptures, thus giving the observer a sense of the artist having been in that very space, physically creating the work for that specific location. People's experience of *Splashing* affords them a more direct sense of the artist as a real person creating the work for their immediate pleasure, rather than of an artist creating some work in a distant place and time and then packing and shipping it to different locations for viewers to see. Serra's work demonstrates how the gallery or museum has become a studio, prompting a significant change in the relationships among the artist, spectators, curators, and works of art. Viewers now get a more immediate sense of the artist's hand in the creation of art. Many art enthusiasts greatly value the sense of intimacy between artist and spectator, as if spectators get to witness the artist creating the work or to see it through the artist's own eyes.

Seeing an artwork through the eyes of the artist who created it has been a stable principle of twentieth-century art conservation. One of the most hotly debated issues in the 1980s art world centered on the cleaning and restoration of the frescoes on the ceiling of the Sistine Chapel in the Vatican.[29] There was tremendous criticism of the efforts to restore the ceiling to its appearance as Michelangelo may have seen it when painting it back in the early sixteenth century. The restored ceiling looked quite unfamiliar to many observers. People questioned exactly what Michelangelo's intentions must have been at the time he created the ceiling. Other critics wondered whether it made any sense to do extensive historical research to make educated guesses as to what Michelangelo may have wanted to present in the finished work.[30]

The furor over the restoration of the Sistine Chapel ceiling illustrates the continual difficulty with the principle that the goal of art conservation should be to present the artwork as the artist originally intended it to be seen.[31] The rise of scientific technique enables conservationists to identify the artist's original intention from later additions by other people or from changes due to the ravages of time. The National Gallery of Art in Washington, D.C., formally adopted this principle in the late 1940s and early 1950s. A conservationist for the National Gallery claimed: "It is presumed to be beyond dispute that the aim of those entrusted with the care of paintings is to present them as nearly as possible in the state in which the artist intended them to be seen."[32] The conservationists job was "to preserve and show to its best advantage every original particle remaining of a painting," and in so doing to be "guided by the master's intentions."[33] But as argued above, interpretation of a master's intentions can be primarily a retrospective, idealized reconstruction of the artist's visually and formally expressed intentions. Art historians may never know what Michelangelo's intentions were as he created the Sistine Chapel frescoes. But historians and critics can propose idealized reconstructions of the artist's formally expressed intentions based on the artwork itself and their understanding of the complex conditions under which it was created.

INTENTIONS AND PERFORMANCE

In performance art, such as in music, dance, and theater, an original artist's conception of the work also involves intentions directed toward another agent – the performer. A performance of a work is a series of actions in which one person (the performer) has intentions to fulfill the intentions of another person (composer, choreographer, or playwright). For instance, the composer's score is the set of indications to the performer about how the music artifact is to be played.

Understanding that an artwork conveys various intentions to both performers and observers is best illustrated by looking at the hierarchy of intentions in musical performances.[34] High-level intentions are those intentions of a composer that are directed toward effects on a listener, such as thoughts or emotions a listener is to have. Middle-level intentions are the means the composer has to bring about these effects, which in a pure musical experience are intended sounds to which the listener is to be exposed. The composer will have clearly conceived intentions about many aspects of these, such as the key, tempos, dynamics, textures, melodic and harmonic content, and so on. How the composer conceives of aspects of sound is radically relative to the culture, the sophistication of the composer, and the existing theoretical language, notably notation, that the composer has to work with. Often the composer also has low-level intentions and expectations regarding how these intentions are to carried out. For a middle-level intention – about the texture or timbre of sounds at a given place in the composition, for example – low-level intentions may be directed at the nature of the instruments to be played, the relative dynamics or balance, how the stringed instruments are to be bowed, how the wind instruments are to be blown, and so on.

Several empirical studies illustrate that musicians generally are aware of the particular intentions they wish to communicate and that listeners often are successful in understanding these expressive meanings. One study compared musicians' performance of a Baroque sonata with their notated interpretations of musical dynamics (patterns of intensity changes).[35] Performers' notated intentions generally corresponded to changes in sound level. For instance, a musician can intend to produce a crecsendo by increasing the intensity sufficiently and gradually. Listeners' perceived dynamics nicely matched performers' intended dynamics, even when underlying acoustic changes were not identifiable. Another study compared performers' interpretation of emotional content with their use of expression.[36] For instance, flute and violin performances of the same music interpreted with different emotional character revealed specific patterns of change in expression. Performances of happy and angry emotions were played at a faster tempo and with larger dynamic range, while sad emotions were played at a slower tempo and with smaller dynamic range. Tone onsets were abrupt in the angry performances and more gradual in the sad performances. Most generally, these empirical studies demonstrate how musicians specifically get listeners to successfully recover different high-level intentions through recognition of middle- and low-level musical intentions.

Contemporary composers often work closely with conductors and musicians in rehearsal to facilitate the realization of low- and middle-level intentions so that audiences may recognize a composer's high-level intentions. In fact, there are examples of composers altering their scores to better realize a high-level intention because of a conductor's feedback. Once, for instance, Aaron Copeland sat in during rehersals of a new piece with the Boston Symphony Orchestra, under the direction of Serge Koussevitzky. Although the conductor is usually subservient to the composer, Copeland often found himself saying *Yes, Dr. Koussevtizsky, it sounds better that way. I will change it in my score*.[37] Koussevitzky also tried to get Bela Bartok to change aspects of his score for *Concerto for Orchestra*, because of the orchestra's difficulties with Bartok's irregular rhythms, but Bartok refused to alter his composition in any way.[38] Conductors and performers may interpret a work according to their own artistic goals and obligations. Critics sometimes complain that conductors and musicians take undue liberties with composers' scores. The musicologist Gunther Schuller recently argued that many cherished symphonies in Western culture are really bastardized, given that conductors have long misinterpreted the true intentions of the composers.[39] Schuller has documented in great detail how twentieth-century conductors have misread many classical composers' intentions, often doing tremendous damage to the original compositions (e.g., Beethoven's Fifth and Seventh Symphonies, Schumann's Second, Brahms's First and Fourth, Tchaikovsky's Sixth).

Yet other scholars have claimed that realizing aesthetic value in performance may conflict with a composer's noted intentions. Thus, Alan Golden finds it "obvious in the case of music" that "artistic value may be lost by strict adherence to the artist's intentions."[40] For example, a musical performance may suffer if musicians are required to use instruments only available to the composer at the time the piece was created. But this view of what a composer had at his disposal at the time of creation paints too narrow a view of the composer's communicative intentions. Musicians might very well better realize a composer's higher-order intention using instruments invented after the time a piece was originally created.[41] Strict adherence to the composer's intentions may, in some critics' and conductors' view, be reasonably sacrificed to enhance people's experience of the work.

In general, some aspects of a performance are traceable to the composer through the intentions of the performer to fulfill the composer's intentions, and some may be traceable only to the intentions of the performer.[42] Yet this conclusion does not tell the whole story about intentions and performance. Consider the case of John Cage, who in his aesthetic philosophy adhered to the belief that "events do not possess discrete facts and discrete perceivers; rather the two are joined in an observation."[43] Cage's philosophy placed the greatest emphasis on the phenomenological experience of performers, performance events, and audience in an evolving, complex interrelationship.[44] In a 1937 manifesto called *The Future of Music*, Cage urged that everyday materials be used in musical performance: "Wherever we are, what we hear is mostly noise. When we ignore it, it disturbs us. When we listen to it, we find it fascinating. The sound of a truck at 50 m.p.h. Static between the stations. Rain. We want to capture and control these sounds, to use them, not as sound effects, but as musical instruments."[45] By exploring how everyday life provides the materials for musical performance, Cage adopted an anti-intentionalist view of music composition. Even though he desired to "capture and control" aspects of these events, Cage also wanted to let "chance" dictate performance rather than assuming that performances are entirely determined by an artist's intentional decisions.

For instance, in Cage's self-explanatory *Demonstration of the Sounds of the Environment*, three hundred people silently followed an itinerary generated by an aleatoric procedure devised from the *I Ching*. Of course, Cage's best-known piece in this genre was his 4′33″, in which silence was a notational device (i.e., a way of framing circumambient sounds). In the performance, a person appeared on stage, opened a score, but played nothing, compelling the audience to attend to whatever sounds were heard in the interval of "silence." One critic noted that attending 4′33″ "was one of the most intense listening experiences you can have," yet what was heard was not determined in any special way by the "composer."[46]

Intentionally removing authorial intentions from the creation of musical performances illustrates the power of listeners to define their own aesthetic experiences. Over the last fifty years, many painters, musicians, poets, dancers, and filmmakers have found great inspiration in spontaneous performances that appear to be beyond the grasps of artists' deliberate intentional meanings. A key event in the history of modern performance was the presentation in 1959 of Allan Kaprow's *18 Happenings in Parts* in New York City.[47] Audiences at Kaprow's "happenings" were seated in three different rooms, where they saw fragmented events performed simultaneously in all three spaces. The events included the showing of slides, the playing of musical instruments, posed schemes, the reading of fragmentary notes from placards, and artists painting on canvas walls. People's meaningful experience of such events are created in sharp contrast to other artistic performances, where what is seen or heard is very much under the control of an intentional agent.

Plays and films also provide interesting cases in which artists' differing intentions toward the performance can affect people's experience of their works. In plays and films, for instance, the author often steps outside the work itself to provide explicit instructions as to how his or her intentions are to be realized. Samuel

Beckett's position was that stage directions, rather than the text's "diction," often *are* the play. His *Acts without Words I and II* is nothing but stage directions! As director Sidney Lumet recently wrote: "Carrying out the writer's intention is the primary objective of the entire production."[48] Yet in movies, unlike plays, directors get all the credit for success and must bear the criticism for any failures. Longtime *New Yorker* movie critic Pauline Kael often critiqued films on the basis of the director's choices in making the film (choice of actors, musical score, camera angles, plot development). Kael went so far as to "re-plot" movies based on what she would have done as director.[49] For instance, in her review of *The Right Stuff*, Kael said:

> I wish that Kaufman [the director] had followed through on the disturbing, awkward qualities of this incident, which grips us at a different emotional level from the other scenes. I realize that I'm asking for a different kind of movie, but if he'd taken a different approach to the Gus and Betty Grissom episode he might have opened up some of the implications of the phrase "the right stuff" that have bothered me ever since Tom Wolfe's book came out.[50]

Many spectators engage in exactly the kind of thinking Kael exhibits in her review when they experience, and later reflect upon, the movies or plays they see. People's experience of performances is very much tied to what they believe are the intentions of those who created the artwork.

There are notable cases where a play's performance clearly violates a playwright's communicative and aesthetic intentions. Consider one production of a play by Arthur Miller. Many critics have argued that Miller's earlier works were far more successful than his later plays, in part, because of his close working relationship with directors like Elia Kazan on plays such as *All My Sons* in 1947 and *Death of a Salesman* in 1949. But later in his career, Miller's casual, agreeable style with directors shifted to a more confrontational stance. Miller even threatened litigation against one director, Elizabeth LeCompte, who attempted to ignore Miller's scripted intentions. LeCompte wished to add something new to Miller's play *The Crucible*, which Miller wrote to mirror the religious rites and spirit of the Puritans in Salem,

Massachusetts. But LeCompte envisioned the play more broadly as a work "that examines political repression as much as religious domination."[51] To realize this idea, LeCompte wanted to present an abbreviated version of Miller's play and embellish it with various film footage, including film of LSD advocate Timothy Leary debating Watergate figure G. Gordon Liddy. Miller voiced alarm that to let LeCompte alter the spirit of *The Crucible* would discourage a possible major revival of the play (the play was made into a movie in 1996). Miller did not wish LeCompte to produce what he perceived as a "blatant parody of his work"– though parodies normally lie beyond the protection of the Dramatists' Guild.[52]

As LeCompte fought Miller for legal rights to her creative use of the play, she reduced her illegal incorporation of the play from forty-five to twenty minutes of pantomime and/or gibberish. Critics noted that LeCompte's performers "drink, smoke, and party while fragments from Act III surface in a fitful rhythm" and that the actors' activity "alternates between the simple act of reading" and a "highly theatricalized mania."[53] Ultimately, with the backing of the Dramatists' Guild, Miller triumphed and LeCompte's production was closed. Miller's fears for his artistic product are understandable in view of the pace at which the theatrical world has moved toward radical alteration of the author's text. Contemporary directors readily tear down traditional walls that once protected classic scripts. Poor William Shakespeare (whoever he really was) might be shocked if he saw how many of his plays have been "cut and rearranged," with characters transmogrified to "everything from voodoo priestesses to American gangsters."[54] Many critics, especially those who have read and studied Shakespeare's texts, note how widely many contemporary productions vary from the original texts. But do ordinary viewers of these new productions recognize which parts of the plays are close to Shakespeare's intentions and what parts can be attributed to what a director has specifically done? Does it really matter who authors the play? Although many people care little about who wrote a play, or film, and instead only wish to get caught up in the experience of watching the performance, to others knowing who wrote a play or film still matters a great deal (see Chapter 8).

INTENTIONS IN IMPROVISATIONAL DANCE

Improvisational dance, where the performers act without benefit of a choreographer's directions, provides an interesting challenge to the idea that intentions underlie meaningful experience. Consider the case of contact improvisation, a dance genre where two or more dancers move spontaneously in close physical contact with each other. Just as two people must coordinate their actions as they improvise in spoken dialogue, contact improvisation, as the name implies, requires dancers to coordinate and cooperate as they lean against and balance on each other, give support or are supported by each other, roll on the floor and over each other, jump up, fall, and perform in various other solo and shared movements. Dancers and observers may not be consciously aware of meaningful patterns as they move and watch. Yet a few moments of reflection on the aesthetic pleasure we receive as dancers and observers clearly suggests that dance, including improvisational dance, taps into important aspects of intentionality. My claim is that the creativity we see in improvisational dance is not the product of unintentional movements, but arises from our perceptions of the intentionality underlying the dancers' individual and shared actions.

The power of intentional meaning in the performance and interpretation of contact improvisation is best demonstrated in terms of an actual performance. Consider my own response to the first few minutes of a contact improvisational dance performance entitled *Julian and Alito's Duet*, originally presented as part of *A Cappella Motion* (1993).

Julian and Alito's performance begins with the two dancers walking onto the stage and Julian lying face down on the floor, hands extended in front, and Alito moving over to squat on the back of Julian's thighs. Julian raises his head and shoulders and looks behind to observe Alito and then Julian extends his arms out in front of him. Julian lies back down and Alito moves upward onto Julian's back, balancing himself, arms extended, then stands on Julian's back as Julian once more rises, this time to his hands and knees. Alito sits on top of Julian, riding him, while Julian slowly raises himself to his knees, soon coupling his hands around

Alito's feet as Alito wraps his legs around Julian's trunk. Julian stands, walks around the stage and twirls Alito around in circles as Alito twists on Julian's back, extending arms and legs outward in different directions, sometimes using Julian's one extended arm as a guide. Julian then stops walking and slowly pulls Alito around in front of him, and, while still standing, cradles Alito in his arms down by his waist. Alito lies back, and with arms extended over his head and legs extended outward. Julian then forcefully attempts to pull Alito up and Alito jerks spasmodically (audience laughing). Julian then makes the same attempt, and again Alito jerks spasmodically (again the audience laughs).

Even within these first few minutes of *Julian and Alito's Duet*, I am struck by several specific movements and several general themes that suggest different levels of intentionality on the part of the dancers. The dancers, both individually and in concert, exhibit through a number of movements and positions great symmetry, balance, support, linkage, and emotional involvement and independence. As the performance proceeds, the dancers appear to be on an improvisational journey heading toward some unknown destination that unfolds in front of them. At several moments, both the dancers and the audience appear to be "taken by surprise" as one movement leads unexpectedly into another position and/or movement. I see the dancers awakening, coming together, struggling over different personal and mutual obstacles, experiencing moments of calm, moments of great elation, moving toward places where they are in tight synchronicity; and, at other times, the dancers appear to be feeling each other out for possible new ways to be joined together for their individual and mutual benefit.

Many aspects of Julian and Alito's performance make use of bodily based metaphors that we recognize for their intentional meaning. For example, various bodily postures and movements express via metaphor different sorts of conventional meanings. Upward movements are suggestive of positive affect, of greater conscious control of one's body and, more generally, of one's life. For instance, there are many moments in Julian and Alito's dance where their upward movements, both while on the ground and while standing, signify positive emotions, especially when they are in balanced positions of contact. On the other hand, downward body postures and movements suggest negative affect, reflecting individuals under stress, in poor health, with little control over their movements or their lives. The opening of Julian and Alito's performance, where Julian lies prone with Alito on top of him, suggests, just for a moment, Alito's control over Julian. At the very beginning Julian lifts his head and looks over his shoulder at Alito as if to question this control. Some of their unsteady movements and positions suggest uncertainty. Falling represents the lack of control, illness, and feelings of debasement. At a later moment in Julian and Alito's dance, Alito runs toward Julian and leaps into his arms, as if wishing to establish a more personal bond between them. But the movement fails because the dancers immediately become unbalanced, yet the two dancers gracefully tumble onto the stage and start anew to establish contact. Throughout the performance, bodily movements that are balanced, whether a dancer is moving or stationed alone or in contact with other dancers, reflect mental, emotional, and moral stability.

In Julian and Alito's dance, movements across the stage reflect aspects of our embodied experience of physical journeys. Here the movements from point A along some path to point B express progress toward some concrete or abstract, sometimes personal, goal. One sees the struggle when the dancers first begin a journey (some movement from point A to point B), the obstacles they encounter along the way, how they try, and sometimes fail, to support each other, the times when they seem to be spinning their wheels (including one moment later in Julian and Alito's performance when Alito actually walks briskly in place), until they break free and almost fly toward their long-anticipated goal. Most generally, many aspects of the movements Julian and Alito perform, the movements observers see in their dance, are not interpreted simply as arbitrary physical acts with no sense of purpose or communicative meaning. The basic images in dance are movement structures that are inherently intentional, imaginatively patterned, and flexible, both in terms of their physical instantiation and their symbolic interpretation.

If one were to ask a dancer why he or she moved in some way at a particular improvisational moment, it is unlikely that any specific aesthetic or communicative intentions would come to mind. Dancers feel the "flow" of their bodily movement – they become the dance they are creating. Most dancers even resist trying to articulate in words what their movements meant. But the deeply rooted patterns of embodied metaphor evident in improvisational dance appear as manifestations of the dancers' intentional minds, working together to create aesthetic meanings.

Dancers do not necessarily create de novo entirely new conceptualizations of experience each time they react spontaneously to create seemingly novel body movements and combinations. Although dancers may perform bodily movements in ways that take us by surprise, they are creatively elaborating in intentional ways the bodily based metaphorical ideas shared by all human beings. We can acknowledge dancers such as Julian and Alito for their creativity in moving, positioning themselves both alone and in contact with others, for their creativity in the moment. In fact, much of the creativity we see in contact improvisation, such as that I observed in watching Julian and Alito's performance, rests on our polysemous understanding of embodied metaphors. For instance, there are moments of great power and happiness as Julian and Alito move down across the floor as, in my immediate reading, they struggle to find harmony between them. This reading might seem to conflict with metaphorical notions that to be down is to be sad, in ill health, unconscious, or even dead. Yet we can take joy in how even those who are down, with great burdens upon their shoulders, as when Alito climbs onto Julian's back, actually reverse the preexisting metaphorical idea and express different emotional nuances than are traditionally expressed by such body positions.

Most important, though, is that we may be aware, as I was, of how the new insights in an improvisational dance are rooted in established patterns of embodied meaning while, at the same time, these same conventional patterns of meaning are overturned and lead to the sense of being "taken by surprise." Some of our appreciation of contact improvisational dance is based on our tacit recognition of the multiplicity of meanings that we construe for particular sets of movements and positions. I like to think that dancers are intentionally communicating narratives or stories via

317

combination of various bodily movements, which are reflective of widely shared metaphors. The movements dancers make create the impression of stories that we can understand, not just in the local sense of watching someone move across a stage, but in broader terms relating to the human story, our own mundane lives as we struggle to find meaning between order and chaos. Recognition of the intentionality in dance is an important element in our experience of the movements not as mere accidents but as beautiful, artistic, meaningful actions.[55]

A CASE STUDY IN ARTISTIC INTENTIONS

A wonderful example of how artists' communicative intentions play a direct role in the interpretation of artworks is illustrated in a series of non-representational paintings by two artists, Marilyn Hammond and Thelka Levin. Because of their concern that the visual impact of contemporary art was getting lost in voluminous verbal statements by both artists and critics, the two painters decided to undertake a project entitled *Epistolary Paint: A Visual Correspondence*, in which they corresponded solely with their paintings. The artists agreed on some ground rules on the size of the paintings and restricted their colors to the simple palette of red, green, white, and gold. They agreed to talk by phone about the logistics of the project, but never about the actual art. Ten times from October 1992 to July 1995, Hammond shipped a finished piece from her Berkeley, California, studio to Levin in Brookline, Massachusetts. In turn, Levin interpreted each of Hammond's ten paintings and responded with a painting of her own for Hammond to then interpret. Back and forth the correspondence went, with each painting raising the stakes for their project. The exhibition of the correspondence in pictures at the Richmond Art Center in Richmond, California, in the fall of 1995 provided a vivid testimony to Levin and Hammond's intellectual and artistic sparrings. The paintings were hung in sequence, starting with Levin's opening piece and ending with Hammond's final response. Walking through the exhibit, a spectator immediately saw a contrast in styles, despite the general similarities in the two artists' work as abstract painters. Levin painted with bold edges and simple patterns, while Hammond, as she later admitted, added complexity to each painting, forming layers of color to make things ambiguous. Her work, as she put it, "asks a lot of questions."

We are fortunate that Levin and Hammond not only created their respective paintings but also that they kept separate journals to record their private thoughts and musings as they painted and reacted to each other's visual "letters." Ignoring Henri Mattise's adage, "Painters, cut out your tongues," the two artists' journals provide a fascinating glimpse into the role of communicative intentions in the creation and understanding of art. Visitors at the Richmond Art Center exhibition spent considerable time reading through these journals (in fact, they spent as much time, if not more, reading the journals as they did looking at the painting dialogue).

How successful was this visual correspondence? Not surprisingly, the two collaborators encountered many moments of confusion, irritation, elation, excitement, and anger, all experienced through and understood in terms of their artistic communication. Consider some of the following journal entries.[56]

Upon receiving painting #4 from Levin (the artists agreed not to give the paintings titles), Hammond recorded her reaction: "Elegant, engrossing, upsetting, denying. Is this correspondence a false situation that creates unrealistic consequences? How much of a dialogue are we trying to build? What is a dialogue? Is a xx from possibility a negation?" Commenting further on #4, Hammond continued, "And it feels like a simplification or negation of the complexity I was attempting to approach." Upon sending #5 in response, Hammond wrote: "So I am violating the... quality of your piece ... I don't know the answers to my questions about the nature of the dialogue, except that certainly this is an exchange, and in that there must be some push/pull – some tension – and then some change."

But Levin was clearly upset with #5 upon receiving it. "But wait! Is it really an answer to my #4? Or is it more of how our interpretation of her new series and its application to our visual dialogue? No! Of course not! It's all unconscious. How can we be so aware of the influences how head tricks play?... [Hammond's #5 is] More of a response to my #2 – very much so. Is she aware that this is so radically different? How could she not be? But then again, we sometimes do things that we don't realize 'til months later."

When painting #6 Levin "threw a monkey wrench," as she put it, into one of her paintings as a not-so-subtle message for Hammond, one that Hammond saw as a vise rather than as a wrench, a vise she felt closing around her neck. "I really didn't understand what the significance of the vise was," she said, "and there was no way to figure it out." When Levin received Hammond's answer, "I didn't see any reference at all to the monkey wrench," she said, "so I began to wonder, is she listening to me and responding?"

When painting #8 Levin said, "Not only will Thelma experience a long time to receive this painting, but when she sees it, she will feel the way it develops. Hopefully she'll understand that the process is very much the reason for this response." When Levin painted #8 she wrote,

> A struggle seems to have developed between us – so we moved closer to the concerns that govern and shape our other work we seem to need to insist on our own identity in the process we are sharing – rather than allowing a dialogue, an exchange, to create a different reality.... I have suggested structured space twice. Twice you have denied it. Is it because you didn't like it? You don't think it important?... The object is completely dismissed as well. Is it because you don't like objects? Do you know what a monkey wrench is? Do you recognize it? Do you object to humor?... I want to be strong enough, secure enough about who I am and what my work is about to be able to enter your world, to open myself up to your painting and allow a truly feeling reaction to your statement.

Later on, Levin wrote upon receiving #9,

> Despair – a profound despair and hopelessness overwhelms me. This painting makes manifest the leitmotif that has haunted me throughout our project – or may be throughout my life – the suspicion that communication between people isn't just difficult, it

is most probably impossible.... I suggest multiplicity, you simplify, I suggest ambiguity, you reduce, object, you insist on nonrepresentational shapes.... I feel that I have been discounted. Denied. Ignored. Refuted. Abandoned. Reduced. Closed out. Maybe we are communicating!

At the end of the series, it is clear that the artists were in close syncopation. For the last paintings in the series, Hammond planted two gold figures on opposite edges of the canvas. "I wanted to show that the space had opened up and was filled with all types of new possibilities, which is what I felt our correspondence had done." The final painting by Levin brings the figures into focus. "I call it the 'Walking in painting'," she said. "There's the two of us moving on to the next step."

These personal observations about their visual correspondence dramatically illustrate how important it was for Hammond and Levin to have their communicative intentions understood. Of course, the very nature of their collaboration forced both painters, and us as observers, to wonder about the interplay of intentions in the creation of artworks. Yet taken as a whole, as Hammond noted at the end of the project, the *Epistolary Paint* exhibition "shows that the paintings could carry all of that conversation, all of that emotion, all of these ideas, and when we started we weren't sure of that."

CONCLUSION

Understanding artwork starts from the premise that these artifacts were intentionally created to count as instances of art. Artworks, after all, are not mere products of nature. The intentional nature of artworks immediately leads spectators to wonder about the purposes and meanings artists wish to express through their work. Although we do not necessarily seek out the subjective intentions of the artist(s) who created an artifact, observers will use any available information about the artist, and the historical contexts in which a work was originally produced, to draw inferences about what makes the artwork meaningful. Even when authorial intentions are presumably divorced from how a work is created (e.g., Cage's 4'33"), people almost immediately hypothesize about the artist's presumed intention in creating the work. Once again, observers may infer meanings that deviate from an artist's possible communicative intentions, and they may even be aware that such interpretations conflict with what the artist intended. But as is the case for spoken language, and written texts, people's experience of meaning of artworks begins as a conversation with the intentional artist.

Part V

Conclusion

Chapter 12

The Intentional Mind

We live in a time when clever folks work long and hard to reveal the hidden meanings of what people have said, written, created, and presented. So much of what we desire to understand remains elusive, hidden, bidding us to "come get me" and "discover my secrets." We experience this sense that some meaning is hidden as much when we interact with people as we do when struggling to interpret literature, law, artworks, and other cultural symbols. Our common reflex is to indulge in the Socratic impulse to tear the covers off things in the hope that opaque meanings will shine transparent.

Consider this excerpt from a work entitled *Men Are from Belgium, Women Are from New Brunswick*, which aims to help readers better understand the secret meanings behind the statements spoken by a man and woman during a dinner conversation. Each statement is followed by an interpretation of what the speaker actually meant by his or her words:

Guy: *Is this meat loaf?* (he actually means "This is meat loaf? Isn't it?")

Gal: *Of course it is, darling.* (she actually means "Do you have a problem with that?")

Guy: *Mmm. It's delicious!* (he actually means "It's awful")

Gal: *I'm so glad you're enjoying it.* (she actually means "Isn't that a damn shame")

Guy: *Did you use a recipe?* (he actually means "Did you just throw all this stuff together randomly or what?")

Gal: *To tell the truth, I was feeling kind of creative, so I made it up.* (she actually means "So what if I did. SO WHAT. SO, SO, SO WHAT!!!")

Guy: *Next time, don't be shy about using a recipe, O.K.?* (he actually means "It's completely inedible, that's what!")

Gal: *Okeydokey!* (she actually means "Your criticism stems from your own feeling of inadequacy. You should seek professional help.")

This excerpt is really a *New Yorker* cartoon parody of the best-selling book about relationships between men and women by John Gray, *Men Are from Mars, Women Are from Venus*.[1] Yet the dialogue rings true for many people who have engaged in conversations like this one, where the main task appears to be to find the hidden messages behind what someone else has said. Bookstores are stocked with hundreds of advice books on how to uncover the hidden or secret meanings of different kinds of speech, writing, actions, and artwork. These self-help books offer explicit translations of different human behaviors into readily understandable terms (e.g., explaining how to tell when a person really means "yes" when his or her words or actions say "no"). This widely held "code" view of human behavior assumes that people interpret the actions of others as if each event, utterance, text, dream, dance, musical piece, or artwork had a secret meaning that can be made transparent given the right access "code." Thus, in the above dinner conversation, the man and woman speak in different codes, which is why the two sexes often experience communication problems when interacting.

My purpose in this book has been to demonstrate that people don't interpret the behavior of others, or understand the meanings of human artifacts, simply by looking up what each discrete event secretly means in a mental "code book." Nor do people generally interpret language or artworks by engaging in idiosyncratic deconstructive practices. Instead, people's experiences of meaning are fundamentally structured by their inferences about the intentions of others. We understand what is meaningful as a result of cognitive operations about the intentional purposes motivating our own and other people's actions in social/cultural contexts. Understanding is not simply a private mental act, however, but a social achievement taking place in the public domain. The intentional meanings that underlie communication arise as much as a product of understanding as they do from the originary sources for what we see as meaningful in life, language, and art.

This book has described some of the arguments and empirical research from the humanities and cognitive sciences on the pervasiveness of intentional meaning and understanding. My working assumption has been that language, art, and many nonlinguistic behaviors are not independent of the minds that created and interact with these human artifacts. Meaning is not transcendent of human experience, but arises from the ways we ordinarily think, reason, and imagine about ourselves and the world around us. My adoption of the cognitive intentionalist premise (i.e., explicitly seeking out through empirical means the possible ways that assumptions about intentionality shape understanding) has allowed me to examine a wide range of ideas about human action, language, and art and to suggest a number of conclusions about the intentional mind.

First, the idea that a person's intentions play no part in the interpretation of human action, language, and artworks is clearly wrong. People judge that speech, texts, or artworks have particular meanings primarily because of their perceptions about what speakers, authors, and artists intended to communicate. People cannot ignore the fact that speech, texts, and artworks arise from human activities that have intentional purposes. Our deeply held, mostly unconscious, assumptions about the link between human agency and human artifacts shape how we think about and understand language and artworks as being relevant to our experiences.

Intentional meaning is relevant in different ways to our understanding of experience. People understand language and art in real time beginning in the earliest unconscious moments when hearing an utterance, reading a text, or observing an artwork, up to later temporal moments when they consciously reflect upon language and artworks over long periods of time. Various cognitive science research demonstrates that recovery of a person's communicative intentions is a fundamental part of our ordinary, immediate comprehension of spoken and written language. Understanding language focuses on the communicative intentions of speakers and writers, and does not obligatorily demand an analysis of what is literally or textually stated. Many empirical studies indicate that people directly infer speakers' and authors' communicative intentions, even when what is literally expressed underdetermines what is meaningfully implied. People can, on occasion, recover a speaker's, writer's, or artist's subjective intentions as part of understanding what is said, written, or artistically created. This ability to infer another person's subjective intentions is most commonly found in spoken conversation. Speakers and listeners often negotiate what is being specifically communicated and may indeed come to a "meeting of minds." Recovery of subjective intentions in the experience of meaning can happen with written language and artworks as well, but clearly less often than is the case with speech.

The most common way of understanding written language and artworks is in terms of hypothetical intentions. Hypothetical intentionalism holds that people find language and artworks meaningful without necessarily knowing the actual beliefs and intentions of the person(s) creating the artifact. Readers and spectators form meaningful interpretations of what is written or created by reconstructing an idealized version of what someone has said, written, or created, given the artifact (i.e., the language or artwork) and an understanding of the conditions under which the artifact was created. Whether language and art are understood by recovering a person's subjective intentions, or by forming hypothetical intentions about what that person must have meant, depends on a large variety of factors. The most important of these is the extent to which sufficient common ground exists to allow speakers and listeners, authors and readers, artists and observers to infer agents' actual intentions.

One of the most important points of this book is that many aspects of meaningful experience arise when various meanings are manifest to listeners and readers given the cognitive environments they share with speakers and authors. People infer loose implications of utterances, texts, and artworks not always because their authors explicitly intended such meanings to be understood. Instead, addressees are often encouraged to explore different contextual assumptions that give rise to a range of weak implicatures. Many aspects of poetic and literary language, as well as of artworks, are best understood in terms of the communication of weak implicatures, which are meanings not explicitly represented in the minds of speakers, writers, and artists. The concept of weak implicatures nicely captures the indeterminacy of literary and artistic effects that appear to go beyond intentional meaning.

A significant claim of this book is that it is quite difficult, and at times impossible, to conceive of interpretations that differ from intentional meanings unless there is some acknowledgment that understanding is fundamentally grounded in human intentionality. Consider one debate about the meaning of a popular song by the Police entitled "Every Breath You Take."[2] The lyrics to the song are:

> Every breath you take
> Every move you make
> Every bond you break
> Every step you take
>
> I'll be watching you
>
> Every single day
> Every word you say
> Every game you play
>
> I'll be watching you
>
> Oh can't you see
> You belong to me
> How my poor heart aches with every step you take
>
> Every move you make
> Every vow you break
> Every smile you fake
> Every claim you stake
>
> I'll be watching you
>
> Since you're gone I've been lost without a trace
> I dream at night I can only see your face
> I look around but it's you I can't replace
> I keep crying baby please

Conclusion

Every move you make
Every vow you break
Every smile you fake
Every claim you stake

I'll be watching you

What is this song about? Most listeners have interpreted this song as a love ballad in which the vocalist, Sting, laments the loss of a dear loved one. But Sting has noted in various interviews that the song was written from the perspective of a spurned lover stalking his ex-girlfriend. Thus, the refrain *I'll be watching you* is not intended to reflect the person's admiration of the object of his affection, but his paranoid obsession with her.

As discussed in many chapters here, one might argue that it doesn't especially matter what the author, Sting, really meant to communicate by his song. Millions of listeners clearly enjoy this song in deeply meaningful ways, even if those meanings diverge from what Sting intended in writing the song. This is a common occurrence in contemporary music. Consider how people misinterpret Bruce Springsteen's "Born in the U.S.A." as a deeply patriotic ballad, when Springsteen wrote it to be critical of aspects of American life. My favorite example of people completely misreading a song is Elton John's "Philadelphia Freedom," which most people interpret as a celebration of this country's bicentennial in 1976, when in fact John was commissioned to write the song in 1975 to honor a World Team Tennis franchise by the name of Philadelphia Freedom.

Each of these misreadings of authorial intentions still reflects the facts that (a) people construct their interpretations in view of what they think might be the original author's intentions, and (b) that the erroneous interpretations are still tightly linked to what the authors did actually wish to communicate. Even if Sting grumbles about fans misunderstanding his song "Every Breath You Take," people's experience of this song as meaningful is tied to many of the communicative intentions Sting hoped would be understood (that the song was about lost love, etc.). One of the great challenges for future work in debates over intentionalism is to explore in greater detail how readings that diverge from authorial intentions are predicated upon recovery of at least part of what authors did intend by their work.

Many of my conclusions about the importance of intentions in the experience of meaning are not commonly held by scholars engaged in interpretive practice (literary and art critics, legal theorists). Many critics deny the fundamental role of intentional meaning in language and art because they fail to view interpretation as a cognitive enterprise and do not seek accounts of interpretation that are consistent with what is generally known about human cognition. For example, some scholars object that subjective and hypothetical intentionalism requires too much guessing about the inaccessible minds of speakers, writers, and artists. These scholars prefer interpretations of meaning based on more objective evidence such as the plain, literal meaning of a text or artwork without considering anything about the person(s) who created the language or artwork or the cultural and historical conditions under which the work was produced. This desire to cement interpretation in "objective" criteria ignores the psychological nature of communication, especially as interpretation involves both conscious and unconscious mental processes, and the recognition that language and artworks are created by particular people for specific audiences in local cultural situations at different historical moments. The empirical evidence clearly shows that interpretation is a collaborative, coordinated activity where all participants have a role in determining the intentional meaning of what is said, written, or artistically created.

A related objection to my conclusions about the importance of human intentions in the experience of meaning might be that I have focused primarily on what people ordinarily do when they engage in conversation, write and read texts, and create and interpret artworks. I have not specifically proposed how language and art *should* objectively be interpreted for purposes of scholarly criticism, legal adjudication, and art appreciation. My advocacy of a pluralistic approach to intentionalism in meaningful experience, one might claim, is too focused on the common person and not enough on scholarly practice.

Conclusion

My preference as a cognitive scientist is to understand how people think and behave, not to dictate how people, especially scholars and intellectuals, must think about different kinds of language and artworks. I believe that theories of interpretation for literature, law, and art would be better served if they were constructed in light of what people ordinarily do, rather than in terms of some idealistic, and often incorrect, view of what scholars should do. Our experience of meaning emerges directly from ordinary and obligatory cognitive process. People often indulge in a large range of optional activities to enhance their meaningful experience of language and art. In many cases, these more reflective, optional interpretive practices are essential to a fuller understanding of language and art in their rich historical and cultural contexts. Yet the fact that people engage in these optional activities does not imply that more fundamental cognitive processes can be legislated away in the manner many scholars might wish.

Debates over intentionalism will undoubtedly rage on in both the cognitive sciences and the humanities. Finding solutions to some of the thorniest problems about intentions in the experience of meaning demands consideration of several factors. At the very least, scholars will need to explore different hypotheses about how authorial intentions may influence people's experience of meaning. Consider some of these possibilities:

1. Assumptions about authorial intentions have nothing to do with people's understanding of human action, language, and art.

2. Assumptions about authorial intentions play an optional role in shaping people's understanding of human action, language, and art. Thus, people may consider something about why another person acted in some way or why someone created some instance of language or art. But people need not infer anything about authorial intentions when creating meaningful interpretations of human artifacts.

3. Assumptions about authorial intentions motivate people's understanding of why human artifacts exist, and why these artifacts may be conventionally thought to express particular meanings. But inference about what authors intended to communicate

does not actually play a significant role in people's ordinary cognitive understanding of artifacts as these are encountered in the real world.

4. Assumptions about authorial intentions motivate both why people value human artifacts and why they find them to be meaningful when consciously reflecting about them. But understanding what someone intended to do when creating an artifact does not play a role in people's ordinary "on-line" comprehension of language and art.

5. Assumptions about authorial intentions are an essential part of our cognitive systems and function automatically in people's interpretation of human artifacts.

These are just some of the complex possibilities about intentionalism that need to be examined in future empirical and theoretical work. Testing the validity of these hypotheses requires that scholars adhere to a commitment to actually look for the possible effects of authorial intentions in meaningful experience (the cognitive intentionalist premise adopted in this book). Much of the work described in this book has specifically sought to explore the relations between authorial intentions and people's experience of meaning. This evidence clearly rejects hypothesis (1) and supports the claims that the search for authorial intentions plays a major role in people's meaningful experience of many human actions, spoken and written language, and artworks (especially hypotheses 4 and 5). Distinguishing between these different hypotheses in future research is extremely important because much of the debate over intentionalism silently slips back and forth among these possibilities, with laypersons and scholars arguing about whether intentions do or don't play a role in their experience of meaning.

There are five additional hypotheses that require greater consideration in future research and discussion about intentionalism:

6. Assumptions about intentionality differ depending on the human artifacts under consideration. Thus, people draw different inferences about communicative intentions when interacting with nonverbal actions, spoken language, written language, literary texts, legal texts, and different forms of artwork.

7. Inferring intentionality, in some instances, happens more as a later product of understanding than as the fundamental groundwork for building meanings out of experience.

8. Assumptions about authorial intentions arise as joint products of people's interactions with one another through human action, language, and artwork. Thus, intentions are not ideas we recover from other people's minds inasmuch as they are created from, and exist as part of, the cultural web of social interaction via human artifacts.

9. Assumptions about authorial intentions occur differentially among people, even within a single sociocultural context. An individual's personal history, motives, and expertise with particular types of artifacts shape in very specific ways the extent to which that person consciously elaborates upon intentional meanings in human action, language, and artworks.

10. Assumptions about authorial intentions differ significantly in contrasting cultural environments. Inferring intentionality is more than a personal act, it is a sociocultural act and may take on differential importance depending on culture.

I believe that my discussion in this book has, at the very least, suggested why each of these additional possibilities is demanding of scholarly attention in future research. Although I have argued that the disposition to seek human intentionality is consistently strong across indviduals, cultures, and artifacts, there may indeed be important differences worth exploring (e.g., seeing how listeners seek out actual subjective intentions, while readers and observers of artwork seek hypothetical intentions). I certainly have my own beliefs and positions regarding these hypotheses, but I see this book as providing a map for the future as much as it may tell us where we have been thus far. Most generally, there remains a great need for further empirical research on the importance of intentions in different interpretive activities. Cognitive scientists should utilize current methods to examine the fast, mostly unconscious cognitive processes operating as people infer intentional meaning in language and art (and clearly need to place greater emphasis on people's experience of artworks).³ But cognitive scientists must also expand their efforts to look at more reflective aspects of experience, such as those involved in the critical appreciation of literary texts and artworks. Scholars in the humanities must acknowledge the importance of the cognitive unconscious in people's experience of meaning. Although literary scholars, for example, do not possess the methods available for examining fast, unconscious mental processes, they certainly can collaborate with cognitive scientists to create new hypotheses for empirical research and should be aware of the empirical work in cognitive science relevant to their own interests in reading and interpretation.⁴ In general, my plea is for greater interdisciplinary cooperation in the study of intentions in interpretation. Part of the motivation for writing this book has been to alert scholars from a wide variety of fields to the important work on intentionalism being done by people in neighboring disciplines.

The evidence presented in this book clearly indicates a picture of intentions as a ubiquitous, systematic, and orderly part of interpretative experience. I close now with a final example showing how each person constructs his or her own meaning by seeking out an intentional relationship with a human artifact. Consider the case of Jorge Luis Borges's story "Pierre Menard." Pierre Menard, the hero of Borges's tale, is a twentieth-century French critic who has written, word for word, several chapters of Cervantes's *Don Quixote*. The essential idea behind Menard's *Don Quixote* is that it is a more difficult, and therefore more valuable, task for a twentieth-century Frenchman to compose this work than for its original author back in seventeenth-century Spain. Menard has firmly rejected the idea that he might become a seventeenth-century Spaniard in his mind, so that, by recovering the original intention of meaning, he might reproduce exactly the same text. That, he claims, is too easy. He wants to produce the same text, with an entirely different meaning, from the point of view of a twentieth-century Frenchman. At one point, the narrator of Borges's story says the following about some differences between Cervantes's and Menard's respective, but identical, texts:⁵

Conclusion

It is a revelation to compare the "Don Quixote" of Menard with that of Cervantes. The latter, for instance, wrote "Don Quixote, Part One, Chapter Nine:" ... truth, whose mother is history, who is rival of time, depository of deeds, witness of the past, example and lesson to the present, and warning to the future.

Written in the seventeenth century, written by the "ingenious layman," Cervantes, this enumeration is a mere rhetorical eulogy of history. Menard on the other hand, writes: " ... truth, whose mother is history, who is rival of time, depository of deeds, witness of the past, example and lesson to the present, and warning to the future."

History, the mother of truth; the idea is astounding. Menard, a contemporary of William James, does not define history as an investigation of reality, but as its origin. Historical truth, for him, is not what took place; it is what we think took place. The final clauses – "example and lesson to the present, and warning to the future" – are shamelessly pragmatic.

Equally vivid is the contrast in styles. The archaic style of Menard – in the last analysis, a foreigner – suffers from a certain affectation. Not so that of his precursor, who handles easily the ordinary Spanish of his time.

The narrator goes on to comment that he is not sure how Menard took years to produce only small portions of *Don Quixote*; he can only report that Menard filled page after page and was in the habit of lighting public fires to destroy his drafts. Finally, though, in his zeal to be Menard's intellectual disciple, the narrator urges a further application of the principle behind the new *Don Quixote*. Readers should approach certain works as if these had been authored not by their actual creators but by other writers with different sets of cultural associations.

The beauty of Borges's story is that Menard's understanding of *Don Quixote* is rooted in his own intentionality as much as it once was in his recognition of Cervantes's communicative intentions in first writing the novel. In this sense, interpreting *Don Quixote*, like understanding any human artifact, does not depend on figuring out the secret "code" to the text, but in recognizing the ways that human intentionality can make the text personally meaningful.[6] Borges's message, in my mind, indirectly leads to a final point:

Debates over intentionalism will not progress beyond endless rhetorical skirmishes *unless* we clearly, systematically attempt to uncover the complex roles that intentionality plays in people's meaningful interpretations of human action, language, and art. My wager is that if we indeed seek to understand the functions that intentions play in a broad range of meaningful experiences, then intentionalism will rightfully be seen as perhaps the most critical factor in how we make sense of our lives and the human artifacts we interact with.

Notes

CHAPTER 1

1. From MacLeish, A. (1962). *The collected poems of Archibald MacLeish*. Boston: Houghton Mifflin.
2. Tannen, D. (1982). *That's not what I meant*. New York: Ballentine Books. Quote is from p. 220.
3. My discussion and the example presented here are based on Tannen, D. (1994). *Gender and discourse*. New York: Oxford University Press. The following conversation is quoted from p. 164.
4. From Graesser, A., Magliano, J., and Haberlandt, K. (1994). Psychological studies of naturalistic text. In H. van Oostendorp and R. Zwaan (Eds.), *Naturalistic text comprehension* (pp. 9–34). Norwood, NJ: Ablex. Quote is from p. 21.
5. From Sibley, G. (1995). Satura from Quintilian to Joe Bob Briggs: A new look at an old world. In B. Connery and K. Combe (Eds.), *Theorizing satire* (pp. 57–72). New York: St. Martin's Press. Quote is from p. 68.
6. See Bach, K., and Harnish, R. (1979). *Linguistic communication and speech acts*. Cambridge, MA: MIT Press. Donnellan, K. (1979). Speaker reference, descriptions, and anaphora. In P. Finch, T. Uehling, and H. Wettstein (Eds.), *Contemporary perspectives in the philosophy of language* (pp. 28–44). Minneapolis: University of Minnesota Press. Gazdar, G. (1979). *Pragmatics: Implicature, presupposition, and logical form*. New York: Academic Press. Grice, H. P. (1989). *Studies in the ways of words*. Cambridge, MA: Harvard University Press. Recanati, F. (1987). *Meaning and force: The pragmatics of performative utterances*. Cambridge: Cambridge University Press. Schiffer, S. (1972). *Meaning*. Oxford: Oxford University Press. Searle, J. (1969). *Speech acts*. Cambridge: Cambridge University Press. Searle, J. (1983). *Intentionality*. Cambridge: Cambridge

339

University Press. Levinson, S. (1983). *Pragmatics.* Cambridge: Cambridge University Press. Sperber, D., and Wilson, D. (1986). *Relevance: Communication and cognition.* Cambridge, MA.: Harvard University Press. Strawson, P. (1964). Intention and convention in speech acts. *Philosophical Review, 73,* 439–460. Allen, J., and Perrault, C. (1980). Analyzing intention in utterances. *Artificial Intelligence, 15,* 143–178. Cohen, P., Morgan, J., and Pollack, M. (Eds.) (1990). *Intentions in communication.* Cambridge, MA.: MIT Press. Grosz, B., and Sidner, C. (1986). Attention, intentions, and the structure of discourse. *Computational Linguistics, 12,* 175–204. Clark, H. (1992). *Arenas of language use.* Chicago: University of Chicago Press. Clark, H. (1996). *Using language.* New York: Cambridge University Press. Gerrig, R. (1993) *Experiencing narrative worlds.* New Haven, CT: Yale University Press. Gibbs, R. (1987). Mutual knowledge in the psychology of conversational inference. *Journal of Pragmatics, 13,* 561–588.

7. Kivy, P. (1993). *The fine art of repetition.* Cambridge: Cambridge University Press. Quote is from p. 121.

8. Wimsatt, W., and Beardsley, M. (1954). The intentional fallacy. In W. Wimsatt and M. Beardsley (Eds.), *The verbal icon: Studies in the meaning of poetry* (pp. 3–18). Lexington: University of Kentucky Press.

9. For example, see Eliot, T. S. (1919). Tradition and the individual talent. In his *Essays.* London: Faber & Faber.

10. Barthes, R. (1977). *Image, music, text.* New York: Hill and Wang. Derrida, J. (1973). *Speech and phenomena.* Evanston: Northwestern University Press. Derrida, J. (1976). *Of grammatology.* Baltimore: Johns Hopkins University Press. Derrida, J. (1978). *Writing and difference.* Chicago: University of Chicago Press. Foucault, M. (1979). What is an author? In J. Harari (Ed.), *Textual strategies: Perspectives in post-structuralist criticism* (pp. 35–51). Ithaca: Cornell University Press.

11. De Man, P. (1983). *Blindness and insight: Essays in the rhetoric of contemporary criticism.* Minneapolis: University of Minnesota Press.

12. Derrida (1973), supra. Quote is from p. 113.

13. Hirsch, E. (1967). *Validity in interpretation.* New Haven: Yale University Press; Hirsch, E. (1976). *The aims of interpretation.* Chicago: University of Chicago Press; Juhl, P. (1980). *Interpretation: An essay in the philosophy of literary criticism.* Princeton: Princeton University Press.

14. Knapp, S., and Michaels, W. (1982). Against theory. *Critical Inquiry, 8,* 723–742. Knapp, S., and Michaels, W. (1987). Against theory 2: Hermeneutics and deconstruction. *Critical Inquiry, 14,* 49–68.

15. Among the many works on intentions in constitutional interpretation are: Berger, R. (1977). *Government by judiciary.* Cambridge, MA: Harvard University Press. Gibbons, J. (1991). Intentionalism, history, and legitimacy. *University of Pennsylvania Law Review, 140,* 613–646. Hoy, D. (1985). Interpreting the law: Hermeneutical and poststructuralist perspectives. *Southern California Law Review, 58,* 135–165. Jaffa, H. (1994). *Original intent and the framers of the constitution: A disputed question.* Washington, DC: Regnery Gateway. Lyon, D. (1990). Basic rights and constitutional interpretation. *Social Theory and Practice, 16,* 337–357. Perry, S. (1985). The authority of text, tradition, and reason: A theory of constitutional interpretation. *Southern California Law Review, 58,* 551–583. Tribe, L., and Dorf, M. (1991). *On reading the Constitution.* Cambridge, MA: Harvard University Press.

16. Bork, R. (1990). *The tempting of America: The political seduction of the law.* London: Collier Macmillan.

17. Originalism has recently been used to support a conservative political morality intended to curtail what Bork, former attorney general Edwin Meese, and others called the Supreme Court's impermissible law making. See Chapter 10.

18. Bugolisi, V. (1974). *Helter Skelter: The true story of the Manson murders.* New York: Norton.

19. One recent interdisciplinary volume on intentions in communication from the cognitive science perspective never touches on this possibility. See Cohen, Morgan, and Pollack (1990), supra.

20. Voloshinov, V. (1973). *Marxism in the philosophy of language.* Translated by L. Matejka and I. Titnik. New York: Seminar Press. Quote is from p. 102.

CHAPTER 2

1. Malle, B. and Knobe, J. (1997). The folk concept of intentionality. *Journal of Experimental Social Psychology, 33,* 101–121.

2. See the entry on intention in Gregory, R. (Ed.) (1987). *The Oxford companion to the mind.* Oxford: Oxford University Press.

3. Adapted from Chisholm, R. (1967). Intentions. In P. Edwards (Ed.), *The encyclopedia of philosophy,* vol. 3 (pp. 201–204). New York: Macmillan and the Free Press.

4. John Searle has defined intentionality as "that property of many mental states and events by which they are directed at or about or of objects and states of affairs in the world." Searle, J. (1983). *Intentionality*. New York: Cambridge University Press. Quote is from p. 1. For example, my current belief that it is raining outside is about the weather, a state of affairs that is "outside my head." This sense of intention, originally suggested by Franz Bretano and given currency by Edmund Husserl, lies at some distance from the question of authorial intention discussed in this book. But see Bretano, F. (1874/1973). *Psychology from an empirical standpoint*. London: Routledge & Kegan Paul. Husserl, E. (1913/1983). *Ideas pertaining to a pure phenomenology and a phenomenological philosophy, Book 1*. Norwood, NJ: Kluwer.
5. See Anscombe. E. (1963). *Intention*. Ithaca, NY: Cornell University Press. Bratman, M. (1987). *Intention, plans, and practical reason*. New York: Cambridge University Press.
6. Searle, J. (1983). *Intentionality*. New York: Cambridge University Press.
7. Bratman, M. (1990). What is intention? In P. Cohen, J. Morgan, and M. Pollack (Eds.), *Intentions in communication* (pp. 15–32). Cambridge, MA: MIT Press.
8. Bruner, J. (1981). Intention in the structure of action and interaction. In L. Lipsett (Ed.), *Advances in infancy research*, vol. 1 (pp. 41–56). Norwood, NJ: Ablex. Quote is from pp. 41–42.
9. Anscombe (1963), supra. Quote is from p. 8.
10. Davidson, D. (1980). *Essays on action and events*. New York: Oxford University Press. Quote is from p. 54. The philosopher John Searle, for instance, distinguishes between "prior intentions" and "intentions in action." For example, I may intend to kill my uncle. By sheer chance I run him over and kill him. However, although my intention has been satisfied I have not killed him intentionally. As Searle puts it, "All intentional actions have intentions in action but not all intentional actions have prior intentions." See Searle (1983), supra, p. 5.
11. For discussion of these and other distinctions about the philosophical characteristics of intentions and action see Bratman (1987), Davidson (1980), and Searle (1983), supra.
12. Malle and Knobe (1997), supra.
13. Ibid.
14. This folk concept model of intentionality may hold only for people of Western cultures. Even if one culture distinguished intentional

from unintentional behavior, the specific conditions for assuming intentionality may vary.

15. See for example Freud, S. (1936). *Inhibitions, symptoms, and anxiety.* London: Hogarth.
16. Oatley, K. (1988). Gaps in consciousness: Emotions and memory in psychoanalysis. *Cognition and Emotion, 2,* 3–18. Quote is from p. 11.
17. Freud, S. (1976/1901). The psychopathology of everyday life. In J. Strachey (Ed.), *The complete psychological works,* vol. 6. Quote is from p. 83.
18. Ibid. Quote is from pp. 89–90.
19. Ibid. Quote is from p. 77.
20. Adopted from Marshall, J. (1968). *Intention – In law and society.* New York: Funk & Wagnalls.
21. Dennett, D. (1991). *Consciousness explained.* Boston: Little, Brown. Jackendoff, R. (1987). *Consciousness and the computational mind.* Cambridge: MIT Press.
22. Dennett (1991), supra. Quote is from p. 253.
23. Ibid. Quote is from p. 113.
24. Minsky, M. (1985). *The society of mind.* New York: Simon & Schuster.
25. See Fraleigh, S. (1993). Good intentions, and dancing movements: Agency, freedom, and self-knowledge in dance. In U. Neisser (Ed.), *The perceived self: Ecological and interpersonal sources of self-knowledge* (pp. 102–111). New York: Cambridge University Press.
26. See Dipert, R. (1993). *Artifacts, art works, and agency.* Philadelphia: Temple University Press.
27. From a translation by Marcel Raymond in his book *From Baudelaire to Surrealism.* New York: Wittenborn, Schultz. Quote is from p. 285.
28. Psychologists have long been interesting in automatic writing. For a review of this work see Koutstaal, W. (1992). Skirting the abyss: A history of experimental explorations of automatic writing in psychology. *Journal of History of the Behavioral Sciences, 28,* 5–27.
29. Dipert (1993), supra.
30. This example is adapted from Ramos, F. Y. (1998). Relevance theory and media discourse: A verbal-visual model of communication. *Poetics, 25,* 293–309.
31. From Yamaguchi, H (1988). How to pull strings with words: Deceptive violations in the garden-path joke. *Journal of Pragmatics, 12,* 323–337. Quote is from p. 332.
32. Deviant causal chains generally create more complex puzzles for theories of intention. In these cases, an intended event is produced

but not in the manner planned. In one such classic case, an individual tries to kill someone by shooting him. The shot misses, but it alarms a herd of wild pigs, which trample the victim to death. Such cases are difficult because the plan can become very detailed and can be enacted much as intended. Even so, the causal chain is probably deviant enough to make observers question the intentionality of the killing.

33. Schutz, A. (1971). *Collected papers I: The problem of social reality*. The Hague: Martinus Nijhoff.

34. Searle, J. (1990). Collective intention and action. In P. Cohen, J. Morgan, and M. Pollack (Eds.), *Intentions in communication* (pp. 401–416). Cambridge, MA: MIT Press.

35. Velman, J. (1997). How to share an intention. *Philosophical and Phenomenological Research, 57,* 29–50. Also see Tuomela, R. (1995). *The assumptions of us: A philosophical study of basic social notions.* Stanford: Stanford University Press.

36. Some philosophers are skeptical about the idea of sharing an intention because they assume that intentions are really only mental events within individual minds. Two people may share a common goal, but this doesn't mean that their intentions must be identical. For instance, you and I may wish to move a couch to another room; so I lift my end of the couch and you lift yours and we take it to the other room. Yet we aren't really sharing an intention, but hold different intentions that yield a single result. See Velman (1997), ibid; and Harman, G. (1986). Willing and intending. In R. Grandy and R. Warner (Eds.), *Philosophical grounds of rationality: Intending, categories, ends* (pp. 363–380). New York: Oxford University Press.

CHAPTER 3

1. Cassell, E. (1985). *Talking with patients, Volume 2: Clinical technique.* Cambridge, MA: MIT Press. See pp. 137–139.

2. My discussion in this chapter focuses primarily upon spoken language. However, the basic principles sketched here also apply to artistic communication (e.g., painting, dance, sculpture), as will be shown in Part IV.

3. Adapted from Haugeland, J. (1985). *Artificial intelligence: The very idea.* Cambridge, MA: MIT Press.

4. Adopted from Krauss, R., and Chiu, C-Y. (1998). Language and social behavior. In D. Gilbert and S. Fiske (Eds.), *Handbook of social psychology*, vol. 2 (4th ed.) (pp. 41–88). Boston: McGraw-Hill.

5. Gibbs, R. (1994). *The poetics of mind: Figurative thought, language, and understanding.* New York: Cambridge University Press.

6. Falwell, J. (with E. Dobson and E. Hindson) (1980). *The fundamentalist phenomenon.* Garden City, NY: Doubleday. Quote is from p. 63.

7. Religious groups such as the men's organization Promise Keepers talk about the importance of interpreting this text in literal terms that all Christians must obey.

8. Gallup, G. (1980). *Public opinion 1980.* Wilmington, Del.: Scholarly Resources. Quote is from p. 189.

9. Ammerman, N. (1987). *Bible believers: Fundamentalists in the modern world.* New Brunswick, NJ: Rutgers University Press. Quote is from p. 51.

10. Ibid. Quote is from p. 51.

11. Ibid. Quote is from p. 52.

12. Reddy, M. (1993). The conduit metaphor. In A. Ortony (Ed.), *Metaphor and thought* (2nd edition) (pp. 164–201). New York: Cambridge University Press.

13. There is little consensus as to the very definition of literal meaning. Within the cognitive sciences there are at least five types of literality – see Gibbs (1994), supra.

    Conventional literality in which literal usage is contrasted with poetic usage, exaggeration, embellishment, indirectness, and so on.

    Subject matter literality in which certain expressions are the usual ones used to talk about a particular topic.

    Nonmetaphorical literality, or directly meaningful language, in which one word (concept) is never understood in terms of a second word (or concept).

    Truth-conditional literality or language that is capable of "fitting the world" (i.e., of referring to objectively existing objects or of being objectively true or false).

    Context-free literality in which the literal meaning of an expression is its meaning apart from any communicative situation or its meaning in a "null" context.

14. This analysis is adapted from Clark, H. (1997). Communities, communication, and convention. In J. Gumperz and S. Levinson (Eds.), *Rethinking linguistic relativity* (pp. 324–355). New York: Cambridge University Press.

15. Kanouse, D. (1972). Verbs as implicit quantifiers. *Journal of Verbal Learning and Verbal Behavior, 11,* 141–147.

16. Horrman, H. (1983). The calculating listener or how many are *einge, mehere,* and *ein paar* (some, several, and a few). In R. Bauerke,

C. Scwarze, and A. van Strechan (Eds.), *Meaning, use, and inter-pretation of language* (pp. 221–234). Berlin: De Gruyter.

17. Searle, J. (1993). Metaphor. In A. Ortony (Ed.), *Metaphor and thought* (2nd edition) (pp. 83–111). New York: Cambridge University Press.

18. Searle, J. (1978). Literal meaning. *Erkenntnis, 13,* 207–224.

19. Ibid.

20. Gibbs (1994), supra. Quote is from p. 78. See Grice (1968) for discussion of how notions of sentence meaning are derived from speaker meaning, not the reverse. Grice, H. (1968). Utterer's meaning, sentence-meaning, and word-meaning. *Foundations of language, 4,* 225–242.

21. Grice, H. (1957). Meaning. *The Philosophical Review, 66,* 377–388.

22. Ibid., p. 53.

23. For discussion of whether such recognition is necessary and sufficient, see Recanati, F. (1987) *Meaning and force: The pragmatics of performative utterances.* Cambridge: Cambridge University Press.

24. The philosopher Peter Strawson separates not two, but three, intentions in Grice's formulation. In Strawson's terms, to mean something by x, S must intend the following:

    a. S's utterance of x to produce a certain response r in a certain audience A;

    b. A to recognize S's intention (a);

    c. A's recognition of S's intention (a) to function as at least part of A's reason for A's response r.

    We can view these intentions as cycling back upon one another: intention (c) is that intention (b) function as at least part of the reason for the fulfillment of intention (a). It is only when the three intentions are activated that an individual is acting as a communicator; it is only when the three intentions are realized that communication has occurred. Thus, to convey a speaker meaning, a communicator makes manifest (displays) the sort of reflexive intention described above. See Strawson, P. (1964). Intention and convention in speech acts. *The Philosophical Review, 73,* 439–460.

25. Levinson, S. (1983). *Pragmatics.* Cambridge: Cambridge University Press. Quote is from p. 16.

26. Sperber and Wilson (1986), supra.

27. This example is adapted from Dipert (1993), supra.

28. Sperber, D., and Wilson, D. (1986). *Relevance: Cognition and communication.* New York: Blackwell. See pp. 50–64.

29. Conversations are prototypical instances of ostensive-inferential communication, although I will argue throughout this book that many aspects of language and art might also profitably be conceived of as ostensive-inferential communication.
30. See Dipert (1993), supra.
31. Grice (1957), supra.
32. Austin, J. (1961). *How to do things with words.* Oxford: Clarendon.
33. These are from Searle (1969), but also include ideas from Palmer (1996) on how the different speech acts reflect different discourse scenarios. See Searle, J. (1969). *Speech acts: An essay in the philosophy of language.* New York: Cambridge University Press. Palmer, G. (1996). *Towards a theory of cultural linguistics.* Austin, TX: University of Texas Press.
34. One analysis of televised conversations of real speech estimated the relative frequencies of different speech act types. Representatives were by far the most common (79 percent), followed by "reactions" (answering questions, assent or dissent to requests, etc.) (52 percent), expressives (28 percent), and then commissives (2 percent) and verdictives (less than 1 percent). See D'Andrade, R., and Wish, M. (1985). Speech act theory in quantitative research on interpersonal behavior. *Discourse Processes, 8,* 229–259.
35. Robertson, S., Black, J., and Johnson, P. (1981). Intention and topic in conversation. *Cognition and Brain Theory, 4,* 303–326. Exchange is quoted from p. 316.
36. See Clark (1996), supra, and Levinson (1983), supra, for further discussion of this point. Clark and Carlson (1982) make another very important criticism of speech act theory. Traditional illocutionary acts are directed at a single addressee. But in all conversations involving more than two people, a second illocutionary act is directed to all "hearers" in the conversation and serves to inform them jointly of the assertion being made. See Clark, H., and Carlson, T. (1982). Hearers and speech acts. *Language, 58,* 352–373.

   A close reading of Austin (1962) suggests that he clearly saw speech acts as social actions involving both speakers and listeners, but most speech act scholars tend to ignore this critical part of Austin's work. For extended discussions on the bilateral nature of speech acts, see Clark (1996), supra. Hancher, M. (1979). The classification of cooperative illocutionary acts. *Language in Society, 8,* 1–14.
37. Adapted from Tracy, K. (1990). Multiple goals in discourse: An

overview of issues. *Journal of Language and Social Psychology, 9,* 1–13.

38. Sperber and Wilson (1986), supra, p. 201.
39. This example and the following analysis are adopted from Pilkington, A., and Clark, B. (1998). Comments on Green (1997). *Language & Literature, 7,* 73–77.
40. Ibid. Quote is from p. 74.
41. Clark (1997), supra, calls these *elective construals*.
42. Hooper, R., and Drummond, K. (1990). Emergent goals at a relational turning point: The case of Gordon and Denise. *Journal of Language and Social Psychology, 9,* 39–65. Quotes are from p. 57.
43. Dascal, M. (1997). Critique without critics? *Science in Context, 10,* 39–62. Quote is from page 62.
44. I recently attended a conference at which a person other than the author read the author's paper. When he finished, and the audience was applauding, a friend sitting next to me leaned over and asked *Are we applauding the author or the person who read the talk?*
45. From *The New Yorker,* May 27, 1996, p. 34.
46. Bakhtin, M. (1981). *The dialogic imagination.* Austin: University of Texas Press. See pp. 293–294.
47. Tannen, D. (1989). *Talking voices: Repetition, dialogue, and imagery in conversational discourse.* New York: Cambridge University Press. See p. 71.
48. See Levelt, W., and Kelter, S. (1982). Surface form in answering questions. *Cognitive Psychology, 14,* 78–106, for experimental evidence on people using the questioner's words and phrases when replying.
49. Scollon, R. (1995). Plagiarism and ideology: Identity in intercultural discourse. *Language in Society, 24,* 1–28.
50. Goffman (1976), supra.
51. Schiffrin, D. (1990). *Approaches to discourse.* Cambridge: Basil Blackwell. See pp. 250–251.
52. Viechnicki, G. (1997). An empirical analysis of participant intentions: Discourse in a graduate seminar. *Language & Communication, 17,* 103–131. The example is found on p. 130.
53. Goffman, E. (1967). *Interactional rituals: Essays on face-to-face behavior.* New York: Pantheon Books. See p. 2. Several conversational analysts, including some of Goffman's former students, nonetheless have criticized Goffman for focusing too much on individuals and their possible intentions in discourse. See the essays in Drew,

P., and Wootton, A. (Eds.) (1988). *Erving Goffman: Exploring the interaction order.* Cambridge: Polity Press.

54. Rommetveit, R. (1974). *On message structure: A framework for the study of language and communication.* New York: Wiley. Quote is from p. 29.

CHAPTER 4

1. This exhibition was held in San Francisco at the Capp Street Project in the spring of 1989.
2. The artist, Ann Hamilton, reported in an interview that the over 700,000 pennies for the exhibit were delivered in several trips by a Brink's truck. After the second delivery, the Brink's driver asked why he was delivering so many pennies to an old San Francisco warehouse. The artist brought him inside, showed him the first five-foot square pattern of pennies in the middle of the room, and the guard immediately responded *Oh, it's art!*
3. I wrote down this conversation soon after it occurred in March 1989.
4. Kenneth Baker in the *San Francisco Chronicle*, March 25, 1989, pp. C3 and C8.
5. Article in the *San Francisco Chronicle*, March 25, 1989, p. C3.
6. Davidson, D. (1984). *Inquiries into truth and interpretations.* Oxford: Clarendon Press.
7. Dennett, D. (1987). *The intentional stance.* Cambridge, MA: MIT Press.
8. Dennett also claims that *any* system whose performance can be predicted and explained is an *intentional system* regardless of whether it is living or nonliving.
9. Weizenbaum, J. (1976). *Computer power and human reason.* San Francisco: Freeman.
10. Ibid.
11. For research showing how people attribute intentionality to the workings of computer software, see Muldar, M. (1996). Perceptions of anthropomorphistic expressions in software manuals. *Journal of Technical Writing & Communication, 26,* 489–506.
12. Hieder, F., and Simmel, M. (1944). An empirical study of apparent behavior. *American Journal of Psychology, 57,* 243–259.
13. Oatley, K., and Yuill, N. (1984). Perception of personal and interpersonal action in a cartoon film. *British Journal of Social Psychology, 24,* 115–124.

14. Faucheux, C., and Moscovici, S. (1968). Self-esteem and exploitative behavior in a game against chance and nature. *Journal of Personality and Social Psychology, 8,* 83–88.

15. Bloom, P. (1996). Intention, history, and artifact concepts. *Cognition, 60,* 1–29.

16. Ibid. Quote is from p. 12.

17. From *Black's law dictionary,* 3rd edition. (1933). St. Paul, Minn.: West Publishing. Quote is from p. 48.

18. Maselli, M., and Altrocchi, J. (1969). Attributions of intent. *Psychological Bulletin, 71,* 233–236. More generally, attribution of intentionality to other people's actions is viewed as a key factor in appraisal or communicative theories of emotion. For instance, if someone kicks you in the leg, your appraisal of this event as intentional or not is a major determinant of whether you will experience anger as opposed to some other emotion. There is a huge literature on this in the psychology of emotions. For two good references, see Lazarus, R. (1991). *Emotion & adaptation.* New York: Oxford University Press. Oatley, K. (1992). *The best laid schemes: The psychology of emotions.* New York: Cambridge University Press.

19. Dodge, K. (1991). The structure and function of reactive and proactive violence. In D. Peper and K. Rubin (Eds.), *The development and treatment of childhood aggression* (pp. 201–218). Hillsdale, NJ: Erlbaum.

20. Shaver, K. (1985). *The attribution of blame: Causality, responsibility, and blame-worthiness.* New York: Springer-Verlag.

21. Tesser, A., Gatewood, R., and Driver, M. (1968). Some determinants of gratitude. *Journal of Personality and Social Psychology, 71,* 445–454.

22. Taylor et al. (1979), supra.

23. Holtworth-Munroe, A., and Hutchinson, G. (1993). Attributing negative intent to wife behavior: The attributions of maritally violent versus nonviolent men. *Journal of Abnormal Psychology, 102,* 206–211.

24. Gordon, M., and Bowlby, R. (1989). Reactance and intentionality attribution as determinants of the intent to file a grievance. *Personnel Psychology, 42,* 309–329.

25. Dyck, R., and Rule, B. (1978). Effects on retaliation of causal attributions incurring attack. *Journal of Personality and Social Psychology, 36,* 521–529.

26. Hewstone, M. (1989). *Causal attribution.* Cambridge, MA: Blackwell.

27. Pepitone, A. (1958). Attribution of causality, social attitude, and cognitive matching processes. In R. Tasiuri and L. Petrullo (Eds.), *Person perception and interpersonal behavior* (pp. 258–276). Stanford: Stanford University Press.

28. Bassili, J., and Smith, M. (1986). On the spontaneity of trait attribution: Converging evidence for the role of cognitive strategy. *Journal of Personality and Social Psychology, 50,* 239–245. Other studies suggest that the fundamental attribution error is not as dominant in non-Western cultures as in Western ones, and that the error may be observed more readily in some individuals than in others. See Fletcher, G., and Ward, C. (1988). Attribution theory and processes: A cross-cultural perspective. In M. Bond (Ed.), *The cross-cultural challenge to social psychology* (pp. 230–244). Newbury Park, CA: Sage Publications. Block, J., and Funder, D. (1986). Social roles and social perception: Individual differences in attribution and error. *Journal of Personality and Social Psychology, 51,* 1200–1297.

29. The literature on this topic is vast. Some examples to consult include Bretherton, I. (1991). Intentional communication and the development of an understanding of mind. In D. Frye and C. Moore (Eds.), *Children's theories of mind: Mental states and social understanding* (pp. 49–76). Hillsdale, NJ: Erlbaum. Frye, D. (1991). The origins of intent in infancy. Ibid., pp. 15–38. Baron-Cohen, S., Tager-Flushberg, H., and Cohen, D. (Eds.) (1993). *Understanding other minds: The perspective from autism.* Cambridge: Cambridge University Press; Zeedyk, M. (1996). Developmental access of intentionality: Toward integration. *Developmental Review, 16,* 416–461.

30. Gergely, G. (1995). Taking the intentional stance at 12 months of age. *Cognition, 56,* 165–193.

31. Beal, C. (1988). Children's knowledge about representations of intended meaning. In J. Astington, P. Harris, and D. Olson (Eds.), *Developing theories of mind* (pp. 315–335). New York: Cambridge University Press. Beal, C., and Flavell, J. (1984). Development of the ability to distinguish communicative intentions and literal meaning messages. *Child Development, 55,* 920–928.

32. Shultz, T., Wells, D., and Sarda, M. (1980). Development of the ability to distinguish intended action from mistakes, reflexes, and passive movements. *British Journal of Social & Clinical Psychology, 19,* 301–310.

33. These judgments of match and mismatch between goal and outcome can be made in the same way for both desire and intention;

they do not require a sophisticated understanding of intentional causation. It may be that such young children's concept of intention is not distinguished from their concept of desire; but intentions are not seen as the causal link between the desire and the goal, as the means to an end.

34. Astington, J., and Gopnik, A. (1991). Theoretical explanation of children's understanding of the mind. *British Journal of Developmental Psychology, 9,* 7–31. Also see Gopnik, A., and Meltzoff, A. (1997). *Words, thoughts, and theories.* Cambridge, MA: MIT Press.

35. Kaye, K. (1982). *The mental and social life of babies: How parents create persons.* London: Harvester Press.

36. See Harding, C. (1982). Development of the intention to communicate. *Human Development, 25,* 140–151; Trevarthen, C. (1979). Communication and cooperation in early infancy: A description of primary intersubjectivity. In M. Bullowa (Ed.), *Before speech: The beginnings of interpersonal communication* (pp. 56–73). Cambridge: Cambridge University Press. Tronick, E. (1981). Infant communicative intent: The infant's reference to social interaction. In R. Stark (Ed.), *Language behavior in infancy and early childhood* (pp. 5–16). New York: Elsevier.

    Some recent research indicates that maternal interpretation of infant behavior changes over the course of infant development. During the early months of a child's life, social behaviors appear to be particularly important as a basis for maternal assignment of intentionality, but as the infant matures, mothers attribute less significance to social behaviors. See Zeedyk, M. (1997). Maternal interpretations of infant intentionality: Changes over the course of infant development. *British Journal of Developmental Psychology, 15,* 477–493.

37. Goffman, E. (1976). Response cries. *Language, 54,* 787–815.

38. Ibid., p. 99.

39. Ibid., p. 120.

40. Watzlawick, P., Beavin, J., and Jackson, D. (1967). *Pragmatics of human communication.* New York: Norton. See p. 39.

41. Watzlawick et al. (1967), supra. Quote is from p. 39.

42. DePaulo, B. (1992). Nonverbal behavior and self-presentation. *Psychological Bulletin, 111,* 203–243. Quote is from p. 205.

43. Ekman, P., and Friesen, W. (1975). *Unmasking the face: A guide to recognizing emotions from facial cues.* Englewood Cliffs, NJ: Prentice-Hall.

44. Cocker and Burgoon (1987), supra.
45. Nonverbal acts may repeat, augment, illustrate, accentuate, or con-
    tradict the words they accompany. Moreover, nonverbal acts may
    precede the words, substitute for them, or be unrelated to them.
    Various detailed studies of gesture and speech suggest that these
    are highly coordinated and arise from the same computational
    source. This seems especially true for pointing gestures, interac-
    tion gestures, and emblems. See McNeil, D. (1992). *Hand in mind.*
    Chicago: University of Chicago Press. Kendon (1990) also con-
    tends that the co-occurrence of gestures with speech primarily
    arises when verbal articulation is difficult. Kendon, A. (1990). *Con-
    ducting interaction.* New York: Cambridge University Press. These
    studies show, at the very least, that gestures accompanying spo-
    ken language often facilitate listeners' understandings of speakers'
    messages. Research indicates that the accuracy of hearing spoken
    sentences is twice as high when the sentences are presented com-
    bined with gestures than when they are not. See Riseborough, M.
    (1982). An investigation into the interrelationship of physiographic
    gestures and speech in seven-year-olds. *British Journal of Psychology,*
    73, 497–503.
46. Ekman, P., and Friesen, W. (1971). Constants across cultures in the
    face and emotion. *Journal of Personality and Social Psychology, 17,*
    124–129. Goffman, E. (1959). *The presentation of self in everyday life.*
    New York: Doubleday.
47. Goffman (1959), (1963), supra.
48. Coupland, N., Giles, H., and Wiemann, J. (Eds.) (1991). *Miscommu-
    nication and problematic talk.* Newbury Park, CA: Sage.
49. Feyereisen, P., van de Wiele, M., and Dubois, F. (1988). The meaning
    of gestures: What can be understood without speech. *Cahiers de
    Psychologie Cognitives, 8,* 3–25.
50. For a negative appraisal of the role of gestures in conversation
    see Rime and Schiartura (1991). They argue, primarily, that ges-
    tures produced by speakers are not for the benefit of their ad-
    dressees, but rather facilitate speakers' formulating meanings in
    lexical syntactic form. Rime, B., and Schiatura, E. (1991). Gesture
    and speech. In R. Feldman and B. Rime (Eds.), *Fundamentals of
    nonverbal behavior* (pp. 239–281). New York: Cambridge University
    Press.
51. Fast, J. (1970). *Body talk.* New York: Lippincott. Poyatos, F. (Ed.)
    (1988). *Cross-cultural perspective in nonverbal communication.*
    Gottingen: Hogrete and Hogrete.

52. See Kendon (1990), supra, for an example of one scholar who views many aspects of nonverbal behavior as natural signs. Several scholars avoid dealing with the issue of intent entirely by arguing that behaviors are typically interpreted as intentional because of preexisting, socially shared code systems. For example, an unintended frown can be regarded as a message because the behavior is one that people typically encode as a signal of displeasure and typically decode as an intentional signal of displeasure. It is easier to identify the "vocabulary" of nonverbal communication than to divine intent on each occasion of a behavior's enactment. See Burgoon, M., Hunsaker, F., and Dawson, E. (1994). *Human communication.* Thousand Oaks, CA: Sage.
53. Cocker, D., and Burgoon, J. (1987). The nature of conversational involvement and nonverbal encoding patterns. *Human Communication Research, 13,* 463–494.
54. Bavelas, et al. (1986), supra.
55. Anderson, K., and Sull, P. (1985). Out of touch, out of reach: Tactile predispositions as predictors of interpersonal distance. *Western Journal of Speech Communication, 49,* 57–72.
56. Motley, M. (1986). Consciousness and intentionality in conversation: A preliminary model and methodological approaches. *Western Journal of Speech Communication, 50,* 3–23.
57. Heath, C. (1986). *Body movement and speech in medical interaction.* Cambridge: Cambridge University Press. Quotes are from pp. 87–91.
58. Kendon, A. (1994). Do gestures communicate? A review. *Research on Language and Social Interaction, 27,* 175–200; Streeck, J. (1993). Gestures as communication I: Its coordination with gaze and speech. *Communication Monographs, 60,* 275–299.
59. Manusov, V., and Rodriguez, M. (1989). Intentionally based nonverbal messages: A perceiver's perspective. *Journal of Nonverbal Behavior, 13,* 15–24.
60. Kraut, R., and Johnston, R. (1979). Social and emotional messages of smiling: An ethological approach. *Journal of Personality and Social Psychology, 37,* 1539–1533.
61. Kraut and Johnston also report in a different study that fans at a hockey game smiled much more when they were friends, regardless of the outcome of their team's play. Another study in this same series looked at the smiling of passersbys both alone and when interacting with others. Smiling depended overwhelmingly upon whether the subjects were interacting and very little upon the pleasantness of the weather.

62. Fernandez-Dols, J., & Ruiz-Belda, M. (1995). Are smiles signs of happiness? Gold medal winners at the Olympic games. *Journal of Personality and Social Psychology, 69,* 1113–1119.

63. Bavelas et al. (1986), supra.

64. Fridlund, A. (1991). Sociality of solitary smiling: Potentiation by an implicit audience. *Journal of Personality and Social Psychology, 60,* 229–240.

65. Gilbert, A., Fridlund, A., and Sabini, J. (1987). Hedonic and social determinants of facial displays to odors. *Chemical Senses, 12,* 355–363.

66. Brighton, V., Segal, A., Werther, P., and Steiner, J. (1977). Facial expression and hedonic response to taste stimuli. *Journal of Dental Research, 56,* B161.

67. For discussions of the traditional view of emotions in the human face see Ekman and Friesen (1975), supra.

68. Bavelas, J., Black, A., Lemery, C., and Mullet, J. (1986). "I show how you feel": Motor mimicry as a communicative act. *Journal of Personality and Social Psychology, 50,* 322–329.

69. See Bavelas et al. (1986), supra. Even when we talk to ourselves and deploy facial displays in the course of these acts, we are being communicative. Thus when we are alone we often treat ourselves as interactants. See Fridlund, A. (1994). *Human facial expression.* San Diego: Academic Press.

70. Anscombe, E. (1963). *Intentionality.* Ithaca, NY: Cornell University Press.

71. Nisbett, R., and Wilson, T. (1977). Telling more than one can know: Verbal reports on mental processes. *Psychological Review, 84,* 231–259. Our inability, at times, to accurately report our intentions may reflect the possibility that intentions are not always qualitatively conscious. Intentional mental states often lack sensory qualities. For instance, imagine that I ask you to perform some action, but delay the moment when you can execute it. When you get ready to run, but right before taking your first step, there is no specific sensory experience of the intention "getting ready to run," even though this intention is foremost in your mind. The complex, nonqualitative character of intentions provides one reason why people sometimes lack accurate awareness of the intentional basis for their actions. See Baars, B. (1997). *In the theater of consciousness.* New York: Oxford University Press.

72. Some scholars argue that accounts of one's intentions are socially constructed products in which face-saving and self-justification

surely play a part. Even if intentions are important, language is a form of social action that can be damaging and can't be undone. As feminist psychologist Mary Crawford claims, "Analyzing conversation in terms of intentions has very important implications; it deflects attention from effects, including the ways that everyday action and talk serve to recreate and maintain current gender arrangements." See Crawford, M. (1995). *Talking difference: On gender and language.* Thousand Oaks, CA: Sage.

73. Heider, F. (1958). *The psychology of interpersonal relations.* New York: Wiley.

74. Langer, E. (1978). Rethinking the role of thought in social interaction. In J. Harvey, W. Ickes, and R. Kidd (Eds.), *New directions in attribution research* (pp. 35–58). Hillsdale, NJ: L. Erlbaum. Also see Lewicki, P. (1986). *Nonconscious social information processing.* New York: Academic Press.

75. According to some psychologists, person-related attributions require that behavior be seen as intentionally committed, and therefore the interpretation of intent is the first step in the attribution process. See Jones, E., and Davis, K. (1965). From acts to dispositions: The attribution process in person perception. In L. Berkowitz (Ed.), *Advances in experimental social psychology* (pp. 219–266). New York: Academic Press. Other psychologists argue that intent is not only a step in the attribution process, it is also an attribution itself. See Weiner, B. (1986). *An attributional theory of motivation and emotion.* New York: Springer-Verlag.

76. Searle, J. (1983). *Intentionality.* New York: Cambridge University Press.

77. Philosopher Elizabeth Anscombe's definition of intentionality makes it possible to determine how many of the effects were intentional. If the end of the chain of events was unforeseen, or better yet unforseeable, then the person cannot take credit for having brought about the outcome intentionally – assuming that the outcome was beneficial and credit would be sought. The intentionality of each should be assessed. See Anscombe (1963), supra.

78. Keysar, B. (1998). The communication of intention: Investigation into the science of conversation. Unpublished manuscript, University of Chicago.

79. Newton, E. (1994). The rocky road from action to intention. Unpublished doctoral dissertation, Stanford University.

80. Ross, L. (1977). The intuitive psychologist and his shortcomings: Distortions in the attribution process. In L. Berkowitz (Ed.),

Advances in experimental social psychology, vol. 10 (pp. 174–221). New York: Academic Press.

81. Ross, L., Amabile, T., and Steinmetz, J. (1977). Social roles, social control, and biases in social-perception processes. *Journal of Personality and Social Psychology, 35,* 485–494.

82. Jones, E., and Harris, V. (1967). The attribution of attitudes. *Journal of Experimental Social Psychology, 3,* 1–24.

83. Barjonet, P. (1980). L'influence sociale et des representations des causes de l'accident de la route. *Le Travail Humain, 43,* 243–253.

84. For a strong supportive view of facilitated communication, see Biklen, D. (1993). *Communication unbound.* New York: Columbia University Press. For a critique history and analysis of facilitated communication, see Twachtman-Cullen, D. (1997). *A passion to believe: Autism and the facilitated communication phenomenon.* Boulder, CO: Westview.

85. Biklen (1993), supra. Passage is from p. 139.

86. Ibid. Quote is from p. 141.

87. Ibid. Exchange is from pp. 177–178.

88. An odd characteristic of facilitated communication is that facilitators ignore, as they are taught to, other aspects of clients' possible communicative intentions, such as the verbal and nonverbal messages that accompany their typing. Ibid.

89. See especially the studies by Wheeler, D., Jacobsen, J., Paglieri, R., and Schwartz, A. (1993). An experimental assessment of facilitated communication. *Mental Retardation, 31,* 49–60. Smith, M., and Belcher, R. (1993). Facilitated communication with adults with autism. *Journal of Autism and Developmental Disorders, 23,* 175–183. Mulick, J., Jacobson, J., and Kobe, F. (1993). Anguished silence and helping hands: Autism and facilitated communication. *Skeptical Inquirer, 17,* 270–280.

90. Mulick et al. (1993), supra. Quote is from p. 275.

91. From Eliot, T. S. (1936). *Selected poems.* New York: Harcourt, Brace & World.

92. Gerrig, R., and Healy, A. (1983). Dual processes in metaphor understanding: Comprehension and appreciation. *Journal of Experimental Psychology: Learning, Memory, and Cognition, 9,* 667–675.

93. Gibbs, R., Kushner, J., and Mills, R. (1991). Authorial intentions and metaphor comprehension. *Journal of Psycholinguistic Research, 20,* 11–30.

94. It is conceivable that people attribute intentionality to a written text only *after* they have completed processing and created a reasonable

interpretation for what they have read. In this case, intentionality would be inferred as a matter of making greater sense of a text. But the Gibbs et al. (1991) data (ibid.) clearly suggest, as will other data described in the following chapters, that inferences about authorial intentions are made quickly, early on during listening and reading.

CHAPTER 5

1. Clark, H. (1978). Inferring what is meant. In W. Levelt & G. Flores d'Arcais (Eds.), *Studies in the perception of language* (pp. 45–71). London: Wiley. Gibbs, R. (1993). The intentionalist controversy and cognitive science. *Philosophical Psychology, 6,* 175–199.
2. Katz, J. (1997). *Propositional structure and illocutionary force.* New York: Crowell.
3. Bransford, J., and McCarrell, N. (1974). A sketch of a cognitive approach to comprehension: Some thoughts about what it means to comprehend. In W. Weimer and D. Palermo (Eds.), *Cognition and the symbolic processes* (pp. 377–399). Hillsdale, NJ: Erlbaum. Johnson-Laird, P. (1983). *Mental models.* Cambridge, MA. Harvard University Press.
4. Bennett, J. (1976). *Linguistic behavior.* Cambridge: Cambridge University Press. Grice, H. P. (1975). Logic and conversation. In P. Cole and J. Morgan (Eds.), *Syntax and semantics 3: Speech acts* (pp. 41–58). New York: Academic Press. Schiffer, S. (1972). *Meaning.* Oxford: Oxford University Press.
5. Clark, H., and Carlson, T. (1981). Context for comprehension. In J. Long and A. Baddeley (Eds.), *Attention and performance XI* (pp. 313–330). Hillsdale, N.J.: Erlbaum.
6. See Clark, H. (1983). Making sense of nonce sense. In G. Flores d'Arcais and R. Jarvella (Eds.), *The process of understanding language* (pp. 297–332). New York: Wiley. Clark, H. (1997). Dogmas of understanding. *Discourse Processes, 23,* 567–598.
7. Ibid.
8. Clark (1983), supra. Clark, E., and Clark, H. (1979). When nouns surface as verbs. *Language, 55,* 767–811.
9. From Roger Kahn in *The New Yorker,* October 4, 1996. Quote is on p. 63.
10. Wason, P., and Reich, S. (1979). A verbal illusion. *Quarterly Journal of Experimental Psychology, 31,* 591–597.
11. Erickson, T., and Mattson, M. (1981). From words to meaning: A semantic illusion. *Journal of Verbal Learning and Verbal Behavior, 20,* 540–552. Reeder, L., and Cleermann, A. (1990). The role of

partial matches in comprehension: The Moses illusion resisted. In A. Graesser and G. Bower (Eds.), *The psychology of learning and motivation: Inferences and text comprehension* (pp. 233–258). San Diego: Academic Press.

12. Johnson, M., Bransford, J., and Solomon, S. (1973). Memory for tacit implications of sentences. *Journal of Experimental Psychology, 98,* 203–205. Schweller, K., Brewer, W., and Dahl, D. (1976). Memory for the illocutionary forces and perlocutionary effects of utterances. *Journal of Verbal Learning and Verbal Behavior, 15,* 325–337.

13. Jarvella, R., and Collas, J. (1974). Memory for the intentions of sentences. *Memory and Cognition, 2,* 185–188.

14. Kvavilashvili, L. (1987). Remembering intention as a distinct form of memory. *British Journal of Psychology, 78,* 507–518.

15. McKoon, G., and Ratcliff, R. (1981). The comprehension processes and memory structures involved in instrumental inferences. *Journal of Verbal Learning and Verbal Behavior, 20,* 671–682. McKoon, G., and Ratcliff, R. (1986). Inferences about predictable events. *Journal of Experimental Psychology: Learning, Memory, and Cognition, 12,* 82–91.

16. Grice, H. P. (1968). Utterer's meaning, sentence-meaning, and word-meaning. *Foundations of Language, 4,* 225–242.

17. Clark, H. (1977). Inferring what is meant. In W. Levelt and G. Flores d'Arcais (Eds.), *Studies in the perception of language* (pp. 259–322). London: Wiley.

18. Clark (1977), supra. Gibbs, R., Mueller, R., and Cox, R. (1988). Common ground in asking and understanding questions. *Language and Speech, 31,* 321–335.

19. Clark, H. (1979). Responding to indirect speech acts. *Cognitive Psychology, 11,* 430–477.

20. Grice (1975), supra.

21. Grice (1975), supra. Quote is from p. 45.

22. Grice (1975), supra. Grice, H. P. (1978). Some further notes on logic and conversation. In P. Cole (Ed.), *Syntax and semantics 9: Pragmatics* (pp. 113–128). New York: Academic Press.

23. Sperber, D., and Wilson, D. (1986). *Relevance: Communication and cognition.* Cambridge, MA: Harvard University Press.

24. Ibid.

25. Sperber and Wilson (1995) define two principles of relevance: (1) "Human cognition tends to be geared to the maximization of relevance" (the cognitive principle), and (2) "Every act of ostensive communication communicates a presumption of its own optimal relevance" (the communicative principle). They now claim that

principle (2) should be referred to as the "Principle of Relevance."
See Sperber, D., and Wilson, D. (1995). *Relevance: Communication
and cognition* (2nd edition). Cambridge, MA: Blackwell. Quotes are
from p. 260.

26. To see why this is so, Sperber and Wilson suggest that we need
to ask two questions corresponding to two parts of the definition
of optimal relevance: (a) could Mary have expected her utterance,
on this interpretation, to achieve adequate effects? and (b) was
there some other utterance (equally easy for Mary to produce)
which would have achieved the intended effects more economically? It seems clear that the answer to question (a) is yes. After
all, by saying *Would you like some coffee?* Peter has indicated that
a yes or no answer would be adequately relevant to him. It seems
equally clear, though, that if all Mary wanted to communicate was
that she did not want any coffee, she could have communicated
it more economically by saying simply *No.* Her utterance of *Coffee would keep me awake* on this interpretation fails the definition of
optimal relevance because it puts the listener to some gratuitous
effort.

27. One important consequence of relevance theory follows from the
definition of optimal relevance. The first interpretation tested and
found consistent with the principle of relevance is the only interpretation consistent with the principle of relevance. Let us assume that,
in interpreting an utterance, the hearer starts with a small initial
context left over, say, from her processing of the previous utterances. She computes the contextual effects of the utterance in that
initial context; if these are not enough to make the utterance worth
her attention, she expands the context, obtaining further effects,
and repeats the process until she has enough effects to make the
utterance optimally relevant in a way the speaker could manifestly
have foreseen. At that point, she has an interpretation consistent
with the principle of relevance, and it follows that she should stop,
or at least that she is entitled to continue on her own account but
is not entitled to assume that the speaker intended to communicate anything more. All the listener is entitled to impute as part of
the intended interpretation is the minimal (i.e., smallest and most
accessible) context and contextual effects that would be enough to
make the utterance worth his attention. Thus, the interpretation
process has an in-built stopping place.

28. See Gibbs, R. (1986). On the psycholinguistics of sarcasm. *Journal
of Experimental Psychology: General, 115,* 1–13. Gibbs, R., and Moise,

J. (1997). Pragmatics in understanding what is said. *Cognition, 62,* 51–74. Happe, F. (1993). Communicative competence and theory of mind in autism: A test of relevance theory. *Cognition, 48,* 101–119. Sperber, D., Cara, F., and Girotto, V. (1995). Relevance theory explains the selection task. *Cognition, 57,* 31–95.

29. Clark, H., and Brennan, S. (1991). Grounding in communication. In L. Resnick, J. Levine, and S. Teasley (Eds.), *Perspectives on socially shared cognition* (pp. 127–149). Washington, DC: APA Books.

30. Ibid.

31. Ibid. Clark, H., and Schaefer, E. (1987). Concealing meaning from overhearers. *Journal of Memory and Language, 26,* 209–225. Clark, H., and Schaefer, E. (1989). Contributing to discourse. *Cognitive Science, 13,* 259–294. Clark, H., and Wilkes-Gibbs, D. (1986). Referring as a collaborative process. *Cognition, 22,* 1–39. Schober, M., and Clark, H. (1989). Understanding by addressees and overhearers. *Cognitive Psychology, 21,* 211–232.

32. One way this is accomplished is by what are called messages transmitted in the back channel. The brief vocalizations, head nods and shakes, and facial expressions produced by the participant who at that moment is nominally in the role of listener are a rich source of information about the state of the common ground. Such information permits the formulation of messages that are extremely efficient because they are based on a reasonably precise assessment of the hearer's current knowledge and understanding.

33. Clark and Schaefer (1989), supra. Schegloff, E., Jefferson, G., and Sack, H. (1977). The preference for self-corrections in the organization of repair in conversation. *Language, 53,* 361–382.

34. Clark, H. (1996). *Language use.* New York: Cambridge University Press. Clark and Schaeffer (1989), supra.

35. Speakers must obtain positive evidence from the addressee in order to continue speaking; otherwise, the speaker will attempt to correct the possible miscommunication. Even when an addressee offers no confirmation that he or she has understood the speaker, this itself constitutes one kind of evidence that the speaker may take as signaling for him or her to continue.

36. In the past, the concept of mutual or shared knowledge has been considered as part of the analysis of speaker meaning and convention in philosophy. See Lewis, D. (1969). *Convention.* Cambridge, MA: Harvard University Press. Schiffer (1972), supra. By definition, a speaker S and an addressee A mutually know a proposition P if and only if

S knows P

A knows P

S knows that A knows P

A knows that S knows P

S knows that A knows that S knows P

... and so on ad infinitum.

This original definition of mutual knowledge raises a serious paradox. The infinite series of belief statements is seen as necessary, although it is highly unlikely that listeners can compute an infinite series of these propositions in a finite period of time. How then do speaker and listener ever coordinate what they mutually believe if there is *always* one more belief statement to be established?

These concerns have been widely discussed within linguistics and philosophy. See Bach, K., and Harnish, R. (1979). *Linguistic communication and speech acts.* Cambridge, MA: MIT Press. Bennett (1976), supra. Harder, P., and Kock, C. (1976). *The theory of presupposition failure.* Copenhagen: Akademisk Forlag. Also see the essays in Smith, N. (Ed.) (1982). *Mutual knowledge.* New York: Academic Press.

The idea that people need to use knowledge of this infinitely regressive sort is very implausible. Psychologically it would result in a processing and capacity explosion that would render communication impossible. Clark and Marshall (1981) propose that mutual belief can be achieved without having to check that an infinite series of mutual belief statements are true. See Clark, H., and Marshall, C. (1981). Definite reference and mutual knowledge. In A. Joshi, I. Sag., and B. Webber (Eds.), *Elements of discourse understanding* (pp. 10–63). Cambridge: Cambridge University Press. They suggest that mutual knowledge can be represented as an unanalyzable concept of the form:

A and B mutually know that P, if and only if some state of affairs G holds such that

a. A and B have reason to believe that G holds.
b. G indicates to both A and B that the other has reason to believe that G holds.
c. G indicates to A and B that P.

G is called the basis for the mutual knowledge that P. Essentially, if A and B make certain assumptions about each other's rationality, they can use certain states of affairs as a basis for inferring the infinity of conditions all at once. Clark and Marshall argue – also see Lewis (1969), supra; Schiffer (1972), supra – that only one piece of evidence is really needed to establish some mutual belief as long as it is the right kind of evidence. For example, if A and B agree before a foot race to start running when a gun fires, this agreement can serve as the only grounds necessary for their mutual belief that at the firing of a gun they are both to start running. It can be formalized by the *mutual induction scheme* as follows:

a. A and B have reason to believe that the agreement holds that they will both start running when the gun fires.
b. The agreement indicates to A and B that A and B each have reason to believe that the agreement holds.
c. The agreement indicates to A and B each that the firing of a gun indicates that they are to start running.

These three conditions provide the grounds for A and B to individually infer the mutual belief that they are to start running when the gun is fired. There is no need to draw on a potentially infinite number of pieces of evidence. There is no need to confirm each and every one of the infinity of conditions, even though in practice this can be attempted. Clark and Marshall's mutual induction scheme prevents the infinite number of iterations usually seen as a necessary consequence of establishing mutual knowledge.

37. Krauss, R. (1987). The role of the listener: Addressee influences on message formulation. *Journal of Language and Social Psychology, 6,* 81–98.
38. For experimental demonstrations of this, see Schober, M. (1993). Spatial perspective-taking in conversation. *Cognition, 47,* 1–24; Schober, M. (1995). Speakers, addressees, and frames of reference: When is effect minimized in conversations about locations? *Cognition, 20,* 219–247.
39. For phonology, see Fowler, C. (1994). Differential shortening of repeated content words in various communicative contexts. *Language & Speech, 31,* 307–319. For syntax in talking to children, see Hu, Q. (1994). A study of common features of mother's vocabularies. In J. Sokolov and C. Snow (Eds.), *Handbook of research in language development using CHILDES* (pp. 110–131). Hillsdale, NJ: Erlbaum. For lexical choice, see Fussell, S., and Krauss, R. (1989). The effect of intended audience on message production and comprehension:

References in a common ground framework. *Journal of Experimental Social Psychology, 25,* 203–219.

40. Fussell, S., and Krauss, R. (1989). Understanding friends and strangers: The effects of audience design in message comprehension. *European Journal of Social Psychology, 19,* 509–525.

41. Planalp, S., and Garvin-Doxas, K. (1994). Using mutual knowledge in conversation: Friends as experts on each other. In S. Duck (Ed.), *Dynamics of relationships.* Thousand Oaks, CA: Sage. Conversation is from p. 6.

42. Clark and Wilkes-Gibbs (1986), supra.

43. Issacs, E., and Clark, H. (1987). References in conversation between novices and experts. *Journal of Experimental Psychology: General, 116,* 26–37.

44. Clark and Schaefer (1987), supra.

45. See Clark and Schaefer (1987), supra. This research on people's task-oriented dialogues clearly shows that speakers and listeners collaborate to facilitate recovery of each other's communicative intentions. Of course, the task itself imposes some constraints, and certain cues such as eye gaze and facial expressions cannot be used to convey agreement or disagreement. But these findings generally show that pairs work together to secure a definite reference. The processes involved in grounding are central not only to these experimental situations but also to other task-oriented dialogues such as telephone calls to directory enquiries and in ordinary conversation.

    In related work, Fleming and Darley (1991) asked subjects to transmit hidden messages to some intended audience while transmitting a contradictory message to a second audience. Subjects successfully transmitted their hidden messages to the intended audience, and hidden messages went undetected by the secondary audience. Subjects relied to a great extent upon private keys to communicate hidden messages. Speakers deliberately tried to use parts of their common ground to transmit messages to which they thought the overhearer would not have access. Fleming, J., and Darley, J. (1991). Mixed messages: The multiple audience problem and strategic communication. *Social Cognition, 9,* 25–46.

    Other experimental research demonstrates the importance of collaboration in the asking and real-time understanding of questions. Speakers show a strong preference to ask questions in conversation that best specify the actual common ground between themselves and potential listeners in short conversational contexts. At the same time, listeners are quicker to comprehend questions that are designed to highlight precisely the type of common ground information that exists between themselves and speakers. See Gibbs et al. (1988), supra.

A number of researchers in Artificial Intelligence (AI) have similarly stressed the importance of intentions in building intelligent dialogue systems. See Allen, J., and Perrault, C. (1980). Analyzing intention in utterances. *Artificial Intelligence, 15,* 143–178. Appelt, D. (1985). *Planning English sentences.* Cambridge: Cambridge University Press. Cohen, P., and Perrault, C. (1979). Elements of a plan-based theory of speech acts. *Cognitive Science, 3,* 177–212. Cohen, P., Perrault, C., and Allen, J. (1982). Beyond question answering. In W. Lehnert & M. Ringle (eds.), *Strategies for natural language processing.* Hillsdale, NJ: L. Erlbaum. Cohen, P., Morgan, J., and Pollack, M. (Eds.) (1990). *Intentions in communication.* Cambridge, MA: MIT Press; Hobbs, J., and Evans, D. (1980). Conversation as planned behavior. *Cognitive Science, 4,* 349–378. Robertson, S., Black, J., and Johnson, P. (1981). Intention and topic in conversation. *Cognition and Brain Theory, 4,* 303–326.

Most of these computer systems emphasize access to a speaker's/author's underlying psychological plans and goals as fundamental elements for both planning and understanding utterances. AI researchers have in more recent years carefully distinguished between discourse intentions and commonsense plans in task-oriented dialogues. See Grosz, B., and Sidner, C. (1986). Attention, intentions, and the structure of discourse. *Computational Linguistics, 12,* 175–204. Littman, D., and Allen, J. (1987). A plan recognition model for sub-dialogues in conversation. *Cognitive Science, 11,* 163–200.

Computer scientists also have developed computational models to handle situations in which there are discrepancies between the beliefs of the conversational participants – see Pollack, M. (1990). Plans as complex mental attitudes. In P. Cohen, J. Morgan, and M. Pollack (Eds.), *Intentions in communication* (pp. 77–104). Cambridge, MA: MIT Press – and to recognize the importance of collective intentions in discourse understanding: Grosz and Sidner (1986), supra. Grosz, B., and Sidner, C. (1990). Plans for discourse. In P. Cohen, J. Morgan, and M. Pollack (Eds.), *Intentions in communication* (pp. 417–444). Cambridge, MA: MIT Press. Even though one can criticize some of this work for making nonpsychological simplifying assumptions – see Bach, K. (1990). Communicative intentions, plan recognition, and pragmatics: Comments on Thomason and on Littman and Allen. In P. Cohen, J. Morgan, and M. Pollack (Eds.), *Intention in communication* (pp. 389–400). Cambridge, MA: MIT Press – it seems clear that most AI models of linguistic behavior attempt to handle people's ordinary abilities to produce utterances with recognizable intentions and to recognize the communicative intentions behind other people's utterances.

46. Gerrig, R., and Littman, M. (1990). Disambiguation by community membership. *Memory & Cognition, 18,* 331–338.

47. Psychologist Boaz Keysar has recently provided an interesting critique of the idea that common ground is automatically assessed during ordinary language use. In several papers, Keysar and associates have suggested that certain experimental methods do not necessarily distinguish between processes that are sensitive to common ground, and processes that are not. For instance, Horton and Keysar (1996) compared the extent to which speakers use contextual information that was shared with addressees as opposed to contextual information that was privileged to speakers. They demonstrated that when speakers plan utterances, they do not necessarily rely on mutual knowledge shared with addressees, but mostly referred to contextual information known to speakers alone. Keysar proposes that two mental processes work during comprehension: an egocentric process and a perspective-adjustment process. Keysar's general criticisms indicate that close attention must be paid to the particular methods used to examine if, and when, common ground constrains speaking and listening. See Horton, W., and Keysar, B. (1996). When do speakers take into account common ground? *Cognition, 59,* 91–117. Keysar, B. (1997). Unconfounding common ground. *Discourse Processes, 24,* 253–270.

48. Sperber and Wilson (1986), supra.

49. Brown, G. (1996). *Speakers, listeners, and communication: Explorations in discourse analysis.* Cambridge: Cambridge University Press.

50. Kosinski, J. (1970). *Being there.* Toronto: Banthem.

51. For empirical work on how discourse assumptions influence metaphorical processing strategies, see Keysar, B. (1994). Discourse context effects: Metaphorical and literal interpretations. *Discourse Processes, 18,* 247–269.

52. Gibbs, R., O'Brien, J., and Doolittle, S. (1995). Inferring meanings that are not intended: Speakers' intentions and irony comprehension. *Discourse Processes, 20,* 187–203.

53. Searle, J. (1969). *Speech acts.* New York: Cambridge University Press.

54. Ochs, E. (1984). Clarification and culture. In D. Schiffirn (Ed.), *Georgetown University Roundtable on Language and Linguistics* (pp. 325-341). Washington, DC: Georgetown University Press. Quote is from p. 338.

55. Duranti, A. (1988). Intentions, language, and social action in a Samoan context. *Journal of Pragmatics, 12,* 13–33. Rosaldo, M. (1982). The things we do with words: Ilongot speech acts and speech act theory in philosophy. *Language in Society, 11,* 203–237. Silverstein, M. (1979). Language structure and linguistic ideology. In P. Clyns, W. Hanks, and C. Hofbauer (Eds.), *The elements: A parasession on linguistic units and levels* (pp. 193–247). Chicago: Chicago Linguistic Society.

56. The former look at "illocutionary" meaning, while the latter emphasize "perlocutionary" effects. See Chapter 2. As Shore (1982) pointed out in his discussion of the Samoan ethos, it is consequences that matter more than intentions. See Shore, B. (1982). *Sala'ilua: A Samoan mystery.* New York: Columbia University Press.

57. Duranti (1988), supra. Ochs, E. (1982). Talking to children in Western Samoa. *Language in Society, 11,* 77–104. Rosaldo (1982), supra.

58. Duranti (1988), supra.

59. Duranti (1988), supra. Exchange is quoted from p. 25.

60. Ochs (1984), supra.

61. Samoans will sometimes explicitly guess about what someone else might have been thinking, but this occurs only in talk about past actions, or when there is doubt about whether a particular action ever took place. See Ochs (1988), supra.

62. Ochs, E. (1988). *Culture and language development: Language acquisition and language socialization in a Samoan village.* New York: Cambridge University Press.

63. Ibid. Quote is from p. 30.

64. Ibid.

65. Rosaldo (1982), supra.

66. Rosaldo (1984), supra. Quote is from p. 146.

67. Levine, R. (1984). Properties of culture: An ethnographic view. In R. Shweder and R. LeVine (Eds.), *Culture theory: Essays on mind, self, and emotion* (pp. 67–87). New York: Cambridge University Press.

68. Levy, R. (1973). *Tahitians.* Chicago: University of Chicago Press.

69. Ibid. Quote is from pp. 352–353.

70. Paul, R. (1995). Act and intention in Sherpa culture and society. In L. Rosen (Ed.), *Other intentions: Cultural contexts and attribution*

of inner states (pp. 15–46). Santa Fe: School of American Research Press.

71. Wagner, R. (1995). Hazarding intent: Why Sogo left Hweabi. In L. Rosen (Ed.), *Other intentions: Cultural contexts and the attribution of inner states* (pp. 163–176). Santa Fe: School of American Research Press.

72. Ibid.

73. Strathen, M. (1995). Disembodied choice. In L. Rosen (Ed.), *Other intentions: Cultural contexts and the attribution of inner states* (pp. 69–90). Santa Fe: School of American Research Press.

74. Kochman, T. (1988). Strategic ambiguity in Black speech genres: Cross-cultural interference in participant-observation research. *Text, 6,* 153–170.

75. DuBois, J. (1987). Meaning without intention: Lessons from divination. *Papers in Pragmatics, 1,* 80–122.

CHAPTER 6

1. Schiller, L., and Willwerth, J. (1996). *American tragedy: The uncensored story of the Simpson defense.* New York: Random House. Quotes are from pp. 557–558.

2. Furman, M. (1997). *Murder in Brentwood.* New York: Regency Publishers. Quote is from p. 280.

3. Ibid. Quote is from p. 284.

4. See Brown, P., and Levinson, S. (1987). *Politeness.* Cambridge: Cambridge University Press. Sperber, D., and Wilson, D. (1986). *Relevance: Communication and cognition.* Cambridge, MA: Blackwell.

5. Clark, H. (1996). *Using language.* New York: Cambridge University Press.

6. Staged communicative acts are just one way of striving for relevance in one's communication. Staged communicative acts, like that seen in Bill and Grant's brief exchange, are interpreted by ordinary listeners as expressions of and clues to the speaker's thoughts. Every utterance is more or less a truthful interpretation of a thought that a speaker wants to communicate. An utterance is *descriptively* used when the thought interpreted is itself entertained as a true description of a state of affairs; it is *interpretively* used when the thought interpreted is entertained as an interpretation of some further thought, say, an attributed thought or utterance, or as an interpretation of some thought that might be desirable to entertain in some context. Bill and Grant's exchange involves staged communicative acts that must be understood interpretively, rather

than descriptively, precisely because these utterances are complex metarepresentations in the sense of being representations of pretend thoughts. See Sperber and Wilson (1986), supra.

7. See Gibbs, R. (1994). *The poetics of mind: Figurative thought, language, and understanding*. New York: Cambridge University Press.

8. Grice, H. P. (1975). Logic and conversation. In P. Cole and J. Morgan (Eds.), *Syntax and semantics, vol. 3: Speech acts* (pp. 41–58). New York: Academic Press. Grice, H. P. (1978). Further notes on logic and conversation. In P. Cole (Ed.), *Syntax and semantics, vol. 9: Pragmatics* (pp. 113–127). New York: Academic Press.

9. John Searle offers a similar rational analysis of figurative language interpretation. He proposes various principles that allow listeners to figure out just how sentence and speaker meanings differ in metaphor, irony, indirect speech acts, and so on. Searle believes that Grice's principles of cooperative conversation and the rules for performing speech acts are sufficient to provide the basic principles for figurative language understanding. See Searle, J. (1979). Metaphor. In A. Ortony (Eds.), *Metaphor and thought* (pp. 92–123). New York: Cambridge University Press.

10. See Gibbs (1994), supra, for a discussion of the claims that figurative language requires special mental processes to be understood.

11. Gibbs, R. (1984). Literal meaning and psychological theory. *Cognitive Science, 8*, 274–304. Gildea, P., and Glucksberg, S. (1983). On understanding metaphors: The role of context. *Journal of Verbal Learning and Verbal Behavior, 22*, 577–590.

12. Psycholinguists employ a variety of experimental tasks to assess the sequence of unconscious mental events used in the ordinary processing of figurative language. Most of these tasks involve recording the time it takes readers to interpret different kinds of figurative language in comparison to literal utterances. Participants in these "reaction-time" studies are presented with linguistic stimuli to which they must make a quick response. For example, participants may be asked to push a button as soon as they comprehend what they have just read, or they may then be asked to judge the similarity of meaning between two sentences. In both cases, the decision made is subjective and is thought to represent something about the "click of comprehension" phenomenally suggested by people's experience of understanding language.

Reaction-time experiments generally show that people take from one to four seconds to read and understand different figurative utterances. These studies often compare the latency period required to read or respond to figurative utterances versus the time needed to process "literal" expressions. Average differences of 200–300 milliseconds in the comprehension latencies of figurative versus literal sentences may appear to be negligible in terms of everyday communication, but such differences can mark important variations in the sequences of mental processes used in understanding figurative language (e.g., early comprehension processes). The traditional assumption that figurative language is deviant because it violates communicative norms suggests that people should take longer to process figurative utterances than to comprehend literal expressions.

For reviews of the numerous studies on this topic see Gibbs (1994), supra; and Hoffman, R., and Kemper, S. (1987). What could reaction-times studies be telling us about metaphor comprehension? *Metaphor and Symbolic Activity, 2,* 149–186.

13. Gildea, P., and Glucksberg, S. (1983). On understanding metaphors: The role of context. *Journal of Verbal Learning and Verbal Behavior, 22,* 577–590. Glucksberg, S., Gildea, P., and Bookin, H. (1982). On understanding nonliteral speech: Can people ignore metaphors? *Journal of Verbal Learning and Verbal Behavior, 21,* 85–98. Shinjo, M., and Myers, J. (1987). The role of context in metaphor comprehension. *Journal of Memory and Language, 26,* 226–241.

14. Gibbs, R. (1986). On the psycholinguistics of sarcasm. *Journal of Experimental Psychology: General, 115,* 3–15. Keysar, B. (1989). On the functional equivalence of metaphoric and literal meanings. *Journal of Memory and Language, 28,* 375–385. Gildea and Glucksberg (1983), supra.

15. See Gibbs, R. (in press). Metarepresentations in staged communicative acts. In D. Sperber (Ed.), *Metarepresentation.* New York: Oxford University Press. Happe, F. (1993). Communicative competence and theory of mind in autism: A test of relevance theory. *Cognition, 48,* 101–119. Sperber, D. (1994). Understanding verbal understanding. In J. Khalfa (Ed.), *What is intelligence?* (pp. 179–198). New York: Cambridge University Press. Not all aspects of figurative language are staged communicative acts. Following Sperber and Wilson's relevance theory, staged communicative acts might be different from metaphor precisely because of the use of metarepresentational reasoning in the production and interpretation of staged acts – something that is not required for understanding metaphor. Irony differs from metaphor in requiring the recognition of a thought about an attributed thought (second-order metarepresentation) in order to

understand a speaker's intentions (and the "weak" implicatures that become manifest from this).

16. Gibbs (1986), supra. Kreuz, R., and Glucksberg, S. (1989). How to be sarcastic: The echoic reminder theory of verbal irony. *Journal of Experimental Psychology: General, 118,* 374–386. Kumon-Nakamura, S., Glucksberg, S., and Brown, M. (1995). How about another piece of pie: The allusional pretense theory of discourse irony. *Journal of Experimental Psychology: General, 124,* 3–21.

17. From Tannen, D., and Wallat, C. (1983). Doctor/mother/child communication: Linguistic analysis of a pediatric interaction. In S. Fisher and A. Todd (Eds.), *The social organization of doctor-patient communication* (pp. 203–219). Washington, DC: Center for Applied Linguistics. Dialogue is from pp. 213–214.

18. Ibid, p. 216.

19. Several scholars, however, have suggested that the conscious intention to deceive may not be the defining mark of deception. These scholars argue that studies of deception too often focus on the liar rather than the lie, and place too much emphasis on the morality of deception rather than on the discourse situation. See Bavelas, J., Black, A., Choval, N., and Mullett, J. (1990). *Equivocal communication.* Newbury Park, CA: Sage.

20. Nyberg, D. (1996). *The varnished truth: Truth telling and deceiving in ordinary life.* Chicago: University of Chicago Press.

21. Bok, S. (1978). *Lying: Moral choice in public and private life.* New York: Pantheon. Ekman, P. (1984). *Telling lies: Clues to deceit in the marketplace, politics, and marriage.* New York: Norton. Knapp, M., and Comadena, M. (1979). Telling it like it isn't: A review of theory and research on deceptive communication. *Human Communication Research, 1,* 15–29.

22. Carlson, P. (1987). The Academy Awards of untruth. *Washington Post Magazine,* July 9, p. 34.

23. Miller, G. (1983). Telling it like it isn't and not telling like it is: Some thoughts on deceptive communication. In J. Sisco (Ed.), *The Jensen lectures: Contemporary communication studies* (pp. 91–116). Tampa: University of South Florida Press.

24. Camden, C., Motley, M., and Wilson, A. (1984). White lies in interpersonal communication: A taxonomy and preliminary investigation of social motivations. *The Western Journal of Speech Communication, 48,* 309–325. Goffman, E. (1974). *Frame analysis: An essay on the organization of experience.* New York: Harper & Row. Hample, D. (1980). Purposes and effects of lying. *The Southern Speech*

Communication Journal, 46, 33–47. Lippard, P. (1988). "Ask me no questions, I'll tell you no lies": Situational exigencies for interpersonal deception. *The Western Journal of Speech Communication, 52*, 91–103.

25. Another interesting reason has been put forward for deceptive behavior. Occasional deception breeds skepticism, which in turn fosters independent thought among communicators. Ideal societies consisting of nothing other than veracity and truth prevent uncertainty and doubt, two conditions that often lead to creative and critical communication processes. Assumptions of honesty can engender tendencies to accept information on face value without careful analysis. Paradoxically, deception keeps people honest. See Kursh, C. (1971). The benefits of poor communication. *Psychoanalytic Review, 58*, 189–208.

26. Venant, E. (1991). Our cheating hearts (lies and honesty in the United States). *Los Angeles Times*, December 10, 1991, p. E1.

27. Hassett, J. (1981). But that would be wrong... *Psychology Today, 15*, 34–50.

28. Cochran, S., and Mays, V. (1990). Sex, lies, and HIV. *New England Journal of Medicine, 332*, 774–775.

29. DePaulo, B, Kashy, D. Kirendil, S., and Wing, M. (1996). Lying in everyday life. *Journal of Personality and Social Psychology, 70*, 979–995. In a separate study, Kirby and DePaulo (1996) analyzed the personalities of the people in the DePaulo et al. (1996) study. They found that people who told more lies were found to be more manipulative, more concerned with self-presentation, and less highly socialized. People who told fewer lies were more highly socialized, and reported higher quality same-sex relationships. People viewed as more manipulative and less highly socialized also told more self-serving lies. People with high quality same-sex relationships told relatively more other-oriented lies (i.e., lies to protect the feelings of others). Kirby, D., and DePaulo, B. (1996). Who lies? *Journal of Personality and Social Psychology, 70*, 1037–1051.

30. However, Ekman (1984), supra, speculated that fewer deceptions are actually motivated by altruistic reasons than are reported. Their motives are more socially acceptable, so communicators may prefer to think that their deceptions are altruistic when in fact they are self-serving. The ability to deceive successfully could be considered a socially competent communication strategy. At times, the truth can be very painful to the target, and sparing the target this painful experience may be the socially appropriate course of action. This

does not imply that targets desire to be deceived. In short, not all deceptions are designed to be cruel and self-serving, and not all deceptions should be considered morally reprehensible without considering the motives behind their use.

31. DePaulo et al. (1996), supra, note however that it remains to be seen whether there is some cumulative effect of telling many little lies over time.

32. See Ekman, P. (1981). Mistakes when deceiving. *Annals of the New York Academy of Sciences, 364,* 269–278. Quote is on p. 271. Leaked indicators are primarily based on physiologically based behaviors that are less controllable by the deceiver. Research has shown that liars display more blinking, pupil dilation or instability, self and object manipulations, higher-pitched voice, vocal nervousness, speech errors and hesitations, and less gesturing. See Ekman, P., and Friesen, W. (1969). Nonverbal leakage and cues to deception. *Psychiatry, 32,* 88–106; Buller and Burgoon (1994).

33. Ekman (1981), supra. DePaulo, B., Stone, J., and Lassiter, G. (1985). Deceiving and detecting deceit. In B. Sclencker (Ed.), *The self and social life.* New York: McGraw-Hill. Zuckerman, M., Larrance, N., and Klorman, R. (1981). Controlling nonverbal clues: Facial expressions and tone of voice. *Journal of Experimental Social Psychology, 17,* 506–524.

34. Miller and Stiff (1993), supra. Stiff, J., and Miller, G. (1986). "Come to think of it...": Interrogative probes, deceptive communication, and deception detection. *Human Communication Research, 12,* 339–357.

35. Depaulo et al. (1985), supra.

36. O'Sullivan, M., Ekman, P., and Friesen, W. (1988). The effect of comparisons on detecting deceit. *Journal of Nonverbal Behavior, 12,* 203–215.

37. Druckman, D., Rozelle, R., and Baxter, J. (1982). *Nonverbal communication: Survey, theory, and research.* Beverly Hills, CA: Sage Publications. Some evidence suggests there are no differences in deception detection of factual lies by strangers and close friends. However, when judging self-feelings, friends are more accurate in detecting deception than ether strangers or spouses. Miller et al. (1986), supra. Studies even show that people are no better at detecting deception from a relational partner than from a stranger. Comadena (1982), supra. Although relational participants have more information about one another, they apparently do not employ this information very effectively when making veracity judgments.

Researchers argue that the relational costs associated with accusing one's partner of deception, combined with a disproportionate number of truthful interactions, lead people in intimate relationships to presume that their partner is usually truthful. McCormack, S., and Levine, T. (1990). When lovers become leery: The relationship between suspicion and accuracy in detecting deception. *Communication Monographs, 57,* 219–230. Levine, T., and McCormack, S. (1991). The dark side of trust: Conceptualizing and measuring types of communicative suspicion. *Communication Quarterly, 39,* 325–340.

38. Daly, J., Diesel, C., and Weber, D. (1994). Conversational dilemmas. In W. Cupach and B. Spitzberg (Eds.), *The dark side of interpersonal communication* (pp. 127–158). Hillsdale, NJ: Erlbaum.

39. Beck, A. (1988). *Love is never enough.* New York: Harpers. Excerpt is from p. 215.

40. Brown, P., and Levinson, S. (1987). *Politeness.* Cambridge: Cambridge University Press. Cupach, W., and Metts, S. (1990). Remedial processes in embarrassing predicaments. In J. Anderson (Ed.), *Communication yearbook 13* (pp. 323–352). Newbury Park, CA: Sage.

41. Bateson, Jackson, Haley, and Weakland (1956) introduced the term "double bind" as a social cause for schizophrenia, theorizing that significant others in the schizophrenic's early life send contradictory verbal and nonverbal messages. The result is that the child feels trapped in terms of how to respond to these messages. See Bateson, G., Jackson, D., Haley, J., and Weakland, J. (1956). Toward a theory of schizophrenia. *Behavioral Science, 1,* 251–264. The double-bind hypothesis has been examined with a rich variety of contexts across many disciplines, including the interpretation of famous plays, such as Albee's *Who's Afraid of Virginia Woolf?* and Shakespeare's *King Lear,* and Heller's novel *Catch-22;* the behavior of individuals in many organizational settings; and the problems that women face when caught between the conflicting demands of their roles at work, at home, and within their culture.

42. Watzlawick, P., Beavin, J., and Jackson, D. (1967). *Pragmatics of human communication.* New York: Norton.

43. Brown and Levinson (1978), supra.

44. See Chapter 3 for additional discussion of this point.

45. Chovil, N. (1994). Equivocation as an interactional event. In W. Cupach and B. Spitzberg (Eds.), *The dark side of interpersonal communication* (pp. 105–124). Hillsdale, NJ: Erlbaum.

46. From Issacs, S., and Clark, H. (1990). Ostensible invitations. *Language in Society, 19*, 493–529.
47. Clark (1996), supra.
48. Dillon, J. (1990). Conducting discussions by alternatives to questions. In W. Wilen (Ed.), *Teaching and learning through discussion*. Springfield, IL: Thomas Publishers.
49. "Locked in the cabinet," by Robert B. Reich, *The New Yorker*, April 21, 1997.
50. Linde, C. (1988). The quantitative study of communicative success: Politeness and accidents in aviation discourse. *Language in Society, 17*, 375–399.
51. Ibid. Excerpt is from p. 379.
52. The symbol # is a transcription convention of the NTSB, indicating "nonpertinent word," most likely when obscenity or profanity has been used.
53. These are adapted from a list given by Brown and Levinson (1987), supra, pp. 211–227.
54. Bach, K., and Harnish, R. (1979). *Linguistic communication and speech acts*. Cambridge, MA: MIT Press.
55. See Bell, D. (1996). Innuendo. *Journal of Pragmatics, 27*, 35–59. Sperber and Wilson (1986), supra.
56. Bell (1996), supra.
57. Strawson, P. (1964). Intention and convention in speech acts. *Philosophical Review, 75*, 439–460. Quote is from p. 297.
58. *New York Times*, Aug 5, 1992, p. A22.
59. This example is from McKellin, W. (1990). Allegory and inference: Intentional ambiguity in Managalese negotiations. In K. Watson-Gegeo and G. White (Eds.), *Disentangling: Conflict discourse in Pacific societies* (pp. 335–372). Stanford: Stanford University Press.

CHAPTER 7

1. Hirsch, E. (1976). *The aims of interpretation*. Chicago: University of Chicago Press. Kay, P. (1977). Language evolution and speech style. In B. Blount and M. Sanchez (Eds.), *Sociocultural dimensions of language change* (pp. 21–34). New York: Academic Press. Olson, D. (1977). From utterance to text: The bias of language in speech and writing. *Harvard Educational Review, 47*, 257–281. Ong, W. (1977). *Interfaces of the word*. New Haven: Yale University Press.
2. Olson (1977), supra.
3. Adapted from Katz, J. (1981). Literal meaning and logical theory. *Journal of Philosophy, 78*, 203–234.

4. Writers must learn how to become naive readers of their own text. A naive reader is one who shares some common ground with the author but who does not know everything the author knows about a topic or about what the author is intending to say. See Traxler, M., and Gernsbacher, M.A. (1992). Improving written communication through minimal feedback. *Language and Cognitive Processes, 7*, 1–22.

5. See Luria, A. (1981). *Language and cognition*. New York: Wiley; Vygotsky, L. (1962). *Thought and language*. Cambridge, MA: MIT Press.

    However, one large study of the cognitive consequences of literacy concludes that literacy per se contributes only marginally to cognitive development. See Scribner, S., and Cole, M. (1981). *The psychology of literacy*. Cambridge, MA: Harvard University Press. Literacy is not adequately understood as proficiency in decontextualized language. "Literacy is not simply knowing how to read and write a particular script, but applying this knowledge for specific purposes and specific contexts of use." Scribner and Cole (1981), p. 236.

6. O'Donnell, R. (1974). Syntactic differences between speech and writing. *American Speech, 49*, 102–110.

7. Poole, M., and Field, T. (1976). A comparison of oral and written code elaboration. *Language & Speech, 19*, 305–316.

8. Ochs, E. (1979). Planned and unplanned discourse. In T. Givon (Ed.), *Syntax and semantics vol. 12: Discourse and syntax* (pp. 51–80). New York: Academic Press. Also see Chafe, W., and Danielewicz, J. (1987). Properties of spoken and written language. In R. Horowitz and S. Samuels (Eds.), *Comprehending oral and written language* (pp. 83–113). New York: Academic Press.

9. Lakoff, R. (1982). Some of my favorite writers are literate: The mingling of oral and literate strategies in written communication. In D. Tannen (Ed.), *Spoken and written language: Exploring orality and literacy* (pp. 239–260). Norwood, NJ: Ablex. Nystand, M. (1986). *The structure of written communication: Studies in reciprocity between writers and readers*. San Diego: Academic Press.

10. Rader, M. (1982). Context in written language: The case of imaginative fiction. In D. Tannen (Ed.), *Spoken and written language* (pp. 185–198). Norwood, NJ: Ablex.

11. Hayes, J., and Flower, L. (1987). On the structure of the writing process. *Topics in Language Disorders, 7*, 19–30.

12. Geisler, C. (1991). *Academic literacy and the nature of expertise: Reading, writing, and knowing in academic philosophy*. Hillsdale, NJ:

Erlbaum. Spivey, N. (1997). *The constructivist metaphor: Reading, writing, and the making of meaning.* San Diego: Academic Press.

13. See Britton, B. (1978). The composing process and the functions of writing. In C. Cooper and L. Odell (Eds.), *Research on composing: Points of departure* (pp. 13–28). Urbana, IL: National Council of Teachers. Writers who compose on computers sometimes print out their texts to make alterations in longhand.

14. Bracewell, R., Fredricksen, C., and Fredricksen, J. (1982). Cognitive processes in composing and comprehending discourse. *Educational Psychologist, 17,* 146–164. Spivey (1997), supra.

15. Nystrand, M. (1982). The structure of structural space. In M. Nystrand (Ed.), *What writers know: The language, processes, and structure of written discourse* (pp. 75–86). New York: Academic Press. Quote is from p. 70.

16. Turner, S. (1994). *The creative process: A computer model of story telling and creativity.* Hillsdale, NJ: Erlbaum.

17. See Mann, P. (1982). *From author to reader.* London: Routledge & Kegan Paul.

18. Some critics have noted the power and effectiveness of gardening catalogues that speak with a clear authorial voice. See White, K. (1979). *Onward and upward in the garden.* New York: Farrar, Strauss & Giroux.

19. Cheever, J. (1978). The ocean. In his *Stories* (pp. 567–583). New York: Knopf. Quote is from p. 567.

20. Rabinowitz, P. (1987). *Before reading.* Ithaca: New York University Press. Quote is from 118.

21. Shields, C. (1990). *Mary Swann.* London: Fourth Estates.

22. Booth, W. (1983). *The rhetoric of fiction* (2nd edition). Chicago: University of Chicago Press.

23. Gerrig, R. (1993). *Experiencing narrative worlds: On the psychological activity of reading.* New Haven: Yale University Press.

24. Booth (1983), supra. Quote is from p. 149.

25. See Ceci, S., and Peters, D. (1984). How blind is blind review. *American Psychologist, 39,* 1491–1494.

26. Sinclair, M. (1993). Are academic texts really decontextualized and fully explicit? A pragmatic perspective on the role of context in written communication. *Text, 13,* 529–558.

27. See ibid. for all of the quotes from Watson and Crick's article.

28. Gilbert, R., and Mulkay, R. (1984). *Opening Pandora's box: A sociological analysis of scientists' discourse.* New York: Cambridge University Press.

29. Ibid. Quote is from pp. 66–67.
30. Ibid. Quote is from p. 67.
31. Ibid. Quote is from p. 64.
32. This study used naturally occurring texts that were written to convey author personality (college admissions applications) and the readers (college admissions officers) were highly skilled at inferring author traits. See Hayes, J. (1992). A psychological perspective applied to literary studies. In R. Beach, R. Green, M. Kamil, and T. Shanahan (Eds.), *Multidisciplinary perspectives on literacy research* (pp. 125–140). Urbana: National Conference of Research in English.
33. Beck, I., McKeown, M., Sandora, L., and Kucas, L. (1996). Questioning the author: A yearlong classroom implementation to engage students with text. *Elementary School Journal, 96,* 385–415. Jacobowitz, T. (1990). AIM: A metacognitive study for constructing the main idea of text (Author's Intending Message). *Journal of Reading, 33,* 620–625. McGee, L. (1983). Perceptions of author's intentions: Effects on comprehension. In J. Niles and L. Harris (Eds.), *Searches for meaning in reading/language processing and instruction* (pp. 148–157). Rochester, NY: National Reading Conference Yearbook.
34. Beck et al. (1996), supra. Quotes are from p. 409.
35. Ibid. Quote is from p. 409.
36. Martin, S. (1987). *The meaning-making strategies reported by proficient readers and writers.* Paper presented at the meeting of the National Reading Conference, St. Petersburg, Florida.
37. Flowers, L. (1987). Interpretive acts: Cognition and construction of discourse. (Occasional paper no. 1). Berkeley: Center for the Study of Writing, University of California.
38. Tierney, R., LaZansky, J., Raphael, T., and Cohen, P. (1987). Author's intentions and reader's interpretations. In R. Tierney, P. Andes, and J. Mitchell (Eds.), *Understanding readers' understanding* (pp. 205–226). Hillsdale, NJ: Erlbaum.
39. Nolen, S. (1995). Effects of a visible author on statistics texts. *Journal of Educational Psychology, 87,* 47–65.
40. Paxton, R. (1997). "Someone with like a life wrote it": The effects of a visible author on high school history students. *Journal of Educational Psychology, 89,* 235–250.
41. Ibid. The following two quotes are from p. 241.
42. Haas, C., and Flower, L. (1988). Rhetorical reading strategies and the construction of meaning. *College Composition and Communication, 39,* 167–183.

43. Wineburg, S. (1991). On the reading of historical texts: Notes on the breach between school and academy. *American Educational Research Journal, 28,* 495–519.
44. Flowers (1987), supra.
45. Shanahan, T. (1992). Reading comprehension as a conversation with an author. In M. Pressley, K. Harris, and J. Guthrie (Eds.), *Promoting academic competence and literacy in school* (pp. 129–148). San Diego: Academic Press.
46. Ibid., p. 431.
47. Ibid., p. 432.
48. Brewer, W.F. (1980). Literary theory, rhetoric, and stylistics: Implications for psychology. In R. Spiro, B. Bruce, and W. Brewer (Eds.), *Theoretical issues in reading comprehension* (pp. 221–239). Hillsdale, NJ: Erlbaum.
49. See ibid; and Sinha, S., and Janisch, C. (1996). A view of reading practices in the intermediate grades: Treatment of discourse types. In R. Kreuz and M. MacNealy (Eds.), *Empirical approaches to literature and aesthetics* (pp. 495–511). Norwood, NJ: Ablex.
50. Cazden, C. (1989). The myth of autonomous text. In D. Topping, D. Crowell, and V. Kobayashi (Eds.), *Thinking across cultures* (pp. 109–122). Hillsdale, NJ: Erlbaum.
51. Evidence for the psychological validity of causal network representations comes from studies showing that statements with many causal connections constitute good summaries of text and that the probability of recall for a statement in a literary text is strongly determined by its number of connections. See van den Broek, P., Rohleder, L., and Narvaez, D. (1996). Causal inferences in the comprehension of literary texts. In R. Kreuz and M. MacNealy (Eds.), *Empirical approaches to literature and aesthetics* (pp. 179–200). Norwood, NJ: Ablex.
52. See Gerrig (1993), supra.
53. From Magliano, J., Baggett, W., and Graesser, A. (1996). A taxonomy of inferences categories that may be generated during the comprehension of literary texts. In R. Kreuz and M. MacNealy (Eds.), *Empirical approaches to literature and aesthetics* (pp. 201–220). Norwood, NJ: Ablex.
54. Magliano, J., and Graesser, A. (1991). A three-pronged method for studying inference generation in literary text. *Poetics, 20,* 193–232. Also see Graesser, A., and Kreuz, R. (1993). A theory of inference generation during text comprehension. *Discourse Processes, 16,* 145–160.

55. See the essays in Graesser, A., and Bower, G. (Eds.) (1990). *Inferences and text comprehension*. New York: Academic Press.
56. The psychologists Douglas Vipond and Russell Hunt have proposed a "point-driven" theory of understanding that describes how readers generate inferences about the author's intent. See Vipond, D., and Hunt, R. (1984). Point-driven understanding: Pragmatic and cognitive dimensions of literary reading. *Poetics, 13,* 261–277. Hunt, R., and Vipond, D. (1986). Evaluations in literary reading. *Text, 6,* 53–71.
57. Garner, J. (1994). *Politically correct bedtime stories*. New York: Macmillan.
58. Pfaff, K., and Gibbs, R. (1997). Authorial intentions and satire understanding. *Poetics, 25,* 45–70.
59. The extent to which this construction of a mental model for texts employs automatic, as opposed to strategic, inferences about an author remains unclear. For further discussion see Graesser, A., Singer, M., and Trabasso, T. (1994). Constructing inferences during narrative comprehension. *Psychological Review, 101,* 371–395. Magliano, J., and Graesser, A. (1991). A three-pronged method for studying inference generation in literary texts. *Poetics, 20,* 193–232.

CHAPTER 8

1. But consider the "blindfold" tests done by *Down Beat* magazine, where jazz muscians are asked to evaluated pieces they hear without being told the identity of the performer.
2. Authors embark on book tours to promote their work, are frequently interviewed on television and by the print media, and often sign autographs for admirers at bookstores and on college campuses. Readers certainly use authorship as a feature of selection in helping them determine what to read. One study that focused on reasons why adults selected particular books from the library showed that 54 percent of the books were selected solely on the basis of authorship, and that the author figured at least partially in the selection 89 percent of the time. See Mann, P. (1982). *From author to reader*. London: Routledge and Keagan Paul.

    Authors are also accepted as "experts," voices of authority on a variety of topics, even in regard to subjects they have not written about. We clearly live in a culture where to be an author is, to some extent, to be a part of the cult of celebrity. A major trend in contemporary publishing is not just to think of authors as celebrities, but to turn celebrities into authors. Note the large number of books on best-seller lists written by entertainers, professional athletes, politicians, and practically anyone who has been in the public spotlight for at least fifteen minutes. Our interest in these books is almost exclusively with what they tell us about their nominal authors (e.g., Madonna, Dennis Rodman, Jerry Seinfeld).

3. Educators have extreme respect for real authors, as evident in the high school and college curriculums organized around themes such as "great authors." Even though the "canon" has been seriously attacked by some educators and literary critics in recent years, especially by those in favor of multiculturalism in the curriculum, these efforts usually focus on including various works by people of diverse backgrounds. Quite significantly, these debates assume the Romantic vision of authorship instead of drawing from alternative writing practices.

4. Michell, J. (1996). *Who wrote Shakespeare?* New York: Thames and Hudson.

5. Felicia Loudre in a GTE VisNet videoconference entitled "Uncovering Shakespeare," September 17, 1992.

6. Heyward, M. (1993). *The Ern Malley Affair*. London: Faber and Faber. Poem is found on p. 56.

7. Ibid., p. 57.

8. See Gates, H. (1991). Authenticity, or the lessons of Little Tree. *New York Times Book Review*, November 24, pp. 1, 26–30.

9. Ibid. Quote is from p. 26.

10. Ibid. Quote is from p. 27.

11. Quotes are from "Aboriginal artist's ruse roils Australia," printed in the *San Francisco Chronicle*, March 8, 1997, p. 11.

12. As philosopher Nelson Goodman points out, in music, unlike painting, there is no such thing as a forgery of a known work. There are, indeed, compositions falsely purporting to be by different composers, but, for example, all copies of Haydn's manuscripts are equally genuine instances of the scores he has written. Performances may vary in correctness and quality and even in "authenticity" at a more esoteric level, but all correct performances are equally genuine instances of the work. A composer's work is finished when he or she has written the score. Performers must then actually realize the work, and in this sense, music is two-stage art. See Goodman, N. (1976). *The languages of art*. Cambridge, MA: Harvard University Press.

13. Ibid. Quote is from p. 101.

14. Goodman's response to this issue is that practice is essential in distinguishing between the true Rembrandt painting and its forgery. As he puts it, there is no aesthetic difference without a perceptual difference based on the features of the painting that we can eventually learn to recognize. There are minute perceptual differences that can make all the difference in how we recognize a particular work. Ibid.

15. Beardsley, M. (1970). *Aesthetics.* New Haven: Yale University Press.

16. Unger, P. (1990). *Identity, consciousness and value.* New York: Oxford University Press.

17. Ibid. Quote is from pp. 315–316.

18. See Cahn, S., and Griffel, L. (1975). The strange case of John Shmarb: An aesthetic puzzle. *Journal of Aesthetics and Art Criticism, 34,* 21–22. Quote is from p. 21.

19. Ibid. Quote is from p. 22.

20. Cope, D. (1991). *Computers and musical style.* Madison, Wisc.: A-R Editions. Cope, D. (1996). *Experiments in musical intelligence.* Madison, Wisc.: A-R Editions.

21. Aiken, J. (1993). Ghost in the machine. *Keyboard, 19,* 25–28. Quote is from p. 25.

22. Cope (1996), supra. Quote is from p. 238.

23. Gopnik, A. (1997). Doubting Vincent. *The New Yorker.* July 28, 1997. Quote is from pp. 36–37.

24. Foucault, M. (1979). What is an author? In J. Harari (Ed.), *Textual strategies: Perspectives in post-structuralist criticism* (pp. 35–51). Ithaca: Cornell University Press.

25. Yule, E. (1918) *Conjectures on original composition* (originally published in 1759). Manchester: Manchester University Press. Quote is from p. 7.

26. Leader, Z. (1996). *Revision and romantic authorship.* Oxford: Clarendon Press. Quotes are from p. 2.

27. Stillinger, J. (1996). Poets who revise, poets who don't, and critics who should. *Journal of Aesthetic Education, 30,* 119–135. Quote is from p. 123.

28. McDonald, K. (1995). "Too many co-authors?" *The Chronicle of Higher Education, 41,* 33, pp. A35–36.

29. Scientists now assume that the complexity of the problems now addressed requires large collaborative teams assembled over many years. Many scientists complain that long lists of authors, which often include technicians as well as scientists, distort the relative contributions of researchers and make it more difficult to make

tenure and promotion decisions at colleges and universities. Imagine one case where an assistant professor of physics was the 370th in the alphabetical listing of 437 authors on one of the papers announcing the discovery of the top quark. Yet one study found that scientists are reluctant to change the present system of assigning authorship, fearing that debates over who should and who shouldn't be listed will lead to nasty fights among collaborators.

30. Gilbert, G., and Mulkey, M. (1984). *Opening Pandora's box: A sociological analysis of scientific discourse.* Cambridge: Cambridge University Press.

31. See Stillinger, J. (1994). *Multiple authorship and the myth of solitary genius.* New York: Oxford University Press.

32. Stillinger speculates that editors resist the label of collaborator to appeal to the vanity of writers who are among the most ardent believers in the notion of single authorship. Ibid.

33. John Feugin quoted by Shteir, R. (1996). Brecht/not Brecht. *Lingua Franca.* May/June. Quote is from p. 40.

34. See Stillinger, J. (1994), supra. Quote is from p. 132.

35. Although acknowledging Pound's help with the editing of infelicities in the poem, many critics emphasize that Pound's work merely helped Eliot express what he already had in mind. Critics in the 1980s and 1990s now have begun to provide a balanced account of Pound's effort. As is said in *The Norton Anthology of American Literature*, "the study of the manuscript before and after Pound's suggestions were incorporated has led some critics to suggest that we should think of 'The Waste Land' as jointly created." See Bayum, N. et al. (Eds.) (1989). *The Norton Anthology of American Literature* (3rd edition). New York: Norton, 2:1266.

36. Bedeian, A. (1996). Improving the journal reviewer process: The question of ghostwriting. *American Psychologist, 51,* 1189.

37. Scollon, R. (1995). Plagiarism and ideology: Identity in intercultural discourse. *Language in Society, 24,* 1–28.

38. Adapted from Hogan, P. (1996). *On interpretation: Meaning and inference in law, psychoanalysis, and literature.* Athens, GA: University of Georgia Press.

39. Bolter, J. (1991). *Writing space: The computer, hypertext, and the history of writing.* Hillsdale, NJ: Erlbaum. Quote is from p. 112.

40. Coover, R. (1992). The end of books (hypertext). *New York Times Book Review,* June 21. Quote is from p. 23.

41. See Bolter (1991), supra.

42. Atkins, R. (1995). The art world & I go on line. *Art in America*

(December). Thirty or so lines into this text someone wrote: *Who do we think we are? James Joyce's great grandchildren*, and someone else responded, *Or some kind of Gertrude* (as in Gertrude Stein).

43. Fowler, R. (1994) The fate on the notion of canon in the electronic age. Paper presented at the Spring meeting of the Western Institute, Santa Rosa, CA.

44. Bolter (1991), supra. Coover (1992), supra. Lanham, W. (1993). *The electronic word: Democracy, technology, and the arts.* Chicago: University of Chicago Press.

45. Plays and films are created over a period of trial-and-error experimentation as audience reaction can be constantly monitored and numerous revisions can be introduced in response to these reactions. A detailed discussion of one such example, Tom Stoppard's *Travesties,* is given in Garkill, P. (1978). *From writer to reader: Studies in the editorial method.* Oxford: Clarendon.

46. Jaszi, P. (1994). The author effect: Contemporary copyright and collective creativity. In M. Woodmansee and P. Jaszi (Eds.), *The construction of authorship: Textual appropriation in law and literature* (pp. 29–56). Durham: Duke University Press.

47. *Feist Publications, Inc. v. Rural Telephone Service*, 111 S. Ct. 1282 (1991).

48. Jaszi (1994), supra. Quote is from p. 42.

49. Ibid., p. 43.

50. Ibid., p. 44.

51. Ibid., p. 47.

52. Ibid., p. 47.

53. From Zenith, R. (1997). Introduction: The drama and dream of Fernando Pessoa. In *Fernando Pessoa & Co.: Selected poems.* Edited and translated by R. Zenith. New York: Grove Press. Quote is from p. 3.

54. Ibid., pp. 13–14.

55. For additional readings on Pessoa's life and work see Monteiro, G. (1982). *The man who never was: Essays on Fernando Pessoa.* Providence, RI: Brown University Press.

56. Livingston, P. (1991). *Literature and rationality: Ideas of agency in theory and fiction.* New York: Cambridge University Press.

57. Ibid., p. 71.

58. Ibid., p. 72.

59. Ibid., pp. 72–73.

60. Ibid., p. 73.

61. Ibid., p. 75.

62. Foucault (1978), supra.

63. Ibid. Quote is from p. 141. As suggested above, authors are not only people to whom the production of a text or another literary work can be legitimately attributed. Even within the realm of discourse, a person can be an author of a tradition or a discipline. To be an author is not a spontaneous product of simply attributing a text to a specific individual. Instead we simply construct what we call an author based on our need to know certain things. Under this view, a philosopher and a poet are not constructed in the same way. Foucault argued that special types of authors, like Freud and Marx, arose in the nineteenth century as "initiators of discursive practices." The characteristic feature of these authors is that they produced, in addition to their own work, the possibility in rules of formation of other texts. Unlike important novelists whose work might create modes of analysis that could be adapted by other writers, initiators of discursive practices influenced not only the works of individual authors, but help to determine higher levels of thinking within an entire discipline.
64. Nehamas, A. (1981). The postulated author: Critical monism as a regulative ideal. *Critical Inquiry, 8,* 133–149.
65. Parini, J. (1997). The lessons of theory. *Philosophy and Literature, 21,* 91–101.
66. Booth, W. (1961). *The rhetoric of fiction.* Chicago: University of Chicago Press.
67. Rosenberg, D., and Bloom, H. (1990). The book of J (excerpts). *American Poetry Review, 19,* 27–32. Quote is from p. 29.
68. Borges, J. (1995). Borges and I. In D. Halpern (Ed.). *Who's writing this? Notations of the authorial I with self-portraits* (pp. 4–5). New York: Ecco.

CHAPTER 9

1. Lessing, D. (1973). *The Golden Notebook.* New York: Bantam Books. Quotes are from pp. xxviii–xxix.
2. These comments are given in a taped lecture, *Required reading and other dangerous subjects,* by Amy Tam, available from Don't Quit Your Day Job productions in San Francisco, California.
3. Rushdie, S. (1988). *The Satanic Verses.* London: Viking.
4. S. Nomanul Haq, letter in the *International Herald Tribune,* February 24, 1989.
5. Webster, R. (1990). *A brief history of blasphemy: Liberalism, censorship, and "The Satanic Verses."* Suffolk: The Orwell Press, p. 89.
6. See Ni Fhlathuin, M. (1995) Postcolonialism and the author: The

case of Salman Rushdie. In S. Burke (Ed.), *Authorship: From Plato to the postmodern* (pp. 277–284). Edinburgh: University of Edinburgh Press.

7. Jussawalla, F. (1990). Resurrecting the prophet: The case of Salman, the Otherwise. *Public Culture, 2.1,* p. 107.

8. See Miller, J. (1990). *Seductions: Studies in reading and culture.* London: Virago; Iser, W. (1974). *The implied reader.* Baltimore: Johns Hopkins University Press. Fish, S. (1980). *Is there a text in this classroom?* Baltimore: Johns Hopkins University Press.

9. Stillinger, J. (1996). Poets who revise, poets who don't, and critics who should. *Journal of Aesthetic Education, 30,* 119–133.

10. Ibid. Quote is from p. 123.

11. Middlebrook, D. (1991). *Anne Sexton: A Biography.* Boston: Houghton Mifflin. Quote is from p. 62.

12. Sexton, A. (1966). *Live or die.* Boston: Houghton Mifflin.

13. Ludwig, A. (1997). *How do we know who we are? A biography of the self.* New York: Oxford University Press. Quote is from p. 42.

14. Stecker, R. (1997). *Artworks: Definition, meaning, value.* University Park: Pennsylvania State University Press.

15. I thank Greg Murphy for his suggestions on this very point.

16. Bain, A. (1969). On teaching English. *Fortnightly Review, 6,* 213–214.

17. Wimsatt, W., Jr., and Beardsley, M. (1946). The intentional fallacy. *Sewannee Review, 54,* 468–488.

18. Eliot, T.S. (1957). *On poetry and poets.* New York: Farrar, Straus, and Cudahy. Quote is from p. 113.

19. Thompkins, J. (1996). *A life in school: What the teacher learned.* Reading, MA: Addison-Wesley. Quote is from p. 83.

20. Wimsatt, W., Jr. (1976). Genesis: A fallacy revisited. In D. Newton-de Molina (Ed.), *On literary intention* (pp. 116–136). Edinburgh: University of Edinburgh Press. Quote is from p. 36.

21. Later Wimsatt conceded that the work itself might display within it the intentions and mind of the author. A text may be properly understood to display the author's intentions without reference to information or material about the author apart from the text itself. Despite these clarifications, however, until recently the enormously influential "The Intentional Fallacy" has been seen as exiling from respectable literary commentary all reference to an author's intention.

22. Austin, J. (1962). *How to do things with words.* Oxford: Clarendon Press. Grice, H. P. (1957). Meaning. *Philosophical Review, 64,* 377–388. Grice, H. P. (1968). Utterer's meaning, sentence-meaning, and

word-meaning. *Foundations of Language, 4,* 225–242. Grice, H. P. (1969). Utterer's meaning and intention. *Philosophical Review, 78,* 147–177. Searle, J. (1969). *Speech acts.* New York: Cambridge University Press. Also see Ohmann, R. (1971). Speech acts and the definition of literature. *Philosophy and Rhetoric, 4,* 1–19. Pratt, M. (1977). *Toward a speech act theory of literary discourse.* Bloomington: Indiana University Press.

23. For Hirsch, once readers and critics have correctly reproduced the author's verbal meaning, they are free to relate that meaning to whatever contexts they want or think will be relevant to their audience. On Hirsch's account, this is the role of interpretation as opposed to understanding. The fact that explications can change over time in different historical contexts by no means implies that the meaning of the text varies from age to age. "The historicity of interpretation is quite distinct from the timelessness of understanding." See Hirsch, E. (1967). *The aims of interpretation.* Chicago: University of Chicago Press. Quote is from p. 137.

24. Juhl, P. (1980). *Interpretation: An essay in the philosophy of literary criticism.* Princeton: Princeton University Press. See p. 14. Barbara Hernstein Smith (1978) disagrees with Hirsch and Juhl. She writes, "All users of language are ethically governed not by the author's intentions but by the conventions of the linguistic community" (p. 135). Precisely, but those conventions are largely reducible to the audience's recognition that "The poet, in composing the poem, will have made certain assumptions regarding his audience, specifically that they are members of a shared linguistic and cultural community, and thus able and willing to abide by relevant linguistic, cultural, and indeed literary conventions" (p. 37). By responding to the conventions the author presumed, the audience is interpreting the author's intentions. Smith, B. (1978). *On the margins of discourse: The relation of literature to language.* Chicago: University of Chicago Press.

25. Some examples of this work include: Vesser, H. (Ed.) (1989). *The new historicism.* New York: Routledge; Belsey, C., and Moore, J. (Eds.) (1989). *The feminist reader: Essays in gender and the politics of literary criticism.* London: Macmillan. Williams, R. (1977). *Marxism and literature.* Oxford: Oxford University Press. Said, E. (1993). *Culture and imperialism.* New York: Knopf. Ashcroft, B., Griffiths, G., and Tiffin, H. (1989). *The empire writes back: Theory and practice in post-colonial literatures.* New York: Routledge.

26. Montrose, L. (1992). New historicism. In S. Greenblatt and G. Gunn

(Eds.), *Redrawing the boundaries: The transformation of English and American literary studies.* New York: Modern Language Association. Quote is from p. 392.

27. Greenblatt, S. (1980). *Renaissance self-fashioning: From More to Shakespeare.* Chicago: University of Chicago Press. Quotes are from pp. 253, 174, and 46.

28. Gilbert, S., and Gubar, S. (1979). *The madwoman in the attic: The woman writer and the nineteenth century imagination.* New Haven: Yale University Press. Quotes are from p. 6.

29. Gilbert, S., as quoted in Showalter, E. (1986). (Ed.). *The new feminist criticism: Essays on women, literature, and theory.* London: Virago. Quote is on p. 5.

30. Barthes, R. (1977). The death of the author. In his *Image-music-text.* New York: Hill and Wang. Derrida, J. (1973). *Speech and phenomena.* Evanston: Northwestern University Press. Derrida, J. (1976). *Of grammatology.* Baltimore: Johns Hopkins University Press. Derrida, J. (1978). *Writing and difference.* Chicago: University of Chicago Press. Foucault, M. (1979). What is an author? In J. Harari (Ed.), *Textual strategies: Perspectives in post-structuralist criticism* (pp. 35–51). Ithaca: Cornell University Press.

31. De Man, P. (1984). *Insight and blindness.* New Haven: Yale University Press.

32. Norris, C. (1987). *Derrida.* Cambridge, MA: Harvard University Press. Quote is from p. 112.

33. Derrida, J. (1977). Limited Inc abc (response to John Searle). *Glyph,* 2, 162–254. Quote is from p. 199.

34. Foucault (1979), supra.

35. Foucault, M. (1972). *The archaeology of knowledge and the discourse on language.* New York: Harper and Row. Quote is from p. 55.

36. Ibid. Quote is from p. 122.

37. Barthes, R. (1974). *S/Z.* New York: Hill and Wang. The following quotes have been adapted from pp. 21–22.

38. Parini, Jay (1997). The lessons of theory. *Philosophy and Literature,* 21, 91–101. Quote is from p. 95.

39. According to the deconstructionist position, I am engaged in a self-defeating enterprise when I try to understand their position.

40. Barnes, A. (1988). *On interpretation.* New York: Blackwell. Quote is from p. 99. As Barnes also suggests, Derrida's own criticisms of others can be decisive only if Derrida's theory is not correct. Derrida is often misconstrued as radically anti-intentionalist. Derrida affirms that intentions is a relevant category of his writing and reading but

insists that it cannot encompass the full range of textual significance. Understanding of authorial intentions will generate its own area of significance but will also confront moments of contradiction whereby the text will open itself to a reading which eludes or evades the conscious purpose of its author.

41. DeMan, P. (1979). *Allegories of reading.* New Haven: Yale University Press. Quote is from p. 6.

42. Derrida, J. (1979). *Spurs: Nietzsche's style.* Chicago: University of Chicago Press. Quote is from p. 125.

43. Iser (1974), supra. Eco, U. (1979). *The role of the reader: Explorations in the semiotics of texts.* London: Hutchinson. Fish (1980), supra. Holland, N. (1975). *Five readers reading.* New Haven: Yale University Press. Thompkins, J. (Ed.) (1980). *Reader-response criticism: From formalism to post-structuralism.* Baltimore: Johns Hopkins University.

44. Gadamer, H-G., (1975). *Truth and method.* New York: Continuum. Quote is from pp. 21–22.

45. Fish (1980), supra.

46. Ibid.

47. Of course, not any string of words will be seen as poetry or literature. One informal study had students read a page from a biology text, which was divided up with the typical spacing and line division of a poem and presented as a poem. The students did not generally find the "poem" to be credible. Thus, telling students beforehand that a text is a poem, as Fish did in his informal experiment, clearly influences students' attempt to find poetic or literary meaning in what they read. See de Beaugrande, R. (1984). Writer, reader, critic: Comparing critical theories as discourse. *College English, 46,* 533–559.

48. Culler, J. (1975). *Structuralist poetics.* London: Routledge and Kegan Paul. Culler, J. (1981). *The pursuits of signs: Semiotics, literature, deconstruction.* London: Routledge and Kegan Paul. Iser, W. (1978). *The act of reading: A theory of aesthetic response.* Baltimore: Johns Hopkins University.

49. Leenhardt, J. (1992). Does there exist a European reader (literature and reading in a unifying Europe)? *Poetics, 21,* 117–128.

50. See, for example, Kintsch, W., and Green, E. (1978). The role of culture-specific schemata in the comprehension and recall of stories. *Discourse Processes, 1,* 1–13. Steffensen, M., Joag-Dev, C., and Anderson, R. (1979). A cross-cultural perspective on reading comprehension. *Reading Research Quarterly, 15,* 10–29. Lipson, M. (1983).

The influence of religious affiliation on children's memory for text information. *Reading Research Quarterly, 18,* 448–457. Pritchard, R. (1990). The effects of cultural schemata on reading processing strategies. *Reading Research Quarterly, 25,* 273–295.

51. Knapp, S., and Michaels, W. (1982). Against theory. *Critical Inquiry, 8,* 723–742, p. 726.

52. Knapp and Michaels (1982), supra.

53. Some linguistic and literary theorists have gone so far as to argue that if the metaphor, or any piece of language, were produced accidentally by nature, then there would be nothing to understand because the squiggles would not constitute language. Without an intentional agent, there can be no such thing as a language. Knapp and Michaels (1981), supra.

54. Knapp and Michaels (1981), supra. Quote is from p. 19.

55. Ibid., p. 12.

56. See Levinson, J. (1992). Intention and interpretation: A last look. In G. Iseminger (Ed.), *Intention and interpretation* (pp. 221–256). Philadelphia: Temple University Press. Nathan, D. (1992). Irony, metaphor, and the problem of intention. In G. Iseminger (Ed.), *Intention and interpretation* (pp. 183–202). Philadelphia: Temple University Press. Tolhurst, W. (1979). On what a text is and how it means. *British Journal of Aesthetics, 19,* 3–14.

57. Levinson, J. (1992). Intention and interpretation: A last look. In G. Iseminger (Ed.), *Intention and interpretation* (pp. 221–256). Philadelphia: Temple University Press.

58. Levinson distinguishes between categorical and semantic intentions, espousing actual intentionalism with regard to the former and hypothetical intentionalism with regard to the latter. Semantic intentions are an artist's intention to mean something in or by a text or artifact, while categorical intentions "involve the maker's conception of what he has provided and what it is for, on a rather basic level; they govern not what a work is to mean but how it is to be fundamentally conceived or approached" (e.g., that a novel should be read as a work of literary fiction). Ibid. Quote is from p. 188.

59. Many critics prefer hypothesized intentionalism over subjective intentionalism because it preserves the idea that literature has a degree of autonomy from its authors. Hypothetical intentionalism and subjective intentionalism both have problems dealing with cases where it is known, or is plausible to suppose, that the author did not intend a certain meaning, and yet the work still conveys

that meaning. But Jerrold Levinson advanced an idea to deal with this by saying that unintended meanings are secondary or non-central. See ibid. Of course, these "secondary" meanings can be as important for what a text means as are the primary ones.

60. See Eco, U. (1992). *Interpretation and overinterpretation*. New York: Cambridge University Press. Overinterpretation of texts often occurs with secular sacred texts. As soon as a text becomes sacred for our culture (e.g., the U.S. Constitution) it becomes subject to the process of suspicious readings and is open to an excess of interpretations. Sacred texts usually have a religious authority or tradition that claims to hold the key to their interpretation.

61. Ibid., p. 150.

62. Rorty, R. (1992). The pragmatist's progress. In S. Collini, (Ed.). *Interpretation and overinterpretation* (pp. 89–108). New York: Cambridge University Press.

63. Carroll, N. (1993). Anglo-American aesthetics and contemporary critics: Intentions and the hermeneutics of suspicion. *Journal of Aesthetics and Art Criticism, 51*, 245–252.

64. Ibid. Quote is from p. 249.

65. Ibid.

66. Sperber, D., and Wilson, D. (1986). *Relevance: Communication and cognition*. Cambridge, MA: Blackwell. Pilkington, A. (1992). Poetic effects. *Lingua, 87*, 29–51.

67. Ibid.

68. Heaney, S. (1966). *Death of a naturalist*. London: Faber and Faber.

69. For discussion of assumption of "thin authorial rationality" see Livingston, P. (1991). *Literature and rationality*. New York: Cambridge University Press.

70. Ibid.

71. Sperber and Wilson (1986), supra. Quote is from p. 39.

72. Pilkington (1992), supra.

73. This study is described in Clark, B. (1996). Stylistic analysis and relevance theory. *Language and Literature, 3*, 163–178. Carver's story is from Carver, R. (1984). *Fires: Essays, poems, stories*. New York: Vintage Books.

74. Wilson, D., and Sperber, D. (1992). On verbal irony. *Lingua, 87*, 53–76.

75. For a different application of relevance theory to literary discourse, see MacMahon, B. (1996). Indirectness, rhetoric and interpretive use: Communicative strategies in Browning's "My Last Duchess." *Language and Literature, 5*, 209–223.

CHAPTER 10

1. *Thompson v. Oklahoma*, 487 U.S. 815 (1988).
2. Ibid.
3. Ibid., 864. Several historians claim that the Eighth Amendment was created only to prohibit barbarous or tortuous punishment, not disproportionately severe punishment such as putting someone to death. See Berger, R. (1982). *Death penalties: The Supreme Court's obstacle course.* Cambridge, MA: Harvard University Press. Grannuci, A. (1969). "Nor cruel and unusual punishment inflicted": The original meaning. *California Law Review, 57*, 839–865.
4. Who really constitutes the "founders" is a complicated question. The founders include those attending the Constitutional Convention in 1787, the First Congress that drafted the Bill of Rights, the Thirty-Ninth Congress that drafted the Fourteenth Amendment, and the state conventions and legislatures that ratified these efforts, among others. The framers of the Constitution, whether in 1787, or 1789, or 1864, or 1915, or 1951, or 1971, have been politicians, no more endowed with virtue than are politicians generally. See Bassham, G. (1992). *Original intent and the Constitution: A philosophical study.* New York: Rowman & Littlefield. Rakove, J. (1996). *Original meanings: Politics and ideas in the making of the Constitution.* New York: Knopf.
5. Nomination of Thurgood Marshall to be Associate Justice of the Supreme Court of the United States: Hearings before the Committee of the Judiciary, 90th Congress, 1st session (1967), p. 49.
6. The Supreme Court of the United States: Hearings before the Committee of the Judiciary, 92th Congress, 1st session (1971), p. 19.
7. A new chief justice: A new court era. *Congressional Quarterly Weekly Report, 27,* (May 23, 1969), p. 798.
8. Quoted from Davis, S. (1989). *Justice Rehnquist and the Constitution.* Princeton: Princeton University Press. See pp. 3–4.
9. Bork, R. (1990). *The tempting of America: The political seduction of the law.* New York: Free Press.
10. Wills, G. (1978). *Inventing America: Jefferson's Declaration of Independence.* New York: Doubleday.
11. See Tribe, L., and Dorf, M. (1991). *On reading the Constitution.* Cambridge, MA: Harvard University Press. Quote is on p. 9.
12. Some scholars contend that a comprehensive reading of a wide range of documents from the eighteenth century support the idea that the state should not be involved in organized religion in any

way. For more on this issue, see Kramnick, I., and Moore, L. (1996). *The godless Constitution: The case against religious correctness.* New York: Norton.

13. Textualists are often referred to as "strict constructionists." See Bobbitt, P. (1982). *Constitutional fate: Theory of the Constitution.* New York: Oxford University Press. Eskridge, W. (1990). The new textualism. *UCLA Law Review, 37,* 621–691.

14. See Bassham (1992), supra.

15. *Giuseppi v. Walling,* 14 F. 2d 608, 624 (2d Cir. 1944).

16. *Riggs v. Palmer,* 115 NY 506, 22 NE 188 (1889).

17. Gates, J., and Phelps, G. (1996). Intentionalism in constitutional opinions. *Public Policy Research, 49,* 245–260.

18. Brennan, William, Jr. (1985). The Constitution of the United States: Contemporary ratification. Speech delivered at the Georgetown University Text and Teaching Symposium.

19. See Maltz, E., (1994) *Rethinking the Constitution: Originalism, intervention, and the politics of judicial review.* Lawrence: University of Kansas Press. Maltz discusses the traditional view that originalism supports conservative political views.

20. *Valley Forge Christian College v. Americans United,* 454 U.S. 464 (1982).

21. See Solon, L. (1993). *The language of judges.* Chicago: University of Chicago Press. Solon urges judges faced with hard cases to acknowledge the indeterminacy of the text and their reliance on nontextual sources in their decisions.

22. Dworkin, R. (1985). *Law's empire.* Cambridge, MA: Harvard University Press.

23. Dworkin, R. (1985), supra. Quote is from p. 163.

24. Ibid.

25. See Powell, J. (1985). The original understanding of original intent. *Harvard Law Review, 98,* 885–948. Tushnet, M. (1988). *Red, white, and blue: A critical analysis of constitutional law.* Cambridge, MA: Harvard University Press.

26. Bassham (1992), supra. Powell (1985), supra. Tushnet (1988), supra.

27. 347 U.S. 483 (1954).

28. *Plessy v. Ferguson,* 163 U.S. 551 (1896).

29. Hirsch, E. (1994). Transhistorical intentions and the persistence of allegory. *New Literary History, 25,* 549–567.

30. *Maryland v. Craig,* 497 U.S. 836 (1990).

31. Ibid. Also see Scalia, A. (1997). Common-law courts in a civil-law system. In his *A matter of interpretation: Federal courts and the law.* Princeton: Princeton University Press.

32. Dworkin, R. (1986). *Law's empire.* Cambridge, MA: Harvard University Press. Dworkin, R. (1997). Comment. In Scalia (1997), supra.
33. Dworkin (1997), supra. Quote is from p. 122.
34. The Court in *Brown v. Board of Education* requested briefs on the question of whether "the Congress which submitted and the State legislatures and conventions which ratified the Fourteenth Amendment contemplated ... or understood . . . that it would abolish segregation in the public schools." On reviewing the evidence, the Court felt that it was "at best inconclusive" as to the subjective intentions of the members of the Thirty-Ninth Congress with respect to segregated education. See *Brown v. Board of Education*, 347 US. 483, 489 (1954).
35. Dworkin (1997), supra.
36. Dworkin (1986), supra, calls this the "semantic intention."
37. Tribe, L. (1997). Comment. In Scalia (1997), supra.
38. Ibid. Quote is from p. 73.
39. Dworkin, R. (1985). *A matter of principle.* Cambridge, MA: Harvard University Press. Lyons, D. (1986). Constitutional interpretation and original meaning. *Social Philosophy and Policy, 4,* 76–101.
40. There is great irony in the desire of "non-originalists" to remove indeterminacy from the interpretation of law by cementing legal meaning entirely in the text itself apart from serious consideration of authorial intentions. By divorcing the author's (or speaker's) meaning from the meaning of the work as a whole, the "non-originalists" have staked out a position favored by deconstructionist critics who favor free play and indeterminacy in the interpretation of texts.
41. The following discussion has been adapted from Mailloux, S. (1990). Interpretation. In F. Lentricchia and T. McLaughlin (Eds.), *Critical terms for literary study* (pp. 121–134). Chicago: University of Chicago Press.
42. Ibid., p. 128.
43. Ibid., p. 129.
44. Ibid., pp. 128–129.
45. Ibid., p. 130.
46. Ibid., p. 128.

CHAPTER 11

1. Tompkins, C. (1996). *Duchamp: A biography.* New York: Henry Holt. Quote is from p. 185.

2. Stiles, K. and Selz, P. (Eds.) (1996). *Theories and documents of contemporary art: A sourcebook of artists' writings*. Berkeley: University of California Press. Quote is from p. 5.

3. Haring, K. Untitled statement. *Flash Art, 116* (March 1984), 20–28.

4. Stiles and Selz (1996), supra. Quote is from p. 772.

5. Ibid.

6. Wilkerson, I. "Test case for obscenity standards begins today in Ohio courtroom." *New York Times*, September 24, 1990, p. A4.

7. Letter dated May 18, 1989, sent by Senator Alphonse D'Amato to Hugh Southern, acting chairman of the NEA.

8. Statement by Senator Jesse Helms to the U.S. Senate, May 18, 1989.

9. Andres Serrano, letter to Hugh Southern, acting chairman of the National Endowment for the Arts, July 8, 1989.

10. Evans, R., and Novak, R. The NEA's suicide charge. *Washington Post*, May 11, 1990.

11. Finley, K. Letter to the editor. *Washington Post*, May 19, 1990.

12. From Wilkerson, I. Curator defends photo exhibition. *New York Times*, October 4, 1990, p. A19.

13. Ibid.

14. Deng, G. (1994). Cindy Sherman: Theory and practice. In J. Roberts (Ed.), *Art has no history: The making and unmaking of modern art* (pp. 257–277). New York: Verso.

15. From N. Fuku's interview with Cindy Sherman entitled "A woman of parts" in *Art in America*, June 1997, p. 81.

16. Ibid.

17. Bloom, P. (1996). Intention, history, and artifact concepts. *Cognition, 60*, 1–29.

18. On the influence of titles on art interpretation, see Levinson, J. (1985). Titles. *Journal of Aesthetics and Art Criticism, 47*, 29–39.

19. Ibid.

20. Wolheim, R. (1987). *Painting as art*. Washington, DC: National Gallery of Art. Quote is from pp. 36–37.

21. Bloom (1996), supra.

22. Levinson, J. (1993). Extending art historically. *Journal of Aesthetics and Art Criticism, 51*, 411–423. Quote is from p. 412. Also see Levinson, J. (1979). Defining art historically. *British Journal of Aesthetics, 19*, 232–250. Levinson, J. (1989). Refining art historically. *Journal of Aesthetics and Art Criticism, 51*, 411–423.

23. Levinson (1989), supra. Quote is from p. 24.

24. Museums are also full of religious and functional artifacts that are

now viewed as "art," even though many were originally intended to be understood as mere objects.

25. Danto, A. (1981). *The transfiguration of the commonplace.* Cambridge, MA: Harvard University Press.

26. Danto, A. (1986). *The philosophical disenfranchisement of art.* New York: Columbia University Press.

27. Stalnaker, N. (1996). Intention and interpretation, Manet's "Luncheon in the studio." *Journal of Aesthetics and Art Criticism, 54,* 121–134.

28. Ibid, p. 30.

29. For one treatment of the cleaning of the Sistine Chapel see Pietrangeli, C. (Ed.) (1994). *The Sistine Chapel: A glorious restoration.* New York: Abrams.

30. Of course, most experts recognize that Michelangelo had many assistants who helped him complete the Sistine ceiling frescoes. Some scholars even go so far as to suggest that each panel of the ceiling be understood as being painted by a particular person, and not just by Michelangelo, and that the historical record be studied to find out what each of their respective intentions or aims were in creating each of the respective panels.

31. Dykstra, S. (1996). The artist's intentions and the intentional fallacy in fine arts conservation. *Journal of the American Institute for Conservation, 35,* 197–228.

32. Maclean, N., and Weaver, A. (1950). Some factual observations about varnishes and glazes. *Burlington Magazine, 92,* 189–192. Quote is from p. 189.

33. Ruhemann, H. (1963). The training of restorers. In G. Thompson (Ed.), *Recent advances in conservation* (pp. 202–205). London: Butterworth. Quote is from p. 202.

34. This is taken from Dipert, R. (1993). *Artifacts, artworks, and agency.* Philadelphia: Temple University Press.

35. Nakamura, T. (1987). The communication of dynamics between musicians and listeners through musical performance. *Perception & Psychophysics, 41,* 525–533.

36. Gabrielsson, A. (1995). Expressive intention and performance. In R. Steinberg (Ed.), *Music and the mind machine* (pp. 35–47). Berlin: Springer-Verlag. Also see Palmer, C. (1989). Mapping musical thought to musical performance. *Journal of Experimental Psychology: Human Perception and Performance, 15,* 331–346.

37. Meek, H. (1997). *Horn and conductor: Reminiscences of a practitioner*

with a few words of advice. Rochester: University of Rochester Press. Quote is from p. 25.

38. Ibid.
39. Schuller, G. (1997). *The compleat conductor*. New York: Oxford University Press.
40. Golden (1990), supra. Quote is from p. 213.
41. Ibid.
42. Krauz, M. (1992). Intention and interpretation: Hirsch and Margolis. In G. Iseminger (Ed.), *Intention and interpretation* (pp. 152–166). Philadelphia: Temple University Press. Jerold Levinson distinguishes between two sorts of interpretation: critical interpretation and performative interpretation. The first (CI) is a theory about a piece of music, an account of the work's structure, qualities, and meaning. The second (PI) is a maximally specific sound sequence, the actual set of sounds generated in a considered performance of the piece. Thus, CI is an interpreted set of remarks, while PI is a type of performance. See Levinson, J. (1990). *Music, art, and metaphysics*. Ithaca, NY: Cornell University Press.
43. Schmitt, N. (1990). *Actors and onlookers: Theater and twentieth century scientific views of nature*. Evanston: Northwestern University Press. Quote is from p. 8.
44. See Carlson, M. (1996). *Performance*. New York: Routledge.
45. Cage, J. (1970). The future of music: Credo. In R. Kostelantz (Ed.), *John Cage*. New York: Praeger. Quote is from p. 54.
46. Revill, D. (1992). *The roaring silence: John Cage – A life*. New York: Arcade. Quote is from p. 166. John Cage conducted many other experiments on intentionless writing in which he tried to "musicalize" written language. For a description of these experiments, see Shultis, C. (1995). Silencing the sounded self: John Cage and the intentionality of nonintention. *Musical Quarterly, 79*, 312–350.
47. Kapreow, A. (1966). *Assemblages, environments, and happenings*. New York: Abrams.
48. Lumet, S. (1996). *Making movies*. New York: Vintage. Quote is from p. 29.
49. For a lovely discussion of Kael's "re-plottings," see Gerrig, R. (1993). *Experiencing narrative worlds: On the psychological activities of reading*. New Haven: Yale University Press.
50. Ibid. Quote is from p. 95.
51. Freedman, S. Play closed after Crucible dispute. *New York Times*. November 28, 1984. Quote is from p. E21.

52. Massa, R. Arthur Miller clings to Crucible. *The Village Voice.* December 27, 1983. Quote is from p. 52.
53. Savran, D. (1985). The Wooster Group, Arthur Miller, and *The Crucible. The Drama Review, 29,* 99–109. Quote is from p. 105.
54. Luere, J. (1994). *Playwright versus director: Authorial intentions and performance interpretations.* Westport, CT: Greenwood Press. Quote is from p. 99.
55. For more on contact improvisation and cognition see Shannon, B. (1993). *The representational and the presentational: An essay on mind and the study of cognition.* London: Harvester Wheatsheaf.
56. The following quotes were taken from the journals presented at the Richmond Art Center during the *Epistolary Paint: A Visual Correspondence* exhibit.

CHAPTER 12

1. "Men are from Belgium, women are from New Brunswick," by Roz Chast, *The New Yorker,* Aug. 25 and Sept. 1, 1997. Quotes are from p. 111. A recently published dictionary provides male/female definitions (i.e., the encoding/decoding view of communication) for a large number of words and phrases. See Bader, J., and Brazell, B. (1997). *He meant/she meant: The definitive male/female dictionary.* New York: Warner.
2. Words and music by Sting.
3. In this regard, it is surprising to see within the field of experimental psycholinguistics how little work has actually been conducted on the recovery of authorial intentions in fast comprehension processes. Part of the reason for this, I suspect, is that pragmatics continues to be viewed as a later, sometimes optional, part of linguistic processing, as well as more difficult to experimentally examine. Yet given listeners' desires to infer speakers' intentions when processing language, for example, it is important to see how, and when, the search for authorial meaning shapes other linguistic and cognitive processes occurring when people interpret speech. The same idea extends to comprehension of written texts as well.
4. The International Association for the Empirical Study of Literature is one example of how psychologists, literary scholars, and art theorists meet to talk about, and conduct research on, shared interests. For examples of work from scholars associated with this interdisciplinary organization, see papers in the journals *Discourse Processes* and *Poetics.* For an edited collection of recent papers, see Kreuz,

R., and MacNealy, M. (1996). *Empirical approaches to literature and aesthetics*. Norwood, NJ: Ablex.

5. Borges, J. (1963). *Ficciones*. New York: Grove Press. Quotes are from pp. 52–53.
6. For additional discussion on how identical texts have different meanings see Shannon, B. (1993). *The representational and the presentational: An essay on cognition and the study of mind*. New York: Harvester Wheatsheaf.

Name Index

Subject Index

clinical psychology, 77
cognitive commitment, 16
cognitive intentionalist perspective, 18, 136
cognitive intentionalist premise, 16, 72, 248, 258, 272, 292, 327
cognitive processes, 5, 15, 99–106
cognitive science, 9, 22, 102, 103, 115, 118, 125, 235, 256, 279, 327, 332, 334
cognitive unconscious, 33, 98, 106, 272, 335
collaboration in conversation, 125–130
collaborative intentions, 14
collaborative view, 124
collective behavior, 37
collective intentions, 36–38
common ground, 110, 118, 122–124, 127, 129, 130, 366
communicative intentions, 3–8, 10, 14–15, 18, 42, 45, 52–53, 59, 61–62, 67–68, 71, 82, 87–88, 94, 103, 105, 107, 110, 121, 128, 134–138, 141–142, 153, 159, 164, 170–171, 174, 176, 201, 208, 212, 238, 241, 244, 265, 268, 272, 275, 292, 308, 318, 322, 327–328, 330–331, 333, 335, 337
communicative misunderstanding, 5, 6
complex intentions, 41, 50
computer science, 9, 74, 182–185
conduit metaphor, 47
conscious experience, 28
conscious intentionality, 90–91, 239
Constitution, U.S., 12, 50, 273–292
constructivist view, 110–111, 114
contextual expressions, 112
contextual, implied, and speaker meanings, 49
conversational dilemmas, 161, 167
cooperative principle, 117–118, 149
"A Country Doctor" (story), 262, 264
criminal law, 76–77

cross cultural perspectives, 15, 135–142, 171–174
Crucible, The (play), 312

Deadman (performance), 304
death of the author, 103, 187, 252, 256
debate over original intent, 275
Decameron, 195–196
deception, 153–160, 372–374
deconstruction, 252, 256, 263
defining art, 302–307
defining communication, 44–45
definition of meaning, 42–44
departing from authorial intentions, 264–272
descriptions of intention, 23
desires, 24, 27–28
"Digging" (poem), 268–269
discourse intentions, 196
Don Quixote, 335–336
"Durer: Innsbruck, 1495" (poem), 207–208

Education of Little Tree, 209
effective intentions, 247
18 Happenings in Parts (performance), 311
ELIZA (computer program), 74
Epistolary Paint: A Visual Correspondence (paintings), 318–321
emotional displays, 87–88
encoding/decoding paradigm, 44–45, 47, 50
English Hours, 248
equivocation, 160–164
Etant Donnes (artwork), 306
evasion, 164–167
experience of meaning, 9, 15, 19, 22–23, 35, 39, 45, 71–72, 98, 106, 145, 205, 235, 256, 331
expressions of intention, 23
expressive intention, 53–54, 105, 196

face-to-face interaction, 7, 58, 82, 109
facilitated communication, 93–97, 357

Subject Index

principle of accumulation, 123
principle of charity, 72
principle of grounding, 123
principle of speaker meaning, 121
principle of utterance design, 122
principles of successful communication, 121–125
private mental acts, 14, 19, 38
Privation and Excesses (artwork), 69–71, 105–106
processes versus products of understanding, 71–72, 102, 104, 140
proverbs, 148, 149
psycholinguistics, 102, 105, 125–134, 369–370, 398
Psychology Today, 158
Psychopathology of Everyday Life, The (book), 29
psychotherapy, 74
Puppies (sculpture), 224–225

radical subjectivist position, 13
reader-response criticism, 256–257
readers' inferences, 197–199
recognition-implies-fulfillment intentions, 51, 54, 85
relevance theory, 118–121, 270–272, 360
Rembrandt–Not Rembrandt (exhibit), 210
rhetorical inferences, 193
Riggs v. Palmer (1889), 279
Right Stuff, The, 312
Rime of the Ancient Mariner, The (poem), 217, 242

S/Z, 254
Samoan discourse, 136–139
Santa Cruz Sentinel, 179
sarcasm, 6, 149
"Sarrasine" (essay), 254–255
Satanic Verses, The, 238–239,
satire, 9, 111, 200–201
Scenes from a Marriage (film), 6
sculpture, 293–294, 296–300, 303
semiotics, 5

Shoot (performance), 296
simile, 148, 149
skill, 27–28
slips of the tongue, 29–30
social psychology, 77–78
social/cultural forces, 326–327
Sounds of the Environment (performance), 311
sources of admissibility, 25
speaker's intention, 5, 6, 9, 109, 111, 113–118, 120, 124, 127, 131–142, 144–175
speaking off-record, 167–171
  association cues, 168
  contradiction, 169
  hints, 168
  hyperbole, 169
  irony, 169
  metaphor, 169
  presupposing, 168
  rhetorical questions, 170
  tautology, 169
  understatement, 168
  vagueness, 170
speech act classification, 55–56
  assertives, 55
  commissives, 56
  declaratives, 56
  directives, 55
  expressives, 56
speech act theory, 55–57
Splashing (sculpture), 306
staged communicative acts, 145–148, 368, 370
stream of consciousness, 30
Storyspace (software), 231
subjective intentionalism, 240–245, 263, 328
Sunflowers (painting), 215
suppression of intentions, 29

TALESPIN (computer program), 182–185
teasing, 149